MW01049717

America's School for War

MODERN WAR STUDIES

Theodore A. Wilson
General Editor

Raymond Callahan
J. Garry Clifford
Jacob W. Kipp
Allan R. Millett
Carol Reardon
Dennis Showalter
David R. Stone
Series Editors

America's School for War

*Fort Leavenworth, Officer Education,
and Victory in World War II*

Peter J. Schifferle

UNIVERSITY PRESS OF KANSAS

© 2010 by the University Press of Kansas

All rights reserved

Published by the University Press of Kansas (Lawrence, Kansas 66045), which was organized by the Kansas Board of Regents and is operated and funded by Emporia State University, Fort Hays State University, Kansas State University, Pittsburg State University, the University of Kansas, and Wichita State University

Library of Congress Cataloging-in-Publication Data

Schifferle, Peter J.
America's school for war : Fort Leavenworth, officer education, and victory in World War II / Peter J. Schifferle.
p. cm. — (Modern war studies)
Includes bibliographical references and index.
ISBN 978-0-7006-1714-2 (cloth : alk. paper)
1. Fort Leavenworth (Kan.)—History—20th century. 2. United States. Army—Officers— Training of—History—20th century. 3. Military education—United States—History—20th century. 4. World War, 1939–1945—United States. I. Title.
UA26.L4S35 2010
355.0071'173—dc22
2009044653

British Library Cataloguing-in-Publication Data is available.

Printed in the United States of America

10 9 8 7 6 5 4 3 2 1

The paper used in this publication is recycled and contains 30 percent postconsumer waste. It is acid free and meets the minimum requirements of the American National Standard for Permanence of Paper for Printed Library Materials Z39.48–1992.

For Sandy,
Rachel,

and

Colonel Tom Felts, U.S. Army,
our friend
CGSC 1996–1997, AMSP 1997–1998, AOASF 2005–2006
Killed in Action
Baghdad, Iraq
November 14, 2006

CONTENTS

ACKNOWLEDGMENTS

I wish to thank Ted Wilson, my adviser, mentor, and friend, for his wisdom, skill, hospitality, and scholarly editorial pen. Professors Phil Schrodt, Chris Gabel, Peter Mancall, Philip Paludan, and Susan Twombly all helped to make me as good a historian and an educator as they could. The faults in this book are entirely mine; the good analysis is frequently theirs.

My colleagues of the School of Advanced Military Studies, U.S. Army Command and General Staff College, where I have the privilege of being on the faculty, gave invaluable support, helping me pursue my research and writing while teaching. In particular, Professor Emeritus Bob Berlin and Professor Jake Kipp taught many classes so I could have the luxury of work and research simultaneously. Candace Hamm, the *godmother* of SAMS, made everything work, always. The directors of SAMS, Brigadier General Robin Swan, and Colonels Jim Greer, Kevin Benson, and Steve Banach took many risks to let me go to Lawrence and elsewhere to work on my studies and this book. That we still succeeded in educating some of the finest young minds in today's military is due to their patience and professionalism.

This book would not have been possible without the support, long hours, and willing assistance of Timothy Nenninger, a friend and colleague whose encyclopedic knowledge of the records in the National Archives is a real national treasure. The encouraging words, sage advice, helpful criticisms, and deep professionalism of Peter Mansoor, Colonel, U.S. Army retired, were and are invaluable. Kathy Buker, Elizabeth Merrifield, Rusty Rafferty, Pam Kontowicz, Ginny Navarro, and Pamela Bennett, the professional researchers and archivists of the Combined Arms Center Research Library (CARL) at Fort Leavenworth, in whose capable hands the curricular archives of the Command and General Staff School rest, were absolutely indispensable and unfailingly friendly. A tireless helper in all circumstances was Susan Fowler, my best contact at CARL. The records they maintain with a gentle care are a storehouse of historical information that is all too infrequently mined.

Paul Jacobsmeyer and I share two things—a friendship longer than the interwar period, and a continual curiosity about why things happened the way they did. Without his help, criticism, and encouragement, this book would not exist.

Steve Bourque and Dan Fullerton share the dedication to ferreting out the truth—at least as we see it.

My former classmates at the University of Kansas are too numerous to name, but the friendship and advice of Walt Kretchik, Randy Mullis, and Mike Stewart helped get us through long days and nights as full-time teachers and full-time graduate students.

Michael Briggs and the staff at the University Press of Kansas were unflinching in their professionalism and dedication. Their frequent words of encouragement were essential.

My wife, Sandy, and my daughter, Rachel, bore the brunt of years of "I'll be in the library." I promise I will get back to the joys of being a husband and a father any day now.

ABBREVIATIONS

AEF   American Expeditionary Forces
CCA   Combat Command A
CCB   Combat Command B
CCR   Combat Command Reserve
CCC   Civilian Conservation Corps
FSR   U.S. Army *Field Service Regulations*

America's School for War

Major General Ernest N. Harmon. World War II photograph. U.S. Army photograph.

Introduction

> A military historian recently asked me how the United States, in-
> different and even contemptuous of the military in peacetime,
> had been able to produce a group of generals proficient enough to
> lead armies successfully against German might. . . . I am now con-
> vinced that the intensive and imaginative training at the Com-
> mand and General Staff College had a great deal to do with it. . . .
> Most of us saw Armageddon as a certainty.
> —Major General Ernie Harmon, *Combat Commander*, 1970

Explanations given for the victory of the U.S. armed forces over the totalitarian
states of Germany, Japan, and Italy in World War II include the logistical and industrial might of the United States, the inherent advantages of democracies
fighting wars of national existence, and the ability of U.S. tactical formations to
fight effectively against German and Japanese veterans.[1] What has not yet been
explained is how the intellectual and educational development of regular officers enabled the fighting effectiveness of the United States Army in World War II.
To borrow historian Gerald Linderman's phrase, how did senior army officers see
and understand doing their job?[2] How did the army maintain the professional
competence of commanders and staff officers in the two decades after World
War I? What were the principles of tactical competence in the army, and how
were they inculcated in a new generation of professional officers?[3] Although historians have assessed the competence of some senior army generals, and have begun to assess the competence of army formations, there has been no comprehensive look at the preparation of the professional leaders who engineered the
victory in World War II.[4] Any such attempt must examine the professional preparation of generals commanding large military formations, as well as the staff officers who did the detailed work required to effectively move, sustain, and employ
large formations.

Ernie Harmon serves as an example of the generation of officers who survived their baptism of fire in World War I and went on to competent performance as senior leaders in World War II. Harmon, born in 1894, was commissioned from West Point in the World War I class of May 1917. As a captain, he,

in effect, commanded a provisional squadron of horse cavalry in both the St. Mihiel and Meuse-Argonne offensives, engaging in frequent combat with German forces. Returning to the United States after the Armistice, but concerned that America would have to return to Europe to complete the "unfinished business" with Germany, Harmon initially stayed with 2nd Cavalry for troop duty at Fort Riley, Kansas, then served as a tactics and horsemanship instructor at West Point, where he competed in the 1924 Summer Olympics in Paris, France. After another few years with the 6th Cavalry, he was assigned as commandant of cadets at Norwich University for four years and then put in two years as a student at the Fort Leavenworth Command and General Staff Course. Harmon remembered his two years at Leavenworth as the "most difficult years of my training." Finishing in the top 10 percent of his course, he was sent to be a student at the Army War College. After graduating from the War College, he returned to troop duty, this time with the 8th Cavalry at Fort Bliss, Texas.[5]

In 1935, Harmon was assigned to the War Department's General Staff in Washington and worked in the G4 section on army logistics for four years. Harmon then asked to be assigned to the First Mechanized Cavalry Regiment at Fort Knox, Kentucky. This was only a brief assignment; in late spring 1941 he was recalled to the General Staff and service in the War Plans Division and then to duty as G4 for Lieutenant General Lesley McNair, chief of staff of General Headquarters. After some six months with McNair, Harmon moved on to be the chief of staff for the Armored Force at Fort Knox, then went back to troops as a brigadier general with a newly formed armored division. During active operations in World War II, Harmon commanded 2nd Armored Division in North Africa, 1st Armored Division in Italy, and then returned to 2nd Armored Division in Western Europe. He ended the war as commander of XXII Corps and went on to command the American Constabulary Forces in Germany until his retirement in 1947.[6]

As for the more junior officers—those who served necessary functions as staff officers at the division level—Hamilton Howze is a good example. Born in the commandant's house at West Point in 1908, he graduated from the United States Military Academy (USMA) in 1930 and served in a succession of troop assignments, from Fort Bliss to Fort Oglethorpe, Georgia, and by 1938 was in the Philippines serving with the 26th Cavalry (Philippine Scouts). Two years later, declining an extension of duty in the Pacific to retrieve the family's Irish setter from a kennel in the United States, Howze and his wife sailed from Manila on the last troopship out of the Philippines, returning to the United States and duty with 3rd Cavalry at Fort Myer, Virginia. Offered command of a mechanized cavalry troop at Fort Bliss, Howze was on a picnic with his wife when the news of Pearl Harbor reached Texas.[7]

Offered assignment to the forming 8th Armored Division, Howze reported to Fort Knox and command of the divisional reconnaissance battalion. "But then, to my amazement," as he reported in his memoir, he was offered assignment as the G3 (Operations) general staff officer of the fully formed 1st Armored Division, already prepared for overseas movement. It may not be coincidental that the commander of this division, Major General Orlando Ward, was related to Howze's wife. Howze recorded his disbelief in being offered the assignment, as "I knew nothing about tank tactics and nothing about staff work—I had not so much as ridden in a tank, and had not been near the Army's Staff College at Fort Leavenworth."[8]

Now in a regular army division, Howze attempted to coordinate the return of training equipment, the packing of combat gear, the movement of the division from Fort Knox to its loading ports, and then its stationing in Ireland prior to movement to North Africa. As he related the story, after nearly nine months of packing, unpacking, and moving, the "sharpness, our cutting edge, was about that of a broom handle." After a punishing experience fighting the Afrika Korps in Tunisia, Howze and the 1st Armored participated in the Mediterranean theater for the rest of the war, with Howze promoted to colonel and command of one of the combat commands of the division. After the end of World War II, he returned to the United States, his wife, and their Irish setter. Sent initially to Fort Riley as an instructor at the Cavalry School, preparing officers for assignment to the Pacific theater, he was selected for attendance at the first class at Fort Leavenworth's new peacetime-schedule Command Course, an experimental War College equivalent course, graduating in 1946 after a five-month course. Howze eventually gained promotion to four stars before his retirement in 1965.[9]

These two officers, separated by fourteen years of experience and a significant gap in peacetime educational preparation, came together professionally during the defeat of the U.S. 1st Armored Division at the Battle of Kasserine Pass in February 1943. Harmon, in Northwest Africa preparing the 2nd Armored Division for the planned invasion of Sicily, was ordered to Lieutenant General Dwight D. Eisenhower's headquarters for "limited field duty." Eisenhower, who apparently preferred officers who lived by "hard—almost slavish—work, team play, self-confidence, and an enthusiasm that amounts to dedication," seemed uncertain of what to ask of the former West Point halfback ("155 pound[s] wringing wet").[10] Told by Eisenhower to either relieve Major General Lloyd Fredendall, the commander of II Corps, or Major General Orlando Ward, commander of 1st Armored Division, Harmon blurted out, in his typically outspoken and aggressive manner, "Well, make up your mind, Ike, I can't do both."[11] Ike told Harmon to place himself in the role of deputy corps commander and to report back. Traveling forward to II Corps' command post, some sixty miles to the rear of the fighting, Harmon recalled: "I have never forgotten that harrowing drive: it was the first—and only—time I ever saw an American army in rout." Fredendall turned over immediate responsibility to Harmon, asking him if the command post was to move. Harmon, shocked by both the question and Fredendall's attitude, said firmly that the command post would not move. Fredendall then handed Harmon a typewritten paper giving him command authority over both U.S. 1st Armored Division and British 6th Armored Division. In Harmon's words, "I had journeyed out there in the dark; at that point I didn't even know where the front was."[12] Nevertheless, he was in command.

Fredendall then informed Harmon it was expected that the Germans would attack at dawn with their "Sunday punch." About 3:00 A.M., Howze (the operations officer of the 1st Armored Division) called, questioning an order from Fredendall. Concerned with the order to send a battalion of tanks forward to meet the Germans, with crews that had no training on their tanks, Howze asked for the order to be rescinded. Harmon recalled, "If I am in command, let me settle this." He told Howze that the tanks would do no one any good if the Germans broke through, so they needed to come forward, even if the crews were untrained.[13]

Angry and eager to do something, Harmon went forward by armored half-track to the command post of 1st Armored Division. Meeting General Ward, Harmon was informed that a division counterattack order for the morning (named "Operation Howze") was being drafted. Harmon decided that first the retreat needed to be stopped; only then was an attack in order. Harmon told everyone to "hold today, counterattack tomorrow." Ward issued an order to the division: "All units will be alerted at dawn for movement in any direction except to the rear." Harmon then moved to the British 6th Armored Division to check on its status, in the process countermanding the order of the overall British commander, General Sir Kenneth A.N. Anderson, for a unit to withdraw. Harmon returned to 1st Armored Division at dawn as the Germans fired a desultory artillery barrage; the front was quiet for the rest of the day. Harmon moved about the units of the division, issuing orders for a counterattack the next day. The counterattack began as scheduled on February 25 but found only mines and booby traps, the Germans having withdrawn during the night. The U.S. forces at Kasserine, after suffering nearly 9,000 casualties in a little more than two weeks, counterattacked, stiffened by Harmon's personality, decisiveness, professional confidence, and competence at handling large military formations.[14]

The defeat of the U.S. 1st Armored Division at Kasserine Pass in February 1943 has become something of a legend—and tends to be overstated.[15] Frequently ascribed to a combination of ineffective leadership, obsolete equipment, inadequate training, and poor basic soldier skills, Kasserine was only a "tactical defeat. . . . Although the Americans had lost heavily, there was no breakthrough as the Germans had planned," in the words of Gerhard Weinberg, the most competent historian of World War II.[16] Misled by erroneous interpretations of ULTRA intelligence radio intercepts, which had forecasted a German attack in another area, and overconfident in the impending collapse of German forces, U.S. and British forces were indeed surprised by the Germans' attacks. At the time of the defeat, in part due to efforts to protect the existence of ULTRA, alternative excuses and reasons for the defeat were generated.[17] Despite some claims that the morale of the U.S. Army in North Africa had been "shattered" by the battle, U.S. forces attacked again and again during the ensuing three months, until the final defeat and surrender of the German and Italian forces in May 1943.[18]

Combat in Northwest Africa in 1943 foreshadowed the structure of combat between U.S. and German forces for the remainder of World War II. This form of combat was familiar to U.S. officers who survived their own baptism of fire in the 1918 Meuse-Argonne offensive. Warfare in both 1918 and 1943 was a combination of relatively stable defensive fronts and shorter periods of mobile warfare. Dangling at the end of a tenuous and ineffective supply chain, U.S. and British forces themselves were not in any condition to attack *before* the German attack at Kasserine. Faced with an unacceptable situation, German commanders decided that a last-ditch effort was needed to change the worsening situation. Gambling on their own ability to maintain strength while bleeding the U.S. and British forces, the Germans attempted a breakthrough. Despite heavy U.S. losses, the Germans failed, suffering grievously; combined with additional losses a few days later, this sealed the fate of the Axis forces in North Africa. The battles between relatively stabilized defensive fronts continued with increasing logistical strength on the Allied side and simultaneous weakening on the Axis side, as well as efforts by both sides to create mobile warfare where battlefield decisions could be achieved. However, not until the generation of heavy — and irreplaceable — losses in German lives and material could mobile warfare be achieved. The Germans' Kasserine offensive, a last-ditch effort to salvage a lost theater, came at a heavy cost and accelerated their own defeat.[19]

The personal qualities of Ernie Harmon ("Old Gravel Voice" was one of his more polite nicknames), including his aggressiveness, outspokenness, and energy, are matters of birth, experience, and upbringing. But where did Harmon gain his intellectual competence as a division commander? To do the right thing under the extreme pressure of combat requires certain personal characteristics and leadership, but it also requires professional knowledge and decision-making skills — and the resulting professional self-confidence.[20] Between World War I and World War II, the United States Army's professional preparation, education, and training of large-formation leadership existed only at Fort Leavenworth, on bluffs overlooking the Missouri River in Kansas. Yet, as will be revealed in this book, of the hundreds of officers responsible for the management of army divisions in World War II, only the most senior actually attended the Command and General Staff Course at Leavenworth before the war began. This influence of the senior commanders, all of whom attended the peacetime Leavenworth course, was the foundation of effective command and staff functioning of U.S. Army divisions during World War II.

The army between the two world wars has been characterized as an institution caught between its traditional role ("long years of patrolling vast American distances against Indians and Mexican irregulars") and its role during World War I (its "brief moment of European intervention in 1917–1918)."[21] Army service during the interwar period was indeed a mixture of experiences. Omar Bradley, a major through most of the 1920s and 1930s, exemplifies the reality of life for a field-grade officer between the wars. Describing his tour of duty in Hawaii in the mid-1920s, Bradley reminisced:

> Peacetime garrison life in Hawaii for a major and his family was pleasant indeed. We worked only half-days and seldom on weekends. . . . My primary concern was tactical training in the field on terrain my battalion was assigned to defend. . . . I played golf on Schofield's fine eighteen-hole golf course four or five afternoons a week. . . . Our pay was still only about $300 a month, but that was sufficient to hire a domestic who made Mary's life easier and gave us considerable freedom.[22]

However, duty with troops was only a small part of officers' professional life between the wars. A larger proportion of their time was spent as student or instructor.

In the schools, U.S. army officers learned valuable and enduring lessons from World War I. Beginning in France in 1917, the basic army staff organization scheme, defined in the years after the 1903 reforms under Secretary of the Army Elihu Root, was completely revamped, modeled primarily after the French staff system.[23] General John J. Pershing had been so unimpressed by the staff work of the U.S. officer corps during World War I that he instituted a training school for staff officers at Langres, France, initially using French and British instructors.[24] After the war, the army incorporated these lessons and reorganized its education system to provide well-schooled staff officers.

World War I was a revolution in military affairs, but analysts still debate the nature of that revolution. Colin Gray's depiction of this revolution as an artillery-based change to the battlefield is compelling, as he describes a completely modern and novel system that explains the changes in fighting during 1917 and 1918.[25] In this modern system, a series of sensors replace the eye of the commander, requiring combined rather than individual judgment (i.e., a staff) to make decisions in order to exploit the industrial tools operating at long distances and in great numbers.[26] Personal leadership on the field of battle was no longer the purview of commanders above the rank of colonel; leadership by general officers was now made even more intellectually challenging by virtue of its disengagement from the battle itself.

The only school in the interwar army that taught the necessary principles, procedures, and techniques for this new form of combined arms warfare (combined infantry-artillery-tanks-airpower, controlled by a staff and led by a commander separated from immediate tactical decisions) was the Command and General Staff School at Leavenworth. Steeped in the lessons of the Great War, it focused consistently on division and corps operations. Thus it was the only school in the army that dealt with field unit general staff procedures. Leavenworth was the critical link in the chain that connected the World War I experience with the command and staff competence necessary for success in World War II. The U.S. officers who performed these critical tasks in World War II were educated chiefly at Leavenworth. How this education occurred, and what effect it had on the combat effectiveness of U.S. forces in World War II, virtually begs for a substantive analysis.

If the idea was to provide qualified officers to serve as the commanders and staff of U.S. divisions in World War II, something seems to have worked. At the conclusion of World War II, the U.S. Army convened a board of officers to investigate the future roles, missions, and organization of the infantry division. This board of officers concluded that significant changes were necessary to keep the infantry division relevant to modern battlefields. They recommended the addition of a tank regiment, the improvement of the artillery organic to the division, and significant changes in the supply and service organizations, antiaircraft, and antitank defenses. Practically the only satisfactory element of the infantry division, they concluded, was "the command and staff organization of division headquarters."[27] Staffed with officers from captain to full general, the board determined at the close of war in Europe that the doctrine and methods of army ground forces, and the organization of the command and staff of the infantry division, had proven themselves in combat.[28] The proof was evident in the intellectual and professional development of the officers who successfully led divisions and served as critical general staff officers.

The central question to be confronted is this: How did the U.S. Army expand forty-fold in officers during World War II while maintaining its professional competence? Part of this professional competence was the effective, if not painless, mobilization of the industrial might of the United States.[29] However, industrial might required military competence to bring power effectively to bear on the Italian, German, and Japanese armed forces. This military competence must have resided in the regular officer corps of the army even through the leanest years of the interwar period, considering the overwhelming presence of regular army officers in senior positions in combat divisions. More significant, this officer corps, hampered by inadequate budgets, insufficient unit training opportunities, and no new battle experience for more than two decades, somehow managed its organizations in extremely challenging global combat.

For commanders and chiefs of staff at the division level, being a long-service regular was practically a prerequisite. Within the boundaries of their profession, these officers perceived required competencies within the framework of a particular view of future warfare, one that was based to a large degree on the experience of the American Expeditionary Forces (AEF). The operational environment they foresaw was also a reflection of the 1917–1918 experience, although modified by developments in technology at home, as well as changes overseas. What emerges is an assessment that, in the U.S. Army of World War II, all commanders from division and above were graduates of Leavenworth. Practically all general staff officers of corps and above were graduates. However, at division headquarters—the primary place where combined arms were coordinated for battlefield effect—practically no general staff officers attended the peacetime courses at Leavenworth. Nevertheless, U.S. divisions were effective organizations for controlling violence on the battlefield.[30]

The major topics of this book include what the World War II division commanders and staff officers experienced from the Great War through the interwar period to combat operations in World War II; how they perceived their profession; how they approached mastering their professional skills; and what they believed the next battlefield environment would look like. The knowledge they gained from the army's educational program at the division and corps levels was based on the army's experience in France in 1917 and 1918.

Chapter 1

The Great War's Effect on the Army Officer Corps

The World War has made of the Army a great school. We are all of us its instructors. We receive instruction in subject matter and take courses in methods of instruction that we may pass our knowledge on to others most efficiently. Indeed, is it not a fair premise to say that in time of peace the major part of the work of the armed forces is instruction? To this end the appropriations are made, to this end all the organization is accomplished and administered— that men may be instructed to battle proficiency.

> —Major Frederick Pond, Pennsylvania National Guard,
> "Supervision of Instruction," *Infantry Journal*, January 1930

World War I changed how U.S. officers perceived modern war, their duties, and their education. The national experience in that conflict, which historians frequently underestimate as a short, relatively minor involvement with minimal casualties, actually caused a profound change within the U.S. Army. This had been a frontier constabulary during the last half of the nineteenth century and an imperial force during the first decade of the twentieth century. World War I was indeed a momentous experience.[1]

The AEF Experience

The U.S. Army was grossly unprepared for World War I.[2] Beginning with fewer than four divisions, formed initially against the threat of Pancho Villa, the army was short in every manpower, materiel, doctrinal, organizational, and educational requirement for modern warfare. Reminiscing shortly after World War I, Colonel George C. Marshall, who was Army Chief of Staff from 1939 through World War II, emphasized the complete lack of professional skill and competence in the first division to deploy to France. Marshall's experience as this division's G3 (operations and training officer) was searing. He reported for duty on the transport ship in New York harbor and met his fellow staff officers literally the day the ship sailed for France. As he wrote after the war, "We found the [division] contained organizations previously unheard of, which were to be armed with implements entirely new to us. Considering that we were starting on an expedition with an objective 3000 miles across the sea, it seemed rather remarkable that we should have embarked without knowledge of the character of the organization we were to fight."[3]

Marshall found himself immersed in tasks he described as "the most strenuous, hectic and laborious in my experience."[4] The new complexity of operations required significantly different competencies across different echelons of command, requirements not experienced by U.S. officers before 1917. Later Marshall commented how "strange" he felt during his transfer from the 1st Division, where he was G3, to the American Expeditionary Forces staff. The problems of the AEF were entirely different from the problems he had encountered in a division. Issues of ocean tonnage, ports, construction, and the myriad necessary details of running an expeditionary force were issues beyond his experience, at least to that date. "To me, this was a different world from which I had lived during the past year."[5]

Marshall, among many others, was experiencing one of the essential characteristics of twentieth-century warfare: the work required of a general staff. The army's nascent staffs of divisions, corps, and armies, never adequately defined in the years since the 1903 Root reforms, slowly gained maturity during execution of the campaigns in France. In this system, common by 1917 to all major European armies, officers performed general staff–like functions (operations, training, logistics, personnel) not only at central headquarters but also dispersed into numerous large formation staffs, an innovation for the U.S. Army.[6] To fulfill this need, from a start of some fifty officers, the total staff officers in the AEF numbered some 88,000 by the Armistice.[7] In his memoir of the war, Pershing wrote that "the development of a satisfactory general staff system required my special attention." He decried those "certain limited class of line officers" who denied the need for a general staff.[8] In the AEF Pershing created a general staff system for the first time in U.S. history.[9]

Some of the new requirements for trained general staff officers could be offset through the effective use of graduates from the Fort Leavenworth schools, but this was not by itself sufficient. The small pool of available graduates, slightly more than 700 since the Spanish-American War, was insufficient for more than 3 million soldiers in the field.[10] Another challenge confronting Pershing and the effective running of the AEF was a perception among nongraduates that the Leavenworth-trained officers were exerting an undue influence on activities, promotions, and military execution. The domination of the AEF staff by Leavenworth graduates cannot be exaggerated. Of twelve staff officers who served as

AEF chief of staff, deputy chief of staff, G3, G4, or G5, nine were Leavenworth graduates. Just as significant was their domination of general staff positions in field units. The chiefs of staff of both field armies and the chiefs of staff of nine of ten of the corps were graduates, as were the chiefs of staff of twenty-three of the twenty-six divisions engaged in combat. [11]

What the graduates of Leavenworth provided—the "leaven" to use Edward M. Coffman's word—was a shared language and attitude toward problem solving.[12] As Charles Herron (Leavenworth class of 1908), chief of staff of 78th Division, stated of another Leavenworth man, "He understood what you said and you understood what he said."[13] This common understanding did not extend to the more senior officers in the AEF, as the majority of them, including Pershing, had never attended the schools. None of the army or corps commanders had attended, and of the fifty-seven officers who commanded the twenty-six divisions committed to combat, only seven were graduates.[14] If there was distrust of the Leavenworth clique, it came not from peers and junior officers but rather some of the most senior commanders of the AEF, reflecting a distrust of their educated subordinate staff officers.[15]

Despite concerns over the Leavenworth clique and the small pool of graduates available, the Leavenworth education was valued by Pershing and the AEF's senior staff. After the war, Marshall remembered that Pershing "crystallized the appreciation of higher education in the Army, particularly Leavenworth, upon whose graduates he leaned very heavily in France, to such an extent that a standing order required that every Leavenworth graduate disembarking in France would be detached from his unit and sent directly to Chaumont—there were very few of them in those days."[16] Personal desires for promotion opportunities available through combat command were unimportant compared to the requirements for qualified staff officers. The overwhelming need for competent staffs is reflected in the nearly continuous combined phrase of "good unit commanders and good staffs" in reports and reminiscences from veterans of the AEF, including General Pershing.[17]

The requirements of the AEF demanded an additional source of officers educated in general staff processes, terminology, and techniques.[18] Hugh Drum was assigned the problem, and he recommended the creation of a staff school in France, modeled directly on the Leavenworth school system before 1917, with minor modifications to better align the AEF staff with the French and British staff systems.[19] During its existence, this general staff course, in the small city of Langres, graduated 500 officers in four classes.[20] U.S. officers proven in combat operations and in demanding staff positions were selected for instructor positions, at a significant cost to the short-term efficiency of the AEF.[21]

The school drew its students from the army in the United States and from

General Staff of General Staff College, Langres, France, December 28, 1918. Orlando Ward, who commanded 1st Armored Division at Kasserine and whom Harmon confronted, is second from the right in this photograph. U.S. Army photograph.

officers already in France. In September 1917, Pershing cabled the War Department asking for the assignment of 100 officers from the United States as students for the first class at Langres. Weeks later, the War Department cabled that they could find only fourteen available officers. The shortfall was made up from divisions already in France, an effort that understandably generated severe opposition from division commanders. Eventually, seventy-five officers began the first course on November 28, 1917; only forty-two graduated three months later. The removal of officers from AEF assignments for student duty at Langres continued through the end of the war. The Langres course graduated its final students in December 1918.[22]

This three-month course anticipated the students' assignments.[23] Officers who would return to a G3 assignment, for example, would be instructed in the duties of operations, with only a brief introduction in general staff procedures for the entire staff system. This focused instruction was markedly different from the general instruction at Leavenworth, which had closed in 1916 and remained closed for the duration of the war. The method of instruction, however, came directly from the program in Kansas. Focused on the practical skills required of particular staff sections, the school continued the practical application of problem solving as the basis of instruction. Emblematic of the source of this approach to education, the main school instruction hall at Langres was named Sherman Hall, the same as the main school structure at Leavenworth.[24]

Although the efforts of the Langres school made up an important part of the increasing competence of U.S. general staff officers, the new staff officers had a difficult time coping with the complexities of modern war after only such a brief education. According to George Marshall, "Many [of our general staff officers] had not previous practical experience, and most had but three months instruction at Langres. . . . Their lack of adequate training and experience, together with their sudden immersion in a tremendous and prolonged conflict, developed weaknesses which intimately affected the troops."[25]

Tremendous and prolonged conflict identified the command and staff weaknesses of the army. Caught between a desire for a uniquely American way of war that was thought by Pershing and others to be superior to the worn-out ways of the French and British, and the horrible reality of the defensive fronts in 1918, officers in the AEF began to learn modern warfare. Attacks by U.S. divisions to blunt the German spring 1918 offensives, by the 1st Infantry Division at Cantigny, the 1st and 2nd Infantry Divisions at Soissons, and the corps-sized offensive at St. Mihiel, were all bloody contests. The fighting at the Meuse-Argonne, the single bloodiest offensive in U.S. history, in its initial stages was disastrous. Key to success on the battlefield was the competence of the corps and division commanders and staff officers; in a single day during the Meuse-Argonne offensive, October 15, 1918, Pershing relieved three division commanders for incompetence. Despite the prevailing awareness by the British and French that artillery coordination was essential to any form of success, artillery support remained incompetent, for the most part, and remained controversial down to the last days of the war.[26]

At the very end of the war, in the last phase of the Meuse-Argonne offensive, the AEF actually began to fully appreciate and account for the requirements of modern warfare—combined arms reliance on massive firepower in an effort to conduct a breakthrough of the defensive front aimed at restoring some form of mobility to combat. Only in the November 1918 attack of V Corps did the AEF accomplish these requirements. Commanded by Major General Charles P. Summerall, this two-division attack was founded on deliberate, intensive fire planning—and was markedly successful. Summerall, an artilleryman, ordered "fire superiority, rather than sheer manpower be the driving force of the attack." The complexity of V Corps' planning can be appreciated when it is understood that army, corps, and division artillery organizations would all coordinate their fires in accord with a four-phased plan. These phases—before the preliminary bombardment, the preliminary bombardment itself, covering fire for the initial infantry assault, and then support of the infantry in subsequent attacks—were all predetermined, coordinated across the corps' staff, integrated with the intelligence of known and suspected enemy positions, and communicated to all firing batteries. The plan was also, of course, communicated to the two divisions, which then conducted thorough planning of their own. When the attacks began on November 1, 1918, the results were spectacularly successful, in comparison with most AEF combat experiences.[27] The U.S. Army, through the bloodiest of all campaigns, had begun to gain competence in modern warfare on the eve of armistice.

The Unfinished, Horrible Business

The sudden end of the Great War shocked many army officers, the unfinished nature of the struggle remaining a concern for these officers through the interwar period. In the words of one assessment, "Among many of the front-line troops in the Allied armies there was therefore an ambivalent mood, elation at the end of hostilities yet frustration that the victory was somehow muddied by a sense that Germany was still on its feet, bloodied but unbowed. Among the AEF there was a widespread sense of having been cheated of real triumph."[28] On November 11, 1918, in the quiet of his office at Chaumont, Pershing remarked to an aide, "I suppose the campaigns are ended, but what an enormous difference a few days would have made."[29]

Many young officers believed that another war would come; Bradford Chynoweth, a regular army officer who spent the war in the United States, called it "the inevitable War of the Future."[30] Lieutenant Colonel Walter Krueger also shared this view and hoped in 1919 that the lessons learned from the experience of the war in Europe would not be wasted. He was concerned that necessary preparedness would be abandoned by the American people, as "we licked them after raising a splendid army in a short time, what we've done once we can do again and therefore why have any large measure of preparedness?" He remained hopeful that the officer corps, "we of the army . . . ought to be heard."[31] Marshall also worried, as early as 1923, about the Armistice's effects on postwar security, referring to the Armistice as an "open question." Marshall admitted the difficulties inherent in continuing to fight after the Germans had requested an armistice, as well as the challenges of dealing with a Germany without a government, which may have resulted in the collapse of the German empire. However, he still regretted that a more decisive end to the war "did not crown the victory with the disarmament of the German troops, and thus have avoided the effect on the German populace of having their armies march home claiming that they had never been defeated."[32]

Americans considered the war with Germany to be over, and they hoped for the end of military adventures overseas.[33] In the officer corps, there was a different perception. Writing a letter to the editor of *Infantry Journal* in May 1920, Captain E. H. Cotcher asked a series of rhetorical questions, the first simply being: "Have we seen the Last War?"[34] Major General Charles P. Summerall, in a 1927 Infantry School graduation speech reprinted in *Infantry Journal*, declared the graduates ready for the future, including a role in bringing "victory to our arms if, unhappily, our agencies of peace again should fail."[35]

Added to the concerns over the hasty end to the war were personal and professional memories of the slaughter. The stress of the massive casualties suffered by the AEF, particularly in September and October 1918, when the majority of combat casualties occurred, can be understood only in relation to the anticipated casualties in the Big Push planned for 1919.[36] The casualties suffered in the last three months of the Western Front, when America lost 17,000 killed in action every month, charred the professional officer corps. In September 1918, those who were killed in action or died of wounds climbed from 1,000 per week to nearly 2,000, then leaped to more than 6,000 in the first week of October, as a result of the Meuse-Argonne offensive.[37] These rates were among the highest of any U.S. war.[38] The sudden armistice was the only thing that prevented the deaths of hundreds of thousands of U.S. soldiers in 1919. The entire war planning and mobilization effort of the United States was based on winning the decisive victory in 1919, including the necessary cost in blood. Huge, devastating, and crushing casualties, both actual and anticipated, affected the officers who planned and executed these offensives. [39]

Added to the perception of another war, and to the personal and professional experience of the slaughter of the Meuse-Argonne campaign, was a deep feeling of professional incompetence. In less than eighteen months, the AEF created two armies, ten corps, and twenty-six divisions and engaged these new large formations in offensive combat against the German defenses.[40] These offensive combat operations came at a significant cost and engendered a reluctant appraisal by army officers of their incompetence at the essential tasks of modern war: planning, logistics, organization, and the "handling of large formations." This incompetence, noted by many senior and junior officers during the war, resulted in numerous efforts to gain these abilities in 1917 and 1918, including the creation of the AEF General Staff School at Langres; it also generated a perceived need to maintain competence in these areas after the Armistice.

Ernie Harmon shared this view. Assigned to the 2nd Cavalry Regiment for both the St. Mihiel and Meuse-Argonne offensives, Harmon found himself in command of a provisional squadron when the titular commander was medically unable to perform his duties. Recalling his experience in his memoir and in two interwar articles for *Cavalry Journal,* he referred to his squadron as a "group of eager amateurs under the command of a captain (myself) who had been a commissioned officer for eighteen months." Harmon described the movement forward for the St. Mihiel offensive as "progress seemed impossible. Congestion on the narrow road was indescribable: artillery, wagons, ammunition trucks, infantry struggled forward in the dark." Encountering Germans for the first time, Harmon and another junior officer grabbed two automatic rifles and personally began firing at the Germans. Meanwhile the rest of the squadron, leaderless, blundered into an ambush and bolted. Harmon barely managed to get them back under control. Learning lessons about personal bravery, leadership, and responsibility, Harmon continued to try to accomplish the squadron mission of reconnaissance and security operations, in the hell of the modern battlefield.[41]

After two weeks in combat in St. Mihiel, Harmon's squadron was ordered to support the next offensive: Meuse-Argonne, even more confusing and bloody than Harmon's first combat experience. He described the wastage of his men and horses in a chapter he titled "The Decisive Battle." Three weeks of confused, bloody, and poorly organized combat operations left his squadron without serviceable horses, and it was disbanded as a unit in mid-October 1918. However, one of the troops of the squadron was "within 3,000 yards of Sedan just before the Armistice." In his 1922 *Cavalry Journal* article, he wrote that toward the end of the offensive the lieutenant in charge of this troop was told by his corps commander that he "wished he had a division of cavalry to send through on the morning." Breakthrough was almost possible, it seemed—except there was no cavalry available after all the casualties of the offensive.[42]

In autumn 1919, the editor of *Field Artillery Journal* called for U.S. officers to "admit that we muddled, but we muddled through, which was as much as anyone had a right to hope for." He then added, looking to the future of the army, "Do we congratulate the country and ourselves that we did no worse in the face of our handicaps? Do we decide to let bygones be bygones and resolve to profit in future by our obvious mistakes? It does not appear that we do. . . . And nobody appears to be giving a thought to the next season." This editorial comment was appended to an open letter to the field artillery community from Major General William J. Snow, chief of field artillery. In this letter, General Snow wrote that the rapidly demobilizing army was "in a business parlance, in the hands of a receiver. But just as receivership in business puts a concern back on its feet, so in military matters, we will emerge from this 'receivership' as a going concern . . . so that when the next war comes—as it will, sooner or later—we may not again be caught unprepared."[43] As Brigadier General Preston Brown put it in remarks to the faculty of the General Staff College, a lack of preparedness for U.S. entry into a general European war was excusable in 1916, but "we could justly be blamed, in 1922, under similar conditions, for bungling again, or for bungling in far worse fashion."[44] Perhaps the most enduring legacy of the wartime experience for the regular officer corps was the assumption that the next war, when it came, would again require, in the words of interwar doctrine, the "maximum mobilized manpower of the Nation."[45]

Preparedness and an Impecunious Army

General Pershing conceived the next war as a war of the entire nation, not of just the regular army. In his address to the 1920 graduating class of the General Staff College, Pershing declared: "It would seem pertinent to emphasize the great importance of general staff instruction and its bearing upon the future war efficiency of the army. Indeed, we should say upon the war efficiency of the country, for it is the nation with all its resources including the army that makes war."[46] Pershing, Congress, and to some extent Americans in general understood that, if war came again, the entire resources of the nation would be required to fight and win. But without any immediate enemies, and with no perceived current threat to the national existence, the maintenance of a large force was politically impossible, indeed not even desired by anyone in authority. The maintenance of a large regular peacetime force would have been unique in U.S. history, and it was not something that Congress contemplated for very long. The lesson of the Great War—that it required the mobilization of the entire nation—presented Congress with a new mandate for national security in the immediate post-Armistice period. The new policy that resulted was, in the words of Allan Millett and Peter Maslowski, "a reasonable response to the risks of the 1920s."[47]

The National Defense Act of June 4, 1920, established a novel military policy for the United States. This act, a result of a vibrant debate in 1919 and early 1920, conceived of the military as a preparatory force and established the expansion base for a war of national mobilization, not for a force ready for immediate combat. This concept—a small regular army designed as a schoolhouse for both the National Guard and a large reserve force with an unusually large proportion of commissioned officers—did not match the perception of some regulars, but it was the appropriate military policy for the nation.[48]

Given the spirit of the times, Congress proceeded to underfund the army it had designed. Although the 1920s were a time of national economic prosperity, they were not years of affluence for the military. Four years after the Armistice, Brigadier General Hanson E. Ely, commandant of Fort Leavenworth, testified before a subcommittee of the U.S. House Committee on Appropriations in hearings on the 1923 appropriations bill for the Army. Ely argued:

> The officers who are sent there as instructors are among the keenest men
> in the Army, and I now work those officers up to 11 and 12 o'clock at night
> for about five nights in the week. It is my desire, if I can, to reduce the
> work of these instructors down to the equivalent of the work of ordinary
> officers of the army. . . . On account of the lack of money we can not hire
> stenographers, so I say to them "You have got to do this work, it must be
> done by a certain time; here is a typewriter, go to it." And they pick on a
> typewriter with one finger, and that is what they are doing now.

Representative Thomas Sisson asked of General Ely, "That does not cost the government anything extra, does it?"[49] Ely, whose 28th Infantry Regiment suffered nearly 1,000 casualties in the Battle of Cantigny, did not share Congress's concerns with the costs of paper and typewriters. He was more concerned with developing the competency of army staff officers in handling large formations than with administrative costs. Ely continued, with a grim determination, to improve the officer education at Leavenworth, even when Congress continued to penny-pinch.[50]

The concerns over seemingly petty financial issues were reflected in professional journals. The June 1923 edition of *Infantry Journal* included a note from the chief of infantry that asked readers to

> look about the orderly room. Our eye rests on the typewriter, among other
> things. You know how hard it is to get a typewriter repaired, or to get a
> new ribbon for it. Has the machine been oiled and cleaned every week as
> required by regulations? If the ribbon is a bit worse for wear, i.e., makes a
> weak impression—has it been turned over? Think of what it means when
> all the orderly rooms in the Infantry want a new ribbon.[51]

These are hardly concerns that should have forced the major general in charge of the infantry branch to write an article for his professional journal, but this was indicative of the lack of resources throughout the interwar period.

The central core of the army—the officer corps—survived these two decades of scarce resources and the failure of all efforts to generate universal military training or peacetime conscription. Officers found refuge from the problems of typewriter ribbons in the mundane life of the Army: troop duty in dusty outposts scattered around the country; occasional (and more challenging) assignments to China, the Philippines, Hawaii, and Panama; and repetitive assignments as either students or instructors with the newly refashioned officer education system and in support of the National Guard and the Reserves.[52] In 1929, as reported in *Infantry Journal*, nearly half of infantry field-grade officers and captains were assigned as instructors or students in the officer education system. Of these officers, one in ten was at a branch school, one in twenty at Leavenworth or the War College, and more than half were teaching ROTC, the Reserves, or the National Guard.[53]

Ernie Harmon, for example, in the two decades of the interwar period spent eight years as an instructor, four at West Point as an instructor of tactics and military drawing (as well as assistant football coach), and four as the commandant of cadets at Norwich College. He was also a student for four years, one at the Cavalry School at Fort Riley Kansas, two at Fort Leavenworth, and one at the Army War College. He served four years on the War Department's General Staff (in G4). His time with the troops was slightly less than four years: two as a junior officer with the 6th Cavalry at Fort Oglethorpe, Georgia; one as a squadron commander in the 8th Cavalry at Fort Bliss, Texas; and a bit less than one year with the 1st Mechanized Cavalry at Fort Knox, Kentucky. He rounded out the interwar period as the G4 of the Army Ground Forces under Lieutenant General Lesley McNair.[54]

These mundane daily activities, including the education of the officer corps, were themselves not necessarily vulnerable to budget cuts or congressional mandates—if sufficiently protected by senior army officers. Senior officers, unable to change the sections of the Army that required extensive resources, chose to change—and to maintain—things within their purview, including the army educational system.[55]

Acceptance of the New Army

Two related factors led to the eventual acceptance of the new role of teacher-student as the norm for professional officers. One factor was the continued declarations by General Pershing of the need for a new form of professionalism in the officer corps. In an Army War College graduation speech published in *Field Artillery Journal* in 1923, he called on the graduates of the Army War College to develop "a breadth of vision essential to the efficient Army officer of today." He continued:

> In no other army is it so imperative that the officers of the permanent establishment be highly perfected specialists, prepared to serve as instructors and leaders for the citizen forces which are to fight our wars. The one-time

role of a regular army officer has passed with the Indian Campaigns and the acquirement of colonial possessions. Our mission today is definite, yet so broad that few, if any, have been able to grasp the possibilities of new fields opened up by the military policy now on the statute books. . . . There are officers, fortunately in constantly diminishing numbers, who cannot turn their minds from concentration on a diminutive regular army, successfully, and gallantly fighting the country's battles as in Cuba and the Philippines, or serving at isolated stations along the Mexican Border. Those days have not entirely passed away, and probably never will pass, but they are now of secondary importance in the general scheme of National Defense.[56]

The other factor was Congress, which stood ready to spend sufficient funds for officer education but not to maintain a large ready force.

This change generated a spirited debate in professional journals. *Cavalry Journal* led with an editorial in its October 1921 edition titled "The Task of Teaching." It called on readers to embrace that "we have entered upon a large field that may be characterized as 'teaching duty'" and to understand that, in peacetime, this was not only necessary but also natural for army professionals. The editor felt compelled to write, "Reduction Must Not Effect [*sic*] Cavalry Spirit," his very next editorial comment, symbolizing the shift in the profession from duty with units to education.[57] The debate had been stimulated by an *Infantry Journal* article in May 1921 by Major Bernard Lentz, a frequent contributor to journals in the 1920s: "Who Is Going to Soldier When Everybody Is Going to School?" His answer was a cautionary note to the army that the soul of the profession had to continue to be troop duty.[58] Elbridge Colby, another prolific contributor, responded by explaining that Lentz's critique reflected a misunderstanding of the purpose of the officer education system. The system was designed not only to begin the education of officers but also to require officers to continue self-development for their entire careers. The in-house schooling was not to replace self-study or the experiences of troop duty but to enhance both.[59]

Other articles recommended development of personal professional libraries, informed readers of policies for school selection, and provided advice for officers recently selected to be students. There were also reprints of instruction memoranda from the various schools.[60] Colby continued to write articles extolling the virtues of the new education system.[61] Eventually, even Major Lentz returned to the discussion, this time in a 1932 article entitled "The Applicatory Method." Lentz, although still critical of the lack of proper teaching skills and methods at army schools, was now much more accepting of the need for education. Where earlier he had called for a reduction in the length and number of courses, now he simply called for optimizing the educational experience through high-quality educational methods.[62] He wrote, "The schools have been worth all the money and all the efforts we have expended"; writing of his earlier article, condemning excessive officer education, he wrote that "'fools who came to scoff, stayed to pray' now aptly describes the change of sentiment that has taken place."[63]

The funding of the officer education system permitted the construction of large school facilities at Fort Benning in the 1920s for infantry and at Fort Sill in the 1930s for field artillery. Usually overlooked by historians of the period, the relatively large investment of funds in the officer education system would be an essential part of the U.S. Army's competence during World War II. As the budget constraints of the 1920s worsened in the 1930s due to the Great Depression, in the words of one historian of the Army in this period,

> the General Staff was inflexible, doctrinaire and adamant on this point; all else, including equipment and material in general, would be willingly reduced, sacrificed, or eliminated. Nothing could deter the General Staff from maintaining its policy that the skeletonized training basis of the mass army must be kept intact at the expense of all other activities and projects. This meant that the highest priority was put on the maintenance of the regular army officer corps, army schools, ROTC, Officers Reserve Corps, and the National Guard.[64]

All other priorities, including unit readiness and equipment procurement, were secondary to this. Perhaps difficult to understand from the view of historians conditioned to the massive standing military and enormous defense expenditures of the cold war, this policy was fully in keeping with the congressional mandate of the National Defense Act of 1920 and the strategic position of the United States until 1939.

Although it is difficult to precisely determine the amount of resources expended on the army schools during the interwar period, given the nature of the published financial records, it is clear that the schools consumed a significant amount of available resources. Fort Benning, created toward the very end of World War I, for example, consumed more than $1 million in constructing the facilities for the Infantry School.[65] After the war, new construction at Fort Benning for the Infantry School consumed some $12 million in the 1920s; and at Fort Sill, nearly $10 million was spent during the Depression.[66] A major construction project had been completed in 1916 at Fort Leavenworth, so there was no comparable expenditure of funds for the Command and General Staff School for this period.[67] Nearly half of all regular army officers were assigned to various school duties, and with payroll accounting for 40 percent of the annual army expenditures, the schools consumed a sizable proportion of officer pay through the period.[68] Although operating expenses for schools were minimal, annually averaging less than $100,000 for all schools combined, the investment was in construction and personnel—and these were considerable.[69]

Promotion's Very Slow

The 1920 National Defense Act did pose some serious challenges for the officer corps, including stagnant promotions, poor training opportunities with troop units, and, despite relatively robust experimentation, little procurement of new equipment for ground forces. Promotions, as explained by Army Chief of Staff Summerall, were an essential component of the profession of arms, as officers look to gain rank as both an indicator of career success and a sign that they will be offered greater opportunities in the future.[70] The almost stagnant system of promotions in the 1920s and 1930s was a major crisis for army leaders and had some effect on the sense of professionalism among officers themselves. This stagnation was generated by an artifact of World War I: a "hump" in the officer corps' promotion list. The accession of thousands of officers through rapid commissioning after April 1917 generated a large population of junior officers who remained in service through World War II. From a strength of 5,960 regular army officers in April 1917, the commissioned strength of the Army reached some 203,786 by the Armistice.[71]

As explained in official War Department testimony before the House of Representatives Committee on Military Affairs,

> The dominant feature of our present personnel is an abnormal group of about 5,800 officers, considerably more than half of the present promotion list, who were inducted into the service between November, 1916 and November, 1918, and who therefore, vary in length of commissioned service by less than two years. . . . The great bulk of them fall within narrow age limits. Under normal conditions the entry into service, and consequently, the difference in length of commissioned service, of this large group of officers would have been spread over a period of about 20 years, and they would be similarly graded by age. Practically all of our difficulties are due to the existence of this "hump" in our personnel.[72]

This hump of officers was 55.4 percent of the total number of commissioned officers in 1926; it would still be there, like a pig in a python, upon the outbreak of World War II.[73] Despite various studies and proposals for reducing the hump, and thereby accelerating the stagnant promotions, only the onset of national mobilization in 1940 solved the problem, with its attendant increase in promotion possibilities (at least in temporary rank).

The effect of the hump and the National Defense Act upon promotions was intense. Although efforts were made to have promotions occur to "first lieutenant at three years of service; to captain, ten years; to major, seventeen years; to lieutenant colonel, twenty-two years; and to colonel, twenty-eight years," this was not achieved for officers within the hump.[74] As told in many memoirs and biographies written by officers in the interwar army, promotions were exceedingly slow for the officers within or behind the hump. Promotions, when they occurred in accordance with the statute, occurred by strict seniority. The interwar promotion system was based on a classification system of officer evaluation reports. Under this system, officers were designated by superiors as either Class A officers qualified for promotion in due course or as Class B officers who should be removed from service for any and all reasons. The Class B category was used rarely, and officers categorized in Class B could appeal their categorization all the way to the White House. As a result, although the population of the officer corps usually exceeded 12,000 during this period, only 350 officers were eliminated from service under this classification system between 1920 and 1937.[75] Officers were always promoted to the next grade, by seniority, unless they had been separated from the service under a Class B board.[76]

Selection by quality, or by merit, was extremely controversial in the interwar army and never became a matter of course. In the words of "Agrippa II" (officers occasionally used pseudonyms) in a 1939 article, promotion by selection "just does not work equitably and satisfactorily to all concerned." Promotion by seniority had one great advantage: everyone was treated the same. The only promotion that was considered influenced by "who you knew" as opposed to "what you knew" was to general officer. With only sixty-eight general officers authorized by statute from an officer corps of almost 9,000, and with mandatory retirement for age at sixty-four years, the chance of making general for someone in the hump was, in peacetime, remote indeed. The article by "Agrippa II" pointed out that officers in the hump would be retired for chronological age while still majors and lieutenant colonels, leaving a huge gap in senior officers by 1949.[77]

Many other authors joined the fray from 1921 through 1940. Part of the initial debate was the proposal of a single armywide list for promotion. After passage of the National Defense Act of 1920, the Army formed a board of officers, which created, from June 1920 to January 1921, in strict accord with the statute, the single promotion list for all army officers. In an effort to educate its readers, *Infantry Journal* published two informative and detailed articles about the statute and this board's proceedings.[78] The editor felt so strongly about the so-called One List issue that he wrote it was necessary for national defense—without it, training of draftees for the next war would be very difficult.[79] Eventually accepted by the army officer corps over complaints by some branches, who thought they were being slighted, the single list remained law through the period. The majority of the debate continued to be about the officer hump. Completely unresolved by several efforts to accelerate attrition and early retirement, among other proposals, the hump marched forward slowly with each passing year, with small numbers of officers off the single list gradually promoted to the next grade by pure seniority. It was, at least, impartial.

In addition to slow promotions within or behind the hump, there existed a perception that officers who had served in France would receive preferential promotions. This perception, on the part of many officers who had not served in France in 1917 or 1918, was moderated by the huge numbers of officers who had not had that opportunity yet remained in service. On the day of the Armistice, slightly more than half the mobilized army had been shipped to France.[80] The percentage of regular army officers who deployed to France was even lower than that of the overall army, as a disproportionate number remained as part of the training and mobilization establishment. Many junior officers, as well as the majority of field-grade officers (major, lieutenant colonel, and colonel), had remained in the continental United States, preparing the remaining divisions for deployment in late 1918 and throughout 1919.[81] Examples of the attitudes of these officers, their desire to learn from those who did deploy, and their awareness of having "missed the war" are related in their memoirs. Many reported that they made every effort to join the AEF, usually without success, and they understood that they "hadn't gotten into" World War I.[82]

Assessing the proportion of officers who served in the AEF would have mitigated some concern. Of the class of 1915 from West Point, 102 of 164 graduating cadets (62 percent) were sent overseas by the Armistice, but only 56 (34 percent) served in actual combat duties in France. Sixty-two (38 percent) of the class were never sent overseas.[83] This assessment was corroborated by Brigadier General Lytle Brown (director, War Plans Division, War Department General Staff), who wrote in a December 14, 1918, memorandum that military instruction in the postwar army should begin with the "nearly 60 percent of the regular officers who had not had service in France."[84] Although a serving officer could assume that the army would reward combat veterans over those who had missed the war, their concerns would eventually be assuaged by the huge needs during World War II for educated and competent officers, regardless of combat experience. Intellectual and professional development was stimulated by more than the changes in the role of the regular army. Training in the understrength units of the interwar force, and a vibrant discussion of professional issues in the branch journals, also stimulated the officer corps.

Training

Unit training during the interwar period was not up to the standards of the officer corps. Many officers criticized the lack of resources available for unit training, and many methods were discussed to optimize what resources were available.[85] However, at the end of these two decades the standard of training for field units in the regular army was woeful. The standard for National Guard units was even lower. Most evocative was a piece in the February 1926 edition of *Infantry Journal* in which the author awakens from a dream of effective training to face another morning of training his battalion with "a total of four or five squads available for instruction! Oh, hell!"[86]

Despite recommendations to make the most of training under the resource constraints of the period, many officers complained about the lack of resources—particularly of soldiers—to train. Leading these complaints, by the 1930s, was the voice of Major General Douglas MacArthur. Usually assessed by historians as one of the few senior leaders who had the courage to take Congress to task for lack of resources, MacArthur came very close to insubordination in at least one speech before he became chief of staff. The episode was reprinted in *Infantry Journal:* MacArthur, while a corps area commander, told an annual convention of the Reserve Officer's Association,

> In vain [George Washington] pointed to the fact that a well regulated army does not menace liberty or peace. . . . What Washington failed to accomplish on behalf of an adequate military establishment has never been fully achieved by any of his successors, and the proper correlation of civil and military power will not be possible until an intelligent public opinion forces the issue. The entire question is largely a matter of money, as indeed are all considerations of government. . . . People who wish to be free must pay for freedom. Parsimony in expenditure . . . amounts in effect to abdication of sovereignty. . . . Accordingly, as a subject for future reflection, perhaps, I give you as a concluding statement: *An invincible Navy, a model Regular Army, an efficient National Guard, a trained Reserve, all correlated to the civil power of the nation and the States, and all nourished and protected by an invincible public opinion.*[87]

As Army Chief of Staff from 1930 through 1935, MacArthur continued to advocate for additional funding, but to little effect. The Army's budgets never allowed for anything other than skeletonized units, despite relatively robust expenditures for the air service and officer education.

Officer-authored requests for additional resources were frequent in the interwar journals, but so were observations that the economies of the National Defense Act, and subsequent minimal appropriations, were the proper policy for the United States, if perhaps carried to an unfortunate extreme of parsimony. As the president of the Reserve Officer's Association wrote in a 1926 edition of *Infantry Journal*, "The essence of the National Defense Act is that it brings the expense within reasonable limits by eliminating all those things which can be done within a reasonable time after the declaration of war and provides for obtaining and having in readiness only those things that take a long time to obtain and prepare."[88] Added to the debate over resources was a nearly constant reference to the need to be prepared for the rapid expansion of the force in the event of a crisis. Usually linked to the lessons of World War I, frequent articles discussed the techniques necessary for mobilizing and training large numbers of conscripts in times of crisis.[89] Other articles discussed the challenges of keeping National Guard units ready for any role in national defense.[90]

One of the rare bright spots for unit training during the interwar period was the occasional large-unit maneuvers and command-post exercises (CPXs) conducted on an annual basis for some units. Although criticized in the journals as being generally unrealistic, these maneuvers did offer training opportunities for assigned officers, as well as for readers of the professional journals (where the results of maneuvers were frequently published). Maneuver reports began soon after the end of the war in Europe, initially about the training of the U.S. occupation forces in Germany.[91] In 1924, Major Adna R. Chaffee reported on the 1923 maneuvers of the 1st Cavalry Division in a detailed and lengthy report. Conducted in the vicinity of Marfa, Texas, on land "roughly that of the land area of the state of Rhode Island," the maneuver included road and rail movements, both horse-drawn and motorized, of the entire 1st Cavalry Division. Using radios for communication, the division deployed distances in excess of 200 miles to the training area. Upon arrival, umpires oversaw the two-sided maneuvers, which included eight days of force-on-force maneuver.[92] Maneuvers like this continued throughout the interwar period, usually at division level but occasionally involving smaller organizations.[93]

These events introduced to the participating officers, and subsequent journal readers, many of the issues involved with long-distance troop movements, command and control over long distances, and forming cohesive organizations from a polyglot group of smaller organizations. For example, the First Army concentration, which occurred August 17–31, 1935, formed units from two corps area commands and five different divisions into a coherent training effort focused on "combined field exercises, training in logistics, and testing active units of the Regular Army as to rapid concentration." Colonel Conrad Lanza, author of this report (and one of the more prolific authors in the period), concluded that the maneuvers demonstrated both the need to update training regulations and that motor-equipped units would "make circles around foot troops." He recommended, as did most observers, that more maneuvers, with larger units and more funding, should be conducted to improve the training level of the entire force.[94]

Command-post exercises were also conducted during this period but were reported on less frequently than were maneuvers. Designed to provide training for unit staffs without the expense involved with large-unit maneuvers, these exercises were held frequently and included National Guard units and officers of the Organized Reserves.[95] These exercises were useful as a training program for modern war, as demonstrated by the criticism of CPXs raised by General H. S. Hawkins, a frequent contributor to *Cavalry Journal*.[96] Hawkins complained that the army had "gone wild over command post exercises." He believed that all such exercises were based on the trench-warfare system taught to the AEF by the French and that "we have continued to use this method ever since our 'successful' campaign in France." Declaring that commanders must get away from the telephone and go to see for themselves what is happening, Hawkins appeared to forget that his topic was exercises that did not involve troops or terrain.[97]

A special category of army officer experience—neither experiment, nor maneuver, nor CPX but rather a large-scale practice run for mobilization—was the Army's involvement in the Civilian Conservation Corps (CCC). Involving huge numbers of young men organized into camps by army officers and soldiers, the CCC experience was an important adjunct to other professional events during the late interwar period. Numerous articles explained how to conduct camp administration, how to lead large groups of young men using the character of military leadership without the stick of legal authority, and how to publicize the CCC experience for the good of the Army.[98] Other articles called attention to the Army's need to rapidly correct some of the deficiencies in the officer corps revealed by the camps, especially a lack of initiative, reflected in the need to relieve many of the camp commanders.

For the author of one article, the CCC camps proved that the army needed to break from its peacetime garrison activities and become a force ready to adapt to the modern "empty battlefield." In concluding "The Assassination of Initiative," he wrote:

> The rigid fulfillment of routine tasks in peace is made the symbol of duty
> in war. Excellence is judged by the "outward and visible sign." The symbols
> of discipline and training have replaced the reality. Colonels and generals
> usurp the captain's commands. Since the World War our organizations and
> our preparations for mobilizing men and industry have improved; staff
> training has become a reality. The form of an army has been provided

without its substance—without true leaders and the discipline of spirit which alone can keep men on the battlefield of today. Before the army is war worthy the dry rot in its core will be burned out in the fires of lost battles, and by then the war may be lost.[99]

Other officers did not share this appraisal. Ernie Harmon, for example, reflected on his CCC experience as another opportunity to understand the human material of U.S. soldiers for the next war. Harmon's experience reminded him that U.S. soldiers needed to be listened to and have things explained to them.[100]

Experimentation

From 1925 through 1939, as the Army focused its intellectual and financial energies on education, it also experimented with motorization, mechanization, airpower, artillery improvements, and developments in radio. The bulk of this was conducted by branch experimentation boards, normally colocated with the branch schools, which frequently reported the findings in their respective journals. Articles explained experimental techniques and results and the possibilities for modern warfare presented by new equipment and tactics.[101] For example, field artillery experimentation began immediately after World War I, and reports on these tests were frequently published in *Field Artillery Journal*. Test results for 155mm self-propelled artillery, on a chassis designed by Walter Christie, were published in late 1919.[102] Results of experiments with new 155mm and 8-inch artillery pieces, with photographs and line drawings clearly identical to the weapons eventually produced for World War II, were published eleven years later in the same journal. Reports on motorization and mechanization for "prime movers" of artillery pieces appeared frequently. Occasionally, experiments resulted in the acceptance of limited numbers of new equipment for issue to troop units. For example, in a 1930 test, four of the new 105mm howitzers were issued to a Field Artillery School troop unit for additional tests and fieldwork.[103] Wholesale acquisition of weapons, however, usually was delayed until the onset of a crisis that demanded national mobilization, as stipulated under the National Defense Act of 1920.

Infantry Journal and *Cavalry Journal* also reported on experimentation. One of the favorite subjects for the infantry branch was the development of the semiautomatic rifle, which would eventually be accepted as the M-1 Garand.[104] Even more popular were articles about experiments in motorizing infantry units, tank developments, and anti–mechanized defense weapons. As early as the mid-1920s, *Infantry Journal* called for extensive experimentation with commercial trucks as well as military-designed cross-country vehicles for infantry regiments. Articles calling for additional experimentation, or reporting on various tests and experiments, continued to appear regularly through 1938.[105]

The cavalry branch, until the advent of the mechanized force experiments, was initially concerned with tanks and armored cars. After tanks were assigned entirely to the infantry branch, cavalry focused on the motorization of supply trains for its regiments and on cooperative experiments with the air service for reconnaissance. The early 1920s discussions on tanks and armored cars were frequent and usually included traditional cavalry missions (reconnaissance and security) using modernized regiments. Additional articles discussed tests and experiments using the air service to coordinate support for traditional cavalry missions.[106]

Experimentation with mechanization was a unique case for ground forces during the interwar period, generating experiments that went beyond just one branch. Although the air service conducted extensive—and expensive—experimentation and development, especially in the 1930s, ground forces had to make do within limits of single-branch experimentation. The one exception was the mechanization experiments that generated smaller modernized troop units within the army.[107] Army officers, writing for the professional journals, endorsed these experiments in mechanization. Although some voices for tradition remained, the concept of mechanized combined arms teams remained a staple in the journals from the late 1920s through World War II. Questions over the role of armored and tracked vehicles in future combat found new focus during and after the experiments with a formed mechanized force.[108] Debate in the journals, obviously stimulated by the War Department decision for experimentation, peaked in the late 1920s. Articles reported on decisions for the mechanized force and the results of experiments; the experiments became a stepping-stone to forecasts of future war and also reported on foreign experiments in mechanization.[109] Editorial comments usually continued to defer to man as the ultimate arbiter of ground combat, but some also admitted increasingly that proper equipment and organization determined victory.[110]

Some officers predicted sweeping changes in future warfare. In a 1930 article published simultaneously in *Cavalry Journal* and *Field Artillery Journal*, Lieutenant Colonel K. B. Edmunds prophesied an all-arms force of 200 tanks, fifty mechanized infantry carriers, and 100 artillery pieces, with approximately the power of a division, all organized primarily for offensive combat. He wrote that the future army would consist of infantry (modernized, motorized, and itself well equipped with all forms of weapons) as the holding or defensive force and the cavalry (mechanized but itself all-arms) as the offensive and mobile force. At the army commander level, infantry forces would contain enemy defensive fronts, thereby permitting the mechanized, combined arms cavalry organizations to either outflank the enemy or conduct the actual penetrations. The editors of *FA* introduced this article by saying "it contain[ed] much sound thought on a subject which has received considerable treatment of a fantastic or even fanatic nature."[111]

Army Chief of Staff Summerall approved a new mechanized program in 1930, establishing a permanent mechanized unit using out-of-date and poor-condition equipment.[112] For the next seven months, this unit, supported by a motorized infantry regiment and air service assets, conducted "command post exercises, field problems, maneuvers, demonstrations and ceremonies. Among the exercises were night tactical and strategic marches, offensive combat against entrenched infantry, offensive operations against another mechanized force, attacks involving wide turning movements, seizure of key positions and operations as a covering force for a larger unit."[113] However, Chief of Staff Douglas MacArthur saw the need for modernization throughout all the branches, not merely a single modernized force. In a change to War Department policy on May 1, 1931, MacArthur declared the mechanized force disbanded and required all branches to work toward motorization, mechanization, and modernization.[114] Branch rivalries and budget issues prevented large-scale alterations to force structures and large-scale acquisition of new equipment for another ten years, but the need for a modern mechanized force was made clear.[115]

Because mechanization was now required of all branches, the branch journals began informing readers of progress in mechanization and some of its challenges. Some reports were from very senior officers, and some reported directly on the decisions of the War Department.[116] Cavalry officers were told that although combined arms were necessary for success they possessed a unique character trait for the use of mechanized forces: "mental mobility."[117] Readers of *Field Artillery Journal* were informed that their branch was also undergoing mechanization, in support of the changing cavalry mechanization and infantry motorization, and that the future looked bright if lack of funding did not prevent progress.[118] Infantry officers were treated to numerous articles on how tanks fit into the mechanization schemes.[119]

These experiments did not change the Army's doctrinal reliance on combined arms conducting integrated fire and maneuver.[120] Unlike the advocates of tank-pure grand maneuvers that would defeat the enemy by snapping his morale, army officers continued to believe in combined arms and the need to close with and destroy the enemy, usually with dominant firepower. This was eminently suitable for the requirements of World War II, where the realities of combat in Europe "shattered illusions of maneuver" (see, in Chapter 9, the section titled "The Influence of the Leavenworth Men).[121]

Maneuvers, CPXs, the CCC experience, and experimentation had marked effects on U.S. Army officers' intellectual development. "Confessions of an Ex-Horseman" (anonymous), published in the July–August 1935 edition of *Field Artillery Journal*, demonstrates this impact. A self-confessed "erstwhile horseman" who "played polo, rode whenever possible," described his absolute conversion to motorized artillery as a process encouraged by "the national scene, [where] I found most of the world using other means of conveyance, yet I still plodded along on the back of a horse," and "with my faith in the horse already badly shaken, it needed but one view of a modern truck-drawn artillery battery rolling along at 35 miles an hour to give me a new lease of professional life. The speed, the grace, the quietness, the assurance with which this battery went about its appointed task convinced me at once that material progress was not a sham." For this field artillery officer, one glimpse of an experimental or recently motorized artillery battery forced his conversion to modern thought. As he closed his article, "Time marches on!"[122] Time was indeed moving on. The army of the interwar period, although desirous of high-quality training, full-complement units, and the acquisition of modern equipment, found itself with poor-quality training, peace-strength units, and obsolete equipment—yet with an intellectual focus on modern warfare.

The Officer Education System

Future combat realities were the primary subject of the officer education system. As Samuel Huntington later observed in *Soldier and the State*, "A technical love for his craft and the sense of social obligation to utilize this craft for the benefit of society" motivate a professional military officer.[123] After World War I, the army officer corps understood that competency in the craft was largely a matter of skill in handling large formations in both stable defensive and mobile offensive operations. They also appreciated a sense of obligation for preparedness and for basic competence, especially in a society where the desire to avoid another major war rapidly deteriorated to an article of faith: "Never again!" This officer competence in handling large formations, and in the organization and effective performance of large-unit staffs, occurred primarily within the education system.

Immediately after World War I, senior officers in both the AEF and the War Department discussed reestablishing the officer education system disrupted by mobilization. A group of officers met in Treves (Trier), Germany, in spring 1919 and launched a series of conversations, orders, boards, and meetings that established a new and comprehensive officer education system.[124] This system remained intact through national mobilization and itself became a basis for the hugely expanded officer education and training systems for mobilization during World War II. On the eve of that conflict, at least one observer saw the system of officer education to be the very foundation of army officer professionalism, with every officer fully schooled in multiple courses. In the words of Major John H. Burns, "It is doubtful if any professional group are so rigorously trained and educated as the American officer."[125]

This comprehensive system had its origins in the meeting at Treves, convened by Major General James W. McAndrew in response to a telegram sent from the War Department to U.S. forces in occupation duty naming McAndrew to be commandant of the General Staff College in Washington, D.C., and Major General Edward F. McGlachlin to be commandant of the General Service Schools at Fort Leavenworth.[126] This telegram ordered McAndrew and McGlachlin to select "from officers now in the AEF as may be approved by you" for duty as assistant commandants, executive officers, directors, and instructors. Officers selected for staff and faculty duty would prepare their materials from items available in Europe and be ready to start teaching duties no later than September 1, 1919.[127] McAndrew proceeded to take command of the General Staff College, but McGlachlin was replaced by Major General Charles H. Muir, commander of 28th Division in the Meuse-Argonne and of IV Corps at the end of the war. Muir had a reputation for imperturbable calmness under pressure.[128]

In the busy days of demobilization and transfer back home from the AEF, the War Department General Staff circulated a seventy-page comprehensive draft plan for reestablishing the schools on March 8, 1919.[129] It recommended a comprehensive system of officer and soldier education, from precommissioning through colonel-level instruction. Included in this plan were discussions of West Point education; company-grade officer education at division schools; branch instruction for officers and some noncommissioned officers at special service schools, usually with a course for lieutenants and a more advanced course for captains and majors; and two General Service Schools: one school of the line for general staff officer education for duty with large units, and a general staff college for education in War Department–level general staff duties.[130] The Special Service branch schools and the two-stage general staff education would be adopted and remain the hallmarks of officer education for the next two decades.[131]

Critical to the post–World War I development of programs of instruction were lessons gleaned from the AEF, including the value of staff processes and the absolute requirement for a general staff system to cope with the new realities of modern warfare. George C. Marshall wrote to the commandant of the Army War College in 1920: "My observation of the General Staff work in France, particularly at G.H.Q. and in the First Army, and my recent experience at the War Department in connection with Army reorganization, has caused me to feel that one of the most serious troubles in our General Staffs [has] been the failure to follow the proper procedure in determining a policy or plan."[132] Marshall continued: "We would do well if we could obtain examples of this character of General Staff work" for use as instruction aids.[133] General McAndrew, commandant of the War College, distributed copies of this letter to his faculty.[134]

In the post–World War I era, the War Department took several steps toward harmonizing the officer education system. These efforts usually took the form of officer boards convened to investigate certain challenges and recommend solutions to the chief of staff. The first board ordered to investigate the school system (after its initial post–World War I establishment) was the McGlachlin board, which convened in February 1922.[135] This board, charged by Pershing to investigate the entire school system with a view toward decreasing expenditures for the programs, making the system as efficient as possible in an era of decreasing resources, and improving instruction for the National Guard and Reserves, traveled to every army school in the country and met with representatives of every chief of branch in Washington.

The McGlachlin board made several recommendations but also reflected a fascinating series of dissenting views based on the majority opinion of the board.[136] The majority recommendations included careful delineation for officer training tour lengths. Additionally, the panel made recommendations on student evaluation, student selection, and time intervals between courses.[137] Colonel Harold B. Fiske's dissent focused on the separation point between the special service schools and Leavenworth, particularly which school that majors should attend, and sought to clarify the roles of Leavenworth and the Senior Service College. His opinion, although a minority dissent from the McGlachlin board, would eventually gain some effect, as majors were less frequently assigned to the advanced courses at the branch schools with the passage of time.[138] General McGlachlin dissented from his own panel in several areas. His primary argument was the difficulty for Fort Leavenworth to teach every echelon from brigade through corps in only one year. McGlachlin recommended that the School of the Line be continued as a one-year program, followed immediately by the General Staff School, with duration there limited to only six months.[139] This issue would continue until mobilization in 1940, as the course at Leavenworth alternated between one-year and two-year classes.

Due to the range of dissenting opinions, many of the recommendations were only partially adopted. In an effort to clarify the content of the courses recommended by the McGlachlin board, Colonel Fiske, who had several times dissented from the view of the majority, was named president of another board of officers within five months of the adjournment of the McGlachlin board. Ordered to develop course schedules for both the general service and the special service schools, this board was chaired by Colonel Fiske and convened in Washington in late July 1922. Composed of officers from every combat branch, as well as representatives of the War Department General Staff, this group drew up schedules and course names for all officer education in the army system. They were ordered specifically to ensure that educations at the branch special service schools properly prepared officers for attendance at Leavenworth and to define "the division of duties between" the Command and General Staff School and the Army War College.[140] The Fiske board made recommendations that delineated the border between the Army War College and the Command and General Staff School as the line between armies and above, which would be taught at the War College, and corps and divisions, which would be the focus at Leavenworth.[141]

After the various boards had made their recommendations, the outline of the school system remained intact until mobilization in 1940. Officers, the majority of them commissioned in peacetime from West Point, would attend a branch basic course, normally eight months in length, within the first several years of their active duty. Later, if selected by their branch, they would attend a branch "advanced course." Still later, if selected by their branch, officers would attend the school at Fort Leavenworth, focusing studies on the army division and corps in combat operations. After the most selective screening, a few officers would then attend the Army War College, the last step in officer education, where studies were at the army, theater, and department levels.

The mission of the Army War College changed during the interwar period from advanced general staff training, primarily under the leadership of Major General James W. McAndrew, to education for command while Brigadier General Edward F. McGlachlin Jr. was commandant, and then to preparation for war and conduct of war under the command of Major General William D. Connor.[142] Instruction under Connor became a series of large-scale problem-solving exercises, with students divided into committees. Each student committee was responsible for a significant contemporary military problem. After a month of study and research, each committee prepared a staff study, briefed the entire War College class on the problem (including their recommended solution), and received the benefit of student and faculty critiques.[143] Although there were frequent lectures by visiting experts and dignitaries, the students only infrequently were taught in classrooms. The War College was less an academic institution and more a problem-solving extension of the War Department, to which it reported. The students were expected to learn, but that learning occurred in extensive problem solving, usually of real-world problems given to the War College by the General Staff.[144]

By July 1925, the mission of the schools at Leavenworth was established by issuance of Army Regulation 350-5—a mission that remained intact until the spring of 1940. The Leavenworth school was ordered to

Prepare officers for command and general staff duty by training them in the following:

1. The combined use of all arms in the division and in the army corps.

2. The proper functions of commanders of divisions, army corps, and corps areas and the techniques of exercising command.

3. The proper functions of general staff officers of divisions, army corps, and corps areas and the technique of general staff concepts.[145]

The critical roles of combining the arms of divisions and corps, of commanding these formations, and of serving as the general staffs of these formations were Leavenworth's, to the exclusion of every other institution in the interwar army. Despite efforts at training, maneuvers, and CPXs, and despite a growing and robust sense of professionalism, officers during the interwar period had to rely on the education system for preparation in division and corps operations.

Significant time spent in officer education, limited troop-unit training, some experimentation, some degree of overseas duty, and nearly nonexistent promotions were the reality of the interwar army. This reality developed a profound sense of professional dedication among the officers who either experienced the Great War, heard about it in the officer's mess, or came of age as young officers in the 1920s and 1930s. This sense of professionalism, dedication to duty, and awareness of the need for individual preparation—coupled with a national defense policy that made nothing possible until crisis—generated the "wonder" of the World War II victory.[146] Many historians believe the National Defense Act of 1920, and the appropriations in the 1920s and 1930s, left America woefully unprepared for the next world war.[147] However, within the army officer corps, a new sense of purpose, and a new idea of how officer competency was created, altered how the U.S. officer corps itself gained and maintained its professional competence.

Chapter 2

The Essence of Modern War

> No one arm wins battles. The combined employment of all arms
> is essential to success. The special characteristics of each arm
> adapt it to the performance of special functions in execution of
> the mission of the unit in which the action of all is combined. It is
> the task of higher commanders to coordinate and direct the action
> of each arm with a view to the most efficient exploitation of its
> powers and their adaptation to the ends sought.
>
> —*Field Service Regulations,* 1923

Combined arms was the dominant tactical principle of the U.S. Army from 1918
through 1945. However, for the officer corps the singular, overarching challenge
of modern war was defeating a formed defense, usually referred to as a "stabilized front," to generate a decisive war of maneuver.[1] This was identified as an issue by the AEF in World War I. Experiences by multiple divisions in the offensives in the summer and fall of 1918 drove U.S. officers to understand that
wishful thinking could not break a stabilized front and that, once broken, the
transition to a war of mobility—although essential to achieving military victory—was much easier said than done. All this was captured in training and operational documents issued by the AEF. Perhaps the best depiction of the overall
challenge was "Tactical Note No. 7," issued by Major General William G.
Haan, 32nd Division commander, in August 1919. A reissue for the division,
"Combat Instructions for Troops of First Army" was written the month before by
the staff of First U.S. Army, and it clearly specified the differences between combat in the forward zone, named "trench warfare," and combat in the open behind this forward defensive zone, labeled "open warfare," which required
markedly different principles, techniques, and equipment. It stated that, "once
the attack debouches through this [trench warfare] zone, the entire character of
the conduct of the operation must be completely changed." Changes included
careful integration of tanks, 75mm artillery closely accompanying the advancing
infantry, mortars, machine guns, and aerial observers for both artillery fire and
air attack on the enemy. Later, the First Army combat instructions stated, "The
foregoing phase of the operation, which depends upon personal initiative, rapid-

ity of decision, resolute daring and driving power, should afford the American officer and soldier the opportunity to display his best known national characteristics to their greatest advantage, provided he does not blindly rush against hostile strong points, ignoring the weak points and the tactical application of fire superiority combined with maneuver."[2] This formula—breaking through a stabilized, or defensive, front followed by fire superiority combined with maneuver to generate the exploitation—remained intact through World War II as the basic principle of the U.S. Army.

The intellectual foundations for meeting this challenge, foundations that allowed the army to cope with rapidly changing technology after World War I, although constrained by perceived shortages of funds and personnel, were established early in the interwar period and remained consistent through 1945. Without this intellectual background, without this basic principle of land warfare, the experience of the U.S. Army in World War II would have been much more difficult.

The Fundamentals of Modern War

It is clear from a review of the three most relevant army journals that the conception of modern warfare from the World War I experience remained critical to the issues confronting the interwar army. One of the most comprehensive immediate postwar analyses in the journals, and one whose solutions remained effective through the end of World War II, was Oliver Spaulding's "The Tactics of the War with Germany." Published in the September 1920 issue of *Infantry Journal*, Spaulding defined the challenge and the solutions and also described techniques for inculcating the solutions into the entire army. The problem was how to instruct the army without "a diversity of training [where] each commanding officer is likely to take his own experience in the war, and build up his own training theories." Spaulding's solution was to develop a unified doctrine for training the force, based on generally agreed principles; he noted that "we do not seem to be very far apart on fundamentals." The tactical challenge, for Spaulding and so many others, was to transition from the "front of a major operation on a stabilized line" to open warfare. Spaulding agreed with those who believed individual infantrymen were the key determinant on the battlefield, stating that open warfare was where "the man with the rifle occupied his rightful place of preeminence."[3] By the onset of national mobilization in 1940, most authors in the journals were completely converted to mobile warfare as a motorized and mechanized phenomenon; the horse, the rifle, and the bayonet had been rightfully accorded their roles as tools, not as the essence of the profession.

The fundamental principle necessary to gain this mobile warfare, and to succeed at it once gained, was combined arms. Spaulding, a field artillery officer, continued that the infantry had the place of "senior partner in the firm," but the other arms were "indispensable to its successful handling." He discussed cavalry, stating that this nearly independent arm could conduct three missions: reconnaissance, cover of the main body from enemy reconnaissance, and detached missions and raids. Artillery protected the infantry, attacked enemy infantry, or conducted long-range interdiction fires. The air service also protected the infantry, attacked the opposing infantry, and conducted deep bombardment missions while fighting enemy aircraft for air superiority. Spaulding closed his discussion of the battlefield array with several pages devoted to the "accompanying gun." This awkward phrase captured the need among infantry forces for an auxiliary weapon that could defeat enemy strongpoints, defend the infantry from machine guns, and destroy enemy tanks. After dealing with the four main possibilities, accompanying light artillery, tanks, direct-fire weapons (like the 37mm gun), and infantry-borne mortars, Spaulding wrote that only the tank "offer(s) a promising field for development; types of material and tactical methods expressly designed for this use can undoubtedly be developed."[4]

Spaulding identified the use of these fundamental principles as the foundation for officer education and army-wide training in the peacetime force. The development, in his terms, of a "concert of action" required a common doctrine of war and a means of communication so that the common doctrine would be shared by all. Part of this common doctrine and shared communication was the appropriate set of relationships established with all the arms. This was not to exclude the other arms from developing their own sets of techniques, which Spaulding called "tactics." "Each arm has to work out its own salvation, and hence the salvation of the rest, in its own way. . . . Each must develop itself, not for itself, but for the Army—which basically, is the infantry." One key ingredient remained for this officer: the education of the officer corps. Officers needed to be thoroughly educated in the tactics of their own arm, and then, at the general service schools, educated in the tactics of combined arms. The education at the branch schools did not, according to Spaulding, require any explanation. However, the education in combined arms, begun at the general service schools, should also include exchange duty with other branches, as well as extensive field experience. The well-educated officer, or the officer of "long practical experience, studies each particular situation and selects his weapons from his mental arsenal which best suits the case; he does not have to hunt for precedents and forms, but makes each punishment fit the crime."[5]

Analysis of the professional journals from the interwar period reveals a fervent and continual quest by junior officers, the senior officers of the next war, for an effective preparation for modern war. This desire remained remarkably consistent throughout the interwar period. Their view—that modern war would essentially be mass armies equipped by industrialized nations waging a war of societal existence—required both shared fundamental principles of battlefield performance and national preparation in peacetime. For the interwar period, the fundamental—and consistent—military issue was the creation of mobile warfare through an exploitable breakthrough in a stabilized front. This basic framework became a key ingredient of the U.S. Army's interwar doctrine as well as officer education.

Voices of Modernity

A rigorous debate over the essence of modern war—defined as a combined arms tactical system using the developing technologies of motorization, mobile heavy field artillery, tanks, mechanized forces, and airpower—was conducted in the pages of the interwar journals from immediately after the Armistice through national mobilization in 1940.[6] The debate between the modernists and the traditional voices did not begin with the blitzkrieg attacks on Poland and France but rather had its origins in the AEF. Traditional voices (frequently, the more senior officers) spoke consistently throughout these two decades, encouraging officers to maintain the values of the individual branches, the spirit of the bayonet, and the tradition of the horse. Voices of modernity (usually junior officers, but also some of the most senior generals) spoke for combined arms, motorization, mechanization, and experimentation. Motorization was arguably the most readily accepted form of modern war, with the need for heavy field artillery a very close second. Even the most traditional voices gave some mention to these modern aspects of warfare in their articles. Some articles took on the traditionalists directly, especially as experimentation with the mechanized force and the increasing motorization of both artillery and infantry began in the late 1920s.

The fundamental concept of the entire period was the need to fully develop combined arms doctrine and experience. Discussion of combined arms was a staple of *Cavalry Journal* and *Infantry Journal*, although some latitude must be given for their respective branch orientations.[7] The calls for infantry-based combined arms began immediately after the Armistice. In early 1921, Major Bradford Chynoweth, destined to be one of the most senior officers captured in the Philippines in early World War II, proclaimed:

> There is no longer a rifle battalion. The techniques and tactics of infantry have been complicated, yet benefited by the introduction of machine guns, light accompanying pieces, and tanks. The officer who understands no

more than the rifle is not fit for command. The battalion commander of today must know his machine gun, his accompanying pieces and his tank as thoroughly as he knows his rifle. The infantry has become a technical arm.

Chynoweth went on to discuss the breaking of the stabilized front and the gain, at war's end, of mobile warfare with "the infantry once more supreme, maneuver regained." For the future, he called for infantrymen's acceptance of the need for complete mechanization and described the future as the time of the "tank infantry," in which infantry would ride into battle, and fight, from mechanized and armored vehicles.[8] Chynoweth's call for combined arms, and for increasing mechanization, resonated in *Infantry Journal* throughout the 1920s and 1930s.[9]

As a fundamental concept, fire superiority was second only to combined arms.[10] An Infantry School conference summary, published in 1925, began with a clear statement: "The principle of fire and movement and the related principle of fire superiority constitute the most important fundamentals in infantry tactics." The summary proceeded to discuss several examples from the Great War of fire superiority providing a means to attain maneuver. This fire superiority came from "coordinated" artillery fire and airplane bombardment, divisional artillery, accompanying guns, automatic weapons, and rifles.[11] Numerous articles in this period discussed the need for careful coordination of supporting artillery fires.[12]

Articles by very senior officers carried the same message of combined arms and fire superiority. In 1939, the chief of infantry, Major General George Lynch, in a somewhat meandering and poorly organized article, discussed offensive and defensive firepower, as well as the use of artillery, machine guns, and tanks, to support infantry assaults. Although he assigned significant potency to the morale factor and the infantry squad leader's role, his article basically was a discussion of combined arms.[13]

The role of artillery in combined arms was also a frequent subject for articles in *Field Artillery Journal*. At least three major threads of discussion appeared in articles about modernized field artillery in the interwar period: the nature of artillery and its battlefield effect, the lessons of AEF artillery in the Great War, and the technical details of future support for the other arms.[14] A review of two decades of *Field Artillery Journal* found little evidence of any "anti–combined arms, artillery-can-win-by-itself" thinking. The effect of modern artillery on the new battlefield, and the need for combined arms, was clearly understood. In 1925, Major General William J. Snow, chief of field artillery, discussed the casualty figures emerging from historical studies of the Great War. According to figures released in a French military journal in 1923, artillery produced 75 percent of casualties in 1914, 77 percent of casualties at Verdun in August 1917, and 68 percent of casualties at Soissons in July 1918. General Snow called these figures "illuminating—they are more; they are startling."[15] Artillery may not have con-quered by itself, but artillery was the most potent killing force on the battlefield. This remained true in World War II.[16]

In 1933, "The Cavalry-Artillery-Aviation Team," written by Lieutenant Colonel Kinzie B. Edmunds, served as a tutorial for readers of *Cavalry Journal* in the combined arms aspects of a fully integrated battlefield.[17] Edmunds dis-cussed, from the perspective of cavalry division operations, artillery observation by aircraft, central control of fire direction of artillery, time and space issues rele-vant to the emplacement of artillery, the logistics of supplying artillery ammuni-tion, the challenges of liaison and radio communication, and, as all light artillery of cavalry divisions remained horse-drawn, the relationship of aviation and horse artillery.[18] This was an article for all seasons.

After discussions of combined arms and fire superiority, the issue of motor-ization occupied the most space—and gained the most consensus. *Field Artillery Journal* led this development by publishing the Westervelt board's report in its July–August 1919 issue. This board of officers, which convened in France in the winter of 1918–1919, called for the adoption of a 105mm howitzer as the stan-dard medium field piece, recognizing the inadequacy of the 15-pound shell from the ubiquitous French 75mm. The board recommended the complete eventual replacement of all horse-drawn batteries, of any type, with motorized transport. In the words of the report, "At some time in the future it is probable that all division artillery will be motorized," and "the country that first utilizes the new capabilities opened up by the mechanical traction and the caterpillar, will have a great advantage in the next war."[19] The Westervelt board's findings, requiring the eventual and complete motorization of artillery, fell prey to the budget constraints of the 1920s and 1930s.[20]

Field artillery led the other branches in discussing motorization. Although some articles continued to address horse-drawn batteries, equipment, and train-ing for some twenty years, the overall conclusion was clear: once motor transport achieved effective cross-country tactical mobility, the horse would be replaced. By the early 1930s, motor transport frequently was the lead article in *Field Ar-tillery Journal*.[21]

Authors in *Infantry Journal* agreed that motorization was an essential ele-ment of modern warfare, although there was disagreement as to the extent of motorization. Articles early in the interwar period focused on the need for mo-torization of infantry supply units, especially considering the ammunition expen-diture rates experienced by the AEF. Some of these articles advocated a family of vehicles with excellent cross-country mobility, necessary to prevent overreliance on congested road nets. Several called for experimentation with full-tracked ve-hicles, even though "the perfection of power transmission, control of direction, spring suspension and track designs offer interesting problems in a practically virgin field of research."[22] The need was obvious. But would technological means develop rapidly enough to fulfill the requirement before the next war?

Infantry Journal articles also called for widespread adaptation of motor transport for infantry movement, either due to an anticipated shortage of horses and mules or for an anticipated need to match the speed of mechanized forces. Captain Charles Bolté, in a 1929 series titled "The Future of Infantry," commented:

> Two of the present governing doctrines . . . have to do with the exploitation of the motorized nature of American life and with the threat which aircraft and gas hold for animals in the combat zone. When it is realized that between eighty and ninety per cent of the world's motor vehicles are in the United States, numbering one for every four or five inhabitants, it becomes clear that we should exploit to the utmost the familiarity with gas engines, motor transportation, and high speeds which is uniquely an American characteristic and which may be of great value on the modern battlefield.[23]

The future gained a clearer vision less than a year later. In 1930, Major L. D. Davis called for a new form of infantry: motorized and mechanized infantry. Unless infantry embraced both motorization (for mobility) and mechanization (for armor protection and mobile firepower), the branch would no longer perform any useful battlefield functions. For Davis, "The time has come when the movement of infantry on foot is to be considered exceptional but movement by truck usual."[24]

By 1938, despite the efforts of traditionalists (see next section), *Cavalry Journal* was well on its way to embracing the concepts of motorization. Even the outgoing chief of cavalry, Major General Leon B. Kromer, in his final message published in the March–April 1938 edition of *Cavalry Journal*, told readers that "battlefield mobility means the ability to move independent of roads and under any conditions of weather and terrain in the area that is subject to enemy action and fire (from the air as well as from the ground)—an area vastly extended in frontage and depth because of the increased effective range of modern means; guns, motors, tanks, and airplanes."[25] Cavalry was not just horses; the branch had accepted the need for motorization, at least in part.[26]

Conservative Voices

Although powerful traditional and conservative voices called for the retention of the bayonet and the horse during the interwar period, they were clearly in the

The Horse. Cavalry troopers practicing jumping, 1930s. U.S. Army Signal Corps photograph, U.S. Army Center for Military History.

minority. Some senior officers spoke up for this minority position, extolling the virtues of the horse and the need for bayonet training.[27] Others ridiculed such ideas, some resorted to anonymous pen names, and many simply took on their seniors in a professional debate by publishing works under their names.

Cavalry Journal, which changed editors in July 1937, turned to retired Brigadier General H. S. Hawkins to lead the charge for the horse.[28] Hawkins wrote a series of columns through 1940 consistently arguing that motorization and mechanization had roles—but only as supporters of horse cavalry. Driven by what he saw as the only practicable solution to tactical mobility—men riding horses—Hawkins accounted for every development in modernization with a simple argument. As long as tracked and wheeled vehicles had limited cross-country performance, the horse would remain the answer to tactical battlefield mobility. In the September–October 1937 issue of *Cavalry Journal,* Hawkins baldly wrote: "We cannot rely on mechanized force to perform this mission of cavalry. It may be an important adjunct, but it can be nothing more. Tanks . . . can never be numerous enough or effective enough to replace the cavalry."[29]

Only after the collapse of France in May–June 1940 did Hawkins see some merit in mechanized forces. However, he still called for horsed cavalry as an essential arm in this modern world of "devilish" warfare where innocents were bombed from the air. In late 1940, he appealed as follows:

> Cavalry is as necessary as ever before. It is only the kind of cavalry that should be changed. Cavalry is composed mostly of horsemen. In my opinion, if it is mechanized, it is not cavalry; it then becomes mechanized troops. It is the armament of cavalry and its tactics that must be changed from time to time. If we discard it wholly we lose its very special advantages—and the army cannot afford to lose those advantages.
>
> We must have *everything* and not run headlong towards one particular arm because a special campaign in Europe emphasized the use of that particular arm. We might as well run headlong over a precipice.[30]

This appeal for maintaining horseflesh was a traditional voice speaking against the tide of change and modernity, a tide rising since 1918.

Hawkins's outspoken advocacy of the horse and of the mounted arm may have been motivated, at least in part, by his own horrendous personal experience in World War I. While serving as chief of staff of 35th Division in the Meuse-Argonne offensive, Hawkins was cited by the recent historian of that division for effectively losing control of the division staff, for becoming separated from his own command post and lost in the night hours during a critical phase of the division's attack, for ignoring a specific order from corps headquarters to attack at a certain time, and for general incompetence. Indeed, at least according to this historian, Hawkins was responsible for many of the failures of 35th Division that led to its eventual collapse and relief from the offensive. Hawkins's experience with modern war had not been professionally satisfactory.[31]

Hawkins was frequently criticized as a voice of excessive tradition in *Cavalry Journal*. One of the more coherent attacks on his defense of horse cavalry came from Major Robert. W. Grow in early 1938. Major Grow, who would command an armored division in World War II, carefully referred to General Hawkins as an "experienced and recognized authority," then proceeded to take him to task for using terminology declared outmoded seven years earlier and for failing to understand that the form of mount, horse or "iron horse," to use Grow's phrase, did not matter to a cavalry force because the missions remained the same. Grow also repeatedly referred to "Mechanized CAVALRY" in the article.[32] Grow was not alone in his desire to correct a senior officer in a public forum. Even the editor of *Cavalry Journal*, who appears to have brought on Hawkins as a regular columnist, placed Grow's article, originally simply a letter to the editor, in a prominent location as a featured article.[33] Obviously, the debate made for good press.

Voices in support of the bayonet, or at least *the spirit of the bayonet,* maintained a refrain similar to the cries to maintain the horse. More contentious than
the debate over horse versus iron horse, the bayonet debate seems to have challenged the very soul of the infantry branch. In part a response to the overwhelming artillery fire of World War I, where artillery typically generated three-quarters
of all casualties, in part a response to the challenges of airpower advocates, and in
part a response to the challenge posed by mechanization, the demand for close
assault by bayonet-armed infantry was a clear theme in the interwar journals.[34] A
large part of the advocacy for the spirit of the bayonet was the perceived need to
train aggression into the souls of soldiers, especially in a mass conscript army.

The discussion of the bayonet, and of the rifle, began immediately after the
Armistice. Captain Francis Woolfley wrote an impassioned plea for the rifle and
the bayonet in the September 1922 edition of *Infantry Journal.* Quoting directly
from Army Training Regulation 10-5, Woolfley stated, "The final method is the
encounter with the *bullet and bayonet;* the human element is the decisive one."
In his own words, he proclaimed: *"The rifle and bayonet are still the dominant
arms of the Infantry."*[35] He added, "The rifleman's task remains the same—*to
take and to hold by personal encounter."*[36]

The discussion continued through the 1920s and 1930s. No less an authority
than Major General J. F. C. Fuller entered the debate in 1931:

> In the American Civil War . . . Surgeon-Major Albert G. Hart, a participant,
> added "I think half a dozen would include all the wounds [by the bayonet]
> that I ever dressed." Half a dozen! Yet in 1914 the spirit of the bayonet was
> the spirit of every army. Half a dozen! And in 1931 it is still the spirit,
> whether the soldiers who have to prod believe in it or not. To put it mildly,
> is this not pitiful?

Fuller continued to rail against the bayonet for another three pages, closing with
a plea for modern armies to replace the infantry assault with a machine-gun and
tank-assault pattern.[37]

By the autumn of 1940 the debate should have been over, yet it continued.
Driven by some of the probayonet discussions, Sergeant Terry Bull wrote "Bayonet Fever," published in the September–October 1940 issue of *Infantry Journal.*
Using the technique of a conversation between a new lieutenant and his platoon
sergeant, Sergeant Bull wrote this impassioned plea by the eager-to-train NCO:

> I'll take plenty of pains teaching 'em to shoot, dig, and scout, but the
> quicker we run through the motions of this bayonet foolishness, the
> healthier it'll be for all of us.

Yessir, that's just what I meant—foolishness! The Skip—uh—the company commander thinks so too, lieutenant, but there's a whole lot of Indian fighters left in this man's army. They believe what the war correspondents have been printing about bayonet attacks—hand to hand fighting, and all the other blah they've been using ever since the first battle of Bull Run. And the G.O.A.P.—I mean the Good Old American Public, still eats it up. Romantic.[38]

Apparently, even on the eve of Armageddon, the Indian fighters still had *the spirit of the bayonet*, despite the reality of modern war accepted by the soldiers actually responsible for training.

Official Concepts

Training regulations and, beginning in the early 1930s, field manuals provided "in a condensed form for ready reference in the field the approved principles, doctrines, and methods that govern the training and employment of the various arms, together with such reference data as they need for mobilization, training and field service. These manuals will be sufficiently comprehensive to be used as a basis for garrison and school training supplemented when necessary by other authorized publications."[39] Doctrine, as stated, applied to both field units and to the educational system. The quantity of prescriptive and authoritative documents was relatively small during the interwar period. Sixty-two training regulations were included in a 1923 *Infantry Journal* listing.[40] In 1930, some two dozen field manuals were in the process of reaching the force. The creation of field manuals in 1930 was an attempt to streamline and to make more coherent the various documents promulgated by the branches and by the General Staff in the 1920s.[41] These doctrinal manuals, frequently written by the staff at Leavenworth, were the foundation of interwar education and were constantly referenced in lectures, conferences, and problem-solving exercises.

Dissatisfied with the European manner of fighting, and reinforced by the experiences of the St. Mihiel and Meuse-Argonne campaigns, the army entirely rewrote its doctrine, the foundation of instruction at Fort Leavenworth, in the early 1920s.[42] This doctrine formulated a battlefield environment in which the challenge was the generation of opportunities for mobile warfare through a systematic reduction of fortified enemy locales and stabilized fronts. Firepower and mobility, attrition and annihilation, were essential and necessary components of twentieth-century warfare.

Large-formation operations for the interwar army were guided by a limited number of doctrinal publications. Chief among the doctrinal documents was the *Field Service Regulations* (FSR), published in 1923, partially superseded in 1930, and revised with new editions in 1941 and 1944.[43] Another influential document was the *Manual for the Commanders of Large Units* (MCLU), published in several forms during the interwar period. The next important manual was the *Staff Officer's Field Manual*. Also influential were texts issued by Leavenworth for the limited purpose of instruction in the Command and General Staff School. The vast majority of other doctrinal publications were technical or single-branch in nature.[44]

These regulations and field manuals reflected the continuity of World War I's lessons of stabilized front and mobile warfare forms of operation through the modernization experiments of the 1920s and 1930s. There was no great change in the regulations or manuals because the experimentation focused on the primary challenge: how to convert a stabilized front, the normal outcome of industrialized warfare, into mobile warfare in which motorized or mechanized mobile forces could achieve an offensive decision. There was no need to revolutionize doctrine, as the battlefield conditions were not seen as being different in form during the interwar period. Modifications based on the development of emergent science and technology were incorporated from the start. There was no need to drastically alter the *principles* when they had been formulated in the AEF experience, and there was no clear and compelling reason to believe that these principles would not suffice for the next war.

The professional journals were not silent on the issue of appropriate doctrine and performed several useful functions. They informed the officer corps when new regulations and manuals were published, generated debate over the role of doctrine in education, and additionally explained existent doctrine and requested updates and changes to doctrine. Identifying new doctrine was the simplest of these tasks.[45] A few articles went into great detail, summarizing and editorializing on new regulations. Some articles simply announced new publications; others described changes in existent regulations and manuals.[46] Some authors added meaningfully to the body of professional knowledge, although often in rather technical and tactical matters.[47] Writers also engaged in criticism of existent doctrine and in calls for the development of new doctrine.[48] However, such calls usually did not describe what the new doctrine should be but rather critiqued existing doctrine for its failure to account for new possibilities, such as mechanized forces.[49] These articles sometimes called to task previously published material for overlooking some real combat element.[50] Other articles discussed the connections between the doctrine, the journals, and the officer education schools, frequently reading like a synopsis of doctrine or like a prob-lem exercise from one of the service schools.[51] Lectures and pamphlets from the service schools, usually quoting extensively from doctrine, also appeared in the journals.[52]

Other articles critiqued existing doctrine as poorly written or for leaving out significant factors. The debate generated some change in doctrine based on technological changes, especially in the mid- to late 1930s, with periodic reviews of materials used at Leavenworth, and the creation of school texts to supplement published doctrine; the 1937 creation of *Tactical Employment of the Mecha-nized Division (Tentative)* is an example.[53] The use of professional journals to promulgate, criticize, and refine doctrine made doctrine a living, developing en-tity during the interwar period, although the total number of significant doctri-nal documents was in reality limited. What did not change were the principles, or the common conception of the form of modern industrialized warfare. War would continue to be won by combined arms teams conducting mobile offen-sive warfare after, if necessary, a deliberate assault on a stable front had gener-ated an open battlefield. These principles were reflected in the most fundamen-tal doctrine: field service regulations.

"Field Service Regulations"

The *Field Service Regulations* of 1923 and 1939 and *Field Manual 100-5* of 1941 and 1944 were the guides for officers working on any problem above indi-vidual branches and below "large units."[54] Focusing on the division, and en-compassing the lowest echelon of combined arms, these were the critical doc-trinal documents for division commanders and general staff officers. From 1923 through 1944, the fundamentals of combat at the division level, as pre-scribed in these four manuals, did not change significantly. The critical ele-ments of modern war, the need for effective command and control, reliance on firepower, and the requirement for offensive operations utilizing combined arms to generate either envelopment or a penetration remained consistent be-ginning with the 1923 *FSR* through the 1944 *FM 100-5*. There was some movement among the principles of combat and the principles of offensive op-erations, primarily changes in the order of listing. There were some changes, usually unhelpful, to the prescriptions on airpower. The mechanized force was added in the 1939 edition, and the armored division was added to the 1941 edi-tion. However, the basic concepts for ground operations at the division level re-mained practically identical from manual to manual. The lessons of the AEF captured in the 1923 *FSR*—notably lessons on stabilized fronts and mobile operations—served as the fundamental system for land operations at the division level through World War II.

The purpose of land warfare remained identical in all four versions of this manual. The 1923 FSR stated, the "ultimate objective of all military operations is the destruction of the enemy's armed forces in battle." The 1939, 1941, and 1944 manuals used identical language.[55] The guideline of operations in all four manuals was that the "fundamental principles of war are neither very numerous nor complex . . . their application may be difficult and must not be limited by set rules. Departure from prescribed methods is at times necessary. A thorough knowledge of the principles of war and their application enables the leader to decide when such departure should be made and to determine what methods bring success."[56]

These principles were not simply a list of single words and short phrases but rather a set of concepts that applied to different forms of operations. Consistently, chapters on specific types of operations began with a short section of two or three pages devoted to a general outline of the guiding themes for the form of operation before leading readers in a more detailed discussion of forms of operations and operations modified by the enemy, the terrain, the forces available, and the intent of the higher commanders.[57]

Consistent throughout the interwar period was a somewhat mechanical approach to the science of warfare, perhaps best expressed by Tasker Howard Bliss, former chief of staff, in a 1923 draft article:

War is, in a sense, a mechanical art. [The goal is to] perform the maximum of effective work in overcoming resistance at a given point in the shortest time with the minimum wear and tear on the machine. . . . In war the man who can accurately determine the point of hard resistance . . . and who can accurately function all parts of the machine to bring maximum power to bear at this point is the successful strategist.[58]

The 1923 FSR emphasized this adherence to a mechanical science of war and disregarded issues of policy and grand strategy. Designed as a general staff operations guide, the FSR considered variants of national security policy and strategy as issues beyond the scope of operational art for fielded forces. For example, readers find only a single reference to discussions of policy, concepts, and ideas for influencing the manner in which strategy is carried out in peacetime or wartime, or any discussion of operations above the army level, in any of these four manuals. Competency resided simply in maintaining the mechanical capability to close with and destroy the enemy. That had been enough in the Great War— and it was enough to train during the lean years.[59] Throughout the period, all these characteristics were fashioned after their initial discussion in the 1923 *FSR*.[60]

The 1923 "Field Service Regulations"

The 1923 *FSR* contained thirteen chapters in the operations section and began by describing the units and formations necessary for land combat. The scope of the 1923 *FSR* was to serve "especially for the government of the operations of large units and of small units forming a part of larger units."[61] The division, the "elementary organic unit of the combined arms," was "the basis of organization of the field armies." The army corps, the next echelon, was "organized primarily for tactical purposes" but had limited administrative functions.[62]

The second chapter addressed command and control or, using the language contained in the manual, "Command and Staff." In one of the shortest chapters of the manual, command was defined as the "lawful authority" of the commander, and leadership was considered an inseparable part of command. The commander "must be the controlling head, his must be the master mind, and from him must flow the energy and impulses which are to animate all under him."[63] The manual required commanders to command, to lead through personal visits to subordinate commanders and units, to demonstrate professional competence, and to ensure that staff worked in his support, not as a council of war. The commander's decisions were "his alone," not to be shared with others or influenced by others.[64] The staff, addressed in three very short numbered paragraphs, existed to support the commander, with significant authorities designated for the chief of staff.[65]

Combined arms was the key to combat operations. The introduction to the manual, the only section appearing directly over the signature block of Major General John L. Hines, Army Chief of Staff, informed readers that "success in war can be achieved only by all branches and arms of the service mutually helping and supporting one another."[66] The 1923 *FSR* addressed each branch. Infantry, addressed first in all four editions, was described as the "essential arm of close combat. . . . Infantry's direct role in combat required high levels of 'fighting spirit, aggressiveness, and initiative.'" Infantry conducted operations using fire and movement, with fire described as the "principal means of destruction." Although the manual stated that the "principal offensive weapon is the rifle and the bayonet," this comment was in a paragraph that described the necessity for automatic weapons, light cannons and tanks, as well as "elements of other arms" needed to accomplish the mission.[67] Tanks were an infantry-support weapon whose "essential mission is to assist the progression of the infantry," although deployment of tanks was important enough to justify eight numbered paragraphs (whereas infantry warranted nine numbered paragraphs). Using firepower, mobility, and shock action, tanks, as a general headquarters force, were assigned to subordinate units for specific tasks.[68]

The centralized control of artillery fire remained an essential ingredient of army doctrine through the entire period. In the 1923 *FSR*, the purpose of artillery was to provide firepower to "contribute to the power of movement of the entire force." Concentration of fire, while very desirable and important to achieving significant morale effect on the enemy, was to be balanced with the need for decentralized close support of infantry and tanks in certain situations. However, the manual warned that even close-support artillery commanders "must retain, as far as practicable, the power to assume centralized control." Although the "principal mission of the artillery is to support the infantry by fire," such support could come in several forms. Artillery was required to perform counterartillery missions, typically using assets at the corps level, as well as both concentration and direct-support fires. Divisional artillery was responsible for direct support of the infantry and had limited capability for counterbattery and destruction missions. Corps artillery, where the majority of medium and heavy artillery was located, had primary responsibility for counterbattery and destruction missions.[69]

Cavalry was specifically assigned the missions of "reconnaissance, counter-reconnaissance and security in service of large units." It could also be employed to strike exposed flanks, conduct attacks into the enemy's rear areas, and "exploit through pursuit successes gained by other arms." To be effective, "large cavalry units [were to be] frequently reinforced by infantry in trucks."[70] Cavalry had no place in the combat conditions of an assault on a prepared defensive position, and it had a very limited role to play in any action along a stabilized front.

Airpower was an adjunct to ground forces and was designed to perform three missions: "combat, observation, and the transmission of information." Combat missions were categorized as "pursuit of hostile aircraft, the attack of hostile ground forces, and the bombardment of terrestrial objectives." Observation included "distant, close, and battlefield" tasks. To accomplish these tasks, aircraft were organized into pursuit, attack, bombardment, and observation units.[71]

The 1923 *FSR* defined nine "general principles" in the chapter titled "Combat." The first principle was that the "ultimate objective of all military operations is the destruction of the enemy's armed forces in battle."[72] Concentration of superior ground and air forces, and achieving decisive results through offensive action, were the second and third principles. The fourth principle, that "superior leadership" and "greater mobility and higher morale" can overcome numerical inferiority, was followed by the principle of surprise. Surprise led to the principle of security, or taking measures against the enemy's surprise. The last two principles, the need to economize force elsewhere to maximize concentration at the decisive point and simplicity, closed out the section on general principles.[73]

Additional principles applied primarily to offensive action. Attacks were subdivided, in principle, into main, or decisive, attacks and secondary, or holding, attacks. The main attack attempted to either turn a flank or to "penetrate a hostile front." Enveloping attacks could be either single or double envelopments, with the possibility that another type, the turning attack, could be used against enemy forces taking up a new defensive position. All of these forms of attack were used when open flanks existed during an operation in which the enemy could be brought into decisive action by "avoiding attacking on the ground selected by the enemy."[74]

Reflecting the AEF experience, the 1923 *FSR* addressed situations in which there were no open flanks and the enemy had settled into defensive positions along a stabilized front. When this occurred, penetration was required. The penetration of a stabilized front was necessary to "force the enemy into open ground with a view to his subsequent defeat by the applications of open warfare."[75] Deliberate penetrations required extensive reconnaissance, preparation of the battlefield, extensive artillery and tank support, and systematic planning. Specifically directing details of the planning for this penetration, the manual specified the plan "is prepared . . . determines the limits of the front of the attack and of the objective, the troops to be employed, the sectors, zones of action and missions to be assigned to the several elements of the command, and the preparations to be made prior to the occupation of the sectors by the attacking troops."[76] This critical section of the manual, and the essential challenge for the interwar army, reflected the experience of the Meuse-Argonne offensive.[77] The manual continues describing in great detail preparation and execution for reducing a stabilized front—the most complex of all forms of combat—for another three pages.

Two forms of initiative were addressed in the 1923 manual. One was necessary for open warfare, the other for "more methodically conducted operations." In open warfare, where decision could be achieved through the destruction of enemy combat forces, orders assigned only "general missions."[78] In methodical operations along a stabilized front or against prepared defensive positions, orders were more specific.[79] "Armies and corps exercis[e] more detailed control over the action of subordinate units. Corps especially take in hand the organization of artillery fire and in the attack regulate the successive advances of infantry in the approach to the position. As soon, however, as the conditions which require centralization of control cease to exist, wider initiative is returned to subordinate units."[80] Initiative was to be the norm; control from higher headquarters was to be tolerated only when conditions required tight command and control.

Tentative "Field Service Regulations" (1939)

The 1939 *Field Service Regulations (Tentative)*, written as a staff coordination document under the supervision of the War Department's General Staff, then issued as "tentative," perpetuated much of the doctrine promulgated in 1923, with only minor changes in the description of offensive operations, the addition of a short description of mechanized cavalry, and emendations to the description of airpower.[81] Structural changes included the separation of the "Combat" chapter into two separate chapters on offense and defense, as well as the addition of two special-purpose operations: guerilla warfare and operations in mountains.[82] Minor language changes to the discussion of offensive operations included a somewhat more precise analysis of the transition period from penetration of the stabilized front to execution of the pursuit.[83]

Significant differences in the 1939 manual were the addition of mechanized forces as a distinct element on the battlefield and weakening the role of ground-support airpower. Mechanized cavalry, characterized in this edition as a subordinate element of the cavalry arm, "finds its principal role in employment on distant missions covering a wide area." Designated as the ideal counterattack force in the defense, and as "the essential means for exploitation of a success," mechanized cavalry was an essential component of the transition from penetration of a stabilized front to the development of open warfare, terms still in use in 1939.[84] In the meeting engagement, the section of the 1939 *FSR* most reminiscent of discussions of open warfare from the AEF's "Tactical Note No. 7," subordinate unit commander initiative, in "consonance with the general mission of the command and intentions of the superior commander," was desired.[85] The 1939 version modified airpower, eliminating the specific role of attack aviation. The mission could be accepted by either light bombardment units or pursuit units, performing missions as assigned, but only if required. There no longer existed a specific type of aircraft or unit of aviation specifically designed and trained for the mission of close air support of ground forces.[86]

"FM 100-5" (1941)

The 1941 version of *FM 100-5*, written at Fort Leavenworth, maintained the basic conceptualization of war found in the 1923 and 1939 FSRs, although now as a field manual rather than a field service regulation.[87] The application of fundamental principles, the purpose of ground combat, and the organization of forces remained unchanged.[88] A new chapter on retrograde movements was added after defense. Special operations were now expanded to eleven, adding attack of a fortified locality, combat in snow, combat at defiles, jungle operations, and desert operations. Combat in towns was now a separate chapter from combat in woods. The chapter on guerilla operations was recharacterized as "partisan operations."[89] Artillery remained intact from the earlier editions, although it was relabeled as "field artillery."[90] Cavalry remained a distinct arm but was now equipped with motorized cavalry as well as horse and mechanized cavalry.[91]

The nine principles of combat, now called "doctrines of combat," were reduced to seven, all of which were identical to the 1923 and 1939 *FSRs*. The principles of economy of force (although it became part of the discussion of concentration) and fire superiority (which appeared in different form as part of the decisive leadership doctrine) were now absent.[92] Command and control, expanded in 1941 by bringing in elements from other sections of the earlier regulations, continued to discuss the same points of command and staff relationships, with minor additions.[93]

The largest substantive addition from 1939 to 1941 was a new chapter, toward the back of the manual, detailing four types of divisions. Unlike the 1923 and 1939 regulations, which discussed infantry and cavalry only as branches and contained little discussion of infantry and cavalry divisions as unique entities, the 1941 manual added several pages on each division type in the force in 1941: infantry, motorized, cavalry, and armored.[94] These discussions of the divisions simply categorized more clearly the functions of infantry and cavalry divisions and added functions for the two newest formations, motorized and armored.[95] Significantly, even though this was foreshadowed in the description of cavalry in 1923 and the discussion of mechanized cavalry in 1939, the 1941 manual included clear doctrine for the employment of mechanized forces, namely the armored division. This new type of division added several concepts to the 1939 discussion of mechanized cavalry. In a fifteen-page section, the 1941 edition describes the armored division as an all-arm, combined arms, highly mobile armored force whose primary mission was to operate against the enemy's rear areas.[96]

Also added, toward the front of the manual, was a small chapter titled "Leadership." Leadership had been an implied part of everything the professional force did during the 1920s and 1930s. In 1941, given the requirements of a rapidly expanding force, some of the commonsense discussions of practical leadership, taught during the interwar period at small posts scattered around the United States, in overseas postings, and at the branch schools during the interwar period, had to be incorporated into doctrine. Much of this chapter appears to have been drawn from portions of the German version of *FM 100-5*, *Truppenführung* (1933). Some sentences and phrases were obviously lifted from the German manual, but the applicability of most comments in the "Leadership" chapter are also simple common sense; they derived from Leavenworth as much as from Berlin.[97]

Airpower continued to decline in its doctrinal ability to integrate with ground-force divisions and corps. In a section retitled "Air Corps," the role of ground attack from the air was further marginalized to the point that no form of aviation was tasked with that role, even as a secondary mission as specified in the 1939 version. The 1941 manual did say that close-support aircraft (the authors used the phrase "air support of ground troops") were essential for mechanized and armored forces operating beyond the range of artillery, but the manual could not name which aircraft would provide ground support. The 1923 variant on attack aviation had been replaced in 1939 by light bombardment. By 1941, only observation aviation still worked in close cooperation with ground forces.[98]

The discussions of combined arms, branches, and offensive combat continued without notable alteration from the 1923 and 1939 regulations, with a noteworthy exception: the inclusion of armored and motorized forces now provided an answer for creating the "break through"—itself a new phrase. Although the techniques required to generate a penetration (extensive planning, air superiority, fire superiority, local tactical control, surprise, and security) maintained the same form as in the 1923 and 1939 *FSRs*, the new addition in the *FM 100-5* (1941) was a prescription for *how* to create the break through and generate an exploitation operation.[99] Although not a replacement for the term *penetration*, break through was considered a necessary initial stage in the conduct of any penetration. If given the opportunity to create a penetration, readers of the 1941 manual were advised to create a wide penetration, as that would make it more difficult for defenders to seal the penetration and would facilitate the creation of secure shoulders for the attacker. The penetration, using similar techniques from the 1923 and 1939 regulations, was now further clarified as consisting of "three separate impulses: a break through the hostile position, a widening of the gap thus created by enveloping one or both of the interior hostile flanks, and the seizure of the objective and exploitation of success." The break through could be accomplished by infantry forces or by armored forces, depending on the situation. Once the penetration had been accomplished, "cavalry, armored and motorized units were considered especially suitable for seizing the objective and for exploitation."[100] This additional clarity in the critical transition phase would be helpful for fast-moving situations—but the penetration still had to occur, using the old techniques of 1923: comprehensive planning, close combined arms assault, and artillery superiority—all for the penetration of a stabilized front to gain a war of movement and the decisive battle.[101]

"FM 100-5" (1944)

The June 1944 edition of *FM 100-5* was a very minor modification of the 1941 edition. The army, with fresh lessons from the Pacific and North Africa, had, in the words of historian Michael Doubler, emerged from these campaigns with "the conviction that its doctrinal and operational concepts were sound."[102] There was little call from the field army to change the concepts or doctrine contained in *FM 100-5*. The largest change was the movement of airpower from a branch to a separate chapter ("Air Forces"); the role of ground support merited only two of twenty-seven numbered paragraphs.[103] Again, as in the 1941 edition, the discussions of principles, command and control, branches, and offensive operations remained relatively intact. The chapter on leadership, new for the 1941 version, survived intact in 1944, with the only change being the addition of italics to three sentences.[104] Offensive operations retained the valuable new insights reflected in the 1941 version while also maintaining the discussions on careful planning, artillery preparation, and infantry assault.

The lessons of the AEF for carefully planned infantry, tank, and artillery assaults on defensive positions arrayed in depth along stabilized fronts, and the need for specific techniques to penetrate stabilized fronts (with the accepted theory that decisive battle was only possible in open warfare, or the war of movement), remained consistent from the 1923 *FSR* through *FM 100-5* (1944). Improvements in technology and technique made the exposition of the transition from penetration to movement much clearer, and by 1944 mobile operations stood some chance of success *if* the penetration could be made with the infantry-artillery-tank-aircraft combat team required since the 1923 *FSR*.

"A Manual for Commanders of Large Units"

Another manual of the period "contemplated the employment of forces varying in strength from a single division to the maximum mobilized man power of the Nation."[105] This controversial manual was *A Manual for Commanders of Large Units*, published in 1930 to supplement the 1923 *FSR*.[106] Apparently, senior army leaders saw that echelons above division, and certainly echelons above corps, were inadequately discussed in the *FSR* and thus needed a manual dedicated to problems relevant to theaters, field armies, and corps. The 1930 *MCLU*, a partial translation of a French army manual from 1921 and partially lifted from the 1923 *FSR*, addressed division, corps, and army operations.[107] In verbose and stilted language, including some painfully poor translations, the manual incompletely served the purpose of providing army doctrine for opera-

The Tank. Troopers practicing the new-style dismount. U.S. Army Signal Corps photograph, U.S. Army Center for Military History.

tions at echelons above division. The 1930 *MCLU* was a combined arms manual, with the arms generally limited to field artillery in support of an infantry assault, supported by tanks if available. Attacks on fortified positions, although not using the terminology of a "stabilized front" found in the *FSRs* and *FM 100-5*, were to be planned and executed in the same deliberate and synchronized fashion as in the *FSRs*. However, the *MCLU* offered little in discussion of the delicate and essential transition operation from break through to exploitation. In a rather simplistic statement, the corps was required to "place great dependence upon the initiative of the division commanders"; the division was required to "push on vigorously to a rapid and successful completion of its mission." Even the minimalist discussions in the earlier publications were superior to the *MCLU*'s uselessly vague prescriptions.[108] Although used as a text at the Army Command and General Staff School and the War College, this manual added little beyond the *FSR* discussions to the understanding of conditions and solutions on modern battlefields.

The 1942 version of this manual (now published as *Field Manual 100-15*) was completely new, written in response to the need to cover corps and armies, groups of armies, and air forces; it was coordinated with the newest version of *FM 100-5*. The 1942 manual "stresse[d] the fundamental doctrine that successful military operations demand *air* superiority."[109] It contained five detailed pages prescribing the techniques of the "break-through" (now hyphenated), as well as a novel chapter titled "Employment of Larger Armored Units."[110] Written in early 1942, the manual reflected the fascination with the new armored warfare that appeared to be happening in Europe and the Soviet Union. It also coincided with the development of the largest armored force the U.S. Army ever fielded: fourteen armored and four motorized divisions existed in the United States by the end of 1942. One year later, running low on resources and critically short of maritime shipping, the army had reorganized the motorized divisions into infantry divisions and added only two additional armored divisions. Warfare would certainly include armored forces, yet infantry divisions outnumbered armored divisions (sixty-seven to sixteen) in the United States Army of World War II.[111] Although updated to reflect the developing concepts of armored warfare, the 1942 manual for echelons above division did not deviate from either the principles of combined arms warfare or the battlefield framework of stabilized fronts and mobile operations.

The "Staff Officers' Field Manuals"

Charged to educate officers to fill staffs at the division and corps levels, the faculty of the General Service Schools, and later at the Command and General Staff School, wrote several texts for staff officers in the early 1920s.[112] By 1925, the War Department had issued instructions to the General Service Schools to write, circulate, and revise a text to serve as the basis of a staff officers' manual.[113] This tentative manual included a fourteen-page section on staff principles. Staffs were, in essence, "*to assist* the commanders in formulating and carrying out their decisions and *to serve* the troops in carrying out their missions."[114] In 1928, the War Department published the *Staff Officers' Field Manual*.[115] According to this, the first official staff officer doctrine published after World War I, staff "consists of those officers specifically provided for the purpose of assisting its commander in exercising his command functions." General functions of the staff were defined as

> assist[ing] the commander in carrying out his command functions. It
> constantly anticipates and provides for the needs of the troops. It secures
> information for the commander, works out the details of his plan, translates
> his decision and plan into orders, causes such orders to be transmitted to the

troops, observes the execution of these orders, and anticipates and initiates action, within the scope of its authority, to complete the carrying out of the commander's intentions.[116]

These essential functions of the staff remained intact throughout the interwar period.

In 1932, the War Department published another version, which prescribed exactly, word for word, the same definition of "staff" and the same functions for staff as in 1925.[117] This manual added 125 pages of forms, reports, order formats, military symbology, and other details for modern staff function. It continued in use at Leavenworth, and throughout the army, until superseded in 1940 by another manual, also authored by the staff and faculty at Leavenworth.

Consistent and Applicable Doctrine

In spring 1940, officers on the Command and General Staff School staff and faculty completed a draft of the *Staff Officers' Field Manual*. It was submitted to the War Department on June 13, 1940, and published, with minor alterations, by the War Department on August 19, 1940. This manual stayed in effect through all of World War II and was superseded by a new version in 1950.[118] Although ten changes were issued during the World War II years, they were minor and did not alter the basic conceptualization of modern warfare.[119] The 1940 manual defined "staff" in similar fashion to the 1928 and 1932 manuals and prescribed staff functions in only slightly different language.[120] This critical publication, essential for the massive industrialized wars for national survival of the early and mid-twentieth century, and again written by the Leavenworth staff and faculty, was the bible for officers at the division, corps, army, and army group levels throughout World War II.

The U.S. Army accepted and used, with practically no change for a decade, a staff officers' manual written before the German rapid defeat of the French in the spring of 1940. Given the common conception that the U.S. Army was shocked into a sense of modernity by the 1940 fall of France, the existence, and persistence, of a manual written *before* the fall of France, published by the War Department more than a year before Pearl Harbor, and that served, with only the most minor of changes, for the next ten years, is, to paraphrase General Snow's comment about artillery casualty statistics from World War I, "startling."

How can one explain the consistency of principles and battlefield framework among these doctrinal publications? Two possibilities appear: either these manuals were so useless as to be ignored, or the doctrine was in step with the nature of modern warfare well enough to function in the modern global context. The answer lies in the value of the lessons learned from World War I that were captured in the interwar doctrine, in the quality of the officer corps' intellectual discussion in the interwar journals, in the interwar experiments and technical developments, and in the intellectual proving ground of the interwar officer school system. The staff and faculty of the Command and General Staff School who composed the 1940 *Staff Officers' Field Manual* were only one part of an extensive school system that energized the intellectual development of the U.S. Army's officer corps from 1919 to 1940.

This vibrant intellectual development existed in spite of the prevailing conditions of the army from the passage of the National Defense Act of 1920 through the advent of national mobilization in 1940. With an armed force that was demobilized, inadequately funded, a shadow of its former size, and less ready at the unit level compared to the pre–Great War army, the professional debate over the role of the regular officer and the army never waned during these two decades. While this debate ensued, officers found their professional center in the officer education system. As evoked by Major General Ernest Hinds at the June 1924 graduation ceremony of the Field Artillery School, it was necessary for officers to not only participate in critical education opportunities at the special and general service schools but also to dedicate themselves to the lifelong study of their profession. He advised the graduates, "You are not forced to study tactics every day, but it is necessary for successful troop leading; and it will help you greatly at the Fort Leavenworth School if you will study, not just the tactics of field artillery alone, but that of the combined arms as well."[121] When these officers studied, either at the schoolhouse or on their own, they studied from doctrinal texts that changed very little in the two decades from 1919 through 1940. That these manuals changed very little mattered very little, since the fundamentals of combat—stabilized front and penetrations using combined arms, firepower, and essential staff work—changed very little as well. It was fortunate for these officers, and for the eventual outcome of the global fight against fascism, that the conceptual and consistently prescribed, in doctrine, battlefield framework of the stabilized front and mobile warfare was a sufficient match for the conditions of 1941 through 1945 in all theaters. It is not every generation of officers that can be prepared, trained, and educated for the last war and still be competent for the next war.

Some have characterized the interwar period as the "rise and fall" of U.S. Army doctrine.[122] The reality was that doctrine was sound, consistent, and based on constant principles. Until the advent of the German offensives in Poland and France in 1939 and 1940, the U.S. Army did not alter its doctrine based on the unfulfilled promises of military visionaries. Even after those German conquests, alterations to doctrine were minor, accounting primarily for the existence and use of armored divisions and airborne troops and, in the case of armored divisions, by bringing earlier texts up to date. The role of combined arms, the need for the offensive, and the necessary teamwork of the artillery, and other fires, with all other services remained the keys to U.S. doctrine. Content to garner the lessons of the stabilized front and mobile operations in World War I, aware of the lack of resources for peacetime large-formation maneuvers, and yet concerned for the future readiness of the officer corps, the education of middle-grade officers was devoted to a future conventional war scenario in which the mobilized manpower of the nation would fight a war based on "modern principles." This education, which for combined arms divisions and corps centered at Fort Leavenworth, was essential to the success of the United States Army in World War II.

Chapter 3

The Leavenworth Mission: Knowledge, Problem Solving, and Confidence

Correct problems. Rainy all day. . . . (??) spent a couple of hours with me . . . find him working on a map problem.

Fiske makes us a good task by way of encouraging theoretical schooling hand in hand with practical work. . . . We must not ape the schools either of French or German tactics but fight along original American lines taking what is sound from all but putting individualism in as befits the different race that we are.

—Major Fay Brabson, instructor, Langres Staff School,
diary entry for May 5 and 6, 1918

Understanding principles, combined with their rigorous practical application, characterized the officer corps' professional concepts, occupational skills, and forecasts of the future battlefield. This was true for Major Fay Brabson at the Langres Staff School during World War I and remained true at Fort Leavenworth throughout the interwar period.[1] Learning how to learn, to use George C. Marshall's adage, and learning the skills necessary to be competent on the battlefields of the next war required clarity of mission, a focus on the appropriate subjects, competent teachers, effective teaching methods, students ready and willing to learn, and courses of sufficient rigor.[2]

The essential mission of the army schools remained consistent throughout the interwar period. The commandant and course directors designed the coursework, as new students were told at one of the first lectures in 1919, to "develop a way to reason through problems."[3] As the lecturer himself related when he became commandant of Fort Leavenworth nearly two decades later, by virtue of the school's role in the education system, and through faculty development of course material, the mission was "to give theoretical and practical instruction in the operation of large units . . . which would place [the graduates] in the ranks of those competent to operate large units in time of war." The student would "have acquired another asset which in value can scarcely be measured. This is an increased confidence in your own ability, definite knowledge that you know how to approach difficult military situations, that you make sound decisions therein, and that you have the nerve to stand or fall with these decisions."[4]

Competence in handling large formations, mastery of problem-solving and decision-making skills, and confidence in those skills were the three fundamental proficiencies taught at Leavenworth during the interwar years. The fourth component, personal qualities such as "nerve," was considered by the interwar faculty as beyond the ability of any school to influence. In the words of the director of the General Staff School in 1922, "There is little a school can do in respect to the development of personality in mature men."[5]

Educating Practitioners in Operational Art

For the interwar army, operational art meant mastering a mechanical set of competencies. The essence of military skill was the methodical application of military force to win. Although operational art is only recently a doctrinal term used in the United States Army, the concept of military professional skill as an art form is not new.[6] Practical applicatory instruction at Leavenworth was a good match for the interwar operational art of mechanical application. Practical mastery of nontheoretical army division and corps staff work, with some education on echelons above corps, meant "professional competence" for the Command and General Staff Course.

Although writing five decades after the interwar period, Colonel Wallace Franz, a member of the Army War College faculty in 1983, offered a definition similar to that used at Leavenworth from 1919 to 1945. He wrote that "operational excellence" for army officers resulted from intimate knowledge and understanding of the "doctrine for the employment of large units." Only practical application and wargaming would make this knowledge useful. According to Franz, the essential difference between mere tactics and the "operational excellence" of large-formation employment is the need to anticipate future situations. "Forecast of maneuver is the special problem and responsibility of the commander of large units. . . . One could say that for the division (small unit) the key word is execute, and for the corps (large unit), anticipate."[7] During the interwar period, Leavenworth consistently taught officers the employment of large units, divisions, corps, and armies. Practical application and wargaming were an essential part of this education, as expressed by Major Stuart Heintzelman in 1920: "You will be convinced as a result of the game and of your personal observation, though both are extremely limited as to time and as to area, that any War Department plan that is not first thoroughly studied, then played, then observed on the ground, and then restructured, as a result of further researches by all sections, is no plan at all."[8]

The education of practitioners—those whose profession is to practice—is different from educating pure scientists or pure academicians. Professions that are expected to solve problems, apply techniques to seemingly unique situations, and provide solutions that actually work need a different kind of education than those whose primary assignment is the acquisition of knowledge. Education theorist Donald A. Schön drew on personal observations of education in architecture, the arts, medicine, urban planning, and other professions when he developed his theory for reflective practitioners.[9] In *Educating the Reflective Practitioner*, Schön wrote that practicing professionals must be educated in a specific sequence: "First the relevant basic science, then the relevant applied science, and finally, a practicum in which students are presumed to learn to apply research-based knowledge to the problems of everyday practice."[10] Problem solving was one of Schön's essential skills, but students must also be taught how to implement solutions—that is, after they have defined the nature of the problem. They must also be taught how to improvise within fluid situations, something that is learned most effectively through a comprehensive set of practical exercises.[11]

Leavenworth's Mission

Immediately after World War I, the mission of the schools at Leavenworth was to educate students in the practical skills required for effective command and control of divisions, corps, and armies.[12] During the interwar period's initial two-year course, the first year was devoted to division operations, the second to corps and army procedures. According to the annual report of Lieutenant Colonel Hugh A. Drum, the School of the Line taught "1st, organization, 2d, tactics, techniques and capabilities of the different arms, separate and in combination; 3d, tactical principles, decisions, plans and orders and their application; 4th, supply principles and their application to the division; 5th, the duties and functions of the commander and the general staff of a division; 6th, details of troop leading within the division."[13] As reported in Colonel William K. Naylor's annual report for the 1919–1920 General Staff Course, the second-year course would

> commence with lectures, conferences and outside work on organization, troop leading, tactics and technique of the corps and Army, and of all the auxiliary arms thereof in order that the student may become familiar with the powers and limitations of the[se] agencies. . . .

The duties of the General Staff and problems involving command and general staff duties of the corps and army will be taken up. Upon completion of this work we hope to find that the student either knows, or that we have just reason to assume that he knows, all about the troops with which he must deal with in the corps and army; all about organization; all about general staff duties and all about command. He then is ready to function as a commander or as a staff officer in combined problems.[14]

Drum also agreed with Naylor's recommendation that the method of instruction, that is, the "applicatory method, so long in vogue in these Schools, will be continued and expanded in the following year and officers will be from time to time impressed with the importance of this method of instruction."[15]

Although course content was modified during the two interwar decades, the fundamental learning objectives of competence in handling large formations, problem-solving and decision-making skills, and confidence in these skills, never changed. Indeed, these three fundamental proficiencies were initiated at Leavenworth before World War I and were maintained at Langres. After World War I, faculty and student experiences in the AEF reinforced the need for such skills. Clear mission statements remained in effect for the entire interwar period with only minor modifications.

The school's mission was made clear by commandants when they welcomed new students. In summer 1922, Brigadier General Hanson Ely advised the incoming class that "the mission of this school is to train officers for higher command and General Staff work in the Division and the Corps."[16] Sixteen years later, Brigadier General Charles Bundel, addressing the graduating class of 1938, reminded the graduates that they had "learned many concrete things. You have seen what makes the big military machine work and why these things are. You have had theoretical and practical instruction in the operation of large units which has immeasurably broadened your grasp of the essentials of our profession and has definitely placed you in the ranks of those competent to operate large units in war."[17]

Adequately educating officers who had only battalion-level experience in large-formation operations was a continuing challenge. The ready acknowledgment of the army leadership that troop duty in the 1920s and 1930s was not sufficient for officer education made Leavenworth the only place where competence in large-formation operations could be acquired. If Leavenworth's education was to be valued by students during a lull when actual field maneuvers were rare, the education had to work in harmony with their combat experiences. Accommodating the lessons from their war experience was essential to the credibility and relevance of the instruction. Immediately after the war, the faculties of the School of

the Line (the first-year course) and the General Staff School (the second-year course) treated students to an inaugural lecture titled "History of the AEF." The lessons learned from this recent experience developed into twelve separate lecture and conference sessions for the General Staff School in September 1919.[18] In addition, every instructor was a veteran of division and higher headquarters during the war. It is clear that the students at Leavenworth, in the immediate postwar years, were steeped in the events, history, and lessons learned from the AEF.[19]

The traditional principles and techniques taught at the prewar Leavenworth and at Langres were still sound. Problem-solving techniques of assessment, course-of-action development, and wargaming, which had been developed at Leavenworth before World War I, remained the foundation of problem-solving.[20] What was novel was the experience of modern combat. The faculty and students were warned that the experience of the students varied greatly and that there was indeed a "lack of broad military training." This shortage of com-

ABOVE: Line Class, Army Service School, Fort Leavenworth, 1919–1920. A typical class photo of the first-year course. U.S. Army photograph.

BELOW: Staff Class, Army Service School, Fort Leavenworth, 1919–1920. Second-year class. U.S. Army photograph.

mon knowledge and experience, however, would not generate a slavish adherence to the lessons of the most recent war, as "such a policy would be a mistake as there are many features of the European War which are peculiar to special situations in that war which have no broad application."[21]

Leavenworth occasionally modified its curriculum for changes in technology and other developments, frequently by writing its own texts. The school generated a large volume of school and special texts during the interwar period. For the class of 1934, Leavenworth issued eleven War Department doctrinal manuals, a binder containing thirty-five training regulations, and twenty-two school texts.[22] The school texts ranged from special digests of historical campaigns to more doctrinal publications like "Offense" that expanded on the principles and techniques of approved formal doctrine.[23]

One of these school texts was *Tactical Employment of the Mechanized Division (Tentative)*, first issued in 1937. Organized in a way similar to sanctioned doctrine, this manual's eleven sections began with a general discussion of mechanized forces, followed by sections on the organization of the mechanized division and suitable missions for divisions. Other sections included marches, offensive and defensive combat, supporting arms (with four sections), and one titled "Air Force and the Mechanized Division."[24] In consonance with the 1923 *FSR*, this manual categorized operations as either offensives in meeting engagements or attacks against prepared defensive positions. Depicting the primary use of mechanized forces as attacking enemy mechanized forces, the manual prescribed specific actions to be taken when mobile or when attempting to attack a defended position. In both cases, the development of a combined arms team of infantry, cavalry (mechanized), and artillery, in close cooperation with the air service, was deemed essential to success. Although a school text and not a formally sanctioned item of doctrine, it, like the vast majority of school publications issued during the interwar period, characterized combat as combined arms, used either in mobile warfare or in attacks on prepared defensive positions.[25] The dual nature of the forms of combat is as clear in these student texts as it was in the 1923 and 1939 *FSRs* and the 1941 and 1944 editions of *FM 100-5*.

The faculty made other modifications in instruction based on student comments (see below). The school also evolved in reaction to changing international and domestic situations.[26] However, the school mission remained the same through the interwar period: educating officers in the practical skills required for commanders and staff officers of divisions, corps, and armies.[27]

The Taught Curriculum

Consistency across texts derived partly from the intensity of the World War I experience, partly from the general lack of any significant fielded-force military revolutions during the 1920s and early 1930s, partly from the lack of significant doctrinal change in the U.S. Army (see Chapter 2), and partly from the reassignment of junior instructors to Leavenworth to more senior positions in later years, whose influence stabilized the curriculum and the method of instruction. However, the single most influential reason was a doctrinal belief that certain warfare principles were immutable. As stated in the introduction to the 1923 *Field Service Regulations*,

> While the fundamental principles of war are neither very numerous nor complex, their application may be difficult and must not be limited by set rules. Departure from prescribed methods is at times necessary. A thorough knowledge of the principles of war and their application enables the leader

to decide when such departure should be made and to determine what methods bring success.

War is positive and requires positive action. All training should, therefore, aim to develop positive qualities of character rather than negative. The basis of training will be the attack.[28]

According to the interwar army, then, war was to be won through the attack, and thorough knowledge of fundamental principles was the first requirement for commanders and staff officers if they were to adjust to new and changing situations. Leavenworth taught these principles; only the next war would provide new situations where "such departures" from accepted principles might become necessary.

The ability of future commanders and general staff officers to adjust to new situations was based on the principles of military problem solving as taught at Leavenworth. As Lieutenant Colonel Charles Bundel, who commanded two artillery brigades during World War I, expressed to the School of the Line class of 1920 on September 17, 1919:

A commander on the battlefield confronted with an emergency or special situation, or an officer given a tactical problem to solve in the classroom, in order to arrive at a sound tactical decision and to initiate the necessary steps to carry that decision into effect, must go through a certain well defined mental process, which includes a consideration of his task, the obstacles to be overcome, and the means at his disposal for overcoming these obstacles.[29]

Eighteen years later, Brigadier General Bundel, now the commandant of Fort Leavenworth, told the faculty that the Command and General Staff School was "one of the most valuable activities in the Army, if not the most valuable." In his view, the value came from the students learning "sound methods of employing [the division] in different tactical situations."[30] The critical need to educate methods of solving special situations had not changed in two decades.

The other critical aim of education at Leavenworth was creating self-confident officers who could become senior commanders and general staff officers in time of war. The students were promised that they would gain confidence at the school. Brigadier General Ely warned the new class in 1922 that students would "be surprised when you see what general staff really means and what command really is. You may think you know pretty well what they are, but after you have been here a few months, you will see these functions in so many varied phases you will be surprised." He then assured the students that they would graduate with their "efficiency increased 20 per cent."[31] General Bundel made it even clearer to the 1938 graduates that the course had given them "an increased confidence. . . . A good military leader must have confidence in himself. Without that, he is a pathetic figure."[32]

Such confidence derived, in part, from complete familiarity with a specific and routine method of problem solving; the majority of instruction time was spent on this subject. Confidence sometimes developed despite the efforts of the instructor. For example, in mid-September 1944, 2nd Armored Division had run into a German defensive line after pursuing it across France and Belgium. German commanders, attempting to establish a coherent defense that could eventually become another stabilized front, brought together the remnants of German units. U.S. Major General Ernie Harmon, remembering his Leavenworth experience, moved a reinforced reconnaissance element with combat engineers from 2nd Armored into a British division's sector. It found an undefended crossing site and breached the Albert Canal in two days, pushing both Combat Command A and B across the canal within forty-eight hours. The German attempt to reorganize and establish a stabilized front had failed, and the Germans pulled back to another canal line to make yet another attempt.[33]

Recalling the situation in his memoir, Harmon planned this crossing of the Albert Canal while

> indelibly fixed in my mind was a problem I had wrestled with years earlier at the Army's Command and General Staff School at Fort Leavenworth. The problem was to plan a river crossing for an army corps. Among the specifics provided in the problem was one which its authors thought of as a red herring: twenty-five miles to the right of the corps' location, the student was told there was a ford across the river. . . . In my solution I seized upon the red herring, and if I might put it so, turned it into a succulent morsel. . . . In the schoolroom, however, my instructor was more interested in extracting the answer he desired than in student ingenuity. I argued in vain to shake his decision that my answer was wrong. I was firmly advised that I had evaded the intent of the question, which was to quiz my knowledge of the technique of a frontal river crossing.[34]

In the heat of combat Harmon seized the initiative, found a bridge outside his division sector, crossed over a combat command, and rapidly outflanked the Germans holding the opposite bank. He well knew the traditional techniques for a frontal river crossing, but instead he chose professional initiative based on self-confidence and relied on his Leavenworth training for the details of execution, even the "red herring" of a flanking movement.

The details of execution, essential for successes like Harmon's adroit crossing of the Albert Canal, became subjects for nearly every class at Leavenworth. For example, students in 1934–1935 began the first-year course with a series of introductory lectures on infantry organization and weapons. Even the very first day of class included a problem-solving exercise—a demonstration of the corps in the attack. This demonstration occurred on the morning of September 11, 1934. Five class days later, the students conducted a problem-solving exercise focused on staff conduct of the estimate of the situation.[35] Two days later, the students were engaged in committee work on a problem involving the infantry brigade in the attack. The students, given a situation in class, had one hour to determine various requirements. Committees 1A and 1B were required to present verbally the "factors of disposition and relative combat strength, numerical strength, combat efficiency (physical condition, morale, training) composition, material means, including supply and equipment, and supporting troops of the opposing forces." They were to "state the conclusion reached with respect to relative combat strength," in a final oral report not to exceed three minutes.[36]

By the end of the first year, the problems were much more complex. On May 22, 1935, the same students had to solve two requirements from a more intricate set of circumstances. The brigade was still the unit size, but now, after a year's coursework, it was a mechanized brigade.[37] In the first requirement of this map exercise, issued to the students at 2:00 P.M. on May 21, all students were to give the "directive of General 'A' (the mechanized brigade commander) to his staff" at 8:00 A.M. the next day. The solution posted in the course records required the student to give "orders, essential information required of the enemy, reconnaissance instructions, information to the mechanized brigade artillery, chemical and engineer sections, and information to the brigade trains."[38]

The second-year course began for these students on September 3, 1935, with opening ceremonies and an address by the course director. The next morning they were all involved in a conference covering the movements and activities of the German and French armies in August 1914. The students had three requirements, the first being to discuss the decision made by the German First Army commander at 9:50 P.M., August 22, 1914. They were also required to address how the scenario would change if "the Germans had modern observation aircraft and . . . a mechanized force." For the second requirement, after a short situation update, they were instructed to discuss the same German Army commander's decisions, but twelve hours later. After another situation update, they were required to discuss the appropriate decisions by the same commander, after five hours more had passed. They were then required to write complete orders for the army, now equipped as a fully mechanized force instead of foot and horse mobile. After this, they had finished their second day back at school.[39]

Nearing completion of the second course year at Leavenworth, students were ready for their final large-scale problem, with all the complexity the faculty thought appropriate.[40] In this maneuver, students played both sides, the Blue side defending the New England coast from an amphibious attack launched from Europe by the Red side. Over six half-day periods, the students provided mission statements, specified troops and locations for defense (or attack), and developed the G2 plan for intelligence and the G4 plan for supply and evacuation. The students also had to describe naval reconnaissance measures, the disposition of mobile seacoast artillery, and the use of mustard gas for three geographic regions of New England, from Newfoundland to New York City.[41] After two years at Leavenworth, the students were conducting what today would be called joint operations, at the land component command level, in a chemical warfare environment, while playing both the attacking side and the defending side in a free *kriegspiel*.

The Untaught Curriculum: Command and Leadership

At Leavenworth during the interwar period, the school's leadership frequently discussed the question of whether to provide an education for commanders and staff officers. These discussions usually began because of either external or internal criticism that the school was overemphasizing staff skills and paying insufficient attention to the skills required of senior commanders. The consistent response was a conflation of the two sets of skills, usually worded in an argument that general officers must know the skills required of their subordinate general staff officers; those same general staff officers of divisions, corps, and armies required the knowledge and skills of the generals commanding these formations to be effective general staff officers.

One example is the discussion in the 1922 annual report by Brigadier General Hanson Ely, school commandant. Reacting to apparent external criticism, General Ely endorsed the comments by the assistant commandant, Colonel Drum, and the director of the General Staff School, Colonel Willey Howell, that the "command phase of the instruction here has been strongly emphasized." However, he continued that the faculty "realized that all commanders to be fully efficient must have detailed knowledge of staff work and that all staff officers to be fully efficient must have intimate knowledge of the commander's viewpoint."[42]

In response to an "impression [that] seems to exist that these schools are primarily intended for training officers in general staff duties," Colonel Drum wrote, "it is our conviction that the efficient commander must know general staff work and the efficient general staff officer must know and have the commander's viewpoint." Any distinction between command and staff education, or capabilities, according to Drum, "does not rest on theoretical knowledge or training, but, rather, on personal qualities and mainly on the factors of experience, judgment, personality, leadership, determination and aggressiveness. However, the fundamental training should be the same for both classes of officers."[43]

Colonel Howell continued this discussion in his report that same year. Howell stated that the "ability to command" is based on three elements: the "physical, the psychological, and the professional. Some of these may be acquired in a school; some may not." Howell agreed entirely with the inherent requirement to educate future commanders and future staff officers in the same manner. He reported,

> But so far as any school can be concerned in the development and furtherance of the growth of military leadership, there can be no practical difference between the training required for command and that required for general staff duty, since the fundamental difference between the two is not one of professional qualification but one of personality and there is little a school is able to do in respect to the development of personality in mature men.[44]

Fifteen years later, Brigadier General Charles Bundel sidestepped the issue of inherent or learned leadership when he gave a lecture titled "Leadership" to the 1937 Command and General Staff School class a few days before graduation. Bundel told the student officers that they would profit from "careful thought" of what they possessed in terms of leadership skills. Bundel believed "the control of human element in our profession is growing more and more difficult," but he also stated that the acme of professional skill was "thorough preparation for the position. No man can be a good leader if he is unprepared."[45] Apparently, the commandant in 1937 still purposefully conflated professional skill acquisition with the requirements of leadership. The senior faculty of the school had not changed its policy of equating preparation for professional handling of large formations with the needs of leadership or of command.

Brigadier General John McAuley Palmer expressed a somewhat different opinion, but one still mindful of the inherent personality requirements for an effective commander, in a 1938 letter to Major General George A. Lynch, chief of infantry. Palmer, an influential writer on U.S. military policy, wrote that "a good general staff officer is primarily a product of education. . . . The gift of command is not. All history proves . . . rugged morale qualities" made great commanders, not education. Palmer had disagreed with changing the name of the General Staff School to the Command and General Staff School, fearing "the same principle of academic eligibility would be applied to command and staff assignments." Palmer did not believe that officers should be selected for high command assignments using the same criteria as selection for staff duty. He was concerned that officers with the gift for command, the innate ability to lead soldiers, would be passed over in favor of officers with book smarts but no talent for command. Some other senior officers also feared the conflation of staff and command, anticipating that it would raise officers to senior command who lacked the inherent moral qualities required.[46]

These arguments found fertile ground in professional journals. Perhaps most evocative of this debate was an exchange in *Infantry Journal* in 1935 and 1936. Begun by "Mercutio" in the "Cerebrations" column (May–June 1936) with a call for making the bottom 10 percent of the school classes into senior commanders—since only they had "men who think and who think along original lines" and the typical officer in the top 90 percent was a "slide-rule tactician, a mechanical brainmaster, a canned commander"—the response was spirited.[47] First to respond was "C.T.L." in the July–August edition. With "Banned Commanders" as his title for the "Cerebrations" column, "L"'s response seemed like a classic from the Leavenworth faculty, stating, "Our service schools neither create nor destroy imagination or originality. They seek largely to teach the mere mechanics of war, to acquaint the student with the brick and mortar of battle. . . . If a conformation to time-tested and axiomatic tactical truths destroys originality and imagination, then every great commander has been devoid of these two great attributes." Concluding with a quote from Bismarck ("Only fools say they must learn by experience. I prefer to learn by other people's experiences"), "L" closed with the following: "According to Mercutio, this procedure would produce 'canned commanders.' But there are others equally confident that it will not produce *banned commanders*."[48]

Next up in the debate was "G.I.," who wrote "Non-Conformists Get a Break" in the November–December issue. Defending the current courseware at Leavenworth, "G.I." wrote that, in looking over the current problems at Leavenworth, "we find stratagems favored in the problems. Students are encouraged to strive for surprise and to endeavor to outsmart the enemy. Mechanized forces, aviation, smoke, motorized infantry movements, feinting the main attack, on a flank and then attacking the opposite flank . . . are all used." Although critical of the course when he took it a decade before, he stated clearly that imaginative solutions were plentiful at Leavenworth in 1935.[49] Another author, "Singlebars," responded with another critique of "Mercutio." This time, the argument was that commanders needed to be intelligent, and the bottom 10 percent of "Mercutio"'s canned commanders had

> forgot[ten] the mission. The mission of the student is to get an "s" [satisfactory rating]. The mission of the school is to teach the right dope. Let the student learn, let the teacher teach. If you don't like it, do it anyway,

because that's the system and that's the way to get high command. If you're so smart that you know a better solution than the school's old obvious solution, you'll know it in time of war.

He also stated that "intellectual capacity is essential for high command and in direct proportion to the highness of the command. . . . Commanders must have mental and physical force. Foch called it 'habit of command.'"[50]

These authors did not seem to draw any distinctions between future commanders learning the art of war and future senior staff officers learning the art of war. Both appear to have required mental and physical energy, and both required knowledge of the "brick and mortar of battle." The debate in the journals was also reflected in two articles on the role of command and staff, one written in 1920, the other in 1940. In the first article, Major R. M. Johnston wrote, "Our Army at the present day is in even greater danger than the German that the Command may become unduly subordinated to the Staff. Both functions are essential and complementary; they both call for an improved system of Staff training and of high military studies."[51] Twenty years later, "General Gripe" wrote,

> No one can deny that the Command and General Staff School does a fine job of teaching men how to analyze a military situation, appreciate the value of terrain, make reasonably sound decisions, get out a complete order and in doing so, act either as a commander or as one of his G's. It teaches the relation between the command and staff by showing how the command gets out a directive for a movement and how the staff amplifies this directive into detailed order.[52]

Command and staff were combined because they were complementary skills, not antithetical approaches to the "brick and mortar of battle."

An analysis of the class schedule for the 1934–1936 two-year course shows, rather starkly, that "brick and mortar" work predominated. Among all courses taught in these two years, listed on the schedule by fifty different types, ranging from equitation to legal principles, only one was devoted to leadership. Taught in the first year, the course in leadership represented only five class hours (among 2,211 total hours over the two years).[53] Although leadership was raised in other classes as a discussion point, a review of the course material, the instructions, and student comments support the assessment that leadership was not a predominant subject at Leavenworth. The senior army leaders during the interwar years either believed that officers with more than twenty years of service knew how to be leaders already or that leadership was an innate character and could not be trained.

Discussions of staff skills dominated the academic courses. The "strategy" course focused on issues more appropriate to a staff officer than a commander. In 1929–1930, it discussed the campaigns of Napoleon, the U.S. Civil War, and the Russo-Japanese War. An analysis of the discussion material reveals that the students assessed and evaluated logistics and administration much more frequently than issues of leadership. Even when required to discuss the decisions of historical commanders, they were required to discuss problem-solving "objectives" rather than leadership or command influence.[54]

The 1923 *Field Service Regulations* also conflated the skills of commander and general staff. Addressing the role of the commander, the manual discussed the estimate of the situation in terms identical to those taught at Leavenworth:

> In estimating a situation, the commander considers his mission as set forth in the orders and instructions under which he is acting, or as deduced by him from his knowledge of the situation, all available information of the enemy . . . conditions affecting his own command . . . and the terrain, weather, climate, morale, and other factors in so far as they affect the particular military situation. He then compares the various plans of action open to him and decides upon the one that will best enable him to accomplish his mission.
>
> In general, it is the function of the staff to elaborate the details necessary to carry the decision into effect.[55]

However, on the next page, the duties of staff are expanded to include all duties of the commander identified in his estimate of the situation. In particular, the duties of chief of staff, the officer in charge of the formation general staff, enumerated "powers of supervision, coordination, and control in the commander's name [that] are coextensive with this responsibility and are exercised to the extent that he [the chief of staff] deems necessary to its discharge." The role of staff was to serve as an extension of the commander, primarily in the areas of control, supervision, and coordination. Limits to the staff's power were established only to the extent they would not imperil the accomplishment of the mission; and according to doctrine, the chief of staff, not the commander, determined those limits.[56] This blend of duties between commander and staff, problematic if personalities clashed, could also be an effective form of teamwork in a division or corps.

The Leavenworth texts made some distinctions between the responsibility of command and the duties of the general staff. According to the 1923 "Command, Staff and Tactics" text, the commander was the "leader of men." His authority was his "lawful exercises over subordinates by virtue of his rank or assignment." His duty was to "produce individual or collective military action or non-action on the part of subordinates, regardless of the will of the latter." The staff included "personnel who help the commander in the exercise of the functions of command by professional aid and assistance."[57]

Fourteen years later, the faculty published another school text, *Command and Staff Principles*, to assist in the instruction of the proper functions of commanders and staffs. This document diluted somewhat the clarity of the 1923 text, informing the students that "the methods of organizing the staff departments will depend, to a great extent, on the personalities of the commander and the members of his staff. Therefore, matters that have to be accomplished by the commander and his staff and the manner in which they can be accomplished are indicated only in general terms." The text also labeled the command element of an organization as "consisting of a single head, or commander, together with such assistants or staff officers as are necessary to relieve him of the burden of details." In the chapter on staffs, the text described the staff as "those officers specifically provided for the purpose of assisting the commander in exercising his command functions."[58]

Students at Leavenworth learned the functions of commanders and staff simultaneously during the interwar period, in part because the doctrine required of the commander an intimate integrated knowledge of staff functions and staff officers needed comprehensive knowledge of the role of commanders. Leadership, the very essence of command, was not taught in the coursework, as the faculty believed command to be an innate skill, and certainly not educable in forty-year-old professional officers.

Untaught Curriculum: Mobilization

Another subject that received surprisingly little instruction was mobilization of the nation's manpower for war.[59] Perhaps considered a task best left to others, perhaps considered only one of many subjects for which there was insufficient time, postmobilization forming, training, and preparation of forces accounted for very little instruction time during the interwar period. Class schedules reflect numerous classes on the division and corps, but even in the 1928–1930 two-year program there was no instruction specifically on mobilization or force preparation. In this program, the army and the army group were taught, with occasional lectures on the national economy in time of war and civil-military relations (especially in domestic use of military force). However, there were no lectures and no practical exercises on forming the "mobilized manpower of the nation" into coherent organizations prior to deployment.[60]

The lack of education at Leavenworth on mobilization, forming, training, and preparation for overseas movement may have a simple bureaucratic explanation. As part of the massive post–World War I study effort in the army, the Chief of Staff of the Army empanelled a board of officers to review the general staff system and the officer education program for the general staff. This panel, known commonly as the Harbord board, recommended a two-section organization to the army General Staff. One division, the Mobilization Branch, would have responsibility for "mobilizing the manhood and the industrial resources of the nation and their preparation, training, concentration and delivery to bases in the theater of operations." The other branch, the War Plans Branch, would have responsibility for "the actual employment of the armed forces against the enemy."[61] War Department General Order No. 41, dated August 16, 1921, "codified the relationship between the Assistant Secretary of War and the General Staff." This order established five divisions within the General Staff, with the Operations and Training Division given primary responsibility for mobilization planning.[62]

The Harbord board recommended that officers who graduated from the General Staff School be assigned for duty with either branch. However, this board also recommended that Fort Leavenworth instruction be under the supervision of the chief of the War Plans Branch.[63] As a result, Leavenworth's mission became the preparation of officers for the "actual employment of the armed forces against the enemy." The Harbord board did not address which school was to provide education for the manpower mobilization mission. The National Defense Act of 1920 charged the assistant secretary of war with responsibility for economic mobilization, and authorized the creation of an Army Industrial College, but the priority given to educating for mobilization was always appreciably lower than that for Leavenworth or the Army War College.[64] The Army Industrial College remained a school for limited numbers of specialists, the rough equivalent of a command and general staff course, not a War College–level development of senior officers. In the words of its most comprehensive assessment, "Throughout the interwar years, the [Army Industrial College] constantly faced hard times. Always inadequately funded and staffed, the college was also plagued by low-grade students because it lacked minimum standards and the prestige for advancing careers. The AIC competed with but was adversely compared to the high-powered [Army War College]."[65] Mobilization of the manpower of the nation was not effectively taught anywhere in the interwar army.

2-1-2-1

Although the mission of the Leavenworth school remained the same during the interwar period, the length of the course changed dramatically three times over less than twenty years. Based on an army-level quest to generate an adequate number of graduates, the original two-year course changed to a single one-year course in 1922, returned to a two-year course in 1929, and changed back to a one-year course in 1935. These changes were meant to meet the needs of the officer corps at large and were not initiated from Fort Leavenworth.[66]

The War Department initially ordered conversion to a single one-year course to generate more graduates. Based on the findings of the McGlachlin board, the War Department sent a letter to the Leavenworth commandant on July 12, 1922, informing him that beginning with the class of 1923–1924 one year of education at Leavenworth and one year of education at the Army War College would constitute the General Service School education system. The driving factor was to increase annual capacity to "275 field officers instead of only 190 at present."[67] In effect, Leavenworth was now required to cram two years of education into one year. The result was to eliminate most discussions of the reinforced brigade, and it shortened the time devoted to corps and army operations.[68]

In 1927 it was believed that a satisfactory percentage of officers had graduated, and the program returned to the two-year format originally established after World War I.[69] This decision was transmitted on verbal instruction by the Army Chief of Staff in December 1927.[70] It stemmed from an initial discussion to return to the two-year program, when the June 1927 Conference of Corps Area and Division Commanders, held in Washington, D.C., determined that the time was right to study this issue.[71] In August 1927, the Ely board convened. The board, ordered to "consider the length and scope of existing courses at the Army War College and the Command and Staff School," recommended that the course at Leavenworth revert to a two-year program as soon as sufficient officers had been educated and the backlog of officers awaiting selection had been reduced to a manageable quantity.[72] The chief of staff directed Leavenworth to return to the two-year program effective with the 1928–1929 school year.[73]

A few years later, additional staff work, this time conducted by students at the Army War College, identified a future shortage of general staff officers for anticipated mobilization requirements. For four class years (1932–1933 through 1935–1936), students at the Army War College were asked to assess the officer development system and to recommend changes necessary to better prepare the Army for future mobilization requirements. Each year, committees of students met to analyze the situation, and subcommittees reviewed the officer education program, with a particular focus on the educational preparation of general staff officers.[74] The October 1932 student and faculty conference on this subject included a review of the "normal career of a commissioned officer" based on a 1922 General Staff study commissioned by General Pershing.[75] Given this "normal career," and the requirements to send every officer through his basic branch school before promotion to captain as well as attendance at the branch advanced course before promotion to major, the committee identified a problem. The effective promotion slowdown of the hump had generated an excess of officers who had not attended both branch courses, although due to the slowness of promotion most were still company-grade officers. The committee believed that a single branch school with double the number of graduates every year would resolve the problem of undereducated branch officers.[76]

A similar challenge existed for Leavenworth. The committee concluded that there were inadequate student openings available for the necessary number of officers.[77] This committee of officers then determined that Leavenworth graduates were grossly overage for mobilization in any future year. Remedying this problem at the current graduation rate (some 115 officers annually) would require an immediate age ceiling for Leavenworth of thirty-seven. This drastic measure, given that the hump had generated a huge number of officers who were overage but underranked, would imperil the chances of at least 1,300 officers ever to attend Leavenworth. In an effort to educate a significant quantity of these officers, and do so before they became superannuated for mobilization, the committee recommended the reintroduction of a one-year course at Leavenworth.[78]

The next year's committee did not make any specific recommendations about Leavenworth but recognized that significant alterations to the promotion system were required. However, their response to a faculty question about Leavenworth was to posit one of three solutions: cut the course to one year, double the enrollment and maintain a two-year program, or shorten the course to six-month segments. They did not recommend maintenance of the two-year program of 200 graduates.[79]

The following year, a student committee conducted a detailed analysis of mobilization requirements. Beginning with information provided by the War Department General Staff, the students, after their own assessment, increased the quantity of general staff officers required for mobilization.[80] They concluded that Leavenworth had to become a one-year course, thereby doubling the number of graduates. However, even this increase in "general staff list eligibles" would leave a shortfall unless officers in the hump were allowed to attend special branch courses that would teach the division level and then be authorized to take an extension course from Leavenworth. The student committee also recommended that the general staff eligible list be discarded, as it prohibited officers who were not Leavenworth graduates from ever attaining high command or responsible staff positions.[81] Both of the recommendations would eventually be approved.

The War Department General Staff was also studying the problem. An extensive project conducted in spring 1932 revealed that the driving issue was the hump and whether Leavenworth could sustain the flow of officers through the course and into the pool available for general staff assignment. According to the numbers cited by the War Department G1, if Leavenworth continued to matriculate only 110 officers each year through a two-year course, only slightly more than one in four officers in the hump could ever attain the general staff eligible list. To make matters worse, officers behind the hump, those commissioned since 1920, would graduate from Leavenworth at an even smaller rate.[82]

General Douglas MacArthur, Army Chief of Staff, did "not believe it advisable to have the matter agitated at this time, due to the unsettled conditions imposed by pending legislation," and the report was filed for reference in June 1932.[83] Three months later, MacArthur again shelved the idea, this time on oral instructions.[84] However, within two years, the compelling case of officers within the hump generated a decision by General MacArthur to return to a one-year course at Leavenworth.[85] Again, the need for student graduation rates in the range of 250 (rather than 100), not the quality of the education, was the deciding factor in the decision.[86] In 1935, General MacArthur's decision, taken over the objections of the Leavenworth faculty, shrank the class to a single year, effectively doubling the number of graduates.[87]

In accordance with a letter dated January 2, 1935, from the War Department Adjutant General Office, the course once again became a single one-year program.[88] Major General Herbert Brees, the Leavenworth commandant when the course reverted to a single year, expressed dissatisfaction. He reported, "It must be remembered that the majority of students are in the junior grades. It may be many years before any of them will be required to make decisions relating to high command."[89] He was wrong. Within a very few years, one of his students, Leslie Groves, would be in charge of the Manhattan Project; another, Carl Spaatz, would be directing the Army Strategic Air Forces in Europe; and others, including William Dean, would be commanding divisions.[90]

Major General Brees reported that the students had arrived for the 1935–1936 single-year class inadequately prepared to study the necessary material in the time allotted. He commented with some asperity that because only twenty-seven students had graduated from both of their branch schools, the class was underprepared. He wrote, "In my opinion the time has arrived when the War Department should make definite announcement as to just what role this School is to play in our future military educational program." Brees recommended that a single-year course require better-qualified students, including attendance at either the basic or advanced branch schools or an entrance examination to cull the unqualified applicants. He concluded, "If the purpose of the

School is to select and train only our best officers for high command and staff positions, then the Two-Year Course should be re-inaugurated and a rigid entrance examination required."[91] Additional criticism by Brees and his replacement, Major General Charles Bundel, continued to call for more highly qualified students for a one-year course, or for resumption of the original two-year course.[92] These criticisms were unanswered until mobilization in 1940 forever altered the schools at Leavenworth.

Controversy continued over the value of a one-year versus a two-year course, but the observations of Major Virgil L. Peterson, honor graduate of the one-year course in 1925, are compelling.[93] Relating his experience to his fellow War College students and faculty in a committee conference report in 1932, Major Peterson observed:

> Remember, as I went through that course I expanded with pride and wisdom in the knowledge I was acquiring, and by graduation day that lump of pride had gotten up to a considerable size. I was kept at Leavenworth as an instructor and when I began to deal with the logistics of the corps and army, and associate with others, this bubble or balloon of pride, by Christmas, had more or less gotten to look like a wart. My thought on the matter is that the one-year course is not sufficient. Our Army needs commanders and staff officers familiar with the logistics of larger units, and the only opportunity given commanders and staff officers or men who are going to be commanders or staff officers to learn this important subject is the system of instruction; the one-year course is insufficient to teach much more than the logistics of a division.[94]

Major Peterson's complaint that the one-year course could only suffice for division education, and that two years were necessary to educate on echelons above division, did not preclude his student committee from recommending a one-year course at Leavenworth. The driving requirement was the number of graduates, not merely the competence of graduates.

Shortening the course caused much concern for the Leavenworth commandants, as they reported in their annual reports. Practically every year that the one-year course existed, the interwar commandants requested a return to the two-year program. Normally, their complaint was that there was too much information and too many exercises required to teach divisions, corps, and army.[95] For the period that the one-year program was in existence, the natural tendency of instruction was to the division, less to the corps, and even less to any echelon above corps.

Criticism and Change at Leavenworth

Even though the mission remained consistent as the school length varied, the faculty actively solicited student input. Student research projects in 1928–1929 and 1935–1936 offered students an opportunity to research the educational system at Leavenworth and then to comment on subject matter, methods of instruction, and evaluation. Only a few students answered the education questions, most preferring to write on tactical subjects, but two students wrote significant research papers on Leavenworth. Major Frank Emery, class of 1930, concluded in his paper that being a member of the first year of the two-year program obviated much of the utility of his comments. However, he did recommend that the current separation, that is, of branch education into special schools and the instruction in division and corps operations at the General Service Schools, be continued. His primary recommendation was to instruct all officers at Leavenworth, not just a selected minority. He offered no recommendations for altering the curriculum as taught.[96] Seven years later, another student wrote a monograph on the methods of instruction at Leavenworth. Major J. P. Cromwell recommended no change to the subject matter; he did recommend that the evaluation system be adjusted to allow for more freedom of thought.[97] The few students who took advantage of the opportunity to critique the Leavenworth education system offered no recommendations for change to subject matter.

In 1937, George C. Marshall criticized the Leavenworth concentration on staff officer training as a general failure to prepare officers for the future. In a memorandum that Marshall prepared for the army deputy chief of staff, he cited the existence of "fundamental practices" at Leavenworth that "lessen[ed] the tremendous benefits which should accrue to the national defense." He specified the problem as being a focus on unrealistic conditions, particularly of items of primary interest to a commander "handling hastily raised, partially trained troops. . . . We must be expert in meeting the confusion and chaotic conditions of the first months in a war where discipline is poor, officers green and information of the enemy invariably lacking. . . . We must be specifically trained when to make decisions rather than concentrating almost entirely on what decisions to make."[98]

Marshall's comments focused on Leavenworth's failure to prepare officers for command; he says little about failures to prepare them for staff work. Indeed, in a letter to the newly appointed commandant, Brigadier General Lesley J. McNair, on February 23, 1939, Marshall urged McNair to make all changes required to update Leavenworth, to move it away from its concentration on "routine procedures" and staff officer duties.[99] Marshall continued writing letters to

McNair. In his last letter before becoming chief of staff, Marshall confided to McNair that "you at the head of Leavenworth are one of the great satisfactions I have at the moment in visualizing the responsibilities of the next couple of years. And, as I told you here, speaking merely as Deputy Chief of Staff, I now tell you as a prospective Chief of Staff that your judgment in what is to be done quietly at Leavenworth is to govern."[100] After he became chief of staff, Marshall wrote to McNair:

> I hear on every hand the most flattering comments regarding your effect on Leavenworth. You apparently, to use a hackneyed word, have vitalized the place and yet in a most harmonious manner. I told you in our last conversation that you had the authority to proceed as seemed best to bring about the general ends we have in mind, and that you could do this without feeling the necessity for securing approval for the various steps. . . . Anything I can do to assist, you command me; but I want you to feel perfectly free to act, and we all have complete confidence in your judgment, your leadership, and your integrity.[101]

Two weeks later, Marshall wrote to McNair asking him to reconsider a request for the reassignment of officers for a repeat tour as instructors. Marshall's concern was his desire to infuse "new blood" into Leavenworth, and he wished McNair to reconsider. He also recommended that McNair shorten the National Guard and Organized Reserve courses.[102]

Marshall frequently informed McNair that he wished to have an opportunity to discuss matters in person. On January 16, 1940, Marshall at last arrived at Fort Leavenworth for a direct conversation with McNair. One hour into the discussion, he was forced by an oncoming snowstorm to hastily fly out of Leavenworth. Drafting a quick note to McNair a week later, Marshall commented that he believed the instructors from the school needed to attend the upcoming large-scale maneuvers, or else they would no longer be the experts teaching the novices.[103]

McNair ordered a survey of student perceptions in June 1939. His 1938–1939 annual report, in condensed form, summarized the results of the survey. Asked which major subjects they thought were "most effective and adequate," students responded that the material in courses on military intelligence, the infantry division, military history, tactical principles, and the corps were the most effective. Least effective were command, troop leading, mechanized units and tanks, aviation, and supply and logistics. A complementary question asking about the least effective subjects garnered the same responses, in reverse order. Another matched set of questions asked if some subjects were "padded" and which subjects were "insufficient." Again, the students believed that instruction in tactical principles, the division, and the corps was the least padded and that instruction in aviation, mechanized units and tanks, staff functions, troop leading, and supply and logistics was insufficiently weighty. The survey asked students their opinion on "minor subjects" as well. Students responded that the course on the solution of problems and estimate of the situation was of "outstanding importance," followed closely by tactics and techniques of separate arms. Forty-seven percent of students recommended the elimination of equitation.[104]

These results reflected the focus of the institution on the division and corps and reflected the conservative nature of that focus. As long as the school concentrated on the infantry division and the corps, and on the tactical principles existing in published doctrine, the new, emergent, and uncertain roles of aviation, mechanization, and tanks would lose out to problem solving and the detail work of infantry divisions and the corps. However, in the seemingly contradictory nature of student surveys, something all too familiar to teaching faculty everywhere, 66 percent students also responded they were "able to apply the school command and staff procedure, including orders, in fast moving situations with modern motorized units."[105] This response may demonstrate the value of teaching techniques in problem solving and the principles of combat operations in uncertain and changing situations — in short, the development of professional confidence. The students had gained enough confidence in their ability to apply the "school command and staff procedure" even in an environment they thought had been insufficiently explained in the classroom. Perhaps they actually were ready to take on the challenge of new types of units in new and unknowable situations.

Chapter 4

The Leavenworth Staff and Faculty

The school consists essentially of a corps of instructors whose primary duty is to assist you in absorbing the subject matter of the course. As to the nature and scope of this work, many of our finest officers have been engaged for years in establishing and revising the course to the end that the student shall be benefited from the greatest amount possible in the time available. Most of the officers now on duty there have held important battle commands.

— "The Leavenworth Course," attributed to D. D. Eisenhower,
Infantry Journal, June 1927

The staff and faculty at Leavenworth, as well as the consistent doctrine of the interwar period, presented a stable worldview to students from 1919 through 1940. The most potent influence was the officers who had seen the bloody cost of amateurism in combat, had experienced the necessary skills of combat staff work, and were then assigned to form the staff and faculty of the schools at Leavenworth.[1] These officers, men in their forties who a few years before had never dreamed of fighting a war on European soil, now firmly believed that another war would come and that they were personally responsible for the efficient conduct of the next war—the second great war.[2] This change, which defined the ethos of the interwar education at the school, occurred during the first three classes after World War I. The faculty of 1919 through 1922 established a system of instruction that endured despite changes in the student population and the modernization of courseware. The immediate postwar faculty in 1919 created the programs, materials, systems, and methods that remained surprisingly intact until the school went to a three-month class in 1940.[3] The continuity in perception of modern war as a combined arms, artillery-heavy, deliberate offensive battlefield framework, designed around penetrations of stabilized fronts and envelopments in mobile warfare, explains the persistence of this system of instruction. This enduring perception, and the enduring system of instruction, were combined with continuity in the Leavenworth mission of training general staff officers for divisions and corps. Although the length of the course changed three times during the interwar period (see Chapter 3), the form of instruction, the rigor of the work, and the Leavenworth ethos did not vary significantly. The faculty, although usually assigned for a three-year tour, was also consistent throughout this period, as many returned for more than one assignment.

The Leavenworth Faculty

The faculty grew gradually over the two decades from 1919 to 1940, beginning with thirty-four officers in 1919 and reaching a total of seventy-nine officers.[4] The senior faculty included the commandant, the officer who commanded the entire faculty, staff, and student body of all the schools at Leavenworth, and his assistant commandant, responsible for the methods of instruction and the system of evaluation for all the schools. In addition, the assistant commandant supervised the preparation of texts, doctrine, and teaching materials and had general supervision over instructors and their management. The school directors had direct charge of instruction, including the initiation and development of new course materials, as well as direct control over the evaluation of students and the management of instructors in their respective schools.[5]

Of the twenty-seven officers who filled these positions—the commandants, assistant commandants, and directors of courses—in the two decades from 1919 to 1940, ten were members of the inaugural faculty.[6] As discussed below, their influence was consistent and personal. The close professional relationships among officers directly involved in education is personified by Karl Truesdell, who commanded Fort Leavenworth for most of World War II. Truesdell had been assigned as the recorder for the 1924 Educational Advisory Board, presided over by Major General Hanson Ely. Ely had commanded 5th Division in the AEF, then served as commandant of Leavenworth from 1921 through 1923.[7]

The faculty had two different organizations in the period, although with little, if any, noticeable affect on the nature of instruction and the form of the curriculum. In the 1920s, the commandant organized the faculty to support the two different classes, the School of the Line and the General Staff Course, the first- and second-year courses at that time. The faculty was composed of sections roughly comparable to the staff sections in a division: command, responsible for terrain exercises and decision-making instruction; G1 and G4 sections, responsible for logistics and legal instruction; G2, which taught military history and intelligence; and G3, which taught classes on orders, organizations, and problem-solving and conducted the map problems. In the 1930s, the faculty changed its organization to mirror the battlefield rather than staff. By 1936, the faculty was organized into offensive and defensive sections. The intelligence and logistics sections were retained, but the command section was eliminated.[8]

The junior faculty—the instructors—taught the vast majority of the course-work. The typical instructor throughout the interwar period was a graduate of the Leavenworth schools; had attended at least one, and usually both, of his branch schools (basic and advanced); and, until the mid-1930s, was a veteran of the AEF. After the teaching assignment, most of the instructors were sent, either immediately or shortly after another assignment, to the Army War College in Washington, D.C. These were generally very reputable officers, frequently finishing as honor or distinguished graduates of their Leavenworth course, and, after such distinctions were no longer used post-1925, were usually in the top half of their graduating class. Knowledge, teaching ability, experience, and personality were all considered when officers were nominated to be instructors. Arguably, the most proficient faculty existed in the 1920s, when many were personally selected by their own teachers to remain on as instructors themselves.

Consistent throughout the historical record are stories of officers selected to remain as instructors at Leavenworth or to return to teach after a single tour following graduation. The story of Troy Middleton's assignment to Leavenworth is typical for the interwar period. A graduate of Mississippi A&M College, Middleton enlisted in the army in 1910 and received a direct commission in 1912. Following service in the AEF, including promotion as the youngest colonel in the army, command of the 39th Infantry Regiment, and award of the Distinguished Service Medal for combat actions, Middleton served on occupation duty until 1919. Assigned as a faculty member at the inaugural Infantry School, Middleton served there until 1921, when he entered the advanced course as a student. After graduating from the Benning course at the top of his class, he was retained as an instructor at Benning—to his disappointment. As a house guest in the home of Major General Farnsworth, chief of infantry, Middleton confided to the general's wife his abject disappointment at having missed Leavenworth. Middleton recalled, "General Farnsworth took me to the train the next day for the return trip to Georgia. Standing there in the deep snow at the station, he turned to me and said, 'Middleton, I think I'll send you to the Command and General Staff School.'"[9]

Troy Middleton and his family arrived at Leavenworth in the summer of 1923. Once the youngest colonel in the AEF at age thirty-four, Middleton became one of the youngest officers in the Leavenworth class of 1924. He became friends with George Patton, who one day told Middleton that he intended to be an honor graduate of the course. Middleton said nothing, but at the end of the year Patton was among the top 10 percent as an honor graduate, finishing fourteenth in the class (Middleton finished eighth). Toward the end of his school year in 1924, Middleton was asked to stay on as an instructor, which he did for the next four years. That year, he was one of the fifteen graduates held over as an instructor. In his group of sixty-eight instructor-officers, sixty-seven were graduates of either the one- or two-year General Staff Course.[10] According to a biographer, Middleton, his wife, and son moved out from crowded student-officer housing into a "comfortable, two-story home of their own" and found "life on the post agreeable and busy." At the end of his four years as an instructor in 1928, he had spent nine consecutive years as a student or instructor. As he had one of the finest reputations among all the infantry officers after World War I, repeat assignments as instructor and student could only have been considered prime assignments. Leaving Leavenworth, Middleton attended the Army War College—with possible future assignment as a general staff officer, marking a tenth consecutive year in the schoolhouse.[11]

The workload as an instructor in the "life agreeable and busy" was significant. The faculty spent long hours teaching, but they also spent many hours refining the extension courses for the school, the texts used in the courses, or actual army doctrine.[12] Instructors created a large volume of texts to simultaneously teach, design courses, and develop teaching materials. By the end of the first year, Colonel Hugh Drum reported that his faculty at the School of the Line had written and distributed thirteen texts, including works on the division in the offense and the defense, combat orders, *General Tactical Principles of Larger Units*, and *Tactics and Techniques of Tanks*.[13] Drum made a specific point in his report that these manuals were the "tactical doctrine to be imparted in this school [that] will be the American doctrine as illustrated by our own teachings and experiences."[14]

Instructors' diligence, continual preparation of new material for lectures and conferences, the onerous task of grading hundreds of written problem solutions, as well as the work conducted to ensure that problems and solutions were appropriate to the mission were all chronicled in the professional journals. Articles extolling the work required for instructor preparation appeared in the October and November 1920 issues of *Infantry Journal* and closed out the period in the January–February 1940 issue of *Cavalry Journal*. Proficiency included becoming a subject-matter expert; knowing one's audience; making contact with every student in class, in smaller group settings, and in conferences; and keeping current. All these were significant issues for the interwar army instructor.[15]

Faculty Selection Policy and Process, 1920–1940

As pointed out by historian I. B. Holley, the selection of personnel is an essential ingredient in the quality of any military education program.[16] In 1920, the War Department, in response to a request from the commandant at Leavenworth, developed a selection process for its faculty.[17] According to this policy, instructor duty at CGSS would be the third priority for assignments, superseded only by duty with the General Staff in Washington and instructor duty at the War College. The policy statement also required the detail of only Leavenworth graduates, preferably lieutenant colonels or colonels, as instructors, typically for a four-year tour. The policy statement forecasted that after the temporary shortage of graduates and general staff officers was alleviated by the graduation of several additional classes from Leavenworth and the War College, instructors could be assigned to duty from sources other than the most recent graduating classes.[18]

Although the Leavenworth faculty was initially assigned in general accord with this War Department policy, exceptions eventually became the rule. The four-year tour, and lieutenant colonel– and colonel-grade policy, became impossible to implement. Detail of officers became a series of negotiations between senior officers at Leavenworth and the Army Chief of Staff, the War Department's G1, the adjutant general, and branch chiefs in Washington. Part of the negotiations included a complex set of public statutes and army rules requiring intervals between assignments, a set time on station before officers were moved to another station, and similar administrative restrictions. Although the Leavenworth commandant remained the primary nominator of faculty candidates, within the negotiation process substitutes were often made or nominated officers arrived after a delay of months or even years.[19]

For example, the 1924 process for faculty assignment, which began in February for assignment that June, required listing officers by branch, then stipulated that each officer's file be validated for time available for detail away from troops, eligibility for foreign service within three years, and time available for detached service. Each of these stipulations was required by statute or regulation. Although officers had been nominated by the commandant, he received a smaller number of the officers whom he had requested. Among the officers denied entry was George Patton, but no reason was noted in the records (except for two question marks penciled in next to Patton's name).[20] The Leavenworth commandant also lost out to the commandant of the War College in the case of Major Joseph A. "Sandy" McAndrew, sought by both as an instructor.[21] Although in direct violation of the 1920 policy, the Leavenworth commandant also lost out to the chief of coast artillery in the case of Major George L. Wertenbaker. Wanted by the Coast Artillery Branch to serve as director of the Coast Artillery School, this officer was denied assignment to Leavenworth.[22] The records for the entire interwar period reflect a similar nomination-negotiation process.[23]

Competition over senior faculty candidates resulted in even more intense negotiations. In June 1924, Brigadier General Harry A. Smith, the Leavenworth commandant, requested that Colonel Herbert J. Brees be assigned as assistant to the commandant to replace Colonel Robert H. Allen, who was being reassigned (as he needed to return to duty with troops by summer 1925). However, Brees, a cavalryman, was only tentatively approved by the outgoing chief of cavalry, who wrote that he wished the matter be deferred until he himself was replaced. After the new chief of cavalry came on duty, Brees was subsequently approved for detail. Then, the commander of Ninth Corps Area requested that Brees serve as a senior umpire for the summer 1925 army-navy maneuvers in Hawaii. Unwilling to see the assistant commandant position go unfilled for several months, General Smith telegraphed the War Department asking if Colonel Allen could be retained until Brees arrived and inquired whether, if Colonel Allen was appointed court-martial duty, it would count as duty with troops, thereby allowing him to stay on for several months. This request was approved, Colonel Brees was allowed to umpire the maneuvers, and Colonel Allen remained at Leavenworth until Brees arrived in late July 1925.[24] This detailed, tedious, and time-consuming back-and-forth, frequently involving chiefs of branches, corps area commanders, the adjutant general, the War Department G1, the Leavenworth and War College commandants, and sometimes even the Army Chief of Staff, was typical of the negotiations for senior staff members at Leavenworth throughout the period.[25]

Turbulence among the faculty was a major concern, as reported by the Leavenworth commandants in their annual reports.[26] In an early effort to ameliorate this issue, a large number of graduates of the General Staff School were retained to become instructors, with twenty-one officers so designated by War Department Order No. 109-0, dated May 11, 1921.[27] In 1922, Major General Hanson Ely reported that a policy of stabilizing faculty members, retaining them for a four-year assignment, and rotating out 25 percent each year was in effect and functioning.[28] By 1924, the entire original faculty had been replaced in keeping with the rotational policy described by Major General Ely.

Assignment as an instructor at Leavenworth became a plum assignment during the interwar years, with selection routinely coming from the highest-rated graduates of the school.[29] Assignment as an instructor was also highly regarded by army officers at large. In a study by students at the Army War College in the early 1930s, infantry branch personnel identified instructor assignment to the school system as the third-best assignment among eleven types of duty in 1924. By 1932, that ranking had increased to second out of eleven.[30] The faculty at Leavenworth included some of the finest officers in the officer corps and was thought to be one of the best postings anyone could receive. Of the thirty-four corps commanders profiled by Robert Berlin in *U.S. Army World War II Corps Commanders*, nearly half had been instructors at Leavenworth during the interwar years. Future corps commanders served as instructors in eighteen of the twenty-one academic years during the interwar period, usually more than one each year. In an average year, nearly 10 percent of instructors would become corps commanders.[31] The faculty was not moribund; it boasted many successful officers who would become critical to the army's effectiveness in World War II.

Supervising Instruction During the Interwar Period

The return of several influential instructors to Leavenworth after World War I ensured the continued use of practical exercises—the applicatory method—as the primary method of instruction at Leavenworth. Many instructors assigned after World War I were returning to duty at Leavenworth. Some of them came back again in the 1930s as course directors, as assistant commandants, and as commandants of the school. Other influential senior faculty came to Leavenworth from instructor and administrator duties at either Special Service (branch) Schools, the War College, or civilian colleges. Many stayed at Leavenworth for five or six years.

Commandant career patterns were similar. All were graduates of at least one course at Leavenworth, and all had at least two years' duty as an instructor. Of the nine interwar commandants, five were members of the immediate postwar Leavenworth faculty, and a sixth taught at the Army War College in 1919 and 1920. Some were veterans of the Spanish-American War, and every one (with the exception of Lesley J. McNair, who was in high school and at West Point at the time) had seen duty in the Philippines. Without exception, all were veterans of the AEF. Of these nine commandants, one had commanded a corps, one had commanded a division, two had been army chiefs of staff, two had been division chiefs of staff, one had commanded the Langres Staff School, one had commanded two artillery brigades, and the youngest had been a division G3.[32]

In addition to the commandants, other officers were influential during the interwar period, including Colonel Joseph A. "Sandy" McAndrew, a senior member of the faculty from 1933 to 1937. He served as director of the first-year class, then as director of the second-year class, and finally as assistant commandant in his last year at Leavenworth. He had been a member of the immediate post–World War I faculty, instructing from 1919 to 1923. He graduated from Leavenworth as one of the few dual-credited instructor-graduates (1922 and 1923).[33] A student who wrote a memoir, Lucian Truscott (class of 1936), described him as "a brilliant thinker, positive in thought and action," whose nickname came not only from his hair color but also "for the determination that he brought to the task of directing the instructors and the instructional matter of the school along approved lines."[34]

The role of these officers with multiple assignments to Leavenworth, particularly those who had served in the formative years (the early 1920s), was to confirm and maintain the applicatory method. Maintenance of the school's focus on practical mastery of the mechanical arts of combat command and staff procedures also helped keep the school from being overly radicalized by revolutionary theories (such as tank-pure mechanization or Giulio Douhet's overreliance on airpower theory). Due to their experience in the AEF, as well as their continued belief that the success of the future U.S. Army was to be based on the firepower-reliant ground force, fighting a war where stabilized fronts would be interspersed with a war of movement, they retained a clear and consistent focus through the period. As a group, they also believed in the utility of the applicatory method and continued instruction in immutable principles. Comparing Charles Bundel's lectures from 1919 to his speeches as commandant nearly two decades later, one can see the system's continuity throughout the interwar years.

During a period of infrequent maneuvers, CPXs, and peace-strength organizations, only Leavenworth provided the opportunity to learn the fundamentals of corps and division operations. Instruction and learning at Fort Leavenworth were therefore essential to the future competence of a mobilized army. Changes did occur, as shown in Bundel's address to the faculty in August 1937: "Changes are constantly occurring in the means and methods of war which must be analyzed and studied so that the doctrines we teach will not lag behind. The School therefore becomes a great military laboratory, the output of which is up to date tactical and strategical doctrines. When these doctrines have been approved, they become, or should become, guiding principles for the Army itself." Leavenworth persisted in teaching the fundamental principles of division and corps operations, based on firepower and on an anticipated future battlefield dominated by artillery. Future war would be resolved, to use Bundel's words from two decades earlier, by a series of "hammering attacks" and through "TEAMWORK, the greatest single element of success in modern battle."[35] Instruction in the basic "hammering attack" was itself based on the principle of the applicatory method, in use at Leavenworth before World War I and also at the Staff School at Langres.

World War I and the Leavenworth Faculty

The influence of the immediate post–World War I faculty cannot be overestimated. Officers in this group established the system of education, the subjects taught, and the methods of instruction and wrote many of the manuals and texts that would stay in use until national mobilization in 1940. Motorization and mechanization were integrated into the Leavenworth program, but the system of education itself did not change for twenty years. Many in this inaugural group of thirty-four would return to Leavenworth as commandants and directors. For every year from 1919 to 1940 (except 1930–1932), at least one was on the senior faculty.[36] This group established practically every technique and procedure used at Leavenworth during the interwar period.

It is clear that service in the AEF was a requirement for faculty and staff when the school reopened in 1919. As described in Chapter 1, Major General McGlachlin, initially appointed as the Leavenworth commandant, Colonel William K. Naylor, director of the General Staff School (the second-year course), and Lieutenant Colonel Hugh Drum, director of the School of the Line (the first-year course), selected the initial faculty from fellow AEF veterans. Of thirty-four total staff and faculty commissioned officers, all had served in the AEF.[37] They also represented a cross section of various echelons of staff and command positions and specific skills. Present in the initial instructor pool were officers from the AEF headquarters; First Army's field headquarters; I, III, IV, V, VII, and IX Corps; several combat divisions; and the Staff School at Langres. Instructors who had held significant commands in the war included the Leavenworth commandant, Major General Charles H. Muir, who had commanded IV Corps in combat in France.[38] Senior AEF staff officers included the director of the School of the Line, Lieutenant Colonel Hugh A. Drum, who had served as chief of staff of First Army; the director of the General Staff School, Colonel William K. Naylor, who had been chief of staff of IX Corps after the Armistice; and the assistant commandant, Colonel LeRoy Eltinge, who had served as deputy chief of staff of the AEF.[39]

Instructors with service as AEF general staff officers included Major Lesley J. McNair, who had served with the artillery section of AEF headquarters, and Major Walter C. Short, who had served in the Training Section.[40] In First Army, Colonel Robert McCleave had been the G3; Lieutenant Colonel Willey Howell, the G2 (Intelligence) and military law staff expert; and Major John W. N. Schulz, chief of the Chemical Warfare Section.[41] At the corps level, Captain Thomas Catron had served as G2 of VIII Corps, Major Royden Beebe had been the G3 (Operations and Plans) of I Corps, and Major Troup Miller served as the G1 (Personnel) with the same organization, all after the Armistice.[42] Several among the 1919 faculty had also instructed at the Langres staff course, including Major Fay Brabson, who ended the war as chief of staff of 88th Division, and Captain Adna R. Chaffee Jr., who had been the G3 of both II Corps and VII Corps.[43] Of the thirty-four members of the staff and faculty in 1919, eighteen had been designated as AEF general staff officers, a designation used to qualify officers for general staff assignments.[44]

The commandant, Major General Muir, took special notice of the quality of the faculty and students after the first year of classes. He described the reopened Leavenworth as "on a much higher plane than ever before occupied, instructor and student personnel not only comprising many who held high command or performed important staff duty during the World War but also reverted to their regular rank, this year's session of these schools has been highly successful."[45] It is difficult to describe the implications for classroom discussion if the instructor had been the chief of staff of a corps in combat, and many of the students themselves had been regiment or battalion commanders or commanded training camps in the United States. Eager to take advantage of lessons from the Great War, the faculty also used the students' broad experiences to define, adjust, and systematize such lessons for the postwar United States Army. The students actually brought a wider range of experiences to Leavenworth than the faculty immediately following the war, as many had served in the continental United States.

In the immediate postwar years, the relationship between faculty and students was unusual, in that many students actually taught some courses due to the instructors' heavy workloads. Colonel Drum, the commandant in 1921, reiterated complaints about the instructors' excessive workload, but he also reported that one solution was to use selected students as instructors. [46] In that same year, Colonel Willey Howell, director of the General Staff School, reported that using students as instructors had achieved tremendous success. According to Howell, using student instructors "involved some personal sacrifice on the part of individuals in giving up part of their formal course in the Staff School, [but] the experience gained more than compensated them." For Howell, the twenty-four students of the Staff School who were assigned additional duty as instructors in the School of the Line gained appreciable professional skills and knowledge as a result. Of these twenty-four, twenty were retained as instructors for the next two years.[47]

Reflecting on the experiences with students and faculty since 1920, Brigadier General Harry A. Smith, the commandant in 1924, summarized what he believed should be the relationship of students, instructors, and the army education system. In his annual report, he stated:

> It is believed that the school system adopted is admirable and working better than ever before. . . . Perfection will be reached when every instructor here is a graduate of a special service school and when every instructor at the special service schools is a graduate of the Command and General Staff School. The cooperation of the Army War College and the Command and General Staff School is excellent. It will improve by adherence to the policy of sending instructors who have completed a tour of duty here as students to the Army

War College. One further step is necessary and that is to each year to send a number of graduates of the Army War College as instructors here.[48]

General Smith eventually achieved much of what he had asked. Recent graduates dominated the instructor pool for much of the 1920s, and in the 1930s graduates still monopolized the faculty (although they were now drawn from many different classes). The use of War College graduates as Leavenworth instructors, however, did not become routine during the interwar period.

The faculty understood the difference between European war recently experienced by instructors and that by students; more than a third of them had served in the United States, usually preparing for deployment to France. Although many faculty members understood the differences in experience, they also made a point of telling students, repeatedly, that they possessed shared knowledge of recent events.[49] In addition, students were informed that the object of coursework was to give all the students a "realization," which they in turn would develop in their subordinate officers, who had not even been in the army in 1917 and 1918. As they were informed in a lecture in the fall of 1919, the course was "to attempt to bring to these young men a realization of the simple fact that success in the military profession means unremitting study and work and that the making of sound tactical decisions is not a haphazard affair or simply guesswork."[50] The course was designed to give students the knowledge and confidence needed to teach and develop their own subordinates, uninitiated in the horrors of war, for decades to come.

Marshal Foch visits the General Service Schools, November 2, 1921. Seated are General John J. Pershing at center; on his right is Marshal Ferdinand Foch. To Foch's right is Brigadier General William D. Connor (not to be confused with General Fox Conner). To Pershing's left is Brigadier General Hanson Ely, commandant of Leavenworth. To Ely's left is Colonel Hugh Drum. Standing behind Pershing is Major George C. Marshall. Colonel Willey Howell is standing, third from right. The dignitaries were in town for the dedication of the Great War Liberty Memorial in nearby Kansas City, Missouri. U.S. Army photograph.

The Lessons of World War I and the Faculty

From the very start, AEF veterans on the faculty imposed on the school, and its students, a robust redesign of the coursework. The faculty introduced texts and materials for the School of the Line and the General Staff Course for the 1919–1920 school year based directly on their AEF experience. [51] An official memorandum required doctrine to be "American Doctrine as illustrated by our own teachings and experience."[52] The memo continued: "Our experiences in the European War have been sufficient and the results so creditable that we have little or no need to borrow tactical doctrines from a foreign country. The tactical principles and doctrines heretofore recognized and taught at the Leavenworth Schools have been tested in the European War and have been found to be as sound today as heretofore."[53] However, new developments in weapons, organization, and tactics experienced by the faculty in World War I required a total rewriting of the *prewar* materials used by faculty and students.

This included the integration of tanks and aircraft, as well as the influence of the telephone and other new techniques for communications. These recent developments in the technology of war were acknowledged in the 1919 official memorandum to faculty and students. "While the books used before the war enumerate sound tactical principles, they do not bring out the new weapons and changes in methods. . . . In addition, the German text-books heretofore utilized cannot be employed for psychological reasons." The officers were informed that an entire set of textbooks would be prepared "during the ensuing school year"; in the interim, although the prewar texts could be used by instructors for lecture and conference preparation, all the exercises, problems, and practical instruction would be new.[54]

The lessons of the war served to modify existing principles. The traditional principles as taught at Leavenworth and at the Staff School at Langres remained sound, but the methods and techniques of employment were new. The traditional problem-solving techniques of assessment, course-of-action development, and wargaming, which had initially been developed at Leavenworth before the war, continued to be the foundation of problem solving.[55] The new factor was the experience of modern combat in Europe. The faculty and students were also cautioned that experience among the students varied greatly and that there was indeed "a lack of broad military training." This lack of common knowledge and experience, however, would not generate a slavish adherence to lessons from the last war, as "such a policy would be a mistake as there are many features of the European War which are peculiar to special situations in that war which have no broad application."[56]

Although the dominance of AEF veterans continued for several years, the proportion of faculty with AEF experience changed through 1940.[57] The percentage of officers with World War I experience gradually declined, from a postwar high of 100 percent to a low of 35.9 percent in 1935–1936. Still, the proportion of AEF veterans remained above the norm for field-grade officers.[58] Thus the faculty continued to be proportionally overrepresented by veterans of the Great War.[59] On the eve of World War II, one-third of faculty members were veterans of the stabilized-front and mobile-warfare challenges of World War I.[60] Clearly, that was the experience of at least one-third, and frequently almost 50 percent, of the faculty at Leavenworth.

Although courses evolved, by 1922 the *system* of instruction and the program of material that would educate senior leaders for the army in World War II had been firmly established. How that material was taught did not change significantly. Basic doctrine also did not change (see Chapter 2); the 1923 and 1939 FSRs remained the guiding doctrine. The influence of the first faculty, its production of texts and doctrinal manuals, and its establishment of the curriculum set the standards at the schools for the next twenty years.

An underlying narrative emerges from this history: U.S. success in World War II was not exclusively the result of industrial might and manufacturing capability. Rather, the ability of the U.S. military to respond to the requirements of fielding a force of 12 million after the nadir of the interwar years was due, to a large extent, to an officer corps educated in the essential tasks of military competence by instructors who personally experienced professional incompetence in World War I. The earnest desire to be prepared, and the motivation to distill the lessons of unpreparedness, so that the next generation of army officers would not be condemned to repeat the mistakes of World War I, made an important contribution to America's preparation for the next great struggle. The faculty at Fort Leavenworth was the nexus of this desire and this motivation. How they taught, the use of the applicatory method, and their influence on students are discussed in Chapters 5 and 6.

Chapter 5

The Applicatory Method

> Great depth of knowledge of war, plus practical application of his knowledge through war gaming, can enable the US officer to conduct successful large-unit operations, to develop operational excellence.
>
> —Colonel Wallace P. Franz, U.S. Army War College,
> "The Art of War: Theory and Practice," 1983

The Leavenworth school attempted to accomplish three basic missions: impart to the students the knowledge of large formation operations; provide problem-solving skills; and imbue professional confidence—all through a system of education called the "applicatory method." The so-called graded problem, the single most cited characteristic of the interwar experience at Leavenworth, was only one aspect of this larger educational method. In the applicatory method, the use of large lectures, smaller conferences that engaged students in dialogue with instructors, formal committees of ten students and two instructors, and graded problem-solving exercises provided students with different forms of learning skills.[1] When added to the recognized need for individual study and reflection, the combination of these many techniques of education augured the later development of adult education theory, in particular the work of Peter Jarvis. According to Jarvis's theory, expounded initially in 1987, adults learn through different variations of three major inputs: "thinking, doing, and feeling." Different people learn at different rates from all three forms of experience, and an educational environment that focuses only on one form of educational experience will not be as effective as an educational experience that uses varied forms of teacher-student engagement.[2]

Sixty years before the formulation of this educational theory, the applicatory method at Leavenworth, with its multivariate forms of educational experience, reached students across the spectrum of learning and generated a learning environment accessible to all students.[3] A circular issued to faculty and students in July 1924 wasted little time in informing readers that "the applicatory method is the basis for all instruction in this school. Instruction is imparted by means of

conferences, lectures, tactical rides, map problems, terrain exercises, map maneuvers, and demonstrations."[4]

The Leavenworth Tradition of Practical Application

This applicatory method was not a new pedagogy at Leavenworth. Initiated in
the 1890s, it had been embraced at the AEF's Staff School at Langres and afterward was sustained at Leavenworth throughout the interwar period. Learning
through individual practical application had been an essential part of the Leavenworth education since before the Spanish-American War. Initiated by Arthur
L. Wagner and Eben Swift in the 1893–1894 school year, the system of practical
exercise of skills became a hallmark of the Leavenworth experience under the
post-1898 leadership of J. Franklin Bell. Although historians disagree about
which man was more responsible for including application in the Leavenworth
education, both Wagner and Swift firmly believed in the need to offer practical
experience to the student officers.[5] It was designed to overcome gaps in the earlier experience and education of Leavenworth students, and both Wagner and
Swift discovered the inherent value of requiring students to solve problems using
the principles and techniques taught just before the problem was assigned. This
discovery was a reaction to an ongoing controversy over the emphasis on theory
within the army's education system. While Swift and Wagner were working on
curriculum reform at Leavenworth, in 1897, the Military Service Institution
awarded the gold medal in its annual essay competition to an article by Captain
James S. Pettit. Pettit wrote that the entire officer education system was paralyzed
by too much theory and insufficient practical application. On February 7, 1894,
before this article was published, and while the controversy was still developing,
Swift delivered the first lecture in the use of the applicatory method. Swift recommended that students, after being lectured on each subject, should be required to solve immediate tactical problems posed by their instructors in map exercises and terrain rides. By 1896, the Leavenworth school year included eighty
such exercises.[6]

   Another part of practical application instruction was a wargame form called
kriegspiel, primarily a variant known as free *kriegspiel*. In this form of simulation,
students solved tactical challenges while an instructor, in the role of umpire,
changed situations, deployed enemy forces, and introduced the friction of combat to the exercise.[7] These *kriegspielen*, added to map exercises, terrain rides, and
other exercises, wrought a huge change on the system of instruction at Leavenworth.[8] In his 1896 annual report, Wagner noted that "the benefit derived from

such exercises can hardly be overestimated. . . . These exercises are well calculated to develop a young officer's self-reliance and confidence, more than any amount of ordinary garrison service."[9]

With the reopening of the Leavenworth schools after the Spanish-American War, instruction using the applicatory method waned for several years. Under a caretaker commandant in the first years after 1898, Leavenworth merely attempted to get the school up and running again. However, the assignment of J. Franklin Bell as commandant in July 1903, when Elihu Root's reforms began, brought to Kansas a reinforced commitment to the applicatory method. Assessing the changes at Leavenworth in the 1902 and 1903 school years, Bell reported to the War Department that too few exercises had occurred due to instructor turbulence, a shortening of the course to one year, and a lack of direction immediately following the war. Bell recommended returning to a two-year program, primarily to allow more time for the return of "application exercises" to the curriculum. Permitted to do exactly that, and assisted by instructors like John Morrison and recent graduates-turned-instructors, including George C. Marshall, Arthur L. Conger, Stuart Heintzelman, Harold B. Fiske, Hugh A. Drum, and LeRoy Eltinge, many of whom would return in the 1920s and 1930s as instructors or senior faculty leaders, Bell generated an intense program of application. Considering practical work to be, in his words, "the most important part of the course," Bell, in a manner similar to Wagner and, later, George C. Marshall, attempted to add significantly to the number of exercises with actual units—with no success.[10]

According to historian Timothy Nenninger, Bell's reforms remained the essential characteristic of Leavenworth through World War I.[11] These reforms were maintained and reinforced through the work of John F. Morrison. Morrison, assigned as an instructor in 1906, remained at Leavenworth until 1912, becoming assistant commandant in 1908.[12] Working through the issues of modernization, curriculum reform, and instructional techniques, Morrison reinforced Bell's applicatory education and added the lessons of the Russo-Japanese War and the Boer War to the curriculum. According to a biographer of Marshall, "A generation after his retirement, his onetime students would proudly call themselves Morrison men."[13]

The Applicatory Method in Practice

Many of "Morrison's men" returned to Leavenworth in 1919, when the schools restarted, and they brought the applicatory method with them. From the 1919 initial session through the changes of World War II, application remained the hallmark of the Leavenworth educational system. Application required individual and small-group work, so the faculty divided students arriving at Fort Leavenworth into groups of ten and assigned committee numbers. These committees remained together for the duration, and they became one of the essential ingredients of the instructional technique. Although students attended lectures as a class throughout the year, and frequently participated in exercises as individuals, the committee of ten was one of the essential components of the education at CGSS. A primary and an alternate instructor taught each committee; both instructors were required to be present during each class. With a student-instructor ratio of 5:1 in the classroom, there was little opportunity for a student to shirk.[14]

Classes at Fort Leavenworth normally began at 8:30 A.M., broke for an hour or so at lunch, then resumed at 1:00 P.M. for another four-plus hours. Instruction was either in Building 52 or outdoors. Building 52—the Clock Tower—consists of Grant, Sherman, Sheridan, and Wagner Halls; it is a yellow limestone building facing north on the bluff overlooking the Missouri River. Constructed in various stages from 1859 to 1916, the buildings housed all the staff, faculty, and classrooms of the General Service Schools throughout the interwar period. Wagner Hall, the easternmost building, constructed in 1916, housed the library, including a book bindery in the basement, and instructor offices on the second floor. Grant Hall, the central structure, completed in 1904, connects Sherman and Sheridan Halls. It is dominated by an ornate eight-story clock tower visible for miles. Grant housed the offices of the commandant, his staff, and, on the third floor, a lecture auditorium that is still in use. Sherman Hall was the primary educational building, with three assembly rooms and a large lecture hall on the first floor, a dozen faculty offices and another large lecture hall on the second floor, and a large map-problem room on the third floor. Sheridan Hall also had a map-problem room on the third floor but was mostly dedicated to faculty office spaces, the bookstore, and administrative and mechanical support rooms.[15]

Students and faculty were primarily housed on Fort Leavenworth itself, which boasted a fine set of single and duplex brick family quarters, most of which are still in use by the Command and General Staff College faculty. Some students lived in the "Rookery," the oldest occupied residence in the state of Kansas. Named for the amazing number of children who occupied this multifamily structure, the Rookery was not desirable housing—too much noise disturbed student concentration. Fort Leavenworth, like most large army posts of the period, had its own school system, theater, post exchange, grocery store, and facilities expected of a residential town. Adjacent to the post is the city of Leavenworth, the oldest in Kansas. Various merchants from the city supported the post

Building 52, General Instructional Building, Fort Leavenworth. Known as the Clock Tower, it was constructed in various phases from 1859 to 1916. This complex of buildings housed the Leavenworth schools through 1945, with other buildings added during mobilization. It remains in use at Fort Leavenworth today as the headquarters of the U.S. Army Combined Arms Center. U.S. Army photograph.

and its school, and many civilian employees lived in Leavenworth proper. A trolley ride away was the more cosmopolitan attraction of Kansas City, Missouri.[16]

Back at the school grind, student-faculty engagements were of five distinctly different types. In the mornings, divided into three one-hour periods, students attended lectures, usually with the entire class; attended conferences, either with the entire class, half the class, or their committee; held committee meetings; executed problem-solving exercises; and conducted horsemanship development class ("equitation," in the terminology of the school). In a typical week during the interwar period, students attended entire student-body lectures on two mornings; on one morning they participated in a smaller conference, where the lecture was combined with a question-and-answer format; a fourth morning was a "free" period to prepare for graded exercises; and on Friday morning they attended a committee meeting. Afternoons were normally dedicated to exercises or graded problem solving.[17]

Lectures usually focused on principles to be applied to a tactical problem. Students were encouraged to take extensive notes and were advised by articles in the professional journals, and by the faculty in residence, to carefully prepare for

Library, Building 52, U.S. Army Command and General Staff School, interwar period. The portrait nearest the camera is of Arthur L. Wagner. U.S. Army photograph.

lectures.[18] Instructors were appointed to conduct lectures in subjects of their expertise. Although there were occasional criticisms of the poor quality of some instructors, the overall effect was exposure to a wide array of subjects, ostensibly by well-qualified instructors. Over the course of the 1925–1926 school year, for example, some 240 lectures and conferences were given by sixty different instructors. The result, according to Major Godfrey, was not students "imbued with the personality of individual instructors" but rather students who received a "distinct impression of a *system* of instruction paramount to any individual."[19] Instructors were required not only to prepare extensive notes, maps, and charts for lectures but also to practice these events before their superior officers before being approved for presentation to students.[20] One observer reported that each instructor, before lecturing, spent eighty hours in preparation.[21]

Conferences were audience-participation events, not rote lectures followed by a question-and-answer session. In these sessions, discussion among several students, focused by the instructors, was encouraged. Student responses in conferences were usually ungraded. These conferences were prepared by instructors in a manner similar to lectures, but the student engagement probably made them more enjoyable for most participants. Conferences, like larger lectures, covered principles to be applied to a specific set of tactical problems and followed the same progression from regiment to corps over the course of the year's instruction.[22]

Lectures and conferences were conducted using a building-block approach, with the subjects beginning at the regimental level—an echelon most students had covered in their special service advanced courses—and ending with the army corps. By beginning with the regiment, the course intentionally began with a subject most students had mastered in their branch schools. Instruction was initially primarily through lectures and conferences and an occasional graded exercise. These initial exercises were called "jitney" exercises and were designed to acquaint the student with the techniques of problem solving. They were graded but weighted much less than more significant exercises later in the course. For example, in Major Godfrey's 1925–1926 experience, by October he had received graded exercises amounting only to some 4 percent of the entire courseload. As the year progressed, faculty began instruction in combined arms at the division level, then at corps, as instruction became increasingly complex. Graded events began to occur with greater frequency, reaching three or four per week by the end of the course.[23]

Occasional free morning periods, weekday evenings, and Sunday evenings were to be used for the review of material already presented and to prepare for the next lecture or conference. When a particularly complex or lengthy map problem was scheduled for the afternoon, then the morning, or a part of the morning, would be left unscheduled so each student could review material. Personal study before lectures and conferences was considered essential to a deep understanding of the material presented in the lectures and during question-and-answer sessions. Dwight D. Eisenhower recommended studying for two hours each evening, most of it in preparation for the next day's lecture or conference.[24]

Different techniques for studying were used, among them individual, partner, and committee. Eisenhower recommended the use of whichever technique met the needs of the individual student but noted that he had found the partnership method the most useful for his year at Leavenworth. The individual system was self-explanatory. The partnership technique meant finding a compatible fellow student, forming a partnership, and then preparing together during most free periods, in the evenings, and on Sunday nights. The student committees, formed voluntarily by compatible officers, were intended to work like partnerships but with more students. Eisenhower encouraged prospective students to avoid this technique, as some officers would provide poor study materials; such groups were prone to failure when "some unfortunate characteristic of any one of them may vitiate the efforts of all."[25]

Official committees, the groups of ten students and two instructors formed early in the school year, normally met on Friday mornings. These formal committees reviewed the week's material, answered student questions in an open dialogue, and served as a review and comment forum on a significant problem exercise of the week. When reviewing older material or engaging in open discussion, all ten students and both instructors were encouraged to participate. Indeed, a journal article from the period advised instructors that any session that did not include every student in participation should not be considered successful.[26] If the session reviewed a problem from that week, one student would be selected to prepare a solution to that problem after consultation with the other students in the committee. This event, which could generate lively discussion, occurred before the school had issued its "school solution" to the problem, which encouraged students to compare their responses and internally select the best set of solutions. Aided by comments from both instructors, the group critique was acknowledged, by at least one graduate, to have stimulated "our sense of critical analysis."[27]

The afternoons were generally devoted to problem solving, with exercises, map maneuvers, map exercises, terrain exercises, and tactical rides. In each of these events, the faculty gave students situations, as well as specific and general updates, and then assigned general and specific requirements for response.[28] The students' responses were frequently graded, usually based on the school solution. The faculty quickly informed students of their performance in these tests. However, tests never required simple recitation of memorized facts. As Eisenhower noted in his "Young Graduate" article, "Knowledge alone will do you no good, because you never get an examination at Leavenworth which consists of a list of questions to answer."[29]

The faculty and students referred to the evaluated problems, which occurred two or three times each week throughout the academic year, as "pay problems."[30] Two forms of practical exercises comprised these pay problems. Students solved map problems in one of the two third-floor rooms designated for such exercises in Building 52, usually absorbing a four-hour period. Students also conducted tactical rides near Fort Leavenworth, riding horses about the landscape as they solved problems while graded by the faculty.[31] These map problems were the heart and soul of the Leavenworth experience, and students dreaded the four-hour tests. Sometimes given general and special situations, and sometimes given no information at all, before the exam, map problems required students to write individual solutions to tactical situations involving divisions, corps, or armies. Instructions for faculty and students were exhaustive. Consistently throughout the interwar period, *Instruction Circular No. 1* and *Instruction Circular No. 2* specified the detailed planning, preparation, and execution of these tests.[32]

Instructors did not hesitate to inform students of the form of the map-problem requirements or to instruct the students in the proper methodology for solving the problems. Examples in the archives of Fort Leavenworth include lectures and conferences given by Major Charles Bundel in 1919 and 1920. The notes and scripts for these lectures offered extensive advice on the methods students should employ to solve the problems. Methods ranged from discussion of problem-solving methods outlined in texts to advice on the types of pencils to use.[33]

Terrain exercises were map problems executed in the open air. Usually scheduled for half-day periods rather than a four-hour block of classroom time, these exercises mounted students on horses provided by the school to tour the Fort Leavenworth post or its surrounding terrain in practical application of the principles taught in lectures and conferences. Instructors provided general and special situations, in a manner identical to the classroom map problems, and required students to solve problems, in writing or verbally, while in the field. Frequently, student reconnaissance of terrain was necessary, and occasionally no maps were provided so they could develop an eye for the military aspects of terrain.

The student requirement for all these tests could be one of eight different types. The solution could be an estimate of the situation; a statement of decision by the division or corps commander; a more complete plan of action to support the decision; the formal orders for such a plan; or a selection of those formal orders, as determined by the responsible instructor. Other forms of solution were "orders as actually issued," the school phrase for having the students actually write out the order as it would be issued by one of the organizations in the problem; summaries of actions taken by a commander or a subordinate commander; or "the actions taken and orders issued" solution. These eight forms of solution remained the same for the interwar period, although map problems had become "map exercises" by the mid-1930s.[34]

Examples from the 1932–1933 first-year course include map problems on the movement of a division by railroad, by motor transport, and at night on foot. Later map problems required student solution of the division's artillery in preparation for an attack, as well as the division orders required for a nighttime withdrawal.[35] With increasing complexity, students solved these requirements during the assigned period, usually four hours, although some map exercises required preparation on the evening before the test, and some terrain exercises took an entire afternoon.

In addition to the graded pay problems, students practiced large-formation commander and staff interaction during map maneuvers, the interwar equivalent of the pre–World War I *kriegspielen*, which usually occurred in large classrooms under intense instructor supervision. The faculty used map maneuvers to teach decision making in fluid situations. These were the primary means for instructing teamwork among commanders and their staffs. During map maneuvers toward the end of the academic year, one student acted as unit commander and other students served as general staff officers for the same organization. These free *kriegspielen* were usually played only as friendly forces against a red force controlled by the faculty.[36] At the very conclusion of each academic year, map maneuvers would involve force-on-force exercises, with students playing Blue (friendly) forces versus Red (enemy) forces.[37]

The faculty carefully constructed map maneuvers to reinforce "principles to be illustrated." The chiefs of instructor sections designed the map maneuvers, then assigned subordinate instructors as group or table instructors and as assistant umpires. The officer in charge of instruction served as chief umpire for all games and assigned other faculty as table umpires for each game table. Students also served as assistant umpires when required. A frequently updated Leavenworth text guided the faculty in its umpire duties.[38] Instructor preparation for map maneuvers was intense and closely supervised. The directors of the school played the game under the supervision of the assigned instructor, placed in charge several days before the game, to ensure that the proper principles were tested by the game and to ensure that all preparations were satisfactory.[39]

The evening before the map maneuver, instructors provided advance reading materials to establish the general and special situations. Students were named as commander, subordinate commanders, or staff officers only on the morning of the problem itself, as instructions to faculty required that all students be able to recite their assessment of the general and specific situations *before* commencement of the game. The faculty carefully designed the execution of map maneuvers to preclude second-guessing. Instructors were prohibited from asking questions like "What do you do now?" as that would cause the student to understand that a decision was expected. The faculty taught students when to make decisions, as well as how to go about assessing what decisions to make, by giving them the option, without prompting, to make decisions or not.[40]

The instructions for planning and executing map maneuvers clearly stated that the purpose of *kriegspielen* was to "afford instruction in the correct application of the principles of tactics and logistics, in the proper exercise of command, in the formulation of decisions, in the issuance of orders and in the operation and coordinated functioning of staffs."[41] Students were required to use colored pins and markers to designate forces as they maneuvered them across the maps. The force markers had to be consistent with the formation frontages, depths, and column lengths, precluding misjudgments of time and space calculations. Student "commanders" were also prohibited from asking "anyone to make a decision for him or pointedly suggest a decision to him. He shall use his staff officers and subordinate commanders as the teachings of the school indicate. There shall be no councils of war."[42] Students were also required to use proper orders and message formats for communicating their decisions. In most map maneuvers, unlike with map problems and terrain exercises, the faculty did not provide formal written evaluations. However, since these exercises occurred toward the end of the school year, students' performance was likely observed intently and used by faculty in making final recommendations for potential service on a general staff (based in large part on how well students had *applied* the *principles* they had learned).[43]

The applicatory method required the application of certain principles to practical problems. These principles all came from the new doctrine, often written by the Leavenworth faculty itself, that was promulgated after World War I. The 1923 *Field Service Regulations* enunciated the principles of combat operations taught at Leavenworth during the interwar period as part of the applicatory method. Each substantive chapter of this manual began with a section titled "General Principles." Chapters on transmission of orders, reconnaissance, security, troop movements, and shelter plainly listed and defined the principles for each type of operation.[44] The chapter on combat did the same, in this case emphasizing the principle of the offensive. According to this manual:

> The ultimate objective of all military operations is the destruction of the enemy's armed forces by battle. . . . Concentration of superior forces, both on the ground and in the air, at the decisive place and time, creates the conditions most essential to decisive victory and constitutes the best evidence of superior leadership.
>
> Decisive results are obtained only by the offensive. Only through offensive action can a commander exercise his initiative and impose his will on the enemy.
>
> A defensive attitude is never deliberately adopted except as a temporary expedient . . . to concentrate superior forces at the point of decisive action.[45]

This emphasis on the offensive was not a mindless call for unlimited and unsupported attacks. Additional principles for offensive combat operations included the need to conduct surprise attacks, the need for feints and demonstrations to deceive the enemy, and a requirement to change procedures and methods of combat to keep the enemy from developing effective countermeasures.[46]

More details on the system for conducting attacks with an infantry division—the primary echelon addressed in this manual—reminded the officer to always establish fire superiority as "the most effective means of destruction" of the enemy. Attacks, the manual informed readers, would be conducted using an axis of attack as the primary control measure, giving maximum latitude to subordinate commanders to take advantage of local situations. Divisions would conduct attacks with a "main or decisive" attack and a "secondary or holding attack" designed to contain the enemy, but subordinate commanders' orders "would not distinguish between the character of attacks." These attacks would be accomplished using the firepower of infantry companies, operating under the covering fire of "artillery, machine guns, and infantry cannon and the mutually supporting fires of units of the rifle companies themselves." Attacks were to be either envelopments or penetrations, with envelopment being the preferred method. Even when attacking an enemy force in "stabilized" positions, reminiscent of the fighting in France, the attack was designed to force the enemy into open ground where he could be more easily destroyed.[47] The fundamental principle taught at Leavenworth was to attack and thereby reduce stabilized fronts in order to generate decisive operations in open, or mobile, warfare.

The School Solution

Although large lectures, large and small conferences, and committee discussions were critical tools in the education process, grading individual student performance two or three times per week was the overriding feature of the Leavenworth experience. The commandant's annual report for 1921, for example, listed the student work schedule in both courses and emphasized practical application of knowledge to problems, based on both map analysis in classrooms and analysis conducted in the field.[48]

Grading map problems, and other parts of the applicatory method, were acrimonious subjects at Leavenworth throughout the interwar period. Representing perhaps the most controversial aspect of the applicatory method and the competitive evaluation system during the interwar period, school solutions were frequently interpreted by historians as well as by contemporary students as a single solution with no possible deviations. To the contrary, however, school solutions were methodically constructed, rigorously tested by faculty, and frequently included students in both their development and application. Usually a "school solution" was used by instructors to evaluate student work, but this was not a case of rote recitation or precise and specific answers; it was more of a rubric designed to provide instructors with a framework for evaluation.

Students poked fun at the absurdness of some solutions offered by the school or fellow students. The 1926 humorous yearbook, *The Horseshoe*, included a cartoon depicting a student who failed a requirement. Although he had successfully "launched a coordinated attack" of a division, he "neglected to establish a Veterinary Collecting Station" and apparently received a "U" (unsatisfactory). At the conclusion of the yearbook, in a section titled "Overheard in the 'Dilemma' Hall," a table director of a map maneuver asks a student, "Why did you envelop his left flank?" The student's response: "Because the map does not cover his right."[49]

Despite (or because of) such lampooning, the school made conscientious efforts to limit the negative influences of "only one right solution." Students themselves participated in designing the school solution. As early as 1920–1921, triggered by instructor turbulence, students in the General Staff Course participated in an "analytic review and a constructive criticism of the tactical solution of a member of the Line school, obtain[ing] a review of the principles worked out the preceding year by himself . . . not less than the ability to discern and appropriately point out tactical errors and erroneous conceptions of technique."[50] Procedures involving second-year students as assistant instructors, and as assistants in the grading of pay problems, continued in the two-year program during the 1930s as well.[51] After 1921, in part as a result of a shortage of instructors and in part because of personality clashes between instructors and students, a committee grading system was used to evaluate student solutions. Combined with anonymous evaluation (student numbers, and not their names, were used on the solutions), this committee process apparently reduced some of the rancor surrounding student evaluations.[52]

Throughout the interwar years, the senior leadership consistently promulgated instructions for the faculty that emphasized the need to teach principles and methods and allowed credit for innovative solutions consistent with those principles and methods. Assistant Commandant McAndrew's 1936 text, *The Art of Instructing*, reminded the Leavenworth faculty

> of necessity, when teaching, we must show a type situation and a type application of principles of war to it, but the student must learn that this "type solution" is applicable to the type situation only. There is no greater truth than the statement that "it all depends on the situation," but we must at least attempt to explain to the student, why under different circumstances, the application of the principles will correspondingly differ.[53]

McAndrew continued by comparing the study of war with the study of medicine. He wrote that students of war, like students of medicine, are taught theory and principles, are given a type problem to solve, and then taught the proper methods of clinical practice, after which they proceed to solve that problem. Like medical doctors, military professionals must "learn to study the diseased conditions and symptoms of the particular case, and then modify the application of the fixed rules of treatment to fit that particular case."[54] Perhaps the most eloquent exposition of the impact of the applicatory method on the Leavenworth students was a remark attributed to an officer in the Chinese Army, a member of the class of 1936. According to Captain Lyman Lemnitzer, his classmate referred to the Command and General Staff School as a "most peculiar school—many questions, no answers."[55]

Ten years before, the 1926 edition of *Instruction Circular No. 1* gave specific requirements for the evaluation of student solutions and the creation of the school solution. An instructor responsible for creating a pay problem was required to include a comment sheet for evaluating student solutions. The instructor reviewed the requirements of the problem, then was instructed to "read over carefully and analyze a sufficient number of [student] solutions assigned him to determine the salient features of the solutions, making notes of errors, both of omission and commission." After the lead instructor had done this, he was required by school policy to meet with a small committee of other instructors, "compare notes," and prepare a single comment sheet, which he then gave to all instructors who would grade the student solutions. After the committee had agreed to the soundness of the school solution for a particular problem, the lead instructor briefed the solution to the department head at least three days before the students took the test.

The instructors generated a "cut sheet" of errors based on their reading of many student solutions, then agreed how to grade student solutions to best reinforce the appropriate principles and methods of the particular block of instruction. Instructors were warned that "the greatest care must be used to give proper value to a workable solution although it may differ from the solution issued by the school. . . . Great care must be exercised to avoid injuring the initiative of officers." Instructors were specifically required to "bear in mind that each problem is susceptible of several sound solutions. Strict adherence to the school solution is a mistake and will be avoided."[56] The students themselves, in accordance with school policy and instructions, actually generated the frequently critiqued "Leavenworth school solution."

Nine years later, the procedures remained similar, although they had evolved into a somewhat greater level of complexity and specificity. The lesson author, the lead instructor, was now required to "proceed to the detailed marking of at least fifteen problems" before discussing his recommended comment sheet with the grading committee. In addition, the grading committee now included "for the One-Year Class problems, four members of the Second-Year Class." The responsible faculty chief of section and the director of the course were also now required to approve each author comment sheet before the grading committee could begin its work. Instructors were still cautioned that "great care must be exercised to avoid injuring the initiative of officers." This circular added the requirement for the instructor to make written comments on each student solution that received "cuts" for errors in the student's solution. These comments had to be limited to critique of violations of the principles, violations of technique or method, or "errors peculiar and personal to each solution."[57]

These regulations for grading were not the only system used to prevent "strict adherence to a school solution." After the majority of graded problems, students attended problem-solution conferences. In these class meetings, frequently held with half the class in attendance in one of the large lecture rooms, instructors would brief the school solution, provide student alternatives, and then encourage student comments, critiques, and suggestions. By 1936, the procedures for these "discussion-of-problem" conferences had evolved to include a requirement for the instructors to encourage "free and frank discussion . . . in order that the salient points intended to be illustrated by these concrete cases may be appreciated by all." The circular required that instructors "shall conduct and enter into [these discussions] with an earnest spirit of securing familiarity with the proper application of principles and the approved practice as to technique."[58]

Students who disagreed with an evaluation were also accorded reclama procedures during the interwar period. Discussed in detail in the annual instructional circulars, these procedures required anonymity of evaluation, fairness of review, input from several instructors, and approval by senior faculty for each student reclama. After procedures had improved in the 1920s, General King reported that reclamas had decreased from "twenty-five to forty per problem to two or three per problem" when he instituted a policy of faculty written explanation of cuts on student solutions.[59]

The preparation required for daily conferences and weekly (at least) monitoring of graded problems, plus the work required to grade students fairly and comprehensively, was very time-consuming for the faculty. Older instructors taught their methodical system of teaching and grading to new instructors before they began to teach.[60] With a significant continuous overlap of older instructors, new instructors found little time to innovate in the preparation or execution of instruction. The system of Leavenworth instruction—the use of lectures and conferences to impart principles, followed by a practical application of these principles in a test, itself followed by a review in conference—generated a coherent and self-reinforcing system that continued without significant change throughout the interwar period.

The need to teach principles, and the conclusion of each class period with a graded pay problem, led to some humorous incidents. General Stuart Heintzelman once took to the podium to disagree with the teaching of an instructor and taught the students his own perceptions of a problem. However, when he finished, he reminded students that the instructor was teaching principles they needed to know and needed to pass the pay problem at the end of the period. Heintzelman was reported to have said, "But you do what the instructor suggests, not what I say, or you will probably get a U on the graded test." According to J. Lawton Collins, class of 1933, most students followed the commandant's advice and passed the tests. Collins believed the course evaluations were "stereotyped" purposefully, because by the 1930s no students had any experience with command or general staff functions at division, corps, or echelons above corps. Although the Leavenworth approach was less "innovative, experimental and testing-and-proving" in climate than the Infantry School under Marshall, where Collins had been an instructor, he believed this approach to teaching and evaluating principles was "probably the most important in the entire system of military education and [was] to prove invaluable in World War II." He also remembered that the instruction was "first rate."[61]

One possible grave weakness in the curriculum at Leavenworth was the minimum attention paid to the development of teamwork and the techniques of staff interaction. Almost all work at Leavenworth was individual, and practically all graded work was individual. Although students were occasionally formed into small groups for research papers, class standing was almost entirely based on individual effort. Harmon wrote two research papers during his second year at Leavenworth. A group research study, the shorter of the two, was an analysis of the Japanese intelligence service during the 1904–1905 Russo-Japanese War. Harmon's group wrote a studious and professional assessment of the advantages and disadvantages of the Japanese use of intelligence analysis, reconnaissance forces, and human intelligence during this war. Its conclusions included comments about the Japanese way of war—for example, "The Japanese as a race are crafty and secretive. They are masters of guile to gain information and deceptive measures to spread incorrect information of their own operations"—that reflect some of the jingoistic and even racist conceptions of the United States in the 1930s.[62]

Harmon's longer paper was an individual research project on German cavalry operations against the Russians in the fall of 1914. This campaign, characterized by Harmon as a breakthrough, was a study in the conversion of a stabilized front into mobile warfare. The Germans successfully initiated the breakthrough but were unable to conduct an operationally significant penetration, in part due to terrible weather. Harmon again focused on the use and misuse of intelligence, but he also expanded his inquiry to include the tactical and operational utility of horsed cavalry, particularly in extremely harsh weather conditions. His conclusions included a careful analysis of the weaknesses of horsed cavalry in mobile operations, drawing specific attention to the lack of fire-power in the German cavalry organizations. In light of his own experiences in the Meuse-Argonne, he also commented on the excessive loss of men and horses in prolonged engagements.[63]

Although some memoirs contain references to team building and learning from classmates, including the group research project, there was little in the way of deliberate effort to teach team-building techniques. It is likely that this focused attention on individual practice was due to the school's long-held opinion that character and leadership could not be taught but were part of an inherent individual personality developed long before students came to Leavenworth.

Student Perceptions and Critiques

Not all agreed that the instruction was "first rate." Brigadier General Lesley Mc-Nair's survey of Leavenworth students in June 1939 revealed their perceptions of teaching techniques and methods. Asked which methods of instruction they found most "contributed to their training as a commander and general staff officer," students responded that the practical application method was by far the most important. Twenty-seven percent believed map exercises were among the three most useful experiences; 22 percent believed map problems were in the top three; and 16 percent responded that map maneuvers were most valuable. Sixty-five percent listed map exercises, map problems, and map maneuvers—the three applicatory method instruction types—as the methods that contributed most to their professional development. However, students found little to recommend lectures; 16 percent listed lectures among the three methods that "contributed least" to training. Somewhat surprising was the evaluation of the tactical ride by 26 percent as among the three least valuable, and that 14 percent listed the terrain exercise as least valuable. This may be explained, in part, by student responses to a later question in the survey. When asked if reconnaissance vehicles could replace horses in the tactical rides and terrain exercises, 95 percent responded "yes."[64] Combined with the 47 percent who favored the elimination of equitation, a general dislike for tactical rides and terrain exercises may have reflected a common belief in the waning effectiveness of the horse.

This 1939 survey confirmed students' appreciation for the applicatory method. Significant majorities believed that applicatory methods had been the most valuable part of their education. However, when asked if student-faculty contact was sufficient, nearly half the students responded that contact opportunities were insufficient. Along with the general scorn for the value of lectures was a desire to decrease the routine class size to some number less than twenty. Thirty percent of students believed that small groups should replace large class presentations, and 61 percent responded that small-group instruction was preferred to instruction in lecture formats.[65]

Some student research papers from the interwar period also used student surveys and questionnaires, commenting on the applicatory method but rarely recommending significant changes. W. G. Simmons's 1932 monograph, which included a survey and responses from seventy of his classmates, concluded that "the five methods of instruction considered in this study be continued in use generally in accordance with the present plan." He recommended that lectures be minimized, with shortened and focused readings assigned in their stead. Although he admitted that the conferences, which he called "Socratic method" classes, required engagement by both teacher and student, which was valuable, they were often exercises in "wandering from the point. . . . Valuable time is spent in attempting to have pupils discover unimportant truths which could have been stated in a few seconds."[66] Whatever value Simmons's paper may have had for the faculty in their discussions of curriculum reform is not recorded. Other student papers reinforced the use of practical application principles but commented that more free and frank discussions of the solutions used in evaluation would increase student learning.[67]

These contemporary student evaluations are borne out by an analysis of the curriculum schedule. An assessment of the time spent by the students in 1925–1926 demonstrates the impact of the applicatory method on student time in class. Of 1,386 hours of instruction, more than 500 hours were expended on map problems, terrain exercises, tactical rides, and map maneuvers. Of the 700 hours not spent directly on practical exercises, nearly 300 hours were taken up by small-group discussions, frequently in preparation for practical exercises. The remaining hours, spent in lectures, were also primarily for preparation in the practical exercises.[68] The applicatory method was used directly in more than one-third of the student contact hours and accounted for much of the remaining time in small-group or large-group preparations for practical exercises.

Eleven years later, students in 1936–1937 attended only fourteen lectures but engaged in more than 150 hours of small-group conferences. The bulk of students' time (total contact hours in 1937 was 1,309 1/2 hours) was spent on map exercises (fifty hours), map problems (fifty), and logistics and technical instruction (fifty-plus). Students participated in forty hours of physical training on horseback and an additional twenty-three four-hour periods on horseback conducting terrain exercises, of which seventeen were evaluated. When categorized by subject matter, more than 100 hours were spent studying the infantry division, more than 200 on the corps, and nearly 150 on army-level operations.

More than 300 hours were formally graded and recorded on student evaluations—nearly 25 percent of all course time.[69]

Other Critiques

Writers in the professional journals occasionally critiqued the applicatory method. Some of the most biting was provided by "Mercutio," writing for *Infantry Journal* in the mid-1930s. In a piece published in the "Cerebrations" column, he proclaimed that army instructors, "whose names are legion," were insufferably boring. "One bright afternoon," wrote "Mercutio," "your cerebrationist counted 37 students frankly and openly asleep before he himself succumbed." He proceeded to recommend that special officers, selected for their speaking ability, become "ghost speakers" and that other officers, noted for their knowledge and subject-matter expertise, become "ghost writers" of the lectures.[70] Other writers were less caustic—but perhaps even more critical.

In 1937, Major John H. Burns wrote a piece for *Infantry Journal* criticizing the essence of map problems and the applicatory method. In "Vitalize the Map Problem," Burns critiqued the system for a lack of incorporating psychological factors, for an unhelpful level of indoctrination, for spending too much time on a problem—two or three hours, whereas in combat the decision would be reached in minutes—and for posing obvious situations when the students had to make a decision of some form—also unlike combat, where the art of decision making meant selecting the right time to make decisions. He recommended a new approach to map problems in which rapid decisions were required by the pace of the situation, thereby acquainting and familiarizing students with the rapid pace of modern warfare. In order to teach students when to make decisions, he recommended that students simply be given a situation but no specific requirement for a decision. This would permit a decision, no decision, or some other form of action, further educating the officer on issues involving combat decision making.[71]

Others criticized the instruction at Leavenworth for making the evaluation of student work too rigorous. A 1935 article by Lieutenant Colonel L. D. Davis complained that the Leavenworth evaluation was blind to the experience of the average student, overly harsh, and, ultimately, the only thing the school cared about. Student learning was not a priority, but grading students' work was all-important.[72] Lieutenant Colonel Bernard Lentz had begun this debate in 1932 with an article that assessed the education at Leavenworth as too much training and not enough education. According to Lentz, although progress had been made, there was still too little freedom of thought and too much hard practical testing.[73]

Adding to the criticism, George C. Marshall, in a 1940 memorandum for then-colonel Omar Bradley, discussed techniques he had used to train and educate officers while he was assigned to National Guard duty in the Chicago area. Unable to use the "too ponderous Leavenworth system," Marshall used local area maps, designed tactical problems for headquarters at echelons above regiment, and "did things as a practicable problem, over the telephone, or by telegraph, or by direct conversations, and it merged into a CPX [command post exercise]."[74]

Official documents also record some criticism of the applicatory method. A case in point was an extensive staff study, conducted in 1936 and 1937 at the orders of the secretary of war, of the instruction methods used at Leavenworth. Based on an initial set of questions directed to General Bundel, the Leavenworth commandant, this staff study included comments by some of the most experienced educators in the army. Three questions were asked. Two involved methods of instruction: Would instruction be improved through a reduction in the number of graded problems? and Would instruction be improved through the addition of more extensive small-group instruction? The other question asked whether a more satisfactory system of student evaluation could be achieved.[75]

General Bundel's lengthy response is informative. He told the War Department that the grading of practical problems was the only factor left in Leavenworth's ability to educate and train professionals. He equated grading students' written work to the grading in law and medical schools, where both evaluation and competition were necessary to a healthy professional learning environment. Evoking the memory of the high-quality staff officers provided by Leavenworth during World War I, Bundel refused to acknowledge any current difficulties with the system of instruction. He did admit that there had been too much rigor in the past but stated that all those issues had been resolved.[76]

Answering the question of additional small-group instruction in lieu of lectures and conferences, General Bundel replied that the quality of instruction at Leavenworth was based on instructors who were especially well qualified, through either their experience or extensive preparation, to teach specific subjects. Moving away from lectures and conferences to small-group instruction would "cause a decline in the present high level of instruction." He then enumerated proposals for the extensive and costly changes that would be required, including doubling the number of instructors assigned to the school and the construction of a new academic building to house the fourteen groups of twenty students he believed would be necessary for small-group instruction.[77] Apparently, Bundel was adding so many costly changes as to make his proposals practically impossible. Just as obviously, he felt strongly that the applied method, including the learning of principles in large lectures and conferences, as well as the evaluated proof of learning in graded written practice, was the superior education.

In answering the question about more effective student evaluation, General Bundel replied that change was unnecessary and would be harmful. He wrote to the War Department that student evaluations were done by highly qualified faculty after careful observation and were considered appropriate ratings of specific professional characteristics that could be evaluated in the classroom. If a more general rating was desired, this would not be possible in the academic environment at Leavenworth and would diminish the value of the ratings.[78]

In a ringing endorsement of Bundel's position, a second "indorsement" was added to the file by the adjutant general based on the "personal attention" of Major General Malin Craig, the Army Chief of Staff. Recording the words of the chief, the adjutant general wrote: "He is in general agreement with your views that the mass of instruction is the most economical and, perhaps, the best for the rapid indoctrination of the student body in the rules and mechanics of staff work and for bringing the group rapidly to 'speak the same language.' By this method, also, a great teacher can bring out *salient principles* and inspire the group." However, "in the later part of the course, [the chief of staff] desires that you find a way by which instruction can be carried out in small groups and by unmarked problems, followed by conferences by groups on the solutions. Leaders of groups may be instructors or, better still, selected members of the class."[79] Ironically, General Craig was telling General Bundel to institute student-led problem discussions that were already being done within student committees, part of the courseware since 1919.

The staff paperwork on this issue circulated for another six months. Bundel pushed back, asking for additional instructors, and in July 1937 the Army Chief of Staff relented. While ordering the study "to be filed for future reference," he continued to state that even though he felt the number of instructors at Leavenworth was already excessive, he hoped that in the future a change to smaller groups could be made.[80] In the intervening discussion, a document created in March 1937 by Colonel E. L. Gruber of the War Department's General Staff G3 stated, "When a change in regime is made at Leavenworth have the new commandant report to the Chief of Staff for instructions and for conference with the War Department concerning the changes it is desired to make." This sentence is triple-lined in the left margin; in the same writing, a penciled comment on the bottom states: "That is the course I think is to be followed." This comment was initialed "G.C.M."[81] Several years would pass before Army Chief of Staff George C. Marshall would have this conversation with Major General Lesley J. McNair at Sherman Army Airfield, at Fort Leavenworth, on January 16, 1940. When that conversation was scheduled, an impending snowstorm forced

Marshall to leave after only one hour.[82] Evocative of the personal quality of the military profession during the interwar period, Edmund L. Gruber, the author of the memorandum annotated by General Marshall, himself replaced McNair as commandant at Leavenworth in May 1940. Afterward, World War II forever altered the instruction at Leavenworth—far beyond any changes considered in the 1936–1937 staff study.

Practice Makes Perfect

The applicatory method was essential to the quality of instruction at Leavenworth. Indeed, if the school had not used this pedagogical technique, it is difficult to see how the vast gulf between the minimal field experience of the typical Leavenworth student and confidence in handling large-formation operations could have been bridged. As most Leavenworth students' experience was primarily in battalion-size units during the interwar period, with occasional maneuvers and CPXs under restricted conditions, the application of new knowledge in practical exercises was the only system available to span this gap. In the penurious army of 1920 through 1940, there were few significant opportunities outside officer education at Leavenworth to practice the employment of any force larger than a battalion, with the evident restrictions on those divisional maneuvers and CPXs that did occur.[83] The army took to the field as regiments or divisions so infrequently during the interwar period that these rare experiences served only a limited role in preparing the officer corps for larger responsibilities. As expressed by Major H. H. Pfeil in 1927:

> The mission of Leavenworth, as I see it, is to discount failure in war by placing a mental hazard in front of every problem it presents for solution. Take away the hazard and the problems are not worth a "hoot." Throw out the problems and the course degenerates into a series of lectures, lifeless, academic and ineffectual. . . . The school attempts, and successfully, to differentiate between principles and rules. War is an art, and not susceptible to reduction to hard and fast rules. . . . Given exactly the same set of circumstances, it is doubtful if any two military leaders would apply the principles of war in exactly the same manner. That in itself elevates war above and beyond the mechanistic. Leavenworth is not a school that teaches mechanics.[84]

The graduates of the Leavenworth program of applied education, when faced by the need to form, train, deploy, and employ large formations in World War II, were the only army officers with any significant education at such levels. The applicatory method, despite its criticisms, remained, throughout this period, as the sole repository in the U.S. Army for division- and corps-level competence.

To accomplish this the school relied on the applicatory method: the combination of principles and practical exercise reinitiated for the 1919–1920 school year. The applicatory method—the hallmark of education at Leavenworth— demonstrates that the focus of instruction was practical tactical problem management. For example, students were frequently required to write operations orders for divisions and corps, including specifically requested details that were based on the specific learning requirements of the block of instruction. If indirect-fire management was the current subject, then the practical application segment would require specific instructions from each student on how indirect fire would be used in support of a division or corps.

Even the act of teaching had become the realm of principles applied in practice, as stated in *The Art of Instructing* (1936): "Unless we know and practice these fundamental principles of education, we will not attain the desired measure of success in our vocation as instructors no matter how well we prepare our discourses, or how eloquent we are in their delivery."[85] Mere exposure to lectures, conferences, committees, map problems, and field exercises at the Command and General Staff School was itself insufficient, that is, if the students were not somehow encouraged to work hard, apply themselves, and be diligent in their studies. Chapter 6 contains an examination of who the students were and how they were selected. Chapter 7 discusses how—and why—they were evaluated.

Chapter 6

The Leavenworth Students

I left Chicago in early morning and drove hard until nearly midnight when I arrived in Leavenworth after a drive of 520 miles in one day. This was close to a record for an amateur driver. Next morning I floated into Fort Leavenworth on Cloud Nine! I had heard so much about this School, and I had covered the surrounding terrain in map problems. In Post Headquarters, I encountered many old friends, including West Point classmates, Swede Anderson and Monte Fox. There were also three other classmates, instructors Duke Edwards, Robert Littlejohn, and Mucker Sibert. A jolly reunion!

—Bradford Grethen Chynoweth, CGSS Class of 1928, in *Bellamy Park*

Bradford Chynoweth's recollection of Leavenworth as a "jolly reunion" is only part of the story. Leavenworth was an assignment that required much hard work. For many students it may have provided the opportunity to meet up with old friends, but it was also an indicator of one's military excellence and professional prospects. The reckoning of one's excellence came with selection to attend, but it was especially strong for those who were selected to remain on as instructors or became students at the War College after graduating from Leavenworth.

Duties as a student and as an instructor were inextricable parts of officer professionalism in the years between the two world wars. Many officers served as both student and instructor, often for extended periods and frequently in repetitive assignments. This system, an outcome of the reorganization of the army under the National Defense Act of 1920, assisted many officers by providing periods of thoughtful reflection, interspersed with periods of troop duty and unit command.

An example of this pattern was Ernest Harmon. He and his family arrived at Fort Leavenworth with the class of 1933. Harmon, a 1917 graduate of West Point, had led a provisional cavalry squadron during combat operations in France in 1918. After his AEF experience, Harmon served a typical interwar assignment pattern, including selection for Leavenworth. Recalling this assignment as a "great honor," Harmon also recalled in his autobiography that he was "convinced that the intensive and imaginative training . . . had a great deal to do with the produc[tion] of a group of generals proficient enough to lead the armies successfully against German might." He also recalled that his two years at Leavenworth were the "most difficult years of my training" and praised his "Yankee wife's calm acceptance of a difficult situation and her physical and moral support" for his successful completion of the two years of study. As Harmon and his wife had five children at the time, his comments are not surprising.[1]

Officers assigned to attend Leavenworth, personally selected by the senior officers in charge of each branch, did not experience a relaxed break from troop assignments. Instead, they could look forward to intense scrutiny, evaluation, and subsequent identification for future attendance at the War College, with possible selection for the General Staff Corps. It was also widely believed, with much apparent justification, that the path to promotion to general officer was through appointment to the General Staff.

The Student Body

Starting from a relatively small student population of slightly more than 100 in the immediate post–World War I years, Leavenworth reached its average of 230 students assigned by 1921. This number stayed consistent for the next twenty years. Throughout the interwar period, students were almost exclusively white, and all were men. The primary exception to this racial homogeneity was the occasional foreign student, usually an officer from China or the Philippines.[2] Cuba sent three officer students, in 1924, 1926, and 1928. Japan sent one officer, who graduated in the class of 1932. Germany also sent one student, Major Hans von Greiffenberg, who arrived in summer 1932 expecting to stay for the two-year course but was informed by the German government that he could attend for only one year. He departed Fort Leavenworth in June 1933 without a diploma. With these few exceptions, all were white Americans from the United States Army or United States Marine Corps.[3] Through the interwar years, there was usually at least one Marine Corps officer in each school year. Except for 1920–1921, when there were no marine students at Leavenworth, and 1927–1928, 1933–1934, and 1935–1936, when there were four marine students, each class had one or two marine officers.[4] No navy officers attended Leavenworth as students between 1919 and 1940.

During the interwar period, the Leavenworth student body was middle-aged or older, with majors averaging more than forty-five years of age in 1933.[5] In the Leavenworth class of 1925, the average student was more than forty years old. Of the 258 graduates in 1925, almost every student had been commissioned before

World War I and had reached various temporary ranks of captain, major, and even lieutenant colonel during the war. Only a small percentage, approximately one in twenty-five, was considered to be in the hump of officers commissioned specifically for service in World War I. Practically all the students had reverted to major by 1920, one of the results of the postwar restructuring of the officer corps. The majority of students were majors (89.9 percent), a few were lieutenant colonels (7.8 percent), and a tiny minority were colonels (.4 percent) or captains (1.9 percent).[6]

The students were evenly divided, in thirds, by source of commissioning; roughly equal proportions were graduates of West Point, had received direct commissions from enlisted service, or had received their commission through competitive examination after graduation from a civilian college or university. Additionally, although every branch of the army was represented, with ninety-four (40.3 percent) of the class composed of infantry officers, forty-one (15.9 percent) cavalrymen, thirty (11.6 percent) field artillery, and forty (15.5 percent) coast artillery, there were two to four officers from every other branch as well. Only nine officers were in the air service, the predecessor of the Army Air Corps.[7]

Students and Their Schoolwork

Leavenworth during the interwar period had a reputation for rigor and hard work. The critical importance of "The School" to officers' careers, the fact that graduates were rank-ordered by academic grades upon graduation, and the keen competition (which contributed to suicides by several students) made for an extremely tense two years.[8] Nearly unanimous in the memoirs of officers who attended Leavenworth during the interwar years are discussions of studying until midnight every weeknight and the need to take breaks from the tedium of the coursework.[9] Such comments about the rigor of the courses and the requirements for intense study were sometimes combined with comments about the dull manner of instruction and the mind-numbing detail of some subjects.

The students' wives also had a perspective on life at army schools. Lois Dunn, writing for *Field Artillery Journal,* recalled how wives looked forward to a school detail with "a feeling of expectancy, and a certain tautness hangs over us all." For the husbands, they have "come here to study, and he means to be serious about the entire affair. He hopes that his neighbor's radio and piano will not be placed next to the wall which separates the two apartments. And he wanders through his entire quarters trying to decide which room to make his study." Lois Dunn, the wife of Sidney F. Dunn (field artillery, Leavenworth class of 1937),

found school life different than troop-unit life; at school the husbands were under greater pressure and occasionally suffered from *"schoolitis,"* a nervous condition where the husband "takes life too seriously."[10]

As difficult as schoolwork was for those eager to do well, living conditions at
Fort Leavenworth were among the finest in the army. Lucian Truscott, class of
1936, in his memoir, *The Twilight of the U.S. Cavalry,* provides the best published description of life for a student and his family during the interwar years.
For the student and his family, life at Leavenworth was a combination of rigorous schoolwork and a wide range of recreational, social, and educational opportunities. Activities that supported family harmony were described as deliberate
planning on the part of army leadership to provide a stimulating family environment to support spouses and children, as the husbands would be more engaged
in duty requirements than they had come to expect in troop assignments. Truscott described Leavenworth as an ideal post for his family and observed that the
"emphasis now was to provide so much for the accommodation, education,
recreation, entertainment, and amusement of the wives and children that the
student officer was relieved of all interference with his studies. At least as far as
that might be possible, School and Post authorities did a magnificent job in that
respect."[11]

Several commandants, in welcoming addresses to new classes, expressed a
desire for students to balance schoolwork and family life. In Brigadier General
Hanson Ely's 1922 welcome address, he reminded students that graduation from
Leavenworth "makes you eligible for selection to the General Staff Eligible List,
and also for the War College." He also reminded students that War Department
orders stated that all general officers would be appointed from graduates of Leavenworth and that placement on the eligible list would be based on class standing
and on performance as judged by faculty. After these none-too-gentle reminders,
General Ely told the students that "if you want to go to Kansas City, go. If you
want to go to the movies, go any night you want to. . . . Do what you like when
you like. All that we look for are results." He then asked the wives for help:

> I have observed that the success or failure of officers here was often
> attributable to their wives. That is one of the reasons I asked the wives of the
> officers to be present today. The nine months here are the most important
> nine months of an officer's career. . . . If perchance an officer's wife has
> been accustomed to let him take a good deal of care of the children, or
> answer the doorbell, or do other similar acts, try and remember these acts
> are an injury to your husband here. If, when the bell rings, he takes five
> minutes to go from his study to the door, that does not mean only five
> minutes wasted. If he was working on a problem and has to stop to answer

the doorbell, it takes him half an hour to get back into the same state of mental concentration in which he was before being interrupted. Heretofore, the wives of officers have been known to blame their husbands because they were not honor or distinguished graduates or because they did not graduate. Had they looked into the mirror, they might have seen they were to blame in part, because they called on their husbands to take little Johnny for a walk, or to answer the doorbell, when the husbands should have been studying.

These remarks were greeted with applause and laughter from the audience.[12]

The following year, Brigadier General Harry Smith echoed Ely's comments, although with less humor. He asked students to take plentiful physical exercise during their year at Leavenworth and advised them to have social contact with classmates and instructors. However, he asked them to limit social interaction to Friday and Saturday nights, thereby allowing for concentration on schoolwork during the remaining evenings. He encouraged the student to take a break from academic work if they began to feel "discouraged, blue" and if their nerves were "somewhat on edge." If taking a day off did not help, he told them to come to him so he could help.[13]

In his address to the class on September 1, 1936, Brigadier General Charles Bundel reiterated the concern for spouses to help husbands develop the proper atmosphere at home to enhance their ability to study. A year later he made similar comments. After telling students and their wives that he considered "the Command and General Staff School [to be] the most valuable thing in the Army," Bundel cautioned them that "your husbands will be very busy men during the year and at times will be a little difficult to handle. The method of handling them I leave to you." Closing his remarks, he reminded students of the post regulation to register all servants, as there had been challenges in recent years with "a number of undesirables who are barred from the Post for one reason or another."[14] This is a telling comment on the social class of middle-grade officers during the 1930s, as well as an observation on the moral attitudes, among some senior officers, that existed at the time in the United States Army.

Student Selection

The alterations in course length, the only major change in the Leavenworth program during the interwar years, had little effect on the system for student selection. Consistently throughout the period, students were selected to attend by branch chiefs, usually general officers, who managed each branch of the army.[15]

This policy, established by army regulations, had advantages and disadvantages. It is apparent that the majority of branch chiefs, eager to put their best officers forward in competition for future general staff selection and general officer promotions, normally selected highly reputable officers. Despite efforts by other senior army officers, congressmen, private citizens, and even members of fraternal and religious organizations to influence these selections, archives show that any influence was routine and minimal. The files contain numerous letters sent to inquiring officials whose responses uniformly stated that the interest was appreciated and the appeal "had been noted and will be given consideration at the time officers are selected for this class." This appears to have been the standard response regardless of the rank or position of the interested party.[16]

Occasional policy changes were made for age and qualifications, usually an adjustment to the changing demographics of the officer corps as a whole. For example, the policy for the 1924–1925 school year stipulated that only officers who had volunteered for the course, who were captain through field grade in rank, and who were not older than forty-seven would be selected. Additionally, at least half of the selected officers would be younger than thirty-eight. Official policy required that "candidates [would be] apportioned to each arm based on the ratio of the number of field officers permanently assigned to the total strength of field officers in all arms." Two years later, policy was amended to further tighten age restrictions, with no officer older than fifty permitted to attend; officers older than forty-five would be accepted only if their branch chiefs certified them as "especially qualified." In 1928–1929, selection was tied to a set of 1,000 names on the central promotion list, with similar age stipulations. In the next year, the branch quota was refined by making it the same percentage of officers that each branch had of qualified officers, not of all field-grade officers. In the early 1930s, the need for higher ratings for officer candidates was specified in policy, with places reserved only for officers rated as excellent, unless the chief of branch gave detailed explanations for waivers. Later, graduation from special service school advanced courses became a prerequisite for certain grades and ages.[17]

Annually, a Student Selection Directive was sent from the adjutant general to the branch chiefs. These directives stipulated the process and qualifications for each year and the number of student positions available for each branch.[18] After receiving these directives, branch chiefs, each according to the process of their individual branches, would create a list of officers qualified for selection. Then, pursuant to the branch process, an order of merit was generated and names were submitted to the adjutant general in order of preference.[19] The vagaries of human nature, the medical condition of prospective students, and statutory rules governing time on station and rotation of assignments made the execution of this process time-consuming and labor-intensive.

Part of the reason that branch chiefs tended to select only the most qualified officers was personal oversight exercised by the Army Chief of Staff over the selection process. For example, in 1922, General Pershing sent a memo to the General Staff G1 asking why four officers whose careers were only "average" should have been selected over officers with better evaluations. Although three of the four officers whom Pershing questioned were eventually sent to Leavenworth, each case required the written response of the branch chief before Pershing approved the final list. One officer, Colonel F. L. Munson, who had graduated from the School of the Line in 1920, was not approved. Pershing overruled the chief of the Coast Artillery Corps in Munson's case, as he was more than fifty years old.[20]

Another reason explaining why branch chiefs selected only the most qualified officers was the existence of a seedier side to the officer corps. A file in the National Archives includes an extensive run of officer efficiency report extracts gathered as part of the 1932–1934 student selection process. From a review of these files, it is clear that a significant proportion of officers had conducted themselves in ways detrimental to the good order of the army. Efficiency reports and letters in official personnel files testified to such derelictions. Some were of a sexual nature, including one officer who had been relieved of duty as a student at the Cavalry School for a dalliance with the wife of a fellow soldier. Other infractions were for excessive public drinking, driving while intoxicated, disregard for proper keeping of unit funds, and assorted vices. Many other officers were rated "below average" simply for sloth, indifference, or some personality flaw.[21] These particular officers were not selected to attend Leavenworth.

The officer corps was kept fully informed of changes in the selection policy and process through the professional journals. Frequent articles appeared from editors or from branch chiefs, informing readers of the precise instructions for annual selection, and they frequently discussed what efforts individuals could undertake to ensure fair consideration.[22]

Officer memoirs describe stories of personal influence, either on individual initiative or the initiative of senior friends, to gain a seat at Leavenworth. Sometimes, these intercessions were made by mutual friends or relatives. For example, Dwight D. Eisenhower's story about his appointment as a student is well known. According to Eisenhower, although serving as an infantry officer, he was advised by General Fox Conner, his senior mentor, to "make no move" and to "be ready" and obey any and all telegrams he received and not to complain, no matter how strange the orders. Shortly thereafter, Eisenhower received a branch change from infantry to the Adjutant General's Corps, a startling and unwanted turn of events. He followed the advice of General Conner and did not complain, and another telegram was shortly received that announced his assignment as a student at Leavenworth, occupying one of the Adjutant General Corps' branch billets. In Eisenhower's words, he "was ready to fly and needed no airplane."[23] After arrival at Leavenworth, Eisenhower then received notification of his reassignment back to infantry.[24]

Eisenhower's charming story appears to be a tale without real substance. Records in the National Archives clearly show that Eisenhower was selected as part of the infantry branch selection process for the 1925–1926 Leavenworth class and was apparently considered to be adequately, but not especially, qualified. He rated the twenty-eighth position out of ninety-four officer allotments for infantry that year. In this file, in the remarks column of a spreadsheet of qualified officers, there is a small notation: "General Conner interested." The staff officer who made the notation then felt the need to clarify which General Conner and added, in parentheses, "Gen Fox Conner."[25] During the 1936 selection process for the 1937–1938 course, Major General Hugh Drum attempted to intervene on behalf of a certain Captain Hamilton F. Searight. Drum's involvement was noted in the record, but the officer was not selected to attend.[26] Apparently having a sponsor was noteworthy, but any specific influence this had is not obvious from official records.

Eisenhower's machinations, although he claimed to have been completely passive and reacted only to what General Conner had told him to do, were interpreted differently by Bradford Chynoweth, Command and General Staff Class of 1928. Chynoweth reminisced that when they both served with Fox Conner in Panama, Ike had told him, "Chen, it is my policy in every post to do just exactly what the Top Man desires. . . . The Commanding Officer is *never* wrong with me."[27] Chynoweth himself was not above politicking for assignments as well, although he claimed in his memoir that his assignment to Panama was arranged without his knowledge. In fact, his assignment was arranged so that General Conner's wife, "an ardent violinist," could play music with Chynoweth's mother, "a talented pianist."[28]

Such machinations by prospective students and their influential friends were frequent, if ineffectual. Other examples include the badgering of personnel officers and branch chiefs by officers who coveted a seat. William Hoge, class of 1927, recalled in a postretirement interview that he had "deviled personnel, man in charge of personnel, Colonel Moore, until he finally threatened to throw me out of his office if I didn't leave him alone." Shortly after this incident, Hoge received orders to Leavenworth.[29] Other officers remembered their selection as a surprise and related that they had done nothing to influence their admission. For example, Walter K. Wilson, class of 1939, recalled that he, while teaching at West Point, was approached by his branch chief, who said, "I think we're going to send you to Leavenworth as a student." Wilson said, "I nearly dropped dead."

Only a first lieutenant at the time, Wilson remembered that he had no expectation of the assignment and had done nothing to get the seat. He believed it might have had something to do with a Soldier's Medal he had received for bravery or for good evaluations of his teaching assignment at West Point. Wilson reported to duty at Leavenworth after a four-year instructor posting at West Point, his second teaching position at the academy. Later, he would return to teach at Leavenworth during World War II.[30]

Other officers recalled their happiness at their selection, an assignment that spoke highly of their professional reputation. Attending an early officer orientation class at Fort Benning's Infantry School in 1920, Captain Manton S. Eddy was told that a normal career pattern was attendance at the basic and advanced infantry officer course and then, some years after the advanced course, "selected officers from all branches, now probably with the rank of major, would attend the General Staff School at Leavenworth. Sometime thereafter, the 'water walkers' among them, by this time lieutenant colonels, would be selected to go to the General Staff College at Washington, D.C. Their instructors stressed the competitive nature of the Army's professional education system."[31]

Selection to be a student at Leavenworth opened opportunities to become a member of the General Staff Corps. Designation as a general staff officer occurred only after graduation from both the Staff Course at Leavenworth and the Army War College in Washington, D.C., and after further consideration of all the graduates. Those designated as eligible general staff officers were then assigned probationary duty on the General Staff Corps in Washington, after which they could be granted designation as General Staff Corps officers.[32] Among many others, Ernest Harmon followed this track. Immediately after he graduated from Leavenworth, he was selected to attend the Army War College. After a stint as commander of a Civilian Conservation Corps camp in Iowa, Harmon moved his family to Washington and attended the War College for a year. After graduation, he commanded a cavalry squadron at Fort Bliss, Texas, and then was assigned to General Staff G4.[33] Harmon's career pattern, and his selection for Leavenworth by the cavalry branch chief, was typical of the interwar period.

It is difficult to establish that branch chiefs selected any unqualified officers to attend Leavenworth. However, as selection was left entirely to the branch chiefs and was based on internal branch selection systems, this was a matter of concern for several Leavenworth commandants. The desire to either require successful completion of branch schools, or the administration of an entrance examination, was frequently stated by commandants. However, the official selection process remained unchanged throughout the interwar period. It is also difficult to prove that branch chiefs sent any officers they knew were unqualified, as

Captain E. N. Harmon's Class, 1932–1933. Harmon is third row from top, seventh
from the left. J. Lawton Collins, who commanded VII Corps during Operation Cobra,
is second row from top, second from the left. Charles H. Gerhardt, who commanded
29th Division, is second row from top, first on the right. Frank W. Milburn, who
commanded XII Corps, is fourth row from top, second from the left. Eugene M.

general officers from each branch would, for all intents and purposes, themselves be among the population of Leavenworth graduates.

However, the common perceptions that selection was highly competitive,
and that only half of each year's group of officers attended Leavenworth, were as
inaccurate as Eisenhower's delightful little story. Before officers within the
hump approached qualification for an assignment to Leavenworth, a surprisingly large proportion of available officers actually attended Leavenworth. Two
staff studies located in War Department records in the National Archives made
this assessment during the late 1930s. One staff study, generated in July 1937 to
determine the number of officers by rank and branch who had attended each
school, demonstrates that Leavenworth had educated the vast majority of regular
army colonels and lieutenant colonels (95 percent and 93 percent, respectively).
However, less than a third of all majors had been educated at Leavenworth (344
of 1,073 total). Only 10 percent of captains had graduated from Leavenworth.[34]
The study did illustrate that selection for the War College was significant, as only
62 percent of colonels and 53 percent of lieutenant colonels had graduated from
one of the senior schools.[35] In an army where promotions through the grade of
colonel were entirely based on seniority, and where the only effective form of re-

SCHOOL 1932-1933

Landrum, who briefly commanded 90th Division, and commanded Adak Island in the Aleutians, is fourth row from top, tenth from the left. Lewis B. Hershey, who was executive director of the Selective Service System in World War II, is third row from top, twelfth from the left. U.S. Army photograph.

tirement was at age sixty-four for all officers, the 95 percent and 93 percent graduation rates for colonels and lieutenant colonels clearly demonstrate that the system allowed for nearly all officers to attend, and graduate from, Leavenworth. The majors, at the lower rate of 32 percent, showed the first signs of influence by the hump on Leavenworth matriculation, as explained in the earlier 1936 interwar study.

In a December 1936 study, the War Department staff attempted to determine the effect of the hump on the army school system. It demonstrated the hump's dramatic impact, noting that the commissioning rate of new officers, which was normally some 350 each year, combined with the evaluation ratings of new officers, would generate an annual population of 346 officers, of whom 243 would be rated exceptional or superior and therefore eligible for general staff schooling. Using the metaphor of a dam, with weirs, pools, and bypasses, the author of the study proceeded to meter the flow of officers using various adjustments to promotion and schooling. With the exception of the hump, which caused a veritable tidal wave in this hydrographic metaphor, the normal flow of officers would result in a relatively high ratio, in the vicinity of 90 percent, of officers qualified to attend Leavenworth. However, the tidal wave—the hump—

was the problem, as many more officers would be ready for assignment to Leavenworth than the school could possibly accept.[36]

An item in *Infantry Journal* corroborated these data. In the "Notes from the Chief of Infantry" column for February 1928, it was reported to the infantry community that of all infantry colonels, 164 had attended Leavenworth and 30 had not. Among lieutenant colonels, 139 had graduated and 40 had not; among majors, nearly 400 had graduated and only 110 had not yet attended.[37] This is a clear demonstration that Leavenworth, before the hump of candidates arrived, was actually matriculating the majority of regular army officers.

With the arrival of the officer hump came a flurry of criticism in the professional journals. Most damning was "The Legion of the Lost," penned by "Invictus" for the November–December 1936 edition of *Infantry Journal*. As "Invictus" described the nonselected, "Their shoulders sag, their eyes are lack-lustre, and they continually weep in their beer." He continued to bemoan not the lack of selection but the reaction to nonselection by otherwise perfectly acceptable professional officers. He admonished the Legion of the Lost to continue their duties and have heart that not going to Leavenworth was a career-breaker only for potential general officers.[38] "Invictus" was joined by several other authors in decrying the effect of nonselection of fellow officers or in critiquing the selection process itself. In an earlier 1936 issue of *Infantry Journal*, Colonel Rowan P. Lemly critiqued the unprofessional authorship of officer efficiency reports, noting that "in most branches of the service the selection of Leavenworth candidates is based squarely on efficiency reports," but the reports themselves were frequently poorly written and not really a good indicator of professional attributes.[39]

By 1937, according to another *Infantry Journal* author, "dissatisfaction with the present system of selecting officers to attend the Command and General Staff School is universal."[40] Critiques that were not raised in the 1920s became strident in the late 1930s as the officer hump arrived at Leavenworth. As these officers commissioned in 1917 and 1918 flooded over Leavenworth, only a small fraction of officers would ever gain admission to the Command and General Staff Course.[41] Only the onset of World War II prevented the collapse of the officer education, selection, and promotion system, which would be inevitable by the late 1940s due to the tidal wave of some 5,000 officers commissioned effectively into two year-groups.

As the hump reached Leavenworth, the demographics of the student population changed. Thirteen years after the Leavenworth class of 1925, the average graduate of the class of 1938, for example, was now nearly a year and a half older, with an average age of 41.48. Of the 226 graduates in this class, more than half (60 percent) had been commissioned during World War I—as part of the hump—but many had reached various temporary ranks of captain or major during the war. Only a small fraction, approximately one in ten, had been commissioned before World War I, and about one in four had received their commission after the Armistice. These students had served as lieutenants for nearly thirteen years, then as captains for an additional five and a half years, before reaching Leavenworth. The majority of students were now captains (61 percent), not majors. Majors remained a significant percentage (37 percent), and tiny minorities were either lieutenants or lieutenant colonels. The students were no longer evenly divided in thirds by source of commissioning. Graduates of West Point now represented 42 percent of the class (usually commissioned after World War I); those with Organized Reserve Corps commissions during World War I were 50 percent of the class; and direct commissions from exams or the ranks were less than 10 percent. Every branch of the army was still represented, but infantry had decreased to 34 percent (a loss of 6 percent), cavalrymen to only 8 percent (a reduction by half), and field artillery had increased to 17 percent (from 11.6 percent), probably at the expense of the Coast Artillery Corps, which had lost 6 percent of its strength.[42]

The hump may have affected student quality. Brigadier General Charles Bundel, commandant in 1936–1937, continued some of the complaints about student quality raised by his predecessor, Brigadier General Herbert Brees, in earlier years. In his 1936–1937 annual report, Bundel recommended the initiation of an entrance examination to select students or, if that was unacceptable, a minimum requirement for all students to successfully complete the correspondence-course version of the CGSS before attending the resident course. However, Bundel's concern about the quality of Leavenworth students was, at least in part, a complaint on the effect of a one-year course on the commandant's ability to impart all necessary instruction to students. A two-year program could overcome student inadequacies much better than a one-year course.[43]

Bundel reiterated his complaint the following year. This time he specifically recommended that each student be a graduate of his branch school and added that officers should in addition attend specially designed courses at the other branch schools. He also requested that students complete a course at an Air Corps training school qualifying them as aerial observers.[44] Neither recommendation was instituted by the War Department. Despite such complaints, and others over the next several years, the one-year course remained in effect until national mobilization in 1940.

Complaints about student quality reached the War Department and generated an inspector general investigation in 1938, which apparently consisted solely of an interview with General Bundel at Leavenworth. The inspector general, Major General W. L. Reed, reported to Washington that General Bundel was dissatisfied with student performance. Bundel recommended that all prospective students be required to satisfactorily complete an extension course, which would then be evaluated by the Leavenworth faculty, ensuring that only high-quality students would attend and that all students would begin the course with the same level of initial instruction. The inspector general's report was filed away, and a memo in response was sent to Bundel. The War Department saw no need to make changes, but it stated in the response to Bundel:

> The objective of the War Department is not to limit Command and General Staff School students to those who are qualified for training in duties of high commanders and staff officers, but, within the designated age groups, to send all promotion list officers to that school, because it is believed that all promotion list officers need the instruction and background furnished by the Command and General Staff School course in their daily work, particularly if they are placed on duty with civilian components.

The response also said it would be a burden, and an impediment to regular work, to require officers to take an extension course before reporting to Leavenworth.[45]

As already noted, the commandants' concerns for balance in the lives of their students were based on the rigor of the coursework, the reputation of the school as a challenging intellectual environment, and the complex subject matter of large-formation operations in modern warfare. Of course, commandants were concerned that students would not be able to achieve their desired class rank and thereby attain the career status that their skills may have warranted. Chapter 7 addresses the rigor of study, competition for class standings, the faculty's evaluation of students and the system of establishing class rank, and nomination to the General Staff Eligible List.

Chapter 7

The Most Difficult Year of Their Careers

The two years I spent at Leavenworth were the most difficult years of my training. About 250 officers matriculated, and some of us had almost lost the habit of study; we were warned the class would be thinned down to 125 for the second year. I was able to make the second year, but only with my wife's encouragement and practical management. There were now five children in a crowded house, five children afflicted with the colics, fevers, and ailments of the very young. I studied upstairs and downstairs, often far past midnight, and my disposition at home became as mean as that of a starving prairie wolf, or—as one of my friends suggested—a cobra without a convenient snake charmer. . . .

There were easier days ahead. Immediately after graduation from Leavenworth, I was informed that I had been ordered to the Army War College in Washington. Only about 10 percent of the top students were chosen for this more generalized postgraduate education, and I was pleased and gratified.

—Ernie Harmon, CGSC Class of 1933, in *Combat Commander*

The Leavenworth schools in the 1920s and 1930s had a deserved reputation for rigor and hard work. The critical importance of "The School" to officers' careers—graduates were rank-ordered by academic grades—and keen competition made for an extremely tense time as an officer student.[1] Nearly universal in the memoirs of officers who attended the course during the interwar years are discussions of studying until midnight every weeknight and the need to take breaks from the rigor of the coursework.[2] Intense controversy swirled around student evaluations between the wars. Some critics' concerns of a "school solution," of overemphasis on only one single right answer, and rewarding students who did not really learn but only "grubbed for tenths," were interpretations of what others called "exhaustive evaluation and criticism" designed to coach Leavenworth students toward confidence in their ability to solve the challenge of large-formation operations.

Evaluation, grading, and rank-ordering of graduates characterized Leavenworth day to day. According to General George C. Marshall, an essential part of the applicatory method was the deliberate and detailed evaluation of students' work. Marshall, routinely depicted by historians as opposed to the Command and General Staff School system in the 1930s, actually supported the fundamentals of the program. Marshall heartily endorsed grading in a memorandum to Major General Stanley D. Embick, deputy chief of staff of the army, in 1937. Marshall wrote, "I am strongly in favor of marked problems," also saying that he was "strongly opposed to the present type and system [of map and other graded application problems]."[3] Although grading evolved over the years from cumbersome letter grades in the 1920s to a simpler system ("S" for "satisfactory" or "U" for "unsatisfactory") in the 1930s, the school continued to record and report to the War Department the order of merit of each student, as well as the individual recommendation ("qualified" or "unqualified") for additional education as a general staff officer.[4]

Evaluation for the Good of the Army

The faculty evaluated Leavenworth students on their potential as general staff officers. In accordance with army regulations, the faculty either recommended graduates for further education or recommended that Leavenworth be their last military education. *Instruction Circulars* issued annually by the staff made this requirement crystal-clear, usually quoting relevant congressional statutes: "The name of no officer will be added to the General Staff Corps eligible list unless upon graduation from the Command and General Staff School (General Orders No. 30, War Department, 1923) he is specifically recommended as qualified for General Staff Duty (National Defense Act, as amended by act of June 4, 1920)."[5] This type of statement appeared annually in materials that the students and faculty were required to read. Achieving the desired recommendation for future education was, by law, essential to future selection to the General Staff Corps as well as promotion to general officer.

The General Staff Eligible List had a perceived importance out of all proportion to its actual use by senior army officers. [6] However, the essential role of selection for the GSEL after graduation from Leavenworth may actually have been apocryphal, as shown by official records. A statement in the records at the National Archives places the GSEL, and school attendance, in perspective. In a 1932 memorandum, Brigadier General Andrew Moses, the assistant chief of staff for personnel (G1), wrote:

All officers are considered for assignment to important commands and for promotion to the grade of general officer on the basis of their entire records.

Attendance and performance at the various service schools being only a part of such records, the extent to which lack of such attendance may or may not be a handicap is evidenced whenever assignments or selections are published to the service. It is not believed that any general announcement on this subject would have any beneficial effect.[7]

The pool of candidates who might be considered for promotion to general officer was not limited to the GSEL. However, it was not considered useful to draw attention to this possibility to the non-Leavenworth officer corps. General Moses's statement appears to be contrary to statute, as stated in the National Defense Act of June 1920. In that act, Congress required "that all brigadier generals of the line shall be appointed from an eligible list. It also provides that eligibility for general staff duty except with reference to those placed on the initial eligible list, require graduation from the General Staff School and, in addition thereto, for the War Department General Staff, graduation from the General Staff College."[8] Of course, if entry on the GSEL became automatic with Leavenworth graduation, regardless of class rank, then doing well in school was not necessary. Apparently, this is what General Moses wanted to keep out of any "general announcement."

A process of reducing the importance of placement on the GSEL upon graduation from Leavenworth began in the mid-1920s. Whereas in the early 1920s officers who graduated from the Staff School were not all named to the GSEL, by the late 1920s it appears that every graduate of the Leavenworth schools, and many officers who were not graduates or who had graduated years before but had failed to initially make the GSEL, had their names placed on the list. Boards were convened regularly, normally in the summer, to review the records of recent CGSS graduates.[9] In summer 1928, the GSEL board named 407 officers to the list, even though the course had graduated only 195 eligible officers that year.[10] Apparently, the army leadership resisted the strict requirements that Congress had stipulated in the National Defense Act of 1920 and gradually allowed more and more officers to be named to the GSEL.[11]

The professional journals were far from silent on the issue. Calls for eliminating the GSEL began several years after the National Defense Act became law and continued until that part of the statute was rescinded in 1938. First to call for its elimination was Colonel Thomas W. Hammond, who argued that even though the law had a salutatory effect (encouraging officers to attend Leavenworth), it also created a second class of citizens—those who had graduated but failed to make the list.[12] Lieutenant Colonel Bernard Lentz joined the discussion in 1932, calling for an increase in the quality of education at the general service schools and, in his opinion, the discontinuation of GSEL selection.[13] The use of the GSEL to assign officers to the General Staff Corps was itself critiqued by the chief of infantry in the July–August 1935 edition of *Infantry Journal*; he decried multiple repeat assignments for a few officers to the General Staff Corps at the expense of the remaining qualified officers who were already on the GSEL.[14]

In the months immediately preceding the rescission of the GSEL in 1938, two articles appeared in *Infantry Journal* recommending that the GSEL be eliminated. Major General (ret.) Johnson Hagood began the debate with "A Bas Eligibility" in the January–February 1937 issue. General Hagood called for eliminating this overly restrictive system of eligibility, writing:

> Every ambitious officer in the Army wants to go to school. He will sacrifice anything for a school detail. But he does not thirst for knowledge. What he really wants is to get the schools on his record. And the sad part of it is that many of the best officers in the Army are eating their hearts out because Father Time has beaten them in the race. While serving in the grade of captain they become forever ineligible for promotion to general. At least that is what they fear.[15]

Following General Hagood, "Zadig" (writing anonymously in the January–February 1938 edition of *Infantry Journal*) argued for an "efficient Eligible List" but not for its outright removal.[16] His call for reforms went unheeded, yet the GSEL would not survive for much longer.

In 1938, Army Chief of Staff Malin Craig requested and received from Congress a repeal of language in the National Defense Act that created the General Staff Eligible List.[17] Craig stated in his annual report that this change "afforded a liberalization of eligibility for General Staff duty. These enactments, which broaden the base of selection of officers for detail to this important duty, should tend towards increased efficiency in administration and also an enhancement in morale." The amended statute, approved on June 3, 1938, deleted any and all references to the GSEL.[18] However, this late action had little effect on Leavenworth's interwar experience and the perceived rigor—and importance—of the course for students' careers.

Evaluation and Competition

The perception remained, throughout the interwar period, that Leavenworth remained essential to career success, for two reasons: the in-house competition for good standing, and the opportunity to attend the War College. In 1922, Hugh Drum, Leavenworth's assistant commandant, who would lose his opportunity to become Army Chief of Staff to George C. Marshall in 1939, waxed eloquent, if somewhat jingoistic and sexist, over the evaluation system:

> After seven years close association with [Leavenworth], I am convinced that the main opposition to this system springs from one or two sources, i.e., failures of officers who fear competition with brother officers.
>
> Competition is the finest and healthiest trait in the American race. In all walks of American life, competition, in one form or another, is a daily incident. From boyhood to mature manhood Americans foster and practice healthy competition. Why should the Army be an exception to this national characteristic? Competition is the life of these schools. Once it is removed, I believe the present high standard will be greatly reduced.[19]

During the interwar years, competition remained the essential ingredient for the rigorous education of the army officer as student.[20]

Competition was designed to select officers for education at the War College, a potent indicator of future promotion to the highest ranks. War Department policy, developed in coordination with the commandant and the Army Chief of Staff, established procedures for qualification and further education. On January 5, 1922, the adjutant general's office released a policy letter that required the commandant of the Leavenworth schools to

> include in his report the names of all students who are recommended for future instruction. The recommendations will be based on the merits of individual students and should not be influenced by efforts to keep the numbers at any particular percentage of the graduating classes. . . . Such a detail or advancement is not in any sense a reward for past efficiency, or to give an officer a variety of service. The question is entirely one whether the officer is young enough and has shown enough professional interest, activity, and capacity in his past service to make it worthwhile for the Government to further educate him.[21]

This policy stayed in effect until it was modified during the 1936–1937 academic year. War Department policy also stipulated that 50 percent of the first-year class was the appropriate percentage to allow progress to the second year, unless the faculty at Leavenworth recommended differently.[22] (This system for admitting students to the second year became moot when the course shrank to one year for the class of 1924; it did not return when the two-year program was restarted in 1927.)

The evaluation system adapted the system in use before the schools were closed in 1916. Colonel LeRoy Eltinge, assistant commandant in 1920, reported to the War Department that the system was, "in its general outlines, satisfactory." According to his annual report, although the actual grades varied "as to the severity of the scale of cuts adopted for [any] particular year, the shape of the curve is constant."[23] Eltinge, graduate of the Leavenworth classes of 1908 and 1909 and an instructor for four years before 1917, compared his statistical analysis to the 1918 Carnegie Foundation's study of engineering education. In that study, the top 25 percent included the best students, the bottom 25 percent was considered deficient, and the middle 50 percent was "mediocre," a trend that looked remarkably like the ubiquitous bell curve. Eltinge reported that the Carnegie Foundation study recommended that some 25 percent of engineering students should be found deficient and thus eliminated from engineering courses. He concluded that this percentage was too high for seasoned officers and recommended that the first-year course authorize a deficiency rate of "not over 8 percent to 10 percent of students." He added that because the school selected the best graduates from the first-year course (the School of the Line) for the second-year course (the General Staff School), deficient students could graduate from the first-year course and then be returned to the army, with no effect on the policies at Leavenworth.[24]

One year later, Colonel Herbert Brees, director of the School of the Line, commented that the competitive nature of the course must be maintained, despite some criticisms, for "in no other way can a just, accurate and impartial comparative estimate of the ability of the officers be determined."[25] The following year, official reports continued to note the positive results of the evaluation system, including high levels of student performance as well as the benefits of competition.[26] Apparently, at least for the time being, this system was accepted by the leadership of Leavenworth and the army.[27]

Final student evaluations were partly based on class standing. During the early interwar period, the course was worth a total of 1,000 points, and class standing was established by deducting points for incorrect solutions to the pay problems. Class standing was determined by an arithmetic tabulation of grades in the marked problems and exercises; however, the summary evaluation as to suitability for the general staff was also a subjective evaluation by the staff and faculty. The unique ability of faculty to evaluate students in their tactical knowledge and decision-making skills was frequently identified in annual reports. In 1923, for example, Major General Hanson Ely commented that the efficiency reports the students received were invaluable to the army. Unlike field evaluations, where only a couple of officers observed the rated officer, at Leavenworth a "board of officers of considerable experience, some twelve or fifteen in number," evaluated every student. Additionally, these evaluations, partly anonymous and limited to tactical skills at the division, corps, and army levels, were not simply matters of "personal opinion" but the result of "the closest supervision of a large number of very experienced instructors." He encouraged the War Department to make full and effective use of student efficiency reports for future selection, promotion, and assignments "for best interests of the service."[28]

Even officers who graduated from the first-year course but were not selected to continue were rewarded, at least according to official policy. A 1921 policy required officers in positions of authority to assign preference to graduates of the School of the Line over officers of similar rank who had not been selected to attend a general service school. In times of peace, these officers were to be considered for commands, details as acting general staff officers, and training in the National Guard before nongraduates. In "time of war or emergency," they could serve as higher commanders or be assigned to General Staff Corps duty.[29] According to the commandant, this policy also defused some of the "bitterness and feelings of disappointment" of some very good officers who had worked hard in the School of the Line, but who were unprepared upon arrival or below average in performance in the first-year course. They were still above-average officers and could serve competently during peace or war.[30]

Upon a student's graduation from Leavenworth, the next critical career step was selection to attend the War College. "Making the cut" after Leavenworth was a discriminatory process. Leavenworth consistently graduated slightly more than 200 officers from its one-year course and slightly more than 100 from its two-year course. The War College, by contrast, consistently graduated fewer than 100 graduates each year. For example, the War College graduated sixty-nine officers in 1927, seventy-five in 1930 and 1935, and ninety in 1936.[31] When Leavenworth was a one-year program (effectively half of the years from 1920 through 1940), the War College accepted significantly less than half of the Leavenworth class graduates. Harmon himself graduated fourteenth in his class of 112 students and was immediately selected to attend the War College. He later served in the General Staff Corps after commanding a cavalry squadron.[32] This was how students made the cut based on quality, and it was, in large part, determined by the evaluations of students at Leavenworth.

Effective use of the applicatory method, creating student confidence in handling large formations, and imparting an understanding that solutions to problems could be reached only through persistent application of fundamental principles and problem-solving techniques were possible only if students applied themselves at Leavenworth. Evaluation, grading, and rank-ordering provided the necessary incentive for most students to strive for full competence in their graded exercises. As stated in the 1936 Leavenworth text for the faculty, *The Art of Instructing*, "Without the will to learn there is no learning."[33] Apparently written by Colonel Joseph "Sandy" McAndrew, this text, used to teach the faculty about adult learning, plainly posited that adults needed to learn not only from practical application but also with a reason for learning as well. Only those students with a stake in their education would apply themselves, and only through individual application in a rigorous course would effective learning result.

Some officers looked forward to the rigor of the Leavenworth course as "getting back to work" after assignments with line troops or National Guard duty. The concept that officer promotions were, at least in part, and as perceived by nearly everyone, dependent on class standings was also considered "part of the course." Manton Eddy, class of 1934, believed that competition among fellow officers was fair and devoid of some of the cronyism of the old army.[34] The faculty also believed that students, for their own good, studied harder and learned more effectively when they recognized the advantage that finishing high in the class enhanced their careers. As *The Art of Instructing* informed the faculty, speaking from the student perspective, "If our work here offered no advantage, we would not apply ourselves so assiduously."[35]

George Patton was not alone when he complained about the constant stress. He wrote to his wife, Beatrice, in 1924, "I never seem to get through anymore. It is now 11:30 and I have just finished. Either I study harder or the lessons are harder."[36] Ernie Harmon, class of 1933, would have agreed with Patton. In his autobiography, he wrote: "Compared to Leavenworth, the War College was 'easier' for many officers."[37] Eight years earlier, Dwight D. Eisenhower had graduated number one in his class. According to biographer Geoffrey Perret, Eisenhower, already proficient in staff duties from his mentorship with Fox Conner, learned some valuable lessons at the school. Eisenhower received "a memorable education in the rewards of remaining calm as the pressure increases, a reaffirmation of the importance in a large organization of common sense over cleverness and an appreciation that even at the highest levels of command nothing could be accomplished without first creating a team."[38] Perret believed that Eisenhower's frequent discussions with faculty were not the "brown-nosing" some classmates ridiculed but instead were a conscious effort to develop a sense of teamwork while learning the profession.[39] Some contemporary observers of Eisenhower, including Bradford Chynoweth, thought such behavior odious.[40] Other graduates recalled that they had learned from classmates, especially those in other branches or services, and developed teams of students designed to reinforce strengths from experience.[41]

Several graduates remarked in their memoirs and oral histories that students knowledgeable in certain subjects frequently challenged the credibility of both the instructors and the instruction. However, from the perspective of postgraduation, these officers realized that they, as students, had been in error. The school had marked these students as "deficient," even in their areas of experience, if they disagreed with the fundamental principles at the heart of the education. This education—designed to elucidate principles, including the conversion of stabilized fronts into mobile warfare, provide methods, and develop confidence—had little patience with "know-it-all" students.[42]

The Red Tape of Student Evaluation

The manuals and programs at Leavenworth before World War II detailed procedures for the administration of graded exercises, the evaluation of students, and the design of school solutions for problems.[43] The details of the grading system, the manner in which grades were tabulated, and how students were notified changed several times over the 1920s and 1930s.

The first significant reform after World War I occurred during the 1921–1922 school year. Officers were no longer informed periodically of their class standing but would instead be informed of standing by quartile. Those in the upper quartile would be awarded A's, the second quartile B's, and the third and fourth quartiles C's. The students at the very bottom of the class received a "CU" grade, or unsatisfactory; too many "CU" grades could result in forced departure from Leavenworth or completion without graduation credit. Officers with A and B grades in the School of the Line were normally selected to continue on to the General Staff School.[44]

Five years later, "with a view to increasing the morale of the student body," Brigadier General Edward King changed the letter grade system to "S" (satisfactory) and "U" (unsatisfactory). He reported that this new system resulted in "the morale of the class [becoming] much increased."[45] General King requested permission to cease designating honor and distinguished graduates, a step beyond his authority as commandant. Because the honor and distinguished awards served only to make those so designated "feel very much pleased," they had no discernible impact on performance in the field and thus no utility for determining future assignments. He recommended these distinctions be replaced with "superior," "above average," "average," "below average," and "inferior" marks in the efficiency reports.[46] The next year, the War Department removed the honor graduate and distinguished graduate distinctions.[47] The following year, King enthused that the removal of these distinctions "has been a complete success. The work of the last class was fully up to standard, while the absence of the unhealthy competition engendered by other methods helped create a most desirable atmosphere."[48]

During his last year as commandant, King defended his replacement of letter grades and the removal of graduate distinctions by reporting that "there has been a marked increase in the standard of the work as is shown by frequency curve cards computed from something over 103,000 solutions of problems." Somewhat disingenuously, King claimed that students were selected for further education based on their performance as measured against school standards, not in competition with fellow students or by class rank.[49] However, the War Department had not changed its policy that 50 percent of each graduating class be considered for the War College or the General Staff Corps.[50]

In 1939, Brigadier General Lesley J. McNair, assuming command of Fort Leavenworth, ordered studies of instructional methods, grading and evaluation, and student satisfaction. In response to student critiques, he recommended a return to evaluation based on quartiles, in a manner very similar to that instituted by General Ely in 1921.[51] The next year, McNair reported that the study had continued, with the result that "it is entirely justified to abandon the meticulous and laborious percentage grades in favor of four or five letter grades." However, changing the evaluation system was delayed when the class of 1940 graduated early, as part of the War Department's adjustment to national mobilization.[52]

The Leavenworth faculty fully understood the controversial nature of the grading system. Although it gradually became a less onerous system during the interwar period, the intent to maintain an order of merit, and to evaluate student officers for potential, remained intact. As Assistant Commandant Eltinge reported in 1920, students who did not do well would always find cause to complain: "As has always been the case, a marking system was found to be somewhat irritating to the members of the classes, though no one has ever been able to recommend a substitute that had the same elements of fairness."[53]

Critiques of the Evaluation System

Journal articles both praising and critiquing the Leavenworth student evaluation system occurred during the interwar period. Writing for *Infantry Journal* in 1922, Major Bernard Lentz, preaching the value of the applicatory method for *instruction*, took the army to task for using it for *evaluation*. Lentz believed that problem solving was naturally superior to lectures and conferences. However, he felt that its use to compare students to each other, or even to a single standard, devalued the education. Students, desiring good marks, cared more about evaluation than learning. For Lentz, commenting on a student's solution was a necessary step under the applicatory system, but when it was confused with evaluative grading it undermined the entire method.[54]

One of the more sober critiques was a 1923 *Infantry Journal* article depicting evaluation as a necessary evil—but an evil the officer was advised not to worry about. According to this author, because officers went to Leavenworth to learn, the students should focus on learning and let the grading of papers occur as they might.[55] Twelve years later, the same author was not so upbeat, perhaps due to the appearance of the officer "hump" at Leavenworth and the increased competition for selection. In "The Marking System at Leavenworth," now–lieutenant colonel Davis complained that instructors marked student work as unsatisfactory solely due to disagreements over tactics. He recommended that unsatisfactory grades be allotted only when work "shows evidence of having been carelessly and indifferently prepared."[56]

In 1936, an article by "Mercutio" criticizing the instructor-based evaluation system provoked a small storm of protest. "Mercutio," stating that instructors could be deceived by a wily student, but that others would quickly sniff out their classmates' moral and ethical merits, recommended that every student in every course write an opinion of every other student and that these "most accurate" evaluations be used for future selections.[57] Protesting this critique of the faculty, "Anti-Gauge," in the November–December 1936 edition of *Infantry Journal*, launched into a screed about the inability of students to judge other students, the lack of concern that very high quality officers had for the opinion of their peers, and the other lamentable problems with the ideas of "Mercutio." In frustration he wrote, "I hope the Editor can gather that I really don't think very much of Mercutio and his gauges."[58]

In the early and mid-1930s, several Leavenworth student monographs discussed evaluation. Although several students complained that discussion of solutions should be less constrained and more frank, only one student commented directly on the overall system of evaluation.[59] In 1930, Captain Francis Heraty opined that all officers should attend the Leavenworth course and that any officer deemed fit to graduate should receive the same promotion opportunities as any other graduate. He recommended that the faculty abandon rigorous and detailed evaluation of every test and, instead, simply use professional judgment to determine whether a student officer was competent enough to graduate. He offered no details on how to administer this plan.[60] Neither the War Department nor the Leavenworth faculty implemented Heraty's recommendations.

Brigadier General Lesley McNair's survey in June 1939 addressed students' perceptions of evaluation and the pay problems. When asked if they favored increasing or decreasing the number of pay problems, 26 percent requested more, 23 percent requested less, and 51 percent thought the quantity was about right. When asked if the instructors had graded the pay problems "fairly and well," 98 percent responded "yes." When asked if students should be assigned to evaluate fellow students without faculty oversight, a resounding 99 percent answered "no." Ninety-seven percent responded "fair" when asked if pay problems "as tests of your ability to apply previous instruction . . . were generally fair or unfair."[61]

The response to one question focused on students' perceptions as to why they had lost points in solutions; most students responded that they had lost credit due to a misunderstanding of the requirement, not to any failure on their part. In a follow-up question, the survey asked if students thought whether this misunderstanding was due to lack of clarity in the problem, to their own carelessness, or for some other reason. In the survey, 52 percent believed their misunderstanding was due to technicalities and lack of clarity in the problem statement; only 15 percent acknowledged their own carelessness. The remaining third gave "indefinite" responses.[62] When asked about course requirements, most students responded that they were "about right," with 86 percent answering that the instructional hours were "about right." Twenty-seven percent believed the course had caused "undue eye strain."[63]

Throughout the interwar period, procedures continued to evolve to provide more oversight of the evaluation process, more involvement by students in classmate evaluations (especially during the two-year program), and more intense supervision of instructors. At the end of the interwar period, students were generally satisfied with the quality of evaluation and instruction. The procedures for student evaluation, the applicatory method of instruction, and the principles immutable to warfare all changed with national mobilization in 1940.

Chapter 8

National Mobilization and the
Leavenworth Schools

> It is believed that the General Staff College cannot be expected to
> continue its courses even under a minor mobilization, the de-
> mand for experienced officers will be too great. . . . It may also be
> mentioned that the Committee considers that in any considerable
> mobilization, the present courses at Leavenworth must be sus-
> pended and short courses put into effect.
>
> — Fox Conner, John McAuley Palmer, and J. L. Dewitt,
> *Harbord Board Report,* July 11, 1921

National mobilization of the U.S. armed forces in 1940 caught Leavenworth unprepared despite army warnings that the existing course structure would have to
be suspended.[1] The War Department ordered Leavenworth, in the middle of its
normal Command and General Staff Course, to graduate the class in February
rather than June 1940. Initially, it appeared that Leavenworth would simply continue the program, only with shortened Command and General Staff Courses.
However, the need for large numbers of educated general staff officers soon became clear, and so the school embarked on an extensive program of shorter and
specialized classes for the duration of the war and overall larger class sizes. From
the first shortened class of 1940 until mobilization classes ended in 1946, Leavenworth graduated more than 18,000 officers, nearly three times the total number of graduates it had produced during the entire period from the 1880s up to
1939.[2]

Mobilization Is Declared

In part due to the frenzy of the Protective Mobilization Period, the effect on the
Leavenworth school was unclear at first. Harmon recalled the period as one with
"a feverish tempo."[3] Harmon himself changed his job three times in less than
two years, from assistant chief of staff for I Corps to chief of staff of the Armored
Force to commander of 2nd Armored Division.[4] Leavenworth's first plan, con-

ceived in the frenetic summer of 1940, was to conduct an eighteen-week course for 800 students. The War Department identified students for two classes, but these never began. Instead, the Leavenworth faculty, in coordination with sections of the War Department, designed a much shorter course focused on staff officer instruction.[5] The first of the new courses began on November 30, 1940, with ninety-seven students. Classes soon increased dramatically in size. By the last wartime course, the twenty-seventh, which finished on May 31, 1946, 1,080 officers were graduated.[6]

In addition to this short General Staff Course, the army created other programs of study at Leavenworth. A monthlong course for newly forming divisions educated the commanders and general staff officers for service in half of the army's divisions. Another course provided CGSS-level instruction for staff officers responsible for logistics and installation support. From June 1943 through August 1945, a joint Army–Army Air Forces–Navy course for senior officers assisted with the education of officers destined for combined staffs during World War II.[7] Other smaller courses, including a course for senior civilians, ran intermittently.

The "Special" ("General Staff") Course: Leavenworth Mobilizes

The short course for general staff officers owed more to the system of classes created at Langres than to the interwar Command and General Staff Course.[8] In this first form, which lasted through the eleventh mobilization class, all officers attended a single course, with each student assigned to a special course of instruction based on his current or likely future assignment. As at the Langres Staff School in France during World War I, officers were organized into G1, G2, G3, or G4 sections, with education oriented specifically to those positions. Although some general instruction occurred, the majority of instruction, and all applicatory exercises, focused on specific duty assignments. In most courses, the first and second weeks provided general instruction to all the students. The instruction in weeks three and four focused on staff skills.[9] In these courses, between one-third and one-half of students were instructed in G3 techniques and procedures, some 20 percent in G2, about 25 percent in G4, and about 20 percent in G1.[10]

For example, in the third week of the Eighth General Staff Class at Leavenworth, students in the G1 group completed six exercises. These exercises, which could last an entire day, were divided into shorter (one- to two-hour) exercise segments concerning postal service, grave registration and burial, medical service operations, employment of military police, development of detailed plans for supply and evacuation, development of an administrative plan, replacements and personnel procurement, assignment and promotion, relations with civilian governments (a task executed in the European Theater of Operations [ETO] by G5 officers in each division), functions of division trains (support units in the division rear area), morale and discipline, and decorations and administration. Friday's class concluded with a tour of the Fort Leavenworth inductee reception station. The third week concluded with a Saturday morning class for all students (G1 through G4) on tactical employment of tanks, airborne troops, and anti-mechanized defense operations.[11] After weeks three and four, the remaining five weeks consisted primarily of applied exercises in which each student played the role pertinent to his anticipated staff assignment.[12]

Although Leavenworth instructed students in the first eleven general staff classes specifically by staff duty position, when committed to combat operations the majority of these officers served in positions for which they had not been specifically educated. Only slightly more than one in three served in a position for which he had been educated. Nearly a quarter of these educated general staff officers ended up commanding regiments in combat, a position specifically educated at the branches' advanced courses, not at Leavenworth.[13]

The drastic change to staff section duties was due to the decreased time available for each course. George C. Marshall expressed his concerns over shortening course length and recommended some remedies in an April 1940 letter to General McNair. Marshall believed that the single gravest error of the peacetime training and education system had been that "our Regular Army methods of training take little account of the economy of time."[14] Marshall recommended decreasing the time for lectures and conferences, especially those where the subject could be covered easily in less time. He also recommended that McNair decrease the amount of time students had for completing graded exams, specifically recalling his experiences at Fort Benning and the need for officers to be able to provide sufficient details for subordinates quickly, thus avoiding laborious written orders and estimates. Marshall informed McNair that even though he had received many complaints about shortening the course length at Leavenworth, such complaints came from officers who failed to understand the needs of the mobilizing army. Marshall closed the letter expressing his faith in McNair and gave McNair freedom of action over Leavenworth, advising him not to "be tied down by policies or regulations which in your good judgment are detrimental to the most efficient arrangement."[15]

The second significant curriculum change was increased reliance on applicatory exercises. In peacetime, the ratio was usually one-third application, two-thirds discussion and preparation. During mobilization, the ratio was drastically higher for application. The Second Special Class spent nearly three-quarters of its

Group A, Fifth Special Class, October–December 1941. These classes were so large that several panoramic photos were required for each class. This is about half of the officers from this one class. U.S. Army photograph.

classroom time on applicatory exercises, a proportion that held constant for the next eight classes. After Class Ten, the proportion increased slightly.[16] Lectures and conferences in the World War II period were used only to inform the students of basic information on each subject, including the appropriate principles and techniques of problem solving. By the Eighteenth General Staff Class, instructors lectured to hundreds of students, covering principles for the first week and a half. The first exercise began on Wednesday of the second week, and exercises dominated the remaining seven weeks of the nine-week course.[17]

Two reasons for the increased focus on application were the postmobilization concentration on staff skills and the complexity of material. The more detailed and complex the instructional material, the more the faculty relied on the applicatory method. For example, a postwar assessment of the wartime Leavenworth courses listed some eighty-eight different subjects and exercise events for a single wartime course. The complexity of the course, all of it taught in only ten weeks, with four separate sections, scattered integrated classes and exercises with several large-scale *kriegspielen* and made the interwar pace seem leisurely by comparison.[18]

A third transformation was the drastic increase in class sizes, with a concomitant increase in the number of students in each classroom. From a postmobilization low of 101 officers in the June 1940 class, the General Staff Course grew to slightly less than 400 students by July 1942, almost doubled by January 1943 to more than 700 students, and increased again to 1,000-plus students for the last few classes educated during the war.[19] These increases were principally from the addition of National Guardsmen and Organized Reserve Officers, as well as the other large source of officers, the non–regular Army of the United States officers.

Unlike the longer interwar courses, in which only regular army officers attended, after mobilization the classes included all four categories of officers.[20]

The material taught in the postmobilization special course also changed according to the lessons learned on the battlefield. The First Special Class (December 1940–February 1941) devoted nineteen hours to the armored division. Within a few months of the publication of the new *Field Manual 100-5* for operations in spring 1941, the General Staff Course increased the instruction on armored divisions, reaching ninety-one hours in practical exercises alone by January 1944. By the end of the war, Leavenworth was carefully teaching the lessons of air-ground cooperation, amphibious invasions, movement of airdromes in support of advancing ground forces, and logistical support of corps, armies, and army groups; it was also fully engaged in teaching the concepts required for the anticipated invasion of Japan.[21]

One aspect of postmobilization Leavenworth was a drastic increase in students' failure to pass. Although some students had failed to complete the Leavenworth course during the interwar years, this usually resulted from physical inability. High student motivation to do well (and thereby make the General Staff Eligible List) was replaced, after mobilization, with a significant number of students who failed for nonmedical reasons. In the faculty course-end report for the eighteenth General Staff Course, there were many reasons explaining why students had failed: "became confused under pressure," "poor attitude," "bad mental health due to death of father," "slow mental processes," "excellent officer who dislikes staff work," "insufficient education and military background," "did not want to come and got off to a bad start," "course was just too hard for him."[22]

The number of failures in the course raised concern.[23] According to the faculty, the failure rate was not, as first suspected, due to the increased age of the students; instead it was due to the disparity in students' military experience prior to coming to Leavenworth. From the first Special Class through the last war class (the Twenty-Fourth General Staff Class), 683 students failed to complete the course, 222 of whom failed "without prejudice," usually for medical reasons. The remaining 461 were failed "with prejudice" and returned to their units, where the local commanders determined their career fate.[24] Extant records summarized the majority of failures "with prejudice" as "slow mental processes" or "inability to grasp the details of staff work." Additional reasons were described in the record: "nervous," "insufficient experience for this course," "in a confused state throughout the course."[25]

The *"General Staff" Course: The Second and Third Forms*

In January 1943, the army's deputy chief of staff, Lieutenant General Joseph T. McNarney, an army aviator, visited Leavenworth.[26] Apparently sent from Washington on an inspection tour to remedy faults in the wartime program, including the high failure rate, General McNarney's visit began with "an air of hostility." He proposed eliminating instruction on operations for air forces, cutting back on the number of students, and lengthening the course.[27] During a series of meetings, discussions, and tours, Major General Karl Truesdell, the Leavenworth commandant, and other faculty convinced General McNarney and his team of senior officers that the school was on the right path. Although the official history calls the outcome of this inspection trip a "great victory for the school," McNarney's report stated that Leavenworth's mission had to change if it was to "provide basic general staff training to meet the requirements of divisions, corps, and similar units, both air and ground."[28] It also recommended that the War Department send only qualified students to Leavenworth.[29]

In reaction to General McNarney's change in mission, Leavenworth taught general staff principles and procedures for ground and air forces simultaneously, commencing with the twelfth class in early 1943.[30] The added requirement of "both air and ground" revolutionized the organization of classes and changed the instruction system. By January 1943, because most of the newly formed divisions had already been established, graduates were assigned as general staff replacements rather than being identified for specific assignments upon graduating. Combined with McNarney's change in mission, the old Langres system of focusing on particular staff sections was no longer sufficient or desired.

Yet McNarney's mission change to "basic general staff instruction" codified only one element of what had been done since 1940. From the first "Special Course" through the final "General Staff Course," command was eliminated as a subject in the course.[31] Indeed, the distinction was so marked between staff and command that field commanders began to ask Leavenworth to educate young captains and junior majors for detailed staff work. In a 1943 conference, the G3 of the European theater command, Brigadier General D. Noce, Leavenworth class of 1933, requested thirty to forty Leavenworth graduates every ten weeks—but stipulating that they were junior-grade.[32]

The most challenging change in the entire mobilization course development was the requirement to teach Army Air Forces staff procedures. A direct result of McNarney's visit, and an indirect result of the termination of the Army Air Corps educational system, Leavenworth became the only institution teaching the army's field-grade aviators the complexities of air staff operations and planning. (The Air Corps Tactical School, roughly equivalent to the branch advanced courses, had completely ceased operations in the summer of 1941. All aviation training was thus conducted as part of the larger mobilization effort, focusing on individual aviation skills and on low-echelon tactical leadership. According to *History of the Air Corps Tactical School*, the "old mission of the school of training senior officers for high command and the acquired mission of serving as a doctrinal center for the air arm had been lost" by summer 1941.)[33]

After the Twelfth Course in early 1943, air and ground became separate and distinct instructional subjects, and thus the course grew considerably more complex. Separate classes for air staff officers (designated A1 through A4) were now required for officers assigned to Army Air Forces organizations equivalent to division and above. The needs of infantry and armored divisions were now taught separately as well. Moreover, the curriculum was made even more complex by further subdividing the infantry class section into subsections: motorized division, airborne division, and coast artillery. The course was now divided into five different simultaneous types of instruction. However, students were no longer subdivided into specific staff sections for instruction. After being divided into air or ground, ground's subordinate five subdivisions students now received identical instruction in each section.[34]

A third significant evolution of the General Staff Course occurred in April 1944, when Service Staff Course students were integrated.[35] From then until the end of the war, all three types of students—army ground forces, army air forces, and army service forces—were combined into a single large class but were instructed separately. Internal to this three-function General Staff Course, ground forces students remained divided based on potential assignment into armored or infantry divisions.[36]

In all three forms, the General Staff Classes graduated a total of 16,565 officers between February 1941 and May 1946.[37] Although this more than tripled the entire output of Leavenworth's regular courses from the 1880s through 1940, the U.S. Army's requirements for officers had, by far, more than tripled. An analysis from the eighteenth General Staff Class (April–June 1944) demonstrates the breadth of postgraduation assignments. Thirty-six graduates were sent to the continental U.S. defense commands. Central Pacific forces gained seventeen ground forces and five air forces graduates. Alaska Department was sent nine officers, South West Pacific six, China-Burma-India two, and army forces in the Pacific five. The North African theater received seven graduates, the Middle East command two, and the European theater eight. From the Tenth Service Staff Course, graduates reported to similarly broad geographic and functional requirements.[38] Leavenworth provided specifically trained staff officers worldwide.

The "New Divisions" Course

On January 17, 1942, the War Department issued a plan for building so-called type infantry divisions, and Leavenworth was tasked to conduct the New Divisions Course for division commanders, general staff, and selected special staff officers.[39] Whereas the commander and selected staff attended the course at Leavenworth as a team-building exercise, other officers from the division cadre reported to branch and other specialty schools.[40] From January 1942 to June 1943, forty-five division command teams went through these classes, representing slightly more than half of the eighty-nine divisions mobilized for the war.[41]

The commander of each division, and selected general and special staff officers, participated in these courses at Leavenworth beginning "before D-70" (i.e., seventy days before the official activation of the division). The staff officers included the chief of staff, G2, G3, and G4, and the artillery commander. Special staff positions included ordnance officer, engineer, judge advocate general, chemical officer, inspector general, and adjutant general—a total of twelve officers per division. Each of these courses finished no later than thirty-eight days before division activation.[42]

The New Divisions Course was a unique undertaking for Leavenworth. Unlike the Langres approach, where teaching was directed at a precise assignment as G1, G2, G3, or G4, and unlike the peacetime course dedication to nonspecific command and general staff principles and techniques, these courses focused on tasks associated with the combat employment of a specific division. As part of the education, New Divisions Courses, among all the mobilization courses, arguably came the closest in presenting instruction similar to the interwar period's intensity and applicatory method. With small classes—about a dozen officers per division—with an average of three divisions per class, and with practical exercises unique to each division, these courses taught students the same curriculum of knowledge and problem solving and the implicit curriculum of confidence as the interwar Command and General Staff Courses.

First Course for
Training Divisions,
January–February 1942.
Officers and division
staffs. *Left*, Brigadier
General H. Terrell Jr.,
90th Division.

Right, Major General
Robert L. Eichelberger,
77th Division.

Left, Brigadier General
Omar N. Bradley,
82nd Division. U.S.
Army photographs.

These classes became a monthlong team-building exercise for the command structure of new divisions. Each course included 175 hours of instruction, tilted toward applicatory exercises. The course material incorporated lessons being taught in the much larger General Staff Course as well as some unique classes for new divisions. The majority of instruction focused on tactical combat operations, with instruction based on division type. The last two weeks of the four-week course were predominantly map exercises and map maneuvers, with each division operating as a team under the command of the new division commander, in preparation for the future end-of-training division-level maneuvers conducted as part of army ground forces training.[43]

Through the knowledge imparted by these classes, Leavenworth, to a degree, corrected one of the interwar period's shortfalls: insufficient instruction in mobilization and training. Although only a limited part of the New Divisions curriculum, with two days during the last week allotted to detailed discussions of the tasks required for forming a division, this issue was also discussed in other class meetings.[44] For example, the agenda of a meeting including the new divisions' commanding generals and chiefs of staff with the Leavenworth commandant, Major General Truesdell, the assistant commandant, Colonel Shallenberger, and four other senior faculty dedicated much of one afternoon to a detailed discussion of procedures for establishing new divisions in new training posts. At the conclusion of this two-hour discussion, participants adjourned to Quarters No. 1, General Truesdell's rambling residence, for tea.[45]

The New Divisions Courses attempted to focus on the development of command teams, yet another shortfall of the interwar education. Although this team-building focus may have been beneficial to the formation and initial training of new divisions for future combat, team building itself proved to be a failure. Personnel turbulence wrecked whatever cohesion was achieved. For example, 78th Infantry Division's command and staff team attended the Fifth New Divisions Course from June 8, 1942, to July 3, 1942; among seven senior officers attending, only one, Major General Edwin P. Parker Jr., was in the same assignment when the division entered combat twenty-six months later. Two other officers were still in general staff positions but had held different positions during the New Divisions Course.[46] Such turbulence was not unusual. Only two divisions did somewhat better at retaining trained and educated officers in specific positions. However, several divisions experienced much worse turbulence.[47]

Designed to "form" the team of the new division commander and his general and special staff officers, these courses attempted, with limited success, to instruct these new command teams. However, the command teams produced by these courses, with some exceptions, did not survive the turbulence of mobilization and the deployment to active theaters. In addition, not all the forming divisions actually sent command and staff teams to these courses. Of the eighty-nine divisions mobilized for World War II, only slightly more than half dispatched teams to Leavenworth to go through the New Divisions Course.[48] Although a step in the right direction to correct some of the interwar deficiencies regarding newly organized divisions, the value of these courses was significantly degraded by personnel turbulence.

The Other Courses

In addition to the General Staff Course and the New Divisions Course, three other courses emerged during mobilization and war. The first and most significant instructed officers for the army's service forces; a second provided education for senior officers who would serve on joint (Army–Navy–Air Forces) theater staffs, and a third oriented civilians about the army. The Service Staff Course, alternatively called the Service of Supply (SOS) Staff Course, which was eventually incorporated into the General Staff Course in spring 1944, taught officers installation logistics, mobilization, and theater-level supply and logistics. Between summer 1942 and spring 1944, 1,621 officers graduated from nine of these eight-week courses.[49] These graduates became logistical staff officers in the continental United States, in secure overseas possessions, or in active theaters overseas.

Beginning with a program partially culled from the "Special Course," the Service Staff Course taught logistical planning and operations at echelons above corps. Incorporating principles and techniques of installation support in the United States, preparation and conduct of deployment movements, and wholesale logistical support overseas, the faculty generated this course from the prewar and postmobilization records of the War College, the Army Industrial College, and various publications. The stated mission of this course was "to train selected officers in military organizations, basic staff principles and in staff functions peculiar to the zone of the interior and theater of operations installations and operations, including service commands, ports of embarkation, and services of supply in general," and included subjects taught nowhere else in the interwar army.[50] Although the National Defense Act of 1920 had established the Army Industrial College, where there was some education in national industrial mobilization, there had been practically no institutional education of theater- or army-level logistics in the interwar army.

Leavenworth's Service Staff Course was a marked improvement in logistical education, but it was not enough to provide the knowledge required of the thousands of officers responsible for large-scale mobilization and logistics for an army of 8.3 million soldiers. By the fourth class, the logistics curriculum had reached

its final form: twenty-two hours for general instruction, ninety-five hours for organization of the nation and army for war and the theater of operations, 158 hours
for continental U.S. installation management, forty hours for deployment to
overseas theaters, and 100 hours for wholesale logistics in active overseas theaters.[51] Although such education certainly helped, it was insufficient for an officer corps tasked to mobilize the nation. The matriculation of slightly more than
1,600 officers from these logistics courses, from an army of more than 8 million,
was grossly inadequate for the requirements.

Two other classes were offered at Leavenworth after mobilization. The Army
and Navy Staff College Course (ANSCOL), a hybrid class of officers from all
services, was taught at several different locations and included a four-week
course in land operations. The other course, the "civilian" course, did not flour-
ish. The initial class in 1941 attracted only thirteen participants among the
thirty-four invited personally by General George C. Marshall. One year later a
similar class was undertaken, this time limited to a single month of education on
the army, with similarly poor results.[52]

The Wartime Faculty

To create all of these courses and teach more than 18,000 students in less than
four years, Leavenworth required a faculty that matched or surpassed the quality
of the interwar years. However, this did not occur. High-quality officers did serve
in senior positions, but many junior instructors were not of sufficient quality.

Second Service Staff Class, September–
November 1942. U.S. Army photograph.

Four officers served as commandants during the mobilization and World
War II. Although he departed in October 1940, Major General Lesley McNair
was arguably the most influential commandant of this period. His work in the
summer of 1940 established the system of instruction for the initial set of mobilization courses and set Leavenworth on the road to a wartime instruction system. McNair changed the basic system of instruction from exposure to command and general staff concepts to a focus on staff skills. This focused system of
instruction had been the hallmark of Langres, which McNair understood from
his service in the artillery section of AEF headquarters. And because McNair
had also been a member of the inaugural faculty in 1919–1920, discussions
about the form of instruction at Langres were undoubtedly one of the topics de-
bated among the instructors. After mobilization, McNair's consultations with
the War Department, coupled with the mobilization of National Guard divisions, resulted in combining the regular army course with the reserve component courses, shortening the course length to nine weeks, and organizing students and instruction by specific staff section.[53] By the time of McNair's
departure in October 1940, the system for the first special course was in place.

After McNair departed Leavenworth, three other officers served as commandant, all of whom were Leavenworth graduates and faculty members during the
interwar period.[54] McNair's replacement, Brigadier General Edmund "Snitz"
Gruber, songwriter of "The Caissons Go Rolling Along," died suddenly shortly
after becoming commandant. The next commandant, Brigadier General Horace
Fuller, was reassigned to a division command. Major General Karl Truesdell assumed command of Fort Leavenworth in March 1942 and remained there until

after V-J Day. Truesdell had served in 33rd, 26th, and 1st Divisions and V Corps in the AEF. A member of the 1920 General Service Schools faculty, Truesdell was an honor graduate of the 1921 School of the Line and the 1922 General Staff Course, one of the few instructor-graduates during the immediate post–World War I period; he remained at Leavenworth as an instructor until 1925. A graduate of both the Army War College (1926) and the Navy War College (1927), he had served in the War Department's General Staff, went to China with 15th Infantry, and commanded 1st Division and VI Corps during mobilization.[55] (Of the eleven senior faculty, the three deputy commandants and eight course directors, all were graduates, and ten had served as instructors.)[56]

Despite the experience of the commandants and the senior staff, however, maintaining the quality of instructors was the most serious challenge at Leavenworth during World War II. Because all of the instructors in 1940 were regular army officers with extensive education and experience, the demand for their services elsewhere in the army was intense. From the last premobilization staff of seventy-one instructors, mobilization pressures reduced the instructor group; by 1942, only nine instructors remained who had taught in the final premobilization course.

In addition to the loss of older experienced instructors, Leavenworth no longer retained graduates as instructors. Although the typical instructor during peacetime had always been a graduate, during wartime this was not true. By 1944, an especially turbulent period when 228 officers served as instructors at some point during that year, only twenty, less than 10 percent, were graduates of a peacetime course.[57] Change in the student-to-instructor ratio exacerbated the problem of undereducated instructors. Class sizes grew continually until 1945, but the number of instructors assigned never increased proportionally. There were seventy-one instructors for 200 students in 1939; when class size peaked in 1945, at more than 1,000 students, there were only 142.[58] Compared to the student-to-instructor ratio in 1939 (less than 3:1), by 1945 Leavenworth reached a low of more than 7:1.[59] The quality of instruction suffered as a result of undereducated instructors and inadequate staffing.

When it proved impossible to maintain regular army officers in the numbers necessary for the faculty, National Guard and Reserve officers, some civilians, and wounded veterans of World War II were assigned to teach at Leavenworth. This approach was not completely successful. The National Guard and Organized Reserve officers, although often dedicated and energetic, had little experience in the echelons they taught, and few were graduates of Leavenworth. The efforts to replace regular army officers with Reserve officers failed. The National Guard was unable to simultaneously mobilize all the divisions in the Guard *and* provide professionally competent field-grade officers as instructors. The failures of National Guard officers to perform effectively in their organic divisions are legion in the World War II historiography, and their experience at Leavenworth proved no different. The recruiting of officers from the Organized Reserve Corps was more successful, but it still failed to provide the large contingent of competent and experienced faculty that was needed.[60]

General Marshall expressed concern for the quality of the faculty several times during World War II. In September 1942, he wrote to Major General Harold R. Bull, commander of the Replacement and School Command, to investigate the quality of officers being sent to Leavenworth. Bull responded to Marshall that some local commanders had been sending mediocre officers to Leavenworth but that the practice was disappearing. In December 1942, Marshall commented in a memorandum to General McNair, now reassigned away from Leavenworth, that the instructors were still not of the high quality that the course required. Commenting that "to train mediocrity for staff positions produces a tragic result as well as being a great waste of the machinery," Marshall asked McNair to influence his subordinate commanders to send the best officers as possible to Leavenworth.[61]

After Pearl Harbor, the senior faculty tried to include experienced officers from overseas in the instructor group. The commandant attempted to acquire officers wounded in combat as instructors during their convalescence. General Truesdell believed that combat-experienced instructors would provide higher-quality instruction than officers without combat experience. The army's surgeon general periodically reported to the Leavenworth staff identifying wounded graduates convalescing in the United States. After release from the hospital, some of these officers were assigned to Leavenworth until full recovery. By 1945, 80 percent of the faculty consisted of veterans of overseas duty in World War II. However, the turbulence among instructors remained intense, with the average tour length being only thirteen months by 1944.[62] Instructors during the interwar period were trainee instructors until their second year; during World War II, an instructor with one year on station at Leavenworth was soon to walk out the door.

Another initiative by the senior staff began in 1942, when teams of instructors traveled to each active theater, visited with commanders, staff officers, and course graduates, and determined the changes required at Leavenworth. Three instructors observed the planning and execution of the invasions of Sicily and Normandy. General Truesdell also made trips to the North African, Italian, and European theaters in 1943 and to the Pacific in 1944. In particular, he asked senior commanders, based on their experience with wartime graduates, what improvements the course needed.[63] Upon return from his overseas trips, Truesdell issued summaries to the faculty. He also required instructors to update their programs and materials based on the field practices he had observed.[64]

Major General Truesdell offered the most acerbic comment on the attempts to acquire faculty from overseas assignments. In a report circulated to all instructors at Leavenworth, Truesdell noted that the commander of 45th Infantry Division, Major General Troy Middleton, urged that Leavenworth instructors be "taken from outstanding officers who have had outstanding service in the Theaters." Truesdell quipped, "But . . . try and get them."[65]

Mobilization and Effective Education

The most common photograph of Leavenworth during the World War II era is of the lecture room inside Gruber Hall, the renovated equitation building, renamed in honor of Brigadier General Gruber after his unexpected death. *Wartime History* included a caption with the photo: "The Commandant . . . speaks to a graduating class of nearly 1,000 students of the General Staff Courses. . . . This scene is repeated every ten weeks."[66] Crippled by inadequate instructors, and faced with increasing numbers of students, Leavenworth expanded its physical plant but barely kept up with demand. In three short years the student capacity had increased from less than 300 to more than 1,000, thanks to a new classroom building (based on the standard gymnasium design at the division mobilization centers), the conversion of the old riding hall into a huge classroom, and an extension into several nonclassroom buildings. From a maximum single-classroom capacity of 150 during the interwar period, the Leavenworth of World War II now had a lecture hall with a capacity greater than 1,000, several facilities with capacity for 600, and numerous rooms that held more than 100.[67] In the World War II period, outsized lectures and the mass conduct of individual exams were the norm; the quality of education suffered as a result.

The pedagogical revolution at Leavenworth, from small-group discussion and individual work on practical application to huge classes of many hundreds gathered in lecture halls, combined with the brevity of the mobilization courses and their focus on specific skill sets, produced graduates who were qualified for sharply different competencies than their fellow officers who graduated between 1920 and 1940. Although both groups were educated in the principles and problem-solving techniques required for combat operations, the mobilization graduates had confidence only in their skill sets either specific to their staff function (in the first form of the course) or specific to their service (in the second and third forms). By contrast, the long-course interwar graduates could function and, most important, *believed* they could function either as commanders or as general staff officers across the entire spectrum of military activities from G1 to G4 and, to a much lesser extent, in ground, air, and service functions.

Officers lining up outside the new large classroom building, Fort Leavenworth, 1943. Constructed from plans for training camp gymnasiums, this could seat some 600 students at a time. This building currently houses the Frontier Army Museum. U.S. Army photograph.

Inside of large classroom facility, Fort Leavenworth, 1943. U.S. Army photograph.

Class inside the former equitation hall, Gruber Hall, Fort Leavenworth. This building could seat as many as a thousand for welcoming and graduation ceremonies. Building is currently the post fitness center. U.S. Army photograph.

Chapter 9

Few Leavenworth Graduates,
a Global War's Needs

I feel that in connection with the work which you have performed
for the past 18 months and are going to continue to perform that
we completely missed the boat 20 years ago. . . .

There are many graduates of this course over here, and able
men, but it was, after all, just an infantry division course. . . .

Our mission [at Leavenworth] is particularly to understand
and to integrate two forces which have grown up since the other
World War and since pre–Pearl Harbor training at Leavenworth.
They are the Air Force and the Services of Supply, neither of
which was comprehended by our professionals in time of peace.

— Major General Karl Truesdell Jr.,
"Notes of Command and Staff Conference," November 1943

General Truesdell made these comments at a staff meeting of the Service of
Supply Headquarters, European Theater of Operations.[1] He closed by apologiz-
ing to the logisticians for not graduating more officers from the Services of Supply Staff Course, for, as he put it, "we were so limited in our vision that we did
not foresee the requirements of the SOS."[2] Truesdell also admitted the lack of
education at Leavenworth for the Army Air Forces, the second of two key aspects
of twentieth-century warfare neglected at the school on the Missouri River after
World War I.

Even for ground forces, Leavenworth's interwar graduations could not satisfy
the demand for professionally educated midlevel and senior officers during
World War II. The output of officers from the shorter "Special Courses" was insufficient given the sheer magnitude of the expansion of the post-1940 army.
Quickly outpacing 1930s projections by the Army War College, army expansion
stretched the educated professionals to the edge of their ability to lead, coordinate, and manage the forces raised.[3] To make matters even worse, all prewar projections, and even the initial projections made after 1940, grossly underestimated the need for large headquarters to form, train, deploy, and sustain ground
forces, grossly underestimated the needs of service forces, and nearly completely

failed to understand the needs of the burgeoning army air forces for senior officers and staffs.

"Armageddon" Arrives

In summer 1941, with mobilization under way, the army began to plan for victory in World War II. Albert C. Wedemeyer, Command and General Staff class of 1936, was assigned the task of developing the force structure necessary for war. Wedemeyer, who had studied at the German Kriegsakademie, a military school equivalent to Leavenworth, immediately following his graduation from the Kansas institution, was a highly qualified combat arms officer, but he was also a man with little logistical or airpower experience. He had served as a staff officer and as a commander, but his understandings of logistics and airpower were only theoretical.[4]

Wedemeyer's experience at the Kriegsakademie exposed him to issues of grand strategy and geopolitics, subjects that were not part of the Leavenworth course. However, even at the Kriegsakademie, he gained little additional appreciation for the industrial, logistical, and airpower aspects of the war to come. Upon his return from Germany, Wedemeyer's report on his assignment found an avid reader: then–brigadier general George C. Marshall, chief of the War Plans Division, Army General Staff. Eventually, Wedemeyer was tasked to draft the strategic estimate and national troop basis of the Victory Plan for the United States.[5]

Wedemeyer's plan called for 215 maneuver divisions, along with supply and services troops.[6] His numbers were simultaneously overoptimistic and inaccurate. The United States by 1943 would actually man less than half the divisions Wedemeyer thought necessary. One reason was the need to provide much larger supporting troop strengths for each division than Wedemeyer had proposed. The War Department G3 staff had provided Wedemeyer an assessment that the proper ratio of division strength to support troop strength was 1:1. Wedemeyer agreed. As historian Charles Kirkpatrick assessed, "While that ratio might have been substantially correct for World War I . . . it was completely outmoded by 1941."[7] Indeed, with the inclusion of army air forces and SOS personnel, the tooth-to-tail ratio by the spring of 1945 was 1:4. When air forces are taken out of the ratio, it was still higher than three support soldiers for every combat soldier.[8] Lacking significant logistical experience and with very little education in logistics above division or corps, Wedemeyer had no basis for changing the ratio provided by the General Staff Corps planners.

Wedemeyer's work, and his failure to account for the needs of logistical and airpower forces, therefore did not change Fort Leavenworth's focus on ground forces.[9] Until the addition of the Army Service Forces Course in summer 1942, Leavenworth concentrated entirely on the Army Ground Forces. Only with the initiation of the SOS courses in fall 1942, six months before Lieutenant General Joseph T. McNarney's inspection visit to Leavenworth, did Leavenworth teach the higher-level logistical fundamentals of modern combat. The Army Service Courses at Leavenworth, begun in summer 1942, graduated 3,546 officers in the logistics of echelons above corps, less than 20 percent of all post-1939 wartime graduates.[10]

McNarney's inspection visit, as discussed above, also brought to Leavenworth the mission of educating air forces officers. Not until General Staff Course Twelve (February–April 1943) did Leavenworth contribute to the air war.[11] From that course through the end of the war, 3,905 officers matriculated at the Air Forces Course. In total, Leavenworth graduated 4,504 officers in the tactical and operational employment of airpower, including the logistical support of air forces in theater.[12]

However, the needs of global war far outweighed the capacity of Leavenworth. In summer 1944, an assessment of the use of Leavenworth graduates was conducted by the faculty. "Painstakingly assembled after contacting every division, corps and army headquarters," the survey found that graduates were in the minority at nearly every echelon of command. At the highest level surveyed, the numbered armies, there were 368 graduates for 1,825 positions (20.2 percent); the corps had 429 graduates for 1,390 positions (30.9 percent); and the army divisions reported 703 graduates for 1,838 general staff positions (38.2 percent), as well as an additional 1,123 graduates in command positions in the divisions. This study, generated by General Truesdell after complaints from the field that Leavenworth graduates were arriving in insufficient numbers, concluded that there existed a need for 11,751 additional graduates, 2,828 for air forces, 2,984 for ground forces, 1,939 for service forces, and a nice round 4,000 for "overhead."[13]

Unlike the woeful shortage of Leavenworth-educated logistical and airpower officers, the education for ground forces officers appears to have met the needs of commanders in active theaters, if only barely. Combined with the interwar graduates, who served as senior commanders (see below), the more junior graduates of the postmobilization courses provided necessary staff skills to ground formations. Similar conclusions cannot be reached for the air forces and service forces. Although some aviators attended Leavenworth during the interwar period, they were too few to efficiently command and staff all the Army Air Forces formations in World War II. Air units were constantly short of educated officers, which McNarney's inspection visit to Leavenworth in January 1943 confirmed. The situation for service forces was worse. Although many senior officers assigned to command service forces attended Leavenworth during the interwar period, they had received no education on any subject appropriate to their actual wartime responsibilities. The relatively large number of SOS Course graduates after mobilization helped to staff the logistical and mobilization headquarters, but the effort could not be considered sufficient.[14]

As assessed by historian Richard Overy in *Why the Allies Won*, much of America's contribution to victory in Europe was the commitment of U.S. airpower to the destruction of German air forces and the German economy and the effective logistical sustainment of allied ground forces.[15] The attainment of air superiority and the effective mobilization and utilization of U.S. economic might owed very little to Leavenworth. It may be speculative, but the war could have been won at a lower cost in treasure and human lives if Leavenworth, and the army at large, had paid more attention to the logistical and airpower aspects of modern war during the interwar period.

Leavenworth Graduates and the Army Ground Forces

For army ground forces, the focus of interwar education, a personnel and senior officer roster for Twelfth Army Group dated December 15, 1944, the day before the Battle of the Bulge, is illustrative.[16] From this roster, which lists every commander, chief of staff, and primary staff officer of every organization subordinate to the army group, an exact account of the presence of Leavenworth graduates is possible. The need for Leavenworth education is absolutely clear from this roster, with graduates occupying every critical position at the highest echelons, gradually diminishing, with graduates very rare at echelons below division.

Twelfth Army Group on that day consisted of three armies, nine corps, twenty-four infantry divisions, eight armored divisions, one tank destroyer brigade, three field artillery brigades, and three antiaircraft artillery brigades. Of the organizations above division, all were commanded by graduates of Leavenworth, as were all of the separate brigades. At the army group level, the chief of staff, his deputy, and all the primary staff officers were graduates of Leavenworth. At army level, of nine staff positions reported on the roster, First Army had four Leavenworth graduates, Third Army had five, and Ninth Army had seven, nearly all from the classes of 1938, 1939, and 1940.[17] The corps chiefs of staff were all Leavenworth graduates; artillery commanders represented 89 percent, deputy chiefs of staff 67 percent, and G2 (Intelligence) staff officers 56 percent. At divisional level, only a few staff positions were filled by graduates. The separate brigades had no primary staff officers with full-course Leavenworth experience.[18] Clearly, the higher the echelon, the more significant and critical the staff position, the greater the chance that it was filled by a Leavenworth graduate.

This is not surprising given the missions of the various echelons and the focus of Leavenworth's education. At its maximum size, the U.S. Army during World War II contained several army groups, eight armies, twenty-four corps, and eighty-nine divisions. In addition, the general headquarters in each theater commanded the overseas forces. Stateside, the army continued to man service schools, garrisons, training camps, logistic sites, and general headquarters. All of these headquarters required trained and educated commanders and staff officers to accomplish their missions in any sort of efficient and effective manner.[19]

Numbered army headquarters performed the administration, logistics, and higher command functions. A typical numbered army contained at least 300,000 soldiers; for example, Patton's Third Army had a strength of 314,814 officers and other personnel at the end of August 1944.[20] An army, which had a much larger headquarters than a corps, operated simultaneously as a tactical headquarters, an administrative and logistic support organization, and a semipermanent home for nondivisional combat and combat support formations.[21]

At the corps level, a small headquarters provided tactical direction and organized special nondivisional units into packages to support the divisions of that corps. Corps frequently contained tens of thousands of officers and soldiers. An example was XX Corps, which in November 1944, in addition to command of three infantry divisions and one armored division, had responsibility for the tactical employment of nineteen battalions of corps-level artillery, five tank destroyer battalions, three separate tank battalions, eight engineer battalions, four antiaircraft battalions, and a cavalry group. The total force of XX Corps included more than 500 tanks and 700 artillery pieces.[22]

To fill only the command and primary general staff positions with Leavenworth graduates of army groups, armies, corps, and divisions would require a minimum of 984 officers. Assistant and deputy staff positions, especially at echelons above division, were also positions where a Leavenworth education was essential. Additionally, commanders of regiments and combat commands, as they were full colonels, were commonly graduates of Leavenworth, even if that education was not specifically focused on colonel-level commands. These numbers fail to account for the needs of the Army Air Forces, the SOS theater requirements, and the needs of stateside headquarters, training bases, and continental logistical requirements. To fill these needs, as identified in Truesdell's 1944 study quoted above, of perhaps 12,000 course graduates, there existed, on active duty in December 1941, some 1,575 long-course graduates.[23] Clearly, graduates were carefully selected to fill particularly critical positions using some form of prioritization.

Leavenworth Graduates and Army Divisions

It is only at the division level, however, that general staff officers were not graduates of the peacetime long courses. Divisions fought the close fight of World War II, being responsible for much of the management of violence that converted strategic goals into battlefield success; the division was the echelon in which the army placed many of its most qualified professionals. A significant number of long-service Leavenworth graduates, the officers who had spent much of their adult life developing and refining professional skills, served as the critical officers at division headquarters and as commanders in component subordinate formations, but not as the primary staff officers.[24]

The divisions—either infantry, armored, cavalry, or airborne—performed the basic management functions necessary for modern combat and were organized only with essential logistical support for short-duration independent operations. The division had to be successful in the very complex business of combined arms combat. That task proved to be beyond the capability of part-time officers, as evident from the nearly unanimous failure of nonregular officers who attempted to command divisions. Of the many National Guard and Reserve senior officers at the start of mobilization, only two remained in command of their units through the war. Practically every other nonregular officer was relieved, retired, or reassigned away from senior combat commands.[25] The regulars who commanded and, to a much lesser extent, staffed these divisions were essential to combat effectiveness, and their story tells much, but not all, of the effectiveness and professional competence of the army in World War II. This effectiveness was due, in large measure, to the mastery of intellectual skills and an understanding of the battlefield as taught at Leavenworth during the interwar period.

Each U.S. infantry division in World War II included a command group with the commander, typically a major general, supported by an assistant commander and a field artillery commander, typically brigadier generals. The division general staff consisted of a chief of staff, typically a full colonel, and a group of general staff officers, who ranged in rank from major to full colonel, for G1 (Personnel), G2 (Intelligence), G3 (Operations and Training), G4 (Supply and Evacuation), and G5 (Civil Affairs and Military Government).[26] According to the operations doctrine of 1941, the commander was "the controlling head; he must be the master mind, and from him must flow the energy and the impulse which are to animate all under him."[27] The staff officers "assisted the commander . . . by providing information, data and advice, by preparing detailed plans and orders in accordance with his direction; and by exercising such supervision over the execution of his orders as (the commander) may prescribe."[28] In the circumstances of modern warfare, the commander alone could not make a division function effectively in combat, as the command-and-control requirements were too vast and complex.[29]

In addition to the commanders and general staff officers at division, full colonels commanded the major combat organizations subordinate to each division. In infantry and airborne divisions, these officers commanded infantry regiments. In armored divisions, they commanded organizations known as combat commands. Combat Command A (CCA) and Combat Command B (CCB) were equivalent to infantry regiments in battlefield use. The other combat command was identified as CCR (a reserve formation or a refit organization, depending on the specific armored division).[30] The commanders of these formations were primarily regular officers. Many had the specialized Leavenworth combined arms education at division and corps levels yet saw combat only while commanding a regiment or combat command.

A sample of divisions in the European Theater of Operations makes possible an analysis of the utilization of Leavenworth graduates.[31] Of the sixty-one divisions assigned to the ETO, fifteen were selected as a sample.[32] These fifteen included divisions of every type except cavalry, as the sole cavalry division (dismounted) was employed in the Pacific. Officers assigned to command and general staff positions in these fifteen divisions are representative of the utilization of Leavenworth graduates, from both the peacetime long courses and the mobilization short courses, across the ETO and around the globe.

Senior Officers

These fifteen divisions, once committed into the active ETO, had twenty-four officers assigned as division commanders.[33] Twenty-three (95.8 percent) had graduated from the peacetime Leavenworth Command and General Staff Course. The only commander who did not graduate before 1941 graduated from the Fifth Special Class on the day before Pearl Harbor was attacked.[34] This exception to the rule that all division commanders were graduates of the peacetime Leavenworth course, Brigadier General George W. Read Jr., assumed command of 6th Armored Division in the last days of the war when the commander of the division, Major General Robert Grow, Leavenworth class of 1929, was hospitalized for a gallbladder operation.[35] Although in command for less than twenty-four hours, he counts as one of the division commanders for this study.

The assistant division commanders were all CGSC graduates. Of the twenty-two officers in this position, nineteen graduated from regular army Command and General Staff Courses before the war, two graduated from short courses after mobilization, and one, Brigadier General Kenneth Buchanan, graduated from one of the Special Command and General Staff classes for officers of the National Guard and Organized Reserves. Buchanan, a member of the Illinois National Guard, graduated in 1930 and later became assistant division commander of 28th (Pennsylvania) National Guard Division. Buchanan so impressed Brigadier General Omar Bradley when Bradley took command of the division during training that he remained in his position throughout the war, leaving the division only in August 1944 to become assistant division commander of 9th Infantry Division.[36] Buchanan was the only officer in the study group to graduate from one of the National Guard peacetime courses at Leavenworth and then to serve as a general or in a general staff officer position. Given the performance of senior National Guard officers in the mobilization for World War II, he was exceptionally competent and physically fit and served effectively in combat in France. General George C. Marshall accurately summarized the plight of the more senior National Guard officers. In a letter to Undersecretary of War Robert P. Patterson, he wrote, "The RA [regular army] units are not bothered by poor morale because the officers have attained professional knowledge either at schools or through practical experience. NG officers have not had these opportunities, and the morale of their units reflects the deficiency."[37]

The army's fascination with artillery as a critical part of the combined arms team led to an unusually high percentage of Leavenworth graduates serving as field artillery commanders.[38] Eleven of seventeen (64.7 percent) were graduates of the interwar course, and one had graduated from the Second Special Course for a total of twelve (70.6 percent) Leavenworth graduates. Compared to the infantry regimental commanders and armored division combat command commanders, a rough equivalent in command responsibility, of whom only one-third (33.3 percent) had graduated from an interwar course and another one-fifth (19.5 percent) from the short courses, the field artillery commanders were twice as likely to have graduated from the interwar course. The regimental and combat command commanders, although included in the 1934 War College study as officers who should have the benefit of a Leavenworth education, usually were not graduates of a peacetime course. Only when added together with the short-course graduates are the majority (52.9 percent) of regimental or combat command commanders considered graduates of the program.

The division chiefs of staff were primarily graduates of Leavenworth, but frequently they were graduates only of the shorter mobilization courses. Of twenty-five officers who served as chiefs of staff, ten (40 percent) were peacetime Leavenworth graduates, and nine (36 percent) graduated after mobilization. Of the six nongraduates, two were long-service professionals, West Point graduates of 1918 and 1923, who did not attend Leavenworth for whatever reason, but three were too young to be peacetime Leavenworth graduates, being very recent graduates of West Point, two from 1934 and one from 1936.[39]

Division General Staff Officers and Subordinate Commanders

Officers who served as general staff officers in combat divisions in World War II usually did not have the benefit of a Leavenworth experience. Although no non-Leavenworth officers commanded divisions, and only one served as an assistant division commander, significant numbers of officers without a Leavenworth education were in the other critical positions. Of the seventeen field artillery commanders, five had no Leavenworth experience.[40] Of twenty-five chiefs of staff, ten were interwar graduates, five were short-course graduates, and six had no Leavenworth education at all.[41]

Officers below the rank of division chief of staff were only infrequently graduates of the peacetime Leavenworth course. Of the general staff officers who served as coordinating staff, G1, G2, G3, or G4 of these divisions, only one graduated from Leavenworth in a peacetime course.[42] The division general staff officers, G1 through G5, had practically no education from the peacetime Leavenworth and display a wide variety in attendance of wartime courses. Slightly more than half of the G1s, responsible for all personnel functions of the division, were mobilization course graduates, leaving nine with no discernible education for their duties. The only officer to attend the New Divisions Course as the G1, and to be retained in that position, Lieutenant Colonel David Arp, was a graduate of General Staff Course Ten.[43] The other staff officers responsible for the logistics of the divisions, the G4s, were more likely to be graduates of Leavenworth's wartime courses than their counterpart G1s, with slightly more than two-thirds of G4s attending Leavenworth. Perhaps somewhat more indicative of the importance of consistency in the realm of logistics rather than personnel, three of the New Divisions Course divisions, from five in the study group, retained their G4 positions from the New Divisions Course through V-E Day.[44]

The G2s, responsible for all intelligence matters, including assessment of enemy capabilities and intentions, were primarily graduates of postmobilization courses, with fourteen of nineteen attending Leavenworth between 1941 and 1944.[45] Their immediate counterparts, the G3s, responsible for the operations and training of the divisions, were almost exactly evenly split between Leavenworth and non-Leavenworth officers. The distinction of the G3s, however, unique among the general staff officers, was their high proportion of regular army officers (nearly half, at 44.5 percent). Unlike the other staff officers, who ranged from a low of 16 percent (G2s) to a high of 19.1 percent (G1s), G3s much more frequently were in the army before mobilization. Indeed, ten of the twenty-seven G3s (37 percent) were West Point graduates, a proportion twice as high as G4s and three times higher than G1s and G2s.[46]

G5s, as a group, were the least educated and represented the fewest prewar professionals among all staff officers. Only two attended postmobilization Leavenworth courses, where as G5s they received little education of value, limited to a single discussion of civil-military relations as part of the G1 section of the course. No G5s were regular army or West Point graduates. None of the G5s were on active duty at the start of mobilization, and none had served in the World War I–era army. Given their lack of military education and relative lack of professional stature, they also tended to be the more junior among the staff officers, with an average rank of major, unlike all the other positions, which were normally lieutenant colonels.[47]

These undereducated officers nevertheless coped with the strains of their critical duties in combat, arguably due to the influence of senior officers, who had the advantage of a Leavenworth education, and on-the-job experience. Experience without some form of expertise, however, would have resulted in chaos in the extremely complex requirements of a division during modern combat operations. The vital difference between chaos and competence was undoubtedly the presence of the Leavenworth men at the chief of staff, division field artillery commander, assistant division commander, and division commander positions.

The regimental and combat command commanders were frequently graduates of Leavenworth, either the peacetime course or the postmobilization courses. Twenty-nine (33.7 percent) were peacetime graduates and twenty-one (24.4 percent) were postmobilization Leavenworth graduates. The remaining thirty-six (41.9 percent) were 80 percent regular army officers, twenty-two of whom were senior enough to have competed for Leavenworth but failed to impress their branch chiefs sufficiently to gain entrance. The other seven regulars were too young to have attended Leavenworth before 1941.[48] Whether the assignment of graduates of the Leavenworth course to duties not covered in the Leavenworth education was an effective use of army officers is a matter of some conjecture. However, division commanders apparently felt the need to assign Leavenworth graduates as regimental commanders, to the point that they sometimes went without adequately educated senior staff officers.[49]

Omar Bradley's experience as a division commander early in the war is a reliable indicator of the paucity of professionals:

I moved over to the 28th Division on June 26, 1942, taking only six men from the 82nd Division: my chief of staff, George Pope, my G3, Willis Matthews; my G4, Tubby Thorson; my two aides . . . and my driver. . . . I inherited two other Regular Army staffers, both West Pointers: Basil H. Perry (Class of 1917), artillery commander, and Forrest Carraway, the G1 (Class of 1931). There was one outstanding senior Guard officer in the Division, Kenneth Buchanan. I promoted him to assistant division commander.[50]

Bradley's experience as the new commander of the 28th Division is indicative of the shortage of qualified officers available, but it does not address the even more critical shortfall in Leavenworth educated officers.

The Influence of the Leavenworth Men

The very high proportion of division general staff officers in the army who had not attended the division-level training and education school at Leavenworth is startling. Although Leavenworth was consistently touted as the school for general staff officer preparation, only one officer among more than 100 general staff officers (G1 through G5) attended the course before the war.[51] Despite this apparently grave shortcoming in educated general staff officers, more than one-third of regimental and combat command commanders had attended Leavenworth before the war, although that school conducted practically no education to prepare them for their command. Similar to the proportion of officers with an interwar Leavenworth education, senior officers at division level were predominantly veterans of the World War I army, and a significant percentage (42.4 percent) of the regimental commanders had been in the army in 1917 or 1918. However, division staff officers had no World War I experience.

This preponderance of division commanders and assistant division commanders from Leavenworth meant they knew more about running division staffs than the staff officers themselves. This technical skill and ability to teach the more junior officers of the division, especially during the long months of training, deployment, and downtime prior to being committed to combat, probably had a marked impact on the ethos of the post–World War II U.S. Army officer corps. From a peacetime world in which duty with troops was considered one of the last places a professionally interested and skilled officer could be found, through the crucible of combat in World War II, to the postwar army in which duty with troops became the most desired of all, there was a fascinating change in the ethos of the profession.[52] It is possible that the ethos of personal command, which was not present in the pre–World War II Army to the extent it is today, in part resulted from the personal professional competency of the educated few who were serving as commanders and assistant commanders of combat divisions in World War II.

One example of a division engaged in mobile warfare demonstrates the competencies required of a division commander and his staff in World War II. The professional competency of Major General Ernie Harmon, the subordinate commanders, and the division staff of 2nd Armored Division came to the fore in critical battles on Christmas Eve and Christmas Day 1944. As the Germans' Ardennes offensive (the Battle of the Bulge) gained speed on the morning of December 21, Harmon, ordered to meet with Lieutenant General W. H. Simpson, Ninth Army commander, warned his staff to prepare the division for movement on short notice. At 4:00 P.M., Simpson returned to his headquarters, met Harmon, and ordered him to move the division. First Army, the gaining army, was working the routes Harmon would need and would provide access to them soon. Harmon then "jeeped" to General J. Lawton "Lightning Joe" Collins, VII Corps commander, and conferred with him while First Army worked the routes. At 8:00 P.M. the route clearances arrived and Harmon drove back to the division, arriving at 10:00 P.M. Harmon collected his subordinate commanders, the division staff, and the officers of the reconnaissance battalion and had the approved routes marked on the reconnaissance battalion officers' maps. Harmon ordered the reconnaissance officers to guide the organizations of the division. These officers moved out at 10:30 P.M. to meet up with the other elements of the division. The entire division was moving by midnight. The division moved 14,000 men and 3,000 vehicles, in two columns, as far as 100 miles, traversing the outskirts of Aachen and Liege, across an army-level boundary and several corps boundaries, under total radio communication blackout, in a sleet storm, all in less than twenty-two hours.[53]

The move was meant to occupy secure areas where the division could prepare for an eventual counterattack to eliminate the front edge of the German offensive; however, events on Christmas Eve rapidly identified the need for an attack. German 2nd Panzer Division was racing for bridges over the Meuse and the vital city of Namur, Belgium. Combat Command A of U.S. 2nd Armored, commanded by Brigadier General John Collier, a field artilleryman who graduated from Leavenworth in 1938, ran into lead elements of 2nd Panzer's reconnaissance battalion near the town of Buissonville and fought them to a standstill.[54] Harmon decided the situation was in doubt and understood that the deliberate attack planned for the future was overcome by the situation on the ground, which he stated was "changing all the time." He ordered a divisional reconnaissance element attached to CCA, ordered CCB to secure the critical road junction in the town of Ciney, and then ordered the attached 4th Cavalry Group to serve as a connective screen between the organic elements of the division.[55]

After Harmon's orders brought U.S. forces into contact with elements of 2nd Panzer Division across the division front, the mood at German headquarters, in the words of the official history, "became more somber as the distance between the particular headquarters and the 2d Panzer Division posted at the tip of the Bulge diminished."[56] Late on Christmas Eve, Lieutenant General Collins and Harmon sat down at Harmon's headquarters to sort out a deliberate counterattack for Christmas Day.[57] Harmon launched the attack at 8:00 A.M. Supported by massive numbers of British and U.S. fighter-bombers, pouring in heavy concentrations of artillery, and using combined arms tactics, U.S. 2nd Armored made short work of 2nd Panzer's reconnaissance battalion. Caught by what the Germans described as a "hellish fire," commanders of the remaining combat power of 2nd Panzer, cut off by U.S. 2nd Armored, were ordered to abandon their vehicles and attempt to escape during the night.[58]

For the next two days, 2nd Armored mopped up the area around Ciney. Total U.S. casualties were seventeen killed, twenty-six missing, and 201 wounded, with five light tanks and twenty-two medium tanks destroyed. German losses were 1,213 prisoners taken, eighty-two tanks and eighty-three artillery pieces destroyed, and some 400 vehicles captured or destroyed. In the words of the U.S. Army official history, it was "an illuminating commentary on the use by a veteran formation of the combined arms, the impossibility of striking power inherent in the piecemeal tactics employed by the enemy, the lack of a strong German artillery to counter the weight of metal always available to the Americans, and the complete absence of German attack planes in skies ruled by the British and American fighter-bombers."[59]

Even when conducting textbook mobile warfare, the keys to U.S. success were combined arms, integrated artillery, effective close air support, and rapid and competent staff work, all under the direction of aggressive and skillful leadership. As exemplified by Harmon's experience in 2nd Armored Division, something seems to have worked in providing effective commanders and staff officers to U.S. divisions in World War II.

However, all World War II combat was not mobile warfare. The reduction of defensive positions was also a key component of warfare in 1944 and 1945. This need to reduce a fortified front, or a stabilized position, in order to create the conditions for mobile warfare—the essential principle of U.S. Army doctrine from 1918 through 1945 and of instruction at Leavenworth during the interwar period—remained the same tactical and operational issue from 1918 to 1945. Some of the tools had improved, but the need to be successful at reducing defensive positions to create the breakthrough remained the realm of the deliberately planned and carefully executed combined arms team.

According to Martin Blumenson, author of the U.S. Army "Green Book" official history of Operation Cobra, the start of the breakout from Normandy, 9th Infantry Division was among the best of the U.S. infantry divisions in the ETO. This unit performed an essential role in Operation Cobra "by penetrating the German defenses, then uncovering the roads in its area to permit unhampered exploitation, and thereby turn an incipient stalemate into fluid, mobile warfare that developed from breakthrough to breakout."[60] *Stalemate, breakthrough, breakout* — these principle forms of combat, conducted by mobile combined arms teams, characterized the battlefields of World War I and World War II. Although a comprehensive analysis is beyond the scope of this book, a brief look at lessons learned by the AEF in the Meuse-Argonne campaign is necessary to better understand how those lessons applied in the U.S. Army's campaigns in Western Europe during World War II.[61]

Despite the rapid victories foretold by radical visionaries of the interwar period like Giulio Douhet, J. F. C. Fuller, and B. H. Liddell Hart, the nature of war and the nature of warfare, seen from 1917 through 1918 and 1939 through 1945, were more consistent than observers of the German victories of 1939 and 1940 would have understood. After Germany's "lightning victories" over Poland, Denmark, the Low Countries, and France, it looked to the world as if a new form of war had arrived: gone were the trenches of World War I, and the rapid decisive victory was once again supreme. Three years later, the reality, if not the lingering mythology, was much different. The year 1945 saw Germany completely exhausted and powerless before the Allies, a victory produced by massive militaries mobilized from all available resources in the belligerent nations. The ground forces of these militaries were dominated by combined arms teams (infantry-artillery-tanks-airpower). Tactical and operational engagements were characterized by a series of stabilized fronts, eventually penetrated through the massive accumulation of firepower and infantry divisions followed by a spectacular, if brief, sprint into mobile warfare, only to be delayed by the reestablishment of yet another stabilized front.

The battlefields of 1917–1918 and those of 1944–1945 had much more in common than is generally thought. The use of combined arms, the command and control of divisions and corps, the use of artillery and other fires to reduce the strength of the enemy, rates of casualties, the pattern of the battlefield, and the requirement to create a breakthrough were all effectively identical in 1918 and 1944. Technology made a difference in how these breakthroughs were achieved, and how the pursuits were conducted, but only as matters of technique. The reality of 1918 — at corps and division headquarters and on the

A Brief Respite for Frontline Mess, February 1945. World War I or World War II?
Only the helmets and uniforms tell the difference. Photo taken during the Siegfried Line
campaign, February 1945. From *Third Army, February: Through the Siegfried Line,
Operations Summary*, ch. 9, n.d., 263. U.S. Army photograph.

ground for the soldier—was the same reality as in 1944. As stated by the foremost historian of artillery, Major General J. B. A. Bailey, "The situation in 1944–45 was analogous to that in 1917–1918."[62]

In the last offensive of World War I, the AEF effectively managed combined arms (at least in the last phase of the offensive), command and control of corps and their subordinate divisions, and effective artillery fires and air attacks to support the combined arms attack and was, arguably, close to a breakthrough when the Armistice was announced. In this multiple-division, multiple-corps, twenty-five-mile-wide stabilized battlefront, using artillery fires and tactics of combined arms teams in an effort to generate a collapse of the coherent German defenses, the AEF established the prototype for the U.S. Army's conceptualization of the nature of warfare for the next two decades. Leavenworth's role was clear, and after Meuse-Argonne the army would never again go into combat without an effective system of combined arms coordination. Because the divisions and corps were the primary locations for coordination, and because these echelons were the bedrock of the Leavenworth mission, the school on the banks of the Missouri was the central location during the interwar period where the lessons of Meuse-Argonne were considered, refined, developed, written about, and instructed.

The experience of battle, from Meuse-Argonne to Normandy in the summer of 1944, was more consistent than different. However, there existed an interlude when it looked like quick, decisive maneuver had returned to the battlefield—the German blitzkrieg. Before this form of warfare became known worldwide as blitzkrieg, one observer called it what it really was: *penetration*. Captain Herbert Ehrgott, in an article titled "Power Plus Speed: The Essence of the Flanders Penetration," referred readers to his two-part article from 1936, "The Battle of Picardy and the Double Penetration."[63] In his earlier piece, Ehrgott had analyzed the Germans' spring 1918 offensives in Flanders as textbook examples of penetration, complete with detailed analysis of the 1923 *FSR*'s statements about creating a penetration. Using the 1918 German campaign as a test case, Ehrgott judged the then-current U.S. doctrine to be sound—with one exception: when attacking to create a penetration, according to Ehrgott, the attacker should immediately attack directly at the defending enemy to generate a vulnerable flank, not worrying so much about the depth of the penetration initially but instead focusing on rolling up flanks to the left and right of the penetration. In his 1940 article, he stated that the German attacks in May and June 1940 used exactly this technique for bringing an effective penetration into effect, which allowed the Germans to effectively exploit the penetration to envelop British and French forces in the Low Countries. Connecting his earlier analysis to the later campaign, Ehrgott described the German attacks as a combination of airpower-based fires, mobile (truck-mounted) infantry, and the "closest cooperation of new fast elements of combat forces." The successful penetration and exploitation were a successful example of "the old problem of concentrating superior combat power at the critical time and place, and *maintaining this superiority throughout the necessary period of time.*"[64]

The most important point, from the view of assessing the effect of Leavenworth on the competence of the U.S. field forces in World War II, is that the blitzkrieg was not a novel form of warfare. Heralded by apologists for the loss of Poland in fall 1939 and for the French-British defeat in 1940, and popularized by the German propaganda machine, blitzkrieg was in reality a common tactic turned into a failed strategy. As pointed out by Shimon Naveh, Karl-Heinz Frieser, Richard Overy, and others, the Germans confused tactics with strategy. When the successful application of German tactics failed to produce a decisive victory in the June 1941 invasion of the Soviet Union (Operation Barbarossa), Germany was caught in a two-front war they could not hope to win.[65] The idea of creating a breakthrough and, through its exploitation, transforming warfare again into a mobile, decisive environment was not the sole creation of the German armed forces. It had been the basic operational concept of the AEF in World War I and of the U.S. Army during the interwar period. The fact that Americans could pursue this concept, and thereby conduct war by efficiently harnessing the entire mobilized resources of a superpower, explains the U.S. victory in World War II.[66] When facing U.S. forces using true mobile combined arms teams in tandem with very powerful and efficiently controlled artillery, the German military stood little chance for survival. Outmatched in positional warfare interludes between attempts to make penetrations, and overmatched also in their penetration and exploitation capabilities, the Germans eventually cracked every time.[67]

Five characteristics of the battlefield in the latter part of World War I remained true for battlefields in 1944 and 1945. The most significant characteristic was the challenge of converting the stabilized front into mobile warfare. The actual stabilized front in both wars was very similar, with rates of advance, and the amount of ground gained by an advance, in 1918 the same as in 1944. Another shared characteristic in stable front situations was the great killer of soldiers on the battlefield: artillery. In order to convert stabilized defensive fronts into mobile war in which decision could be achieved, in both wars, armies needed to use combined arms tactics. They also had to effectively harness the command and control of large formations, including the effective use of combined arms at the division level, to generate the breakthrough or penetration. Then armies had to be able to change to a command-and-control system and have adroit organizations, effective in mobile warfare.

World War I Practices on World War II Battlefields

Like the Meuse-Argonne offensive, the invasion of Normandy and the buildup to a breakthrough were an operation characterized by a stabilized front. After successfully landing on June 6, 1944, the Allies built up their own strength and reduced German strength by combining air and ground attacks. By late July, the Allies had managed to gain some twelve to twenty miles of depth into France and had seized Cherbourg, twenty-seven miles from the westernmost invasion beach. In doing this, U.S. forces had suffered nearly 90,000 casualties, including 23,000 dead. Rates of advance in this period were slower than in the Meuse-Argonne offensive.[68] What caused the slow rates of advance were the persistent challenges inherent to advancing against a reasonably fresh opponent that possessed modern weapons and deployed combined arms teams (mainly artillery-infantry-tank).

In World War I, taking into account casualties across all campaigns, the loss to artillery fire accounted for more than 60 percent of casualties. To quote Philippe Petain, the French marshal, "Artillery conquers, infantry occupies."[69] Artillery was also the single greatest killer on World War II battlefields.[70] The weight of artillery support for the U.S. Army in the European theater during World War II is not something that historians frequently remark upon. In an endnote, writer John Thomas Broom revealed the overwhelming quantity of U.S. artillery simply by counting battalions assigned to the European theater: 583 infantry battalions, eighty-five tank battalions, and 523 *artillery battalions.*[71] Artillery dominated the battlefield, even in the close terrain of *bocage* and Swiss Normandy.[72] For the soldier on the ground, or the infantry company commander, the artillery was often the support that made all the difference. During the Battle of Mortain in August 1944, an infantry company commander in the Lost Battalion of World War II recalled: "Our artillery plastered every available route of withdrawal and was very effective, as was evidenced by the screams and hysterical cries of the enemy. There was no doubt now that relief was certain, and the battalion rested and listened to the constant singing of the outgoing artillery."[73]

However, rates of advance, casualties, and artillery firepower were not the only common characteristics from 1918 to 1944. The organizations that formed the backbone of the U.S. Army, although modified from World War I, were still armies, corps, and divisions. At the time of the Operation Cobra breakthrough, U.S. forces in Normandy consisted of 12th Army Group, First and Third Armies, and V, VII, VIII, and XIX Corps, with four armored divisions and nine infantry divisions—a force comparable in command-and-control functions (although now with wireless communications) to AEF First Army in Meuse-Argonne.[74] Most important, as these units struggled to overcome strong German resistance—and to learn the difficult art of combat while under fire—many of these units were green; thus they relied on commanders, who in turn relied on their own interwar experience with corps and divisions, that is, their days at Leavenworth.

The coordination of combined arms attacks was one of the critical tasks of divisions and corps. By November 1944, tactical attacks by 30th Infantry Division, conducted at the end of a tenuous supply chain after the dash across France, were delivered with remarkable success. The attack by 117th Infantry Regiment on St. Jory and Kinzweiler captured both villages and 223 German soldiers, including the commanders and staffs from two battalions, in less than forty-five minutes while suffering only four killed and thirty wounded in action. Supporting the four attacking U.S. infantry companies were two platoons of tanks with supporting artillery fires from six divisional artillery battalions firing 1,128 105mm rounds, six XIX Corps heavy artillery battalions firing 672 240mm and 8-inch rounds, one mortar company launching 468 4.2-inch rounds, and one company of attached self-propelled tank destroyers firing 150 rounds. These successful attacks formed the basis of a visit to the battlefield by officers of XIX Corps in December 1944 for a demonstration. These training events were a prelude to further operations to reduce the Siegfried Line and to penetrate into the heart of Germany.[75]

Effectively commanding forces that conducted both the breakthrough and the exploitation was identified as the critical challenge during the interwar period. The coordinated use of commanders and staff officers to handle the myriad decisions and mind-numbing details required for modern combat was the essential skill taught at Leavenworth. This skill, notoriously missing in much of the Meuse-Argonne offensive, was mastered by the interwar army, primarily at Fort Leavenworth, and was put into effect during combat in World War II. However, a key change was that breakthrough was not to be achieved solely through some form of local superiority. In modern mechanized and motorized warfare between fully mobilizing nations, an effective breakthrough that would lead to decisive mobile exploitation was possible only after a prolonged period of attrition had caused the weaker side to lose combat capability everywhere along the stabilized front. Once penetration was achieved and exploitation began, the weaker side no longer had the resources, mobile or otherwise, to prevent the exploitation from achieving strategic success or halting due to logistical overstretch. To quote from Captain Ehrgott's 1940 assessment of modern warfare, it was necessary to "concentrat[e] superior combat power at the critical time and place, and *maintain this superiority throughout the necessary period of time.*" By 1944, maintaining superiority required both air superiority and sufficient attrition of enemy forces to enable the exploitation.[76]

The U.S. Army in World War II learned its most valuable and enduring lessons from the last major engagement of World War I. The fact that these lessons were sufficient for U.S. military competence in World War II is clear from the statements of participants and is unambiguous from an analysis of the manner of combat in the Meuse-Argonne campaign and the stabilized front operations of 1944 and 1945. The lessons learned from Meuse-Argonne, the professional dialogue in the journals, the doctrine developed as a result of these lessons and dialogue, and the rigorous instruction in this doctrine, primarily at the Leavenworth schools, all prepared the U.S. Army very well for the battlefields of World War II.

The proof of military effectiveness, however, was in the intellectual and professional development of the divisions' officers, not the paper organization of divisions. How did the army simultaneously expand thirty-fold in soldiers and forty-fold in officers while maintaining its professional competence? Part of this professional competence was the effective, and difficult, mobilization of the industrial might of the United States.[77] However, U.S. industrial might required military competence to bring that power to bear effectively against the Axis forces. This military competence must have persisted within the regular officer corps of the army even throughout the lean years of the interwar period, that is, considering the overwhelming presence of regular army officers in senior positions in the combat divisions. More significant, this officer corps, hampered by inadequate budgets, insufficient unit training opportunities, and no battle experience for more than two decades, somehow managed its organizations in combat worldwide. The sample of officers studied in this book provides part of the answer. What the World War II officer division commanders experienced from World War I through the interwar period to their combat operations in World War II, how they perceived their profession, how they approached mastering professional skills, and what they believed the next battlefield environment would be like—all were consistent from 1918 to 1945. What they learned in the army's educational program at the division and corps levels was based, to an unheralded degree, on the experience the army had in France in 1917 and 1918.

The requirement for educated officers beginning in 1940 exceeded every expectation. Barely able to field enough officers to fill half of the critical positions identified before World War II, and then only able to fill something less than half of the shortfall of education through the postmobilization courses, U.S. Army divisions were still competent in the critical tasks of battle management. Leavenworth played a necessary role in this competence. The explicit study of general staff principles and procedures at division and corps, the implied acquisition of confidence in staff skills, and the uneducated aspects of leadership, which these officers had learned in nonacademic environments beginning in

1917, were the foundations for battlefield success in World War II.[78] However, the story of Leavenworth as the educational institution for field-force effectiveness in World War II was hardly an unmitigated success. Significant failures occurred, primarily the inability to graduate officers in the numbers required when the "mobilized manpower of the nation" was called to war, as well as the inability to cope with the increased needs of airpower and high-level logistics.

Conclusion

I cannot understand these Americans. Each night we know that
we have cut them to pieces, inflicted heavy casualties, mowed
down their transport. But—in the morning, we are suddenly faced
with fresh battalions, with complete replacements of men, ma-
chines, food, tools and weapons. This happens day after day.

—German division commander in Normandy,
quoted in Richard Overy, *Why the Allies Won*

Massive amounts of men and material seen by German division commanders in
1944, and their effective use in combat, were essential for warfare in the first half
of the twentieth century. The U.S. Army officer corps learned this lesson in modern warfare in World War I, particularly its experience in the 1918 Meuse-
Argonne offense. However well understood these lessons were by the U.S. Army
officer corps, and how completely integrated they were into the classes at Fort
Leavenworth after World War I, the exigencies of national policy precluded
rapid readiness for World War II. From the small and unready army required by
the National Defense Act of 1920, within three years of President Franklin D.
Roosevelt declaring a limited national emergency on September 8, 1939, the
army expanded from some 200,000 soldiers to more than 8.3 million. The officer corps, less than 14,000 in 1939, numbered 600,000 by the end of World War
II, with officers taken from civilian ranks outnumbering regular army officers
40:1.[1]

It is incomplete and unsatisfactory to explain the U.S. success in World War
II solely from the perspective of industrial might and manufacturing capability.
An effective army in the first half of the twentieth century required massive mobilization to withstand the inevitable casualties, but it also required some level of
competence at the essential military task of coordinating the combined arms battle. The ability of the U.S. Army to respond to the requirements of fielding an effective force of more than 8.3 million men and women from the nadir of the interwar years is due to more than the Ford Motor Company. The earnest desire to
be prepared, and the motivation to distill the lessons of World War I so the next
generation of army officers would not be condemned to repeat the mistakes of

1917 and 1918, were essential contributions to the nation's ability to win the next great struggle. Given America's political decision not to spend the resources necessary to maintain a large and ready army, the U.S. military needed time to rebuild before undertaking the decisive commitment overseas. However, rebuilding, and the eventual effective use of military force, required a foundation of officer capability. The schools at Fort Leavenworth were the nexus of this capability at echelons above regiment.

Several conclusions emerge from this examination of the interwar army and the Leavenworth schools. The most significant, and frequently overlooked, conclusion is the overwhelming influence that World War I had on the interwar army officers. Unheralded by historians dazzled by the more recent magnitude of World War II, U.S. Army officers during the interwar period expected to return to Europe to finish the "unfinished business of the world war" and also expected that the tactical and operational challenges of the Meuse-Argonne offensive would be repeated, in essence, in the next great war. For these officers, from the perspective of 1938, the thing to be avoided at all costs was a repeat of the disasters and near-disasters that the AEF experienced in 1917 and 1918.

The key to understanding the lessons of World War I was the operational framework of stabilized fronts and mobile warfare. Reflecting the experience of the bulk of the AEF in the Meuse-Argonne offensive, officers understood warfare to be decisive only in mobile open warfare and that modern war between industrialized nations would frequently, if not always, devolve into some form of stabilized operation. They were unsure from the Meuse-Argonne experience as to how the transition to mobile warfare should be accomplished, as it failed to appear fully before the Armistice in November 1918. Mobile warfare remained something to achieve through a combined arms, artillery-intensive penetration. The concept that penetration could be made only after lengthy and bloody reduction of the enemy's reserves and frontline combat power was not conceived of during the interwar period. More effective, more powerful, better-planned combined arms appeared to be key—but few were absolutely certain of that. This debate crowded the pages of the professional journals, as did debates about the meaning of professional service, the role of officer schools, and the nature of future warfare. All these debates were influenced, directly and deeply, by the AEF experience and the bloodiest single campaign in U.S. history, the Meuse-Argonne offensive.

These lessons from World War I overwhelmingly influenced the instruction at Leavenworth from 1919 through World War II. Echoing the overlap and continuity of the faculty, overwhelmingly World War I veterans, and combined with the combat and noncombat experiences of student veterans, Leavenworth embraced the lessons of the war in France. The army itself, as reflected in the interwar doctrine that was written, did not deviate significantly from the lessons of the AEF. Field service regulations, field manuals, staff officer manuals, and school texts all were consistent and clear: certain immutable principles emerged from 1917 and 1918, principles that would suffice for the next war. Without transformative alternative choices, and given the near-total lack of any significant military event until the mid-1930s, Leavenworth continued to educate officers as it saw fit—from the perspective of the AEF. Despite the turbulence of alternating one- and two-year courses and changing commandants every three or four years, Leavenworth remained the same much more than it changed from 1919 until 1940.

This conservative existence, however, was not entirely pejorative. Officer students, frequently coming to Leavenworth from ROTC or National Guard assignments or from duty at isolated single-battalion garrisons, managed to practice the principles and techniques of large-formation combat operations (division, corps, army) through the two decades of peace. With some minor exceptions, this practice at Leavenworth was the only experience that the interwar army had in large-formation operations. Although they routinely critiqued classroom events as less effective than field exercises, senior officers in the interwar army fully understood that with such tight budgets the only alternative to schoolhouse practice was no practice at all. Student officers at Leavenworth continued to plow through reading assignments, sit attentively (or not) at lectures and conferences, and endure the continually evaluated map exercises and map problems. Although students were not always encouraged to be innovative, student solutions that did not mimic the instructors' rote answers were possible and did not necessarily result in a lower grade. What every graduating class gained at Leavenworth were not cutting-edge technological advances or new, doctrine-shaking ideas about combat. They gained the three essential elements of the Leavenworth educational system: skills in problem solving, the principles and techniques of handling large formations in combat, and, of inestimable value, the confidence that they could manage these large-formation command and staff tasks that had so greatly challenged officers in the AEF.

Perhaps the greatest irony of the interwar General Staff School education was that the failure to resolve a very controversial issue—whether to focus on teaching future commanders or teaching future staff officers—was itself of great benefit to the fielded force in World War II. The conflation of commandership and staff officer skills, exemplified in the name change in the early 1920s to the Command and General Staff School, actually assisted the leaders of combat divisions in World War II. They were educated like the dragoons of old who, when on foot, were told they could defeat any mounted force and, when on horseback, were told that they could defeat any dismounted unit. Leavenworth students were continually informed that as general staff officers they needed to know everything the generals had to know so they could assist them with proper staff work. As potential generals, they were told they would need to know everything that their staff knew to better teach less qualified subordinates and to better appreciate the estimates they would receive from a staff during combat. After December 7, 1941, many Leavenworth graduates became commanding generals and found themselves teaching undereducated junior officers to be general staff officers, or as chiefs of staff at the division level, bridging the gap between Leavenworth-educated division commanders and junior general staff officers, who were commonly not educated at Leavenworth. Without the conflation of duties during interwar schooling, many officers may not have been able to move from role to role and teach subordinates how to assume ever greater responsibilities. This combination of command and staff skills, like the operational principles and military problem-solving skills taught at Leavenworth, was the source of the absolutely critical professional self-confidence in these soon-to-be senior officers.

The Leavenworth schools reinforced self-confidence through the applicatory method of instruction, in combination with rigorous evaluation and ranking of students. Practical exercises, usually weekly, were the hallmark of the education. Preceded by lectures and conferences on the principles and details of each week's subject, these exercises frequently stressed students and were nearly always evaluated by instructors. Because every student knew that his chance of pinning on a general's stars was officially dependent on evaluations at Leavenworth, competition was intense, at least among those who felt they stood a chance of making the General Staff Eligible List. The instructors were also well aware of this ranking system, for during the interwar period they themselves were, almost without exception, graduates of Leavenworth and had usually made the GSEL.

The realities that practically every graduate, and some nongraduates, made the GSEL, and that in 1938 the list was actually eliminated, seemed to have no effect on the perception of the officer corps that doing well at Leavenworth was essential. This perception, in part the myth of the rigor of being selected for the GSEL, in part the emergent reality of the officer hump finally reaching (or not) Leavenworth, and in part the "hard cut" that only 50 percent of graduates would attend the War College, helped maintain high standards of student engagement at Leavenworth. Rigor, and a strong desire to excel, were continually present at Leavenworth, at least among the top half of each class, plus those students who thought they could manage to get into the top half by working diligently at their studies. There were undoubtedly slackers, as well as some officers who were simply happy to graduate, but these probably represented only the bottom third of each class.

Effective education was certainly enabled by the high-quality faculty at Leavenworth from 1919 to mid-1940. Officers were frequently selected from the best students, then sent off to another duty for two or three years before returning as an instructor. They were the heart of the education process and, in faculty member Troy Middleton's phrase, lived a "life agreeable and busy" at Fort Leavenworth.[2] Frequent return assignments by the best instructors to serve as senior members on the faculty, including many veterans of the 1918 campaigns in France, added a level of experience and skill to the faculty at Leavenworth that has not been matched in the army since 1940. Of course, of great value to the army were the increased skills of the instructors themselves, many of whom served as senior commanders during World War II. Teaching was, indeed, a very effective way of learning, especially when the material is relevant to future challenges.

The school above the Missouri River in Kansas could not educate as many graduates as the army would need in the event of another war. The army fully realized this challenge, as well as the related challenge of satisfying the career expectations of the hump of officers commissioned in 1917 and 1918. Although these problems eventually proved too great for the resources available in the 1920s and 1930s, the army made diligent efforts to ameliorate the problems. The result was the initiation of the one-year program and the effective doubling of the graduates. This reform, the adoption of a one-year program, could have and should have been the norm during the interwar years. If it had been, then the number of graduates would have increased markedly, with no discernible decline in the education quality. Because the one-year course focused on the division, the essential echelon for the coordination of combined arms and the essential element for battlefield success, there is little evidence that graduates of the one-year course were significantly less prepared for effective combat operations compared to the graduates of the two-year course.

Brigadier General Hanson Ely, as commandant, reported to the new class in September 1923 that "had we at the outbreak of [World War I] even such preparation as we now have, the use of graduates of our schools would have saved billions of dollars and many thousands of lives."[3] General Ely was correct, and prophetic, for the preparation of Leavenworth students *did* "save billions of dollars and many thousands of lives." The future brought improved technology, including greatly better tanks and aircraft, and the requirement to add mechanized and airborne forces to the doctrinal mix. However, the significant changes to doctrine and equipment, frequently assumed to have occurred after the German victories in Poland in 1939 and France in 1940, never happened. By the mid- to late 1930s, Leavenworth was teaching mechanized operations and fully integrating, if in a somewhat cursory fashion, air support of ground troops. Adaptation to some tactical lessons happened in the first engagements of the war, in the Pacific and in North Africa, *but the base doctrine of the U.S. Army did not change from 1923 to 1945.* The Leavenworth schools taught this valid and relevant doctrine from 1919 through 1945.

Even so, Leavenworth absolutely failed to meet, and even understand, three of the greatest challenges that the army would face during World War II. Starting with a faculty drawn *without exception* from officers deployed to the AEF, Leavenworth never assumed the task of educating officers for mobilization duties. Perhaps an oversight due to the organizational changes mandated by the National Defense Act of 1920, and perhaps due to the personal experiences of the faculty or the desires of students, or even an ethos in the officer corps that combat operations were the true measure of skill for professional officers, this cleft in the professional education system was never even *perceived* during the interwar period. This was arguably the worst failure of all the interwar army's errors, and only the fortuitous prophylactic of national mobilization exposed the gross unreadiness of the officer corps for mobilization and caused the army to assume the responsibilities of mobilization and training.

The second great failing was also due, in part, to the overwhelming presence of line combat veterans in the inaugural faculty. The lack of appreciation for Service of Supply education occurred because few of the initial faculty had any experience in logistical matters above corps level; the school's mission itself focused on division and corps operations, and so Leavenworth students received no preparation to speak of for logistics for echelons above corps. Slow to remedy this situation, Leavenworth did not begin to address the issue of educating officers for the service forces until well into 1942—and then only in inadequate quantities. The army never fully recovered from its inability to prepare for service support, material replenishment, and combat casualty replacement. Leavenworth was partially to blame.

The issue of airpower was also shortchanged at Leavenworth during the interwar period, for understandable reasons. Through much of the interwar period, senior officers in the army considered the Army Air Corps (which in the 1920s was nascent and rapidly grew through the 1930s) merely another branch and therefore not a distinct part of the school's mission. Flying officers attended their own special service courses at Maxwell Field, Alabama, and this instruction frequently explored theoretical and strategic challenges far above the tasks required of company-grade officers. Part of the blame could very well be laid on the doorstep of Maxwell Field, as the Army Air Corps did not seem to make an official attempt to change the instruction at Leavenworth. It is likely that the desire within the Army Air Corps to effect strategic air domination allowed little in the way of supporting ground forces, which is what Leavenworth would have taught—the direct support of divisions and corps. Moreover, when Maxwell's school closed upon mobilization, Leavenworth did not immediately pick up the task of producing the staff officers necessary for the air armada promised by President Franklin Roosevelt. Only after the inspection trip by one of the most senior aviators in the army, Lieutenant General Joseph McNarney, did Leavenworth begin to teach modern airpower practice. Grievous shortages of educated staff officers hampered air operations for the remainder of World War II.

When committed to combat operations in Western Europe in 1944, the army served competently due in no small measure to the professional competence of Leavenworth graduates. Leavenworth men, without exception, commanded every echelon above regiment and, almost without exception, served as general staff officers at all echelons of corps and above. Critical to combined arms success, Leavenworth graduates commanded practically every division and filled many of the critical assistant division commander and field artillery commander positions. Graduates performed a valuable service by educating junior officers in general staff duties while assigned as division chiefs of staff.

Major General Ernie Harmon, commanding an armored division, was only one example of this generation of division commanders, all educated at Leavenworth, who competently managed divisional command and control during combat in the European theater. Assisted by their chiefs of staff, also predominantly graduates of Leavenworth, they provided educated and mature leadership to the U.S. Army. Despite the need to relieve officers who were not emotionally or physically able to handle the stress of combat, those officers who remained in command of divisions and corps were, as a group, remarkably competent. No less an authority than Winston Churchill remarked:

> To create great armies is one thing; to lead them and to handle them is another. It remains to me a mystery as yet unexplained how the very small staffs which the United States kept during the years of peace were able not only to build up the Armies and the Air Force units, but also to find the leaders and vast staffs capable of handling enormous masses and of moving them faster and farther than masses have ever been moved in war before.[4]

This competence in leading corps and divisions is explained by officer education. As Major General Ely, quoted in the November–December 1940 edition of *Infantry Journal*, believed:

> The American soldier in the World War was excellent material. . . . With nearly 200,000 officers in France only a few thousand of whom had had over a few months' training, it is really surprising that they acquitted

themselves as well as they did. In the next war, if we have a next, we will be tremendously better prepared — 12,000 or more Regular officers instead of about 5,000 as at the beginning of the World War. A National Guard larger than the Regular Army whose officers and men are excellently trained — vastly superior to the National Guard of the World War. Over 100,000 Reserve officers quickly available. The best military schools in the world which will assure us of the best initial leadership until the final school of war makes the changes found necessary by actual battle experience.[5]

When the relative lack of corps and division maneuvers in the 1920s and 1930s is understood, the role of Leavenworth in educating competence looms still larger.

The competence of U.S. corps and division commanders was also remarked upon by the defeated Germans. Secretary of War Henry L. Stimson reminisced:

> I shall never forget the difference between the confusion and hurry at home and later inefficiency at the battlefield in 1918, and the smooth swiftness with which Eisenhower's armies swept across France and Germany to victory. The contrast was epitomized when in 1945 we captured [Field Marshal Gerd von Rundstedt], one of the Commanders of the German forces, who said to one of his captors something like this: "We cannot understand the difference in your leadership in the last war and in this. We could understand it if you had produced one superior corps commander, but now we find all of your corps commanders good and of equal superiority."[6]

More than anyone, perhaps, von Rundstedt would have understood the quality and competence of the U.S. Army's corps and division commanders during World War II. How these officers gained such competence — their experience in the interwar army and education at Leavenworth — offers new interpretations for much of the history of World War II.

However, there were not enough Leavenworth men to fill the officer ranks. In World War I, Leavenworth men were usually staff officers and very rarely division commanders; in World War II the experience was precisely the opposite. It is tempting to postulate that much of the post–World War II army ethos, in which the position of commander is seen as the ultimate duty and other positions always scorned, is due to the influence of division commanders who knew the duties of their staffs much better than the staff officers themselves. This may very well be the original source of a current adage within the army that units do well only what the commander inspects personally. This remains a concept worthy of additional exploration, as is the rich historical goldmine of the professional journals, which are generally untapped to date and provide an incredibly powerful source of insight into the intellectual processes of the U.S. Army officer corps during the two decades between the wars.

The national decision not to maintain large-unit readiness in the U.S. Army, with resultant losses in the Philippines and the western Pacific, did not preclude the eventual victory in World War II. The sheer ability of the army, and the nascent Army Air Corps, to handle huge, newly built formations, the forces that eventually turned the tide in World War II, was learned during World War I and was saved from extinction during the interwar years at Leavenworth.

NOTES

Acronyms

In addition to specific acronyms listed in the notes, the following are generally used:

AWCCA   Army War College Curricular Archives, located at MHI
CARL   U.S. Army Combined Arms Research Library, Archives, Fort Leavenworth, KS
CGSC   U.S. Army Command and General Staff College, Fort Leavenworth, KS
CGSCP   U.S. Army Command and General Staff College Press, Fort Leavenworth, KS
CGSS   U.S. Army Command and General Staff School, Fort Leavenworth, KS
CGSSP   U.S. Army Command and General Staff School Press, Fort Leavenworth, KS
CSFG   U.S. Army Command and General Staff College, *Commandants, Staff, Faculty, and Graduates of the Command and General Staff School, Fort Leavenworth, Kansas* (Fort Leavenworth, KS: Command and General Staff School Press, 1939)
GSS   U.S. Army General Service Schools, Fort Leavenworth, KS
GSSP   U.S. Army General Service Schools Press, Fort Leavenworth, KS
MHI   U.S. Army Military History Institute, Carlisle Barracks, PA
NAII   U.S. National Archives, College Park, MD

Introduction

1. There exists an extensive literature on military effectiveness and efficiency in the inter-war years and for World War II. However, this literature is divided into two camps: the first (usually earlier literature) believes the German Army in World War II possessed the acme of professional competence, and the second (more recent) believes the U.S. Army more than held its own against the Germans. Russell A. Hart provides a very useful summation of the historiography debate in his introduction to *Clash of Arms: How the Allies Won in Normandy* (Boulder: Lynne Rienner, 2001), 1–10.

2. Gerald F. Linderman, *The World Within War: America's Combat Experience in World War II* (Cambridge: Harvard University Press, 1997), 48–55.

3. Another critical question that calls for its own book-length study is whether the changes in military art and science from 1918 to 1945 were so great as to make World War I's lessons learned incompatible with the World War II battlefield, or whether they were in fact similar enough to enhance professional competence in the second struggle. Some initial thoughts on this are posed in Chapter 9.

4. Perhaps the best work to date is Harold R. Winton's *Corps Commanders of the Bulge: Six American Generals and Victory in the Ardennes* (Lawrence: University Press of Kansas, 2007). Although Winton only briefly addressed the interwar period, wishing to get on with his compelling narrative of the Ardennes offensive, many of his conclusions are sound. As his

focus was on personal leadership qualities, he did not address the core competencies of tactical and operational professional knowledge gained during the interwar period. Among the other studies of senior army generals are Robert Berlin, *U.S. Army World War II Corps Commanders: A Composite Biography* (Fort Leavenworth, KS: Combat Studies Institute, 1989); J. D. Morelock, *Generals of the Ardennes: American Leadership in the Battle of the Bulge* (Washington, DC: National Defense University Press, 1993); and Gary Wade, "World War II Division Commanders" (Fort Leavenworth, KS: Combat Studies Institute, 1983).

5. E. N. Harmon with Milton MacKaye and William Ross MacKaye, *Combat Commander: Autobiography of a Soldier* (Englewood Cliffs, NJ: Prentice-Hall, 1970), 14, 32–50; quote is on 50.

6. Harmon, *Combat Commander*, 56–252 passim. Harmon recalled that he actually commanded three armored divisions: 1st, 2nd, and, for two days, 3rd after the death of Major General Maurice Rose; see 252.

7. Hamilton H. Howze, *A Cavalryman's Story: Memoirs of a Twentieth-Century General* (Washington, DC: Smithsonian Institution, 1996), 1–34. After the troopship sailed, only dependents were allowed to return home from the Philippines, the soldiers staying with their units as a precaution against Japanese attack.

8. Howze, *Cavalryman's Story*, 36.

9. Ibid., 74–147; quote is on 43.

10. Eisenhower quoted in Matthew F. Holland, *Eisenhower between the Wars: The Making of a General and Statesman* (Westport, CT: Praeger, 2001), 63–64. "Wringing" wet from Harmon, *Combat Commander*, 12.

11. Not every officer appreciated Harmon's profane and direct way of talking. For an opposing view from a memoir, by a colonel who did not appreciate Harmon's leadership traits, see William S. Triplet (edited by Robert H. Ferrell), *A Colonel in the Armored Divisions* (Columbia: University of Missouri Press, 2001), 123–124.

12. Harmon, *Combat Commander*, 113–116.

13. This story is told in many places, but this account is from Harmon, *Combat Commander*, 111–116; Carlo D'Este, *Eisenhower: A Soldier's Life* (New York: Henry Holt, 2002), 396–397; and Rick Atkinson, *An Army at Dawn: The War in North Africa, 1942–1943* (New York: Henry Holt, 2002), 387–389.

14. Losses from D'Este, *Eisenhower*, 393. Casualties were 6,000 killed or wounded, 3,000 missing in action. The story of Operation Howze is from George F. Howe, *The Battle History of the 1st Armored Division* (Washington, DC: Combat Forces, 1954), 197–198. Also see the official U.S. Army history, George F. Howe, *Northwest Africa: Seizing the Initiative in the West: United States Army in World War II, Mediterranean Theater of Operations* (Washington, DC: Office of the Chief of Military History, Department of the Army, 1957), 471–474.

15. The history of Kasserine has been distorted by the works of Martin Blumenson, one of the authors of the "Green Book" series. From his very critical essay on Kasserine in *America's First Battles* through his later revision of his 1966 book *Kasserine Pass*, Blumenson has continued to see the negative side of the U.S. Army in World War II. See Charles E. Heller and William A. Stofft, *America's First Battles, 1776–1965* (Lawrence: University Press of Kansas, 1986). With subsequent books titled *The Battle of the Generals: The Untold Story of the Falaise Pocket, the Battle That Should Have Won World War II; Sicily: Whose Victory?; Bloody River: The Real Tragedy of the Rapido; and Anzio: The Gamble That Failed*, Blumenson continued to write pessimistic views of U.S. military competence in World War II. His view is skewed to one side—there are other interpretations.

16. Gerhard L. Weinberg, *A World at Arms: A Global History of World War II* (New York: Cambridge University Press, 1994), 443.

17. For part of the ULTRA story, see F. W. Winterbotham, *The Ultra Secret* (New York: Dell, 1974), and Anthony Cave Brown, *Bodyguard of Lies: The Extraordinary True Story Behind D-Day* (Guilford, CT: Lyon's, 1975). We still do not have a complete accounting of the issue of ULTRA and the Kasserine Pass battles—see Weinberg, *World at Arms*, note 104 on 1044. Eisenhower did relieve his G2, British Brigadier E. E. Mockler-Ferryman, after the battle. Mockler-Ferryman had made the error of overreliance on ULTRA. See D'Este, *Eisenhower*, 391 and 395.

18. "Shattered" from Carlo D'Este, *Eisenhower: A Soldier's Life* (New York: Henry Holt, 2002), 394.

19. See "Report, Operations Section, German Italian Panzer Army C.P., 22 February 1943, to German General in Rome," General Situation paragraph 1a. Reprinted in U.S. Army Center of Military History, *Kasserine Pass Battles, Readings, Volume I, Part 2* (not dated).

20. As examined in detail below, it was clear in the interwar officer education system that personal qualities were not something that could be affected during a year in the schoolhouse. Leadership was generally not directly taught, particularly at Fort Leavenworth, the only U.S. Army school that focused on division and corps field operations. Instead that school focused on doctrinal principles, techniques, and procedures. For a somewhat different interpretation, focused more on the education at the Army War College, see Winton, *Corps Commanders*.

21. Russell F. Weigley Jr., "The Interwar Army," in Kenneth J. Hagan and William R. Roberts, eds., *Against All Enemies: Interpretations of American Military History from Colonial Times to the Present* (New York: Greenwood, 1986), 257.

22. Omar N. Bradley and Clay Blair, *A General's Life* (New York: Simon and Schuster, 1983), 58–59.

23. Russell F. Weigley, *History of the United States Army* (New York: Macmillan, 1967), 387; J. D. Hittle, *The Military Staff: Its History and Development* (Harrisburg, PA: Military Service Publishing, 1949), 190; and James G. Harbord, *America in the World War* (Boston: Houghton Mifflin, 1933), 8. Also see Peter J. Schifferle, "The Prussian and American General Staffs: An Analysis of Cross-Cultural Imitation, Innovation, and Adaptation" (MA thesis, University of North Carolina, 1981), 113.

24. This school graduated 500 officers and was modeled after the pre-1917 Leavenworth school system and the French and British staff college systems.

25. Several types of revolutions in military affairs are possible. Some occur in part as revolutions from below, when practitioners determine that a new way of warfare is either necessary or has occurred and must be recognized. See Andrew N. Liaropoulos, "Revolutions in Warfare: Theoretical Paradigms and Historical Evidence—the Napoleonic and First World War Revolutions in Military Affairs," *Journal of Military History* 70 (April 2006): 363–384; Colin S. Gray, *Strategy for Chaos: Revolutions in Military Affairs and the Evidence of History* (London: Frank Cass, 2002), ch. 7.

26. Gray, *Strategy for Chaos*, ch. 7.

27. Board report summarized and quoted extensively in Virgil Ney, *Evolution of the U.S. Army Division, 1939–1968* (Fort Belvoir, VA: Headquarters, United States Army Combat Developments Command, Technical Operations, Incorporated, Combat Operations Research Group, DA Contract No. DAAG-05-67-C-0547, January 1969), 53–56.

28. Ney, in ibid., 51–56, provides lengthy quotes from the General Board. There was practically no discussion of changing the organization of the division command group or of its

education. These officers, all combat veterans of the European theater, apparently felt confident in both the structure and the preparation of the division commanders and their staffs. This is an indicator of contemporaneous perceptions of combat effectiveness.

29. For this part of the U.S. effort in World War II, see Paul A. C. Koistinen, *The Military-Industrial Complex: A Historical Perspective* (New York: Praeger, 1980), and Koistinen, *Planning War, Pursuing Peace: The Political Economy of American Warfare, 1920–1939* (Lawrence: University Press of Kansas, 1998).

30. For the best single volume on the issue, see Peter R. Mansoor, *The GI Offensive in Europe: The Triumph of American Infantry Divisions, 1941–1945* (Lawrence: University Press of Kansas, 1999).

Chapter 1. The Great War's Effect on the Army Officer Corps

1. Robert Doughty, "Viewing the Great War through a Prism," in Steven Weingartner, ed., *Cantigny at Seventy-Five: A Professional Discussion: Proceedings of a Professional Discussion Held at the First Division Museum at Cantigny* (Chicago: Robert R. McCormick Tribune Foundation, 1994), 13–36. Also see Meirion and Susie Harris, *The Last Days of Innocence: America at War, 1917–1918* (New York: Random House, 1997), 5–7.

2. The best discussion of the lack of preparation of the United States is John Patrick Finnegan, *Against the Specter of a Dragon: The Campaign for American Military Preparedness, 1914–1917* (Westport, CT: Greenwood, 1974). Also see James L. Abrahamson, *American Arms for a New Century: The Making of a Great Military Power* (New York: Free Press, 1981).

3. Quoted in John T. Nelsen II, "George C. Marshall as Chief of Staff, U.S. Army 1939–1941: The Influences of His World War I Experiences," in *Cantigny at Seventy-Five*, 111. Also see George C. Marshall, *Memoirs of My Services in the World War, 1917–1918* (Boston: Houghton Mifflin, 1976).

4. Marshall, *Memoirs*, 2.

5. Larry I. Bland, ed., *The Papers of George Catlett Marshall, Volume 1: "The Soldierly Spirit," December 1880–June 1939* (Baltimore: Johns Hopkins University Press, 1981), 152; also see Marshall, *Memoirs*, 121.

6. Russell F. Weigley, *History of the United States Army*, enlarged ed. (Bloomington: Indiana University Press, 1984), 387; J. D. Hittle, *The Military Staff: Its History and Development* (Harrisburg, PA: Military Service Publishing, 1949), 190; and James G. Harbord, *America in the World War* (Boston: Houghton Mifflin, 1933), 8. Also see Ronald J. Barr, *The Progressive Army: U.S. Army Command and Administration, 1870–1914* (New York: St. Martin's, 1998); Timothy K. Nenninger, *Leavenworth Schools and the Old Army: Education, Professionalism, and the Officer Corps of the United States Army, 1881–1918* (Westport, CT: Greenwood, 1978), 134–151; and Douglas V. Johnson II and Rolfe L. Hillman, *Soissons 1918* (College Station: Texas A&M University Press, 1999), 19–36.

7. James G. Harbord, *The American Army in France, 1917–1919* (Boston: Little, Brown, 1936), 579–581. See statistical analysis in Marvin A. Kreidberg and Merton G. Henry, *History of the Military Mobilization in the United States Army, 1775–1945*, Department of the Army Pamphlet no. 20-212 (Washington, DC: Government Printing Office, 1955), 247. Also see the strength of the AEF in November 1918 and the percentage of officers serving in GHQ and general staff assignments in American Battle Monuments Commission, *American Armies and Battlefields in Europe: A History, Guide, and Reference Book* (Washington, DC: Government Printing Office, 1938), 502.

8. John J. Pershing, *My Experiences in the First World War* [publ. c. 1931 *as My Experiences in the World War*] (New York: DaCapo, 1995), vol. 1, 102–103.

9. Holley described Pershing's victory in establishing a general staff system for the army as "far more enduring" than the victory in World War I, as the general staff system became an "integral part of the nation's military tradition." I. B. Holley, *General John M. Palmer: Citizen Soldier and the Army of a Democracy* (Westport, CT: Greenwood, 1982), 330. Also see Pershing, *My Experiences*, 102–105, 150–156, 259. Also see Michael D. Pearlman, *Warmaking and American Democracy: The Struggle over Military Strategy, 1700 to the Present* (Lawrence: University Press of Kansas, 1999), 187–220, and David F. Trask, *The AEF and Coalition Warmaking, 1917–1918* (Lawrence: University Press of Kansas, 1993), 168–175. Also, see David Trask, "The Entry of the USA into the War and Its Effects," in Hew Strachan, ed., *World War I: A History* (New York: Oxford University Press, 1998), 239–252. Despite efforts by both the French and British governments, Pershing, with the strong support of Woodrow Wilson, resisted nearly every attempt to provide replacements directly to the engaged armies. Pershing, *My Experiences*, 30–36. See Edward M. Coffman, *The War to End All Wars: The American Military Experience in World War I* (New York: Oxford University Press, 1968), 137–138, for discussion of the AEF schools at Langres, France.

10. Seven hundred graduates cited by Jonathan M. House in "The Fort and the New School, 1881–1916," in John W. Partin, ed., *A Brief History of Fort Leavenworth, 1827–1983* (Fort Leavenworth, KS: Combat Studies Institute, U.S. Army Command and General Staff College, 1983), 47. See Hugh Drum's comment cited in Edward M. Coffman, "The American Military Generation Gap in World War I: The Leavenworth Clique in the AEF," in William Geffen, ed., *Command and Commanders in Modern Warfare: The Proceedings of the Second Military History Symposium, U.S. Air Force Academy, 2–3 May 1968* (Washington, DC: U.S. Air Force Academy, 1969), 38.

11. Coffman, "Leavenworth Clique," 35–43.

12. Ibid., 42.

13. Ibid., 39.

14. Ibid., 38.

15. The most infamous example of the conflict between nongraduate commanders and Leavenworth men was the experience of Alfred Bjornstad. Nenninger, *Leavenworth Schools*, 143.

16. Memorandum, George C. Marshall to General Surles, "Subject: General Pershing Story for Armistice Number of *Time*," dated November 1, 1943, in Bland, *Aggressive and Determined Leadership, June 1, 1943–December 31, 1944, The Papers of George Catlett Marshall* (Baltimore: Johns Hopkins University Press, 1996), vol. 4, 174. Also see Nenninger, *Leavenworth Schools*, 135.

17. See Pershing, *My Experiences*, 18–19; Harbord, *American Army*, 91–94; Edward M. Coffman, *The Hilt of the Sword: The Career of Peyton C. March* (Madison: University of Wisconsin Press, 1966), 60–61.

18. For a discussion of the magnitude of the challenge facing the AEF, see Johnson, *Soissons*, 25–28.

19. Nenninger, *Leavenworth Schools*, 136. See detailed discussion by James J. Cooke, *Pershing and His Generals: Command and Staff in the AEF* (Westport, CT: Praeger, 1997), 9–10. Drum, as a member of the AEF G3, had earlier advised the creation of large divisions due in part to a shortage of qualified commanders and staff officers. Drum later became chief of staff of First Army, working with Colonel George C. Marshall as his G3. Harbord, *American Army*, 103, 225.

20. For a discussion of Langres, see Cooke, *Pershing and His Generals*, 36–37.

21. Holley, *Palmer*, 328–329.

22. Cooke, *Pershing and His Generals*, 36. Marshall later wrote to General Pershing in 1930: the "staffs of these inexperienced divisions were absolutely scalped a few days before the assault, in several cases I believe the day before—*in order that the next class at Langres might start on scheduled time.*" Letter, George Catlett Marshall, Fort Benning, Georgia, to General John J. Pershing, October 24, 1930, reproduced in Bland, *Soldierly Spirit*, 360, emphasis in original. Cooke, *Pershing and His Generals*, 34–43.

23. Cooke, *Pershing and His Generals*, 35–38. Also see lengthy discussion of Langres in Holley, *General Palmer*, ch. 28.

24. On the closure of the Leavenworth schools in 1916 as a reaction to the crisis with Mexico, see House, "The Fort and the New School," 47. Cooke, *Pershing and His Generals*, 36–37. Nenninger, *Leavenworth Schools*, 137.

25. Lecture to the Army War College by George C. Marshall, September 19, 1922, reproduced in Bland, *Soldierly Spirit*, 214–217; quote on 215.

26. Johnson and Hillman, *Soissons*. Also see comments by Mark Ethan Grotelueschen, *The AEF Way of War: The American Army and Combat in World War I* (New York: Cambridge University Press, 2007), 28. Reliefs described in Paul F. Braim, *The Test of Battle: The American Expeditionary Forces in the Meuse-Argonne Campaign* (Newark: University of Delaware Press, 1987), 131–135; Johnson, *Soissons*, 129–130; Grotelueschen, *AEF Way of War*, 129–130.

27. Mark E. Grotelueschen, *Doctrine Under Fire: American Artillery Employment in World War I* (Westport, CT: Greenwood, 2001), 116–130. Summerall quote is from page 117.

28. Gary Mead, *The Doughboys: America and the First World War* (New York: Overlook, 2000), 397.

29. Quoted in Byron Farwell, *Over There: The United States in the Great War, 1917–1918* (New York: Norton, 1999), 257.

30. Bradford Grethen Chynoweth, *Bellamy Park* (Hicksville, NY: Exposition, 1975), 91.

31. Quoted in Kevin C. Holzimmer, *General Walter Krueger: Unsung Hero of the Pacific War* (Lawrence: University Press of Kansas, 2007), 29–30.

32. Marshall, *Memoirs*, 203–204.

33. William Pencak, *For God and Country: The American Legion, 1919–1941* (Boston: Northeastern University Press, 1989), 42.

34. E. H. Cotcher, "Have We Seen the Last War?" Varied Ground (letters to the editor), *Infantry Journal* 16, no. 11 (May 1920): 994–995.

35. Charles P. Summerall, "A Message to the Infantry," *Infantry Journal* 31, no. 1 (July 1927): 2.

36. Alfred W. Crosby Jr., *Epidemic and Peace, 1918* (Westport, CT: Greenwood, 1976), 145–171, and table on 213. The U.S. offensive of 600,000 soldiers in the Meuse-Argonne region, in late September through November 1918, alone claimed 20,472 killed in action and 81,886 wounded in action. See *American Armies and Battlefields*, 327–328.

37. Colonel Leonard P. Ayres, *The War with Germany: A Statistical Summary*, 2nd ed., with data revised to August 1, 1919 (Washington, DC: Government Printing Office, 1919), cited in Mead, *Doughboys*, 348.

38. The casualty rate in September and October 1918 was 130 percent of the American Civil War rate (12,916 per month) and 250 percent of the rate to be seen in World War II (6,489 per month); the Korean War rate would be 1,320 deaths per month, Vietnam only 667, and the war in Iraq from 2003 thru March 2007 a remarkably low rate of .3 percent (at 54.3 deaths per month). Compared to a consistent population of 250 million, the effect is even

more pronounced. The American Civil War rate was 100,000 deaths per month; World War I was 18,000, World War II 11,500, Korea 2,100, Vietnam 830, and Iraq from March 2003 to March 2007, 45.25. Calculations drawn from a comparison of casualties over time from R. Ernst Dupuy and Trevor N. Dupuy, *The Encyclopedia of Military History from 3500 B.C. to the Present*, 2nd rev ed. (New York: Harper and Row, 1985), 990, 1198, 1221, 1251–1252. Iraq casualty figures from globalsecurity.org/military/ops/Iraq_casualties.htm, accessed March 21, 2007. See Harris and Harris, *Last Days of Innocence*, 407, for the effect of these casualties on the populace.

39. See lengthy discussion of Pershing's disquiet during initial armistice discussions in Harbord, *American Army in France*, 518–529. For forces, see Kreidberg and Henry, *Military Mobilization*, 304–305. See Mead, *Doughboys*, 356, for a discussion of divisions in France and the United States. Mead gives slightly different quantities in an appendix at 429–430. J. H. Johnson, *1918: The Unexpected Victory* (London: Cassell, 1997), 190.

40. *American Armies and Battlefields*, 502. James H. Hallas, *Squandered Victory: The American First Army at St. Mihiel* (Westport, CT: Praeger, 1995).

41. Major General E. N. Harmon with Milton MacKaye and William Ross MacKaye, *Combat Commander: Autobiography of a Soldier* (Englewood Cliffs, NJ: Prentice Hall, 1970), 25–31. He also told the story of his experiences earlier in Captain Ernest N. Harmon, 2nd Cavalry, "The Second Cavalry in the St. Mihiel Offensive," *Cavalry Journal* 30, no. 124 (July 1921): 282–289.

42. Harmon, *Combat Commander*, 32–45. Quote about the Armistice on 44. He also told the story of his Meuse-Argonne experiences earlier in Captain Ernest N. Harmon, "The Second Cavalry in the Meuse-Argonne Offensive," *Cavalry Journal* 31, no. 126 (January 1922): 10–18, quote about the corps commander on 18.

43. Editorial, and Wm. A. Snow, "An Open Letter," *Field Artillery Journal* 9, no. 4 (September–October 1919): 477–485. Also see Major C. M. Busbee, Field Artillery, "Liaison between Infantry and Field Artillery Within a Division—Methods in Use to Date and Developments Pending," *Field Artillery Journal* 18, no. 1 (January–February 1928): 25–35.

44. General Preston Brown, "Preliminary Remarks" to General Staff College faculty conference, Military History Institute, U.S. Army War College Curricular Archives, 1919–1920, Box 003 062.1 1.34, 2. Collection hereafter cited as MHI, AWCCA. The General Staff College shortly after changed its name to the Army War College.

45. U.S. Army, *A Manual for Commanders of Large Units (Provisional), Volume 1: Operations* (Washington, DC: Government Printing Office, 1930), iii. This phrase is from the introduction to this manual.

46. "Address of General Pershing," "Addresses Delivered at the Graduating Exercises, General Staff College, June 29, 1920," MHI, AWCCA, 1919–1920, Box Curriculum 1919–1920, Volume 6: Special Course Volume 8 Field Exercises, 3. Also see Allan R. Millett, *The General: Robert L. Bullard and Officership in the United States Army, 1881–1925* (Westport, CT: Greenwood, 1975), for the discussion of postwar national defense policy (at 439–449).

47. Kreidberg and Henry, *Military Mobilization*, 377–380; Allan R. Millett and Peter Maslowski, *For the Common Defense: A Military History of the United States of America* (New York: Macmillan, 1984), 363–372; quote on 363.

48. Summerall Testimony to House Committee on Military Affairs, December 16, 1926, printed in "Promotion and Retirement," *Report of Secretary of War on Promotion and Retirement in Pursuance of the Provisions of Section 4 of the Act Approved July 2, 1926*, 69th Cong., 2nd sess. (Washington, DC: Government Printing Office, 1926), 307.

49. Congress, House, Subcommittee of House Committee on Appropriations, *Army Appropriation Bill, 1922: Hearing Before the Subcommittee*, 66th Cong., 3rd sess., January 26, 1922, 144. Ely's position as division commander of 5th Division is identified in *American Armies and Battlefields*, 500.

50. A photograph reproduced in John Eisenhower's *Yanks* documented the "grim determination" for which Ely was known in the officer corps. John S. D. Eisenhower, *Yanks: The Epic Story of the American Army in World War I* (New York: Free Press, 2001), 125–132, photo with "grim determination" caption in photographs on 178–179. Ely was commandant of Fort Leavenworth from August 1921 through June 1923. See CGSS, *Commandants, Staff, Faculty, and Graduates of the Command and General Staff School, Fort Leavenworth, Kansas* (Command and General Staff School Press, 1939), 7. Hereafter cited as CSFG.

51. Notes from the Chief of Infantry, *Infantry* 22, no. 6 (June 1923): 680–681.

52. See Edward M. Coffman, *The Regulars: The American Army, 1898–1941* (Cambridge: Belknap Press of Harvard University, 2004).

53. Of 2,307 regular infantry colonels, lieutenant colonels, majors, and captains on active duty, 622 (27 percent) served in units, 319 (14 percent) served overseas, ninety-one (4 percent) served on the staffs in Washington, D.C., and 1,125 (49 percent) served in some capacity in the army education system. Also, 262 (11 percent) served at the Infantry and Tank Schools, 101 (4 percent) at Fort Leavenworth, sixty-two (2 percent) at the Army War College, and, by far the largest numbers, a total of 647 (28 percent) served with the Reserve Officer Training Corps detachments (281, or 12 percent), the National Guard (198, 9 percent), or the Army Reserve (168, 7 percent). Notes from the Chief of Infantry, "Duties of Infantry Officers," *Infantry Journal* 34, no. 1 (January 1929): 80.

54. Harmon, *Combat Commander*, 46–58.

55. See Millett, *Bullard*, 439–442. Also see Cooke, *Pershing and His Generals*, ch. 10.

56. Current Field Artillery Notes, "General Pershing on the United States Army," *Field Artillery Journal* 13, no. 4 (July–August 1923): 360–362.

57. Editorial Comment, "The Task of Teaching," *Cavalry Journal* 30, no. 125 (October 1921): 416–418.

58. Major Bernard Lentz (incorrectly spelled "Lenz" in the byline), Infantry, "Who Is Going to Soldier When Everybody Is Going to School?" *Infantry Journal* 18, no. 5 (May 1921): 441–443. A filler piece on the closing page of this article was a reprint from *Harper's Weekly* titled "The Reduced Army."

59. Captain Elbridge Colby, Infantry, "The School of the Officer," in Varied Ground, *Infantry Journal* 19, no. 3 (September 1921): 327–328.

60. Examples include Major B. G. Chynoweth, Infantry, "The Infantry Library," *Infantry Journal* 19, no. 2 (August 1921): 156–159; "Details to the Infantry School," *Infantry Journal* 18, no. 6 (June 1921): 15–17; Lieutenant Colonel Harris Pendleton Jr., "The Business of Going to School," *Infantry Journal* 25, no. 2 (August 1924): 129–134; "Instruction Memorandum, General Service Schools," *Infantry Journal* 19, no. 2 (August 1921): 189–195; and "Information for Officers Detailed for Duty at the Infantry School," *Infantry Journal* 19, no. 2 (August 1921): 196–199.

61. Captain Elbridge Colby, "Teaching in the Army," *Infantry Journal* 19, no. 5 (November 1921): 527–533, and "Teaching Methods at the Infantry School," *Infantry Journal* 20, no. 3 (March 1922): 284–289.

62. Major Bernard Lentz, "The Applicatory Method," *Infantry Journal* 19, no. 6 (December 1921): 604–609; quotes are on 355.

63. Lieutenant Colonel Bernard Lentz, Infantry, "A Decade of Army Schools," *Infantry Journal* 39, no. 5 (September–October 1932): 355–357.

64. The block quote is from the best study of the effect of the Depression on the army. See John W. Killigrew, *The Impact of the Great Depression on the Army* (New York: Garland, 1979), Concl-2 through Concl-3. See, for examples, Major Thomas W. Hammond, Infantry, "Why Not?" *Infantry Journal* 19, no. 6 (December 1921): 638–642, for general comments about money from Congress for the school system.

65. *Report of the Secretary of War to the President, 1921* (Washington, DC: Government Printing Office, 1921), table 1.

66. Lieutenant Colonel A. B. Warfield, QMC, "Fort Benning, the Home of the Infantry School," *Infantry Journal* 33, no. 1 (June 1928): 573–580; Major Edwin P. Parker Jr., Field Artillery, "New Construction at Fort Sill," *Field Artillery Journal* 24, no. 1 (January–February 1934): 5–14.

67. See Elvid Hunt, *History of Fort Leavenworth, 1827–1937*, 2nd ed. brought up to date by Walter E. Laurence (Command and General Staff School Press, 1937), 261, 269.

68. Of 2,307 regular infantry colonels, lieutenant colonels, majors, and captains on active duty, 622 (27 percent) served in units, 319 (14 percent) served overseas, ninety-one (4 percent) served on the staffs in Washington, D.C., and 1,125 (49 percent) served in some capacity in the army education system. Numbers and percentages in Notes from the Chief of Infantry, "Duties of Infantry Officers," *Infantry Journal* 34, no. 1 (January 1929): 80.

69. The $100,000 figure was for 1922. *Report of the Secretary of War to the President* (Washington, DC: Government Printing Office, 1922), table 1.

70. Title of this section taken from "Benny Havens," a West Point song written in 1838, available at www.west-point.org/greimanj/west_point/songs/bennyhavens.htm. Accessed June 16, 2007. *Promotion and Retirement*, 306–307.

71. Kreidberg and Henry, *Military Mobilization*, 221, 247.

72. *Promotion and Retirement*, 2.

73. Ibid., 23–24 and 31.

74. Ibid., 8.

75. Edward M. Coffman and Peter F. Herrly, "The American Army Regular Officer Corps between the World Wars," *Armed Forces and Society* 4, no. 1 (November 1977): 58.

76. A very useful summary, and interpretation, of the hump from the perspective of June 30, 1938, is by "Agrippa II," "Promotion," *Cavalry Journal* 48, no. 3 (May–June 1939): 200–203; quote is on 202.

77. Ibid., 202–203.

78. Captain Thomas Marshall Spaulding, "The Creation of the Single List." *Infantry Journal* 17, no. 2 (August 1920): 132–141, and Major Thomas Marshall Spaulding, Coast Artillery Corps, "The Promotion List," *Infantry Journal* 18, no. 4 (April 1921): 356–361.

79. See Colonel G. V. S. Quackenbush, Infantry, "One List for Promotion," *Infantry Journal* 16, no. 1 (July 1919): 17–18. Editor's comment is on 18.

80. Troops in the United States and its overseas possessions numbered 1,679,000 (some 46 percent of the total), while troops deployed to France numbered 1,944,000, with some 10,000 at sea en route to France. Kreidberg and Henry, *Military Mobilization*, 307.

81. By November 11, 1918, only 36 percent of all officers listed in the official Army Register were or had been assigned to the AEF. U.S. War Department, Adjutant General's Office, *Army Directory, November 1, 1918* (Washington, DC: Government Printing Office, 1918).

82. See, for example, Chynoweth, *Bellamy Park*, at 84 and 115; and Kenneth S. Davis,

Soldier of Democracy: A Biography of Dwight Eisenhower (Garden City, NY: Doubleday, Doran, 1945), 178.

83. Omar N. Bradley and Clay Blair, *A General's Life: An Autobiography* (New York: Simon and Schuster, 1983), ch. 5, p. 680, n. 10.

84. Brigadier General Lytle Brown, Director, War Plans Division, War Department General Staff, Memorandum for the Chief of Staff, "Subject: Occupancy of Quarters by Officers Not on Duty at the Army Service Schools, Fort Leavenworth," December 14, 1918, NAII, RG 165, Box No. 13, Folder 58, Army Service School, 1.

85. Lieutenant Colonel J. E. Lewis, Field Artillery, and 1st Lieutenant Champlin F. Buck, Field Artillery, "An Additional Training Medium," *Field Artillery Journal* 27, no. 4 (July–August 1937): 302–304.

86. Among many examples, see Major L. D. Davis, Infantry, "What Strength Units?" *Infantry Journal* 26, no. 3 (March 1925): 247–251; Captain Richard M. Sandusky, Infantry, "Skeletonized Drill," *Infantry Journal* 28, no. 4 (April 1926): 406–409; Colonel P. L. Miles, Infantry, "Training of Peace Strength Units," *Infantry Journal* 35, no. 4 (October 1929): 336–339; and the satirical piece by Major Ralph E. Jones, Infantry, "These Recent Factors," *Infantry Journal* 28, no. 2 (February 1926): 148–151, in which the author awakens from a dream of effective training. "Oh, hell!" quote is on 151.

87. Major General Douglas MacArthur (incorrectly spelled "McArthur" in the byline), "The Necessity for Military Forces," *Infantry Journal* 30, no. 3 (March 1927): 327–331. Quote is on 330–331. Italics in original.

88. Brigadier General John Ross Delafield, Ordnance Reserve, "National Defense of the United States," *Infantry Journal* 28, no. 2 (February 1926): 145–146. Quote is from last paragraph on 126.

89. Major General William J. Snow (ret.), "Training for War," *Field Artillery Journal* 30, no. 4 (July–August 1940): 249–260, is one example.

90. Brigadier General Sumter L. Lowry, Jr., 56th FA Brigade, "Is This Perfection?" *Field Artillery Journal* 27, no. 5 (September–October 1937): 333–336.

91. Major C. B. Hodges, General Staff, "Fall Maneuvers, 1921: American Forces in Germany," *Infantry Journal* 19, no. 6 (December 1921): 620–625.

92. Major Adna R. Chaffee, General Staff Corps, "The Maneuvers of the First Cavalry Division, September–October 1923," *Cavalry Journal* 33, no. 135 (April 1934): 133–162.

93. Brigadier General H. B. Fiske, "Maneuvers of the Second Division," *Infantry Journal* 31, no. 3 (September 1927): 225–235; Major George S. Patton Jr., Cavalry, "The 1929 Cavalry Division Maneuvers," *Cavalry Journal* 39, no. 158 (January 1929): 7–15; "The Cavalry Maneuvers at Fort Riley, Kansas 1934," *Cavalry Journal* 43, no. 184 (July–August 1934): 5–14; and Major James T. Duke, Cavalry, G.S.C., "Third Army Maneuvers, Fort Bliss, Texas," *Cavalry Journal* 47, no. 6 (November–December 1938): 528–535.

94. Colonel Conrad H. Lanza, "The First Army Maneuvers," *Field Artillery Journal* 25, no. 6 (November–December 1935): 540–565. Quotes on 541 and 565. Conclusions are on 565. See Lieutenant Colonel John S. Wood, Field Artillery, "Maneuvers and the Umpire System," *Cavalry Journal* 48, no. 3 (May–June 1939): 208–209, and Hanson W. Baldwin, "Maneuvers Reveal Deficiencies," *Cavalry Journal* 48, no. 5 (September–October 1939): 390–391.

95. Examples of reports on CPXs include the Regular Army Infantry, "1st Division Command Post Training," *Infantry Journal* 34, no. 4 (April 1929): 429–430; Organized Reserves, "The Command Post Exercises," *Infantry* 34, no. 2 (February 1929): 214–215; Colonel W. K. Naylor, Infantry, "Command Post Exercises," *Infantry Journal* 36, no. 1 (January 1930): 83–85; Colonel Arthur S. Conklin, General Staff Corps, "III Corps Area Command Post Exer-

cise, Fort George G. Meade—5–19 July, 1930," *Infantry Journal* 37, no. 3 (September 1930): 237–242; Colonel Conrad H. Lanza, Field Artillery, "The First Army CPX," *Field Artillery Journal* 27, no. 6 (November–December 1937): 405–414.

96. See below for more articles by Brigadier General (retired) Hawkins and for a brief description of his service in World War I as chief of staff of 35th Division during its disastrous experiences in the Meuse-Argonne.

97. Brigadier General H. S. Hawkins, "Command Post Exercises," *Infantry Journal* 35, no. 4 (October 1929): 339–345; quotes are on 340 and 342.

98. For a few examples, see Major John J. Bohn, Cavalry, "The Civilian Conservation Corps," *Cavalry Journal* 42, no. 178 (July–August 1933): 41–42; Corporal George Chancellor, 1st Cavalry (Mechanized), "The C.C.C. at Fort Knox, Kentucky," *Cavalry Journal* 42, no. 178 (July–August 1933): 36; Colonel Duncan K. Major Jr., "Yes, Sir, the Army Can!" *Infantry Journal* 40, no. 4 (July–August 1933): 283–288; Representative James W. Wadsworth, New York, "The Army Gets the Job," *Infantry Journal* 40, no. 4 (July–August 1933): 292–293; Captain Leo Donovan, 12th Infantry, "The Establishment of the First Civilian Conservation Camp," *Infantry Journal* 40, no. 4 (July–August 1933): 245–249; and Captain George A. Hunt, 16th Infantry, "Army Publicity Objectives in Connection with the C.C.C.," *Infantry Journal* 40, no. 5 (September–October 1933): 330.

99. "Colonel X," "The Assassination of Initiative," *Infantry Journal* 45, no. 5 (September–October 1938): 412–417.

100. Harmon, *Combat Commander*, 50–53.

101. For a defense of the competitive system, see C. F. Summerall, Chief of Staff, "Field Artillery Progress," *Field Artillery Journal* 20, no. 6 (November–December 1930): 604–608, especially paragraph on bottom of 607.

102. Current Field Artillery Notes, "The Christie Self-Propelled Mount," *Field Artillery Journal* 9, no. 5 (November–December 1919): 603–604.

103. Captain Elmer C. Goebert, Ordnance Department, "Post War Development of the 155mm. Gun, 8" Howitzer," *Field Artillery Journal* 21, no. 3 (May–June 1931): 275–285; Field Artillery Notes, "F. A. Experimental Prime Mover Makes Extraordinary Run," *Field Artillery Journal* 20, no. 6 (November–December 1930): 718; Field Artillery Notes, "105mm Howitzers Issued to Troops," *Field Artillery Journal* 20, no. 6 (November–December 1930): 719.

104. See, among others, Lieutenant Colonel W. P. Coleman, Infantry, former director of experiment at the Infantry School, "The Self-Loading Shoulder Arm," *Infantry* 26, no. 3 (March 1925): 241–266; General Charles P. Summerall, "Infantry Fire," *Infantry Journal* 37, no. 6 (December 1930): 583–586; Captain Bernice M. McFadyen, Infantry, Department of Experiment, "The Present Status of Infantry Development," *Infantry Journal* 38, no. 3 (March–April 1931): 167–173; Major General Stephen O. Fuqua, Chief of Infantry, "Summary of the Infantry," *Infantry Journal* 40, no. 2 (March–April 1933): 140–141; and Major General George A. Lynch, Chief of Infantry, "Current Infantry Developments," *Infantry Journal* 45, no. 1 (January–February 1938): 3–9. Acceptance of the M-1 was announced in the journals; see Frank J. Jervey, Ordnance Engineer, "The New Semiautomatic Rifle," *Cavalry Journal* 47, no. 6 (November–December 1938): 524–527.

105. Notes from the Chief of Infantry, "Cross Country Transportation," *Infantry Journal* 28, no. 1 (January 1926): 69. This particular recommendation for a test of cross-country mobility was, in the next issue of *Infantry Journal*, announced as "laid aside for lack of funds." Notes from the Chief of Infantry, "Motorization of Infantry Regiment," *Infantry Journal* 28, no. 2 (February 1926): 195. Examples include Anonymous, "Accompanying Arms for

Infantry," *Infantry Journal*, 26, no. 6 (June 1925): 621–626; Captain Bernice M. McFadyen, Infantry, Department of Experiment, "The Present Status of Infantry Development," *Infantry Journal* 38, no. 3 (March–April 1931): 167–173; Colonel Alfred T. Smith, General Staff Corps, "Motorization of the 34th Infantry," *Infantry Journal* 38, no. 3 (March–April 1931): 218–221; Brigadier General Campbell King, "The Progress of Infantry Development," *Infantry Journal* 38, no. 3 (March–April 1931): 165–166; Lieutenant Colonel C. H. White, "Motors and Infantry," *Infantry Journal* 40, no. 1 (January–February 1933): 10–13; Major General George A. Lynch, Chief of Infantry, "Current Infantry Developments," *Infantry Journal* 45, no. 1 (January–February 1938): 3–9; and Captain Joseph I. Greene, Infantry, "The Case for Antitank," *Infantry Journal* 45, no. 3 (May–June 1938): 213–222.

106. Two examples are Major Bradford Chynoweth, Infantry, Tanks, "Cavalry Tanks," *Cavalry Journal* 30, no. 124 (July 1921): 247–251 and Major G. S. Patton Jr., "Armored Cars with Cavalry," *Cavalry Journal* 33, no. 134 (January 1924): 5–10. Major Leo C. Hefferman, Air Service, "Co-operation between Cavalry and Air Service," *Cavalry Journal* 34, no. 139 (April 1925): 147–154.

107. Timothy K. Nenninger, "The Experimental Mechanized Forces," *Armor* 78, no. 3 (May–June 1969): 33–39. Also see Robert S. Cameron, *Mobility, Shock, and Firepower: The Emergence of the U.S. Army's Armor Branch, 1917–1945* (Washington, DC: U.S. Army Center of Military History, 2008), 32–43.

108. Captain Dwight D. Eisenhower wrote an article typical of the early discussion for the November 1920 edition of *Infantry Journal*. Captain D. D. Eisenhower, "A Tank Discussion," *Infantry Journal* 17, no. 5 (November 1920): 453–458.

109. Some examples included Topics of the Day, "Mechanized Force Recommended," *Cavalry Journal* 3, no. 158 (January 1929): 112–113; Editorial Comment, "Progress in Material," *Infantry Journal* 30, no. 5 (May 1927): 531–533; and General C. P. Summerall, "New Developments in Warfare," *Infantry* 38, no. 2 (February 1931): 91–93; and a simultaneous publication by Summerall, "New Developments in Warfare," *Cavalry Journal* 40, no. 163 (February 1931): 8–10. Reports on the actual experimental force were numerous. Examples include Captain Arthur Wilson, Field Artillery, "The Mechanized Force: Its Organization and Present Equipment," *Cavalry Journal* 40, no. 165 (May–June 1931): 7–10, simultaneously published in *Infantry Journal* 38, no. 4 (May–June 1931): 252–256, and "With the Mechanized Force on Maneuvers," *Cavalry Journal* 40, no. 166 (July–August 1931): 5–9.

110. Editorial Comment, "Mechanization of Military Forces," *Infantry Journal* 30, no. 5 (May 1927): 533–535.

111. Lieutenant Colonel K. B. Edmunds, "Tactics of a Mechanized Force: A Prophecy," *Field Artillery Journal* 20, no. 4 (July–August 1930): 387–395; simultaneously published as "Tactics of a Mechanized Force: A Prophecy," *Cavalry Journal* 39, no. 160 (July 1930): 410–417. A similar article: Major C. C. Benson, "Tank Divisions," *Infantry Journal* 38, no. 1 (January 1931): 15–19. For the British view, see Colonel J. F. C. Fuller, British Army, "Tactics and Mechanization," *Infantry Journal* 30, no. 5 (May 1927): 457–476; Captain B. H. Liddell Hart, "The British Army Exercises of 1930," *Cavalry Journal* 40, no. 163 (February 1931): 39–44; and "Foreign Views on Mechanization," *Cavalry Journal* 40, no. 166 (July–August 1931): 39–40, 64. The German view was presented by, among others, Major General Heinz Guderian, German Army, in a two-part series in *Infantry Journal*, "Armored Forces, Part One," *Infantry Journal* 44, no. 5 (September–October 1937): 418–421; and "Armored Forces, Part Two: Co-operation between Armored Forces and Other Arms," *Infantry Journal* 44, no. 6 (November–December 1937): 522–528.

112. Nenninger, "Experimental Mechanized Forces," 33–39, quote on 34.

113. Nenninger, "Experimental Mechanized Forces," 33–39, quote on 39.

114. Timothy K. Nenninger, "A Revised Mechanization Policy," *Armor* 78, no. 5 (September–October 1969): 45–49.

115. For a participant's view, see Peter R. Mansoor and Kathy Cast Garth, eds., "Ten Lean Years: From the Mechanized Force (1930) to the Armored Force (1940)," by Major General Robert W. Grow, *Armor Magazine* 96, no. 1 (January–February 1987): 22–30; 96, no. 2 (March–April 1987): 25–33; 96, no. 3 (May–June 1987): 21–28; and 96, no. 4 (July–August 1987): 34–42.

116. For example, see Major General Leon B. Kromer, "Address of Major General Leon B. Kromer, Chief of Cavalry, at Fort Riley, Kansas, During the April-May Maneuvers," *Cavalry Journal* 43, no. 183 (May–June 1934): 44–46; and, reporting on the War Department decision, "Mechanized Force Becomes Cavalry," *Cavalry Journal* 40, no. 165 (May–June 1931): 5–6.

117. Kromer, "Address," 46.

118. "Forecast of Field Artillery Progress During the Next Five Years," *Field Artillery Journal* 23, no. 6 (November–December 1933): 508–513; and Major B. H. Perry, 68th Field Artillery, "Mechanized Field Artillery: Its Organization, Functioning, and Tactical Equipment," *Field Artillery Journal* 38, no. 2 (March–April 1938): 96–108.

119. Colonel Fred H. Wagner, ORC, "Possibilities of the Tank," *Infantry Journal* 38, no. 4 (May–June 1931): 273–277; and Captain Lee Baylor Stanton, Infantry Reserve, "Horsepower vs. Manpower," *Infantry Journal* 44, no. 6 (November–December 1937): 540. Also see Major "Knutson Boltz," Tank Corps, "Development of Tank Tactics, 1937–1939," *Infantry Journal* 42, no. 4 (July–August 1935): 327–332; and the *Field Artillery Journal* 1936 prize essay contest winner, Captain John P. Eckert, Field Artillery, "Trace Chains and Caissons Farewell," *Field Artillery Journal* 26, no. 2 (March–April 1936): 117–140.

120. See, for example, "Fortissimo," "Close Harmony," in "Cerebrations" column, *Infantry Journal* 44, no. 3 (May–June 1937): 261, for the view that combined arms, despite the claims of various branches, remained the ultimate battlefield requirement—the requirement for "close harmony."

121. Matthew Darlington Morton, "Men on 'Iron Horses': The Death and Rebirth of Modern U.S. Cavalry," Ph.D. diss., Florida State University, 2004, 501.

122. "Confessions of an Ex-Horseman," *Field Artillery Journal* 25, no. 4 (July–August 1935): 343–344. For the same perspective, see Observer, "Motors in Mississippi," "Cerebrations," *Infantry Journal* 45, no. 5 (September–October 1938): 456–457.

123. Samuel P. Huntington, *Soldier and the State: The Theory and Politics of Civil-Military Relations* (Cambridge: Harvard University Press, 1957), 15.

124. Major General James McAndrew, "Introductory Remarks by the Commandant," in "Addresses Delivered at the Graduating Exercises, General Staff College, June 29, 1920," MHI, AWCCA, Box Curriculum 1919–1920, Volume 6: Special Course Volume 8 Field Exercises, 1.

125. Major John H. Burns, "The American Professional Soldier," *Infantry Journal* 47, no. 5 (September–October 1940): 418–423. Quote from page 422.

126. The Treves meeting is discussed in passing in Harry P. Ball, *Of Responsible Command: A History of the U.S. Army War College* (Carlisle Barracks, PA: Alumni Association of the U.S. Army War College, 1983), 155–156. It is also mentioned briefly in Colonel Harry A. Smith, Infantry, "General Staff College Course," *Infantry* 18, no. 1 (January 1921): 51–57. McAndrew had served as the chief of staff of the AEF from May 1918 through the end of the war, had been commandant of the general staff schools at Fort Leavenworth, and was first

commandant of the AEF schools. Ball, *Responsible Command*, 154; Nenninger, *Leavenworth Schools*, 136. For a tribute to McAndrew, see "Varied Ground," "General Pershing's Tribute to General McAndrew," *Infantry Journal* 20, no. 6 (June 1922): 665–666. Ball, *Responsible Command*, 176.

127. Telegram no. 3253R, dated April 19, 1919, recorded on April 20, 1919, in NAII Record Group 120, Records of the American Expeditionary Force, Box 20 of 1918–1919 Cables.

128. Memorandum for the Chief of Staff, May 24, 1919, from Lytle Brown, Brigadier General, Director, WPD, "Subject: Names of Officers selected from AEF for duties connected with the School of the Line." NAII RG 165 (Records of the War Department General Staff), Office of the Chief of Staff Correspondence, 1918–1921, 1275–1292, Box 169, folder 1277, School of the Line. For information on Muir, see *CSFG*; Eisenhower, *Yanks*, 207–208; Harbord, *The American Army in France*, 444, 448; Cooke, *Pershing and His Generals*, 149.

129. "Memorandum to Accompany Proposed Revision of Article XIV. Compilation of Orders—Embracing the Subject of Military Education," Office of the Chief of Staff, War Plans Division. Cover letter dated March 8, 1919, signed by George F. Baltzell, Colonel, General Staff, War Department Office of the Chief of Staff. NAII RG 407, Box 808, folder 352 (10-13-19) to (10-4-18).

130. "Memorandum—Military Education," 1–3.

131. Brigadier General Lytle Brown, Memorandum for the Chief of Staff, "Subject: Occupancy of Quarters by Officers Not on Duty at the Army Service Schools Fort Leavenworth," December 14, 1918, NAII RG 165, Box 13, Folder 58, Army Service School.

132. Letter, George C. Marshall, Washington, D.C., July 9, 1920, to Major General James W. McAndrew, reproduced in Bland, *Soldierly Spirit*, 195–196. Letter available in MHI, AWCCA, Box 003 062.1 1.34, Letter, George C. Marshall to Major General McAndrew, July 9, 1920, with marginal note in pencil requiring copies to be furnished to directors at the War College.

133. Bland, *Soldierly Spirit*, 197.

134. Ibid. Corroborated in "Notes of Conference of Directors General Staff College, July 12, 1920," MHI, AWCCA, Box 003, 062.1 1.34.

135. A very useful summary of the McGlachlin and Fiske boards, and a précis of student selection criteria for the Leavenworth schools and the Army War College, are found in Memorandum for the Chief of Coast Artillery, "Subject: Operation of the School System with Special Reference to the Coast Artillery Corps, December 28, 1931." Located in NAII RG165, WDGS G1 (Personnel) Numerical File 1921–1942, 12311–12675, Box 85, Folder 12585–12600. Both boards are also addressed in Ball, *Responsible Command*, 180–186 and 194–195.

136. NAII RG 407, Office of the Adjutant General, Central Decimal Correspondence File, Bulky Packages, 352.01 (2-4-22) (1) "Report of Board of Officers Re-Study of Army School System" (hereafter cited as McGlachlin Report).

137. There was at least one dissenting opinion on every major recommendation. McGlachlin Report, 4–6.

138. Colonel H. B. Fiske, General Staff, "Minority Report," in McGlachlin Report.

139. "Dissenting Opinion by General McGlachlin as to Certain Majority Recommendations," in McGlachlin Report.

140. U.S. War Department, "Special Orders No. 175, July 28, 1922," and "Letter of Instructions for Board, August 16, 1922," paragraphs 2 and 3. Documents found in NAII RG 407, Bulky Packages, 352.01 (9-5-22) (1) Pro. B/O Record Board of Officers, Package No. 1066 (hereafter cited as Fiske Report).

141. The service schools, each run by their own branches, were required, according to the board's recommendations, to "train competent leaders of [each branch's] units and provide instructors for the Regular Army, National Guard, Organized Reserves, R.O.T.C. and C.M.T.C." Fiske Report, pp. 5, 12, and 15. There also existed, for a brief period, an Educational Advisory Board, but it was ineffectual. Educational Advisory Board (EAB), "Report, 22 October 1924." NAII RG 407, Box 806, Folder 352 (11-3-24) to (10-30-24). This appears to have been the only formal meeting of this board. See discussions for the 1925 EAB in NAII RG 407, Box 806, Folder 352 (7-28-25) to (11-24-24); for the on-again off-again EAB of 1926, see RG 407, Box 808, folder 352.01 (10-13-25) to (6-26-25). For the 1927 EAB, see RG 407, Box 2045, which contains the records of the June 20, 1927, Corps Area and Division Commander's Conference.

142. The role of these commandants, and others as well, is told by George S. Pappas, *Prudens Futuri: The U.S. Army War College, 1901–1967* (Carlisle Barracks, PA: Alumni Association of the U.S. Army War College, 1967), 89–129.

143. Much higher-quality analysis than Pappas is Ball, *Of Responsible Command,* 210–214.

144. Ibid., 212–213.

145. U.S. War Department, "Army Regulations, No. 350-5, Military Education," Washington, D.C., July 1925, 8.

146. The most recent and, in some respects, the most comprehensive discussion of this issue is in Coffman's *The Regulars,* ch. 7, "The Army in Limbo." For the professionalism and competence of regular army officers, see the works of Keith Bonn, Peter Mansoor, and John Sloan Brown, among others.

147. See, as a single example, Abrahamson, *America Arms,* 186.

Chapter 2. The Essence of Modern War

1. The critical framework of stabilized front versus mobile warfare I owe to Paul J. Jacobsmeyer. Addressed in his master's thesis, "Intelligence in the American Expeditionary Force: The Experience of the Thirty-Second Division, September 1917–November 1918," University of Wisconsin, 1986, and further clarified in classes he has taught at the School of Advanced Military Studies, U.S. Army Command and General Staff College, from 2005 through 2008. This author found reflected in the interwar professional journals the concepts that Jacobsmeyer identified in several critical AEF documents.

2. Headquarters, Thirty-Second Division, AEF, "Tactical Note No. 7," September 24, 1918. NAII, Record Group 120, 32nd Division Records, 50.4/56.3, Box 14, folder 232-50.4, block quote on 4, other quotes from 1 and 5. For a different interpretation, see Mark Ethan Grotelueschen, *The AEF Way of War: The American Army and Combat in World War I* (New York: Cambridge University Pres, 2007), ch. 1.

3. All quotes from Lieutenant Colonel Oliver L. Spaulding, General Staff, "The Tactics of the War with Germany," *Infantry Journal* 17, no. 3 (September 1920): 228–240. For several of his lectures, see the CARL electronic sources at www.cgsc.army.mil/carl/resources/archival/lectures.asp; accessed June 6, 2007. For his background, see Stetson Conn, "Historical Work in the United States Army 1862–1954" (Washington, DC: U.S. Army Center of Military History, 1980).

4. Spaulding, "Tactics," 228–240.

5. Ibid., 235–235.

6. "Motorization" is generally used in the interwar period to describe transportation using internal combustion engine vehicles. "Mechanization" usually describes armored combat vehicles, frequently but not always tracked, for all arms. Major H. A. Flint Jr., Cavalry, "What a Cavalryman Should Know of the Air," *Cavalry Journal* 42, no. 178 (July–August 1933): 5–11; and an editorial, "War Turns Its Full Face," *Infantry Journal* 47, no. 3 (May–June 1940): 283–287, among many others. Also see Captain H. E. Fuller, Infantry, "On Divorcing the Air Service," *Infantry Journal* 28, no. 3 (March 1926): 243–249, and Dallas D. Irvine, "The Misuse of Air Power," *Infantry Journal* 44, no. 3 (May–June 1937): 255–256; Major Leonard R. Boyd, Infantry, and 1st Lieutenant Joseph I. Greene, Infantry, "Infantry vs. Attack Aviation," *Infantry Journal* 36, no. 5 (May 1930): 461–474; Major John D. Reardan, Air Service, "Action of Attack Aviation," *Infantry Journal* 28, no. 2 (February 1926): 129–134. Air Liaison for artillery fires was an occasional topic, including "Aerial Observation," *Field Artillery Journal* 30, no. 5 (September–October 1940): 355. Artillery liaison as reconnaissance is discussed in an editorial comment, "Will the Airplane Supplant the Cavalry," *Infantry Journal* 29, no. 5 (November 1926): 553–555. Also of note is Brigadier General Lesley J. McNair, "And Now the Autogiro," *Field Artillery Journal* 27, no. 1 (January–February 1937): 5–17.

7. When combined arms were discussed in *Infantry Journal*, it was frequently couched in terms of other branch support for infantry.

8. Major B. C. Chynoweth, Infantry, "Tank Infantry," *Infantry Journal* 18, no. 5 (May 1921): 504–507. Block quote and description of war's end on 504, description of tank infantry on 507.

9. Major General J. F. C. Fuller, British Army, joined in with an article in 1931 that outlined the need for careful planning, by all arms, for any successful attack on the modern battlefield. Major General J. F. C. Fuller, "Co-ordination of the Attack," *Infantry Journal* 38, no. 1 (January 1931): 12–14.

10. As mere examples, in 1922, Major Owen Meredith, a chemical warfare officer, called on infantrymen to embrace automatic weapons as a means of achieving fire superiority, not the rifle alone. Major Owen R. Meredith, CWS, "If Not, Why Not!" *Infantry Journal* 21, no. 4 (October 1922): 410–421.

11. "Fundamentals of Infantry Tactics," *Infantry Journal* 26, no. 1 (January 1925): 47–52. Block quote from first paragraph, on 47.

12. One example of many is Captain R. H. Case, Infantry, "Artillery Support in the Attack," *Infantry Journal* 42, no. 3 (May–June 1935): 247–252. This issue was one of the most extensively covered in both *Infantry Journal* and *Field Artillery Journal*.

13. Major General George Lynch, Chief of Infantry, "Firepower. Man Power. Maneuver," *Infantry Journal* 46, no. 6 (November–December 1939): 498–505, 606.

14. Examples of the three types include Major General William J. Snow, Chief, Field Artillery, "Interesting Diagrams," *Field Artillery Journal* 15, no. 4 (July–August 1925): 323–329; Major General Edward F. McGlachlin, "Army Artillery in Meuse-Argonne," *Field Artillery Journal* 28, no. 5 (November 1923): 544–552; Major Elmer Yeager, Field Artillery, "Supporting Artillery," *Field Artillery Journal* 19, no. 3 (September 1921): 307–311.

15. Snow, "Interesting Diagrams"; quote on 329, figures from chart on 328.

16. See, among others, the discussion in Major General J. B. A. Bailey, *Field Artillery and Firepower* (Annapolis: Naval Institute Press, 2004), 317–327; and Russell A. Hart, *Clash of Arms: How the Allies Won in Normandy* (Boulder: Lynne Rienner, 2001), 277–280. For the effect of artillery fire in World War II on a tactical engagement, see Mark J. Reardon's masterful *Victory at Mortain: Stopping Hitler's Panzer Counteroffensive* (Lawrence: University Press of Kansas, 2002), especially ch. 9.

17. Major Leo G. Hefferman, Air Service, "Co-operation between Cavalry and Air Service," *Cavalry Journal* 34, no. 139 (April 1925): 147–154; Major George Dillman, GSC, "Joint Cavalry and Air Corps Training," *Cavalry Journal* 36, no. 149 (October 1927): 560–567; Major H. H. Arnold, "The Cavalry-Air Corps Team," *Cavalry Journal* 37, no. 150 (January 1928): 70–76; and Major H. A. Flint, Cavalry, "What a Cavalryman Should Know of the Air," *Cavalry Journal* 42, no. 178 (July–August 1933): 5–11. Another theme of the interwar journals was cooperation between artillery and cavalry. Two examples are Major Edmund L. Gruber, Field Artillery, "Field Artillery with Cavalry," *Cavalry Journal* 37, no. 150 (January 1928): 80–93; and First Lieutenant John F. Greco, Field Artillery, "The Cavalry-Artillery Team," *Field Artillery Journal* 29, no. 2 (March–April 1939): 130–141.

18. Lieutenant Colonel Kinzie B. Edmunds, Cavalry, Instructor, Field Artillery School, "The Cavalry-Artillery-Aviation Team," *Cavalry Journal* 42, no. 176 (March–April 1933): 7–11.

19. Westervelt Board, "Study of the Armament and Types of Artillery Material to Be Assigned to a Field Army," *Field Artillery Journal* 9, no. 3 (July–August 1919): 289–347. Quote on 105mm optimum weapon on 295, probable future motorization on 300, discussion of caterpillar advantage on 311, motorization progress in 1919 on 331–332. Due to the 4,500-pound horse-drawn weight limit, all AEF corps and army artillery was already motorized out of sheer physical necessity. In fact, the motorization program for divisional 75mm batteries had already begun and would have been completed "had the war lasted a few months longer, or if ship bottoms had been available during the war." Only some of the divisional batteries were to be left horsed, to retain cross-country capable "accompanying guns" for immediate infantry support.

20. Motorization of artillery for the occupation forces in Germany in 1919 and 1920 continued, at least for the heavy artillery regiments. See James Scott Wheeler, *The Big Red One: America's Legendary 1st Infantry Division from World War I to Desert Storm* (Lawrence: University Press of Kansas, 2007), 109.

21. The following articles were all lead pieces for their issues of the *Field Artillery Journal*: Captain M. R. Cox, Field Artillery, "Truck-Drawn Artillery," *Field Artillery Journal* 21, no. 3 (May–June 1931): 223–244; Captain W. C. Dunckel, FA, "The Truck-Drawn Battery," *Field Artillery Journal* 22, no. 3 (May–June 1932): 245–263; and Major J. H. Wallace, Field Artillery, "Test of the Truck-Drawn 75mm Battery," *Field Artillery Journal* 23, no. 4 (July–August 1933): 301–319. There were many more articles about motorization in *Field Artillery Journal*.

22. Major Stuart H. Clapp, Infantry, Officer Reserve Corps, "Motor Transportation of the Future," *Infantry Journal* 26, no. 1 (January 1925): 34–36.

23. Captain Charles L. Bolté, Infantry, "The Future of Infantry, Part III," *Infantry Journal* 35, no. 5 (November 1929): 458–465, quote on 463.

24. Major L. D. Davis, Infantry, "M^2.I.," *Infantry Journal* 36, no. 6 (June 1930): 655–658, quote on 656.

25. Leon B. Kromer, "A Message," *Cavalry Journal* 47, no. 2 (March–April 1938): 145.

26. Major General Herr, the new chief of cavalry, was quoted in a *Cavalry Journal* reprint of congressional testimony that getting mechanical-minded soldiers was easier than getting horse-minded soldiers: "we have become mechanically minded people because this is a motor country." Herr pointed out that even in a horse cavalry division all supplies and the entire reconnaissance unit were motorized and all antitank guns and mortars were carried on motor vehicles. Herr continued by admitting that horse cavalry still exceeded mechanized cavalry, in his opinion, in cross-country mobility. The future, however, was open to adjustment in the percentage of cavalry that was "partly mechanized." Major General John K. Herr, "Cavalry

Affairs in Congress," *Cavalry Journal* 49, no. 3 (May–June 1940): 201–206, quotes from 201 and 206, motorization of cavalry division elements from 203.

27. See, as examples, Brigadier General Henry J. Riley, "Horsed Cavalry and the Gas Engine's Children," *Cavalry Journal* 49, no. 1 (January–February 1940): 2–9; and Colonel H. S. Stewart, Late 15th Lancers, Indian Army, "Mechanization and Motorization: The Final Chapter Has Not Yet Been Written," *Cavalry Journal* 49, no. 1 (January–February 1940): 35–44.

28. Part of the Hawkins story is told in Alexander M. Bielakowski, "General Hawkins's War: The Future of the Horse in the U.S. Cavalry," *Journal of Military History* 71 (January 2007): 126–138.

29. Brigadier General H. S. Hawkins, "We Must Have Cavalry," *Cavalry Journal* 46, no. 5 (September–October 1937): 405.

30. Brigadier General H. S. Hawkins, "Air and Mechanized Warfare," *Cavalry Journal* 49, no. 5 (September–October 1940); comment about aerial bombardment on 434, block quote from end of article on 435.

31. Robert H. Ferrell, *Collapse at the Meuse-Argonne: The Failure of the Kansas-Missouri Division* (Columbia: University of Missouri Press, 2004), 45, for Hawkins's failure to relieve a commander as ordered; 48–49 for ignoring the corps order; 52 for getting lost; 60 for Hawkins looking for something to do; 64 for general failure of coordination within the division, obviously a primary task of the chief of staff; and 111 for a list of the failings of the division and division staff. Brigadier General H. S. Hawkins, "General Hawkins' Notes," *Cavalry Journal* 49, no. 3 (May–June 1940): 268.

32. Major R. W. Grow, Cavalry, "Mechanized Cavalry," *Cavalry Journal* 47, no. 1 (January–February 1938): 30–31. For a biography of Grow, see George F. Hofmann, *Cold War Casualty: The Court-Martial of Major General Robert W. Grow* (Kent, OH: Kent State University Press, 1993). All uppercase CAVALRY in original.

33. From note at bottom of first page of Grow's article, "Mechanized Cavalry."

34. For a stimulating discussion of artillery casualties in World War I, see John Mosier, *The Myth of the Great War: How the Germans Won the Battles and the Americans Saved the Allies* (New York: HarperCollins, 2001), 2–3 and passim.

35. Captain Francis A. Woolfley, "Queen of Infantry Weapons," *Infantry Journal* 21, no. 3 (September 1922): 308–310. Quotes on 308, italics in original.

36. Ibid., 310. Italics in original.

37. Major General J. F. C. Fuller, "The Infantry Muddle and a Solution," *Infantry Journal* 38, no. 5 (July–August 1931): 327–330. Quote is from 327.

38. Sergeant Terry Bull, "Bayonet Fever," *Infantry Journal* 47, no. 5 (September–October 1940): 457–461. Quote on 457–458. Bull's identity remains a puzzle—it may have been a nom de plume.

39. Notes from the Chief of Infantry, "Field Manuals," *Infantry Journal* 30, no. 4 (April 1930): 418–421. Quote on 418.

40. Varied Ground, "Training Regulations Published," *Infantry Journal* 23, no. 6 (December 1923): 699–700.

41. Chief of Infantry, "Field Manuals," 418–421.

42. For an innovative and compelling assessment of some of Pershing's peculiar ideas as strategic national policy requirements, see Michael D. Pearlman, *Warmaking and American Democracy: The Struggle over Military Strategy, 1700 to the Present* (Lawrence: University Press of Kansas, 1999), ch. 6.

43. See William O. Odom, *After the Trenches: The Transformation of U.S. Army Doctrine,*

1918–1939 (College Station: Texas A&M University Press, 1999). Odom's interpretation, focusing on the 1923 *FSR* and the 1939 *FSR*, is markedly different from the one offered in this book.

44. For a listing of the field manuals, see U.S. War Department, *Staff Officers' Field Manual, Part One: Staff Data, September 26, 1932* (Washington, DC: Government Printing Office, 1932). The only book-length assessment of these technical manuals is Kenneth Finlayson, *An Uncertain Trumpet: The Evolution of U.S. Army Infantry Doctrine, 1919–1941* (Westport, CT: Greenwood, 2001), an assessment limited to the infantry branch.

45. Two examples included a simple list, Varied Ground, "Training Regulations Published," *Infantry Journal* 23, no. 6 (December 1923): 699–700; and a more detailed description of the new doctrine in Major C. G. Helmick, Field Artillery, "The New TR 430-85, Gunnery for Field Artillery," *Field Artillery Journal* 20, no. 5 (September–October 1930): 481–490.

46. Examples in the journals include Major C. G. Helmick, Field Artillery, "The New TR 430-85, Gunnery for Field Artillery," *Field Artillery Journal* 20, no. 5 (September–October 1930): 481–490, an article that goes into great detail about a new training regulation; Varied Ground, "Training Regulations Published," *Infantry Journal* 23, no. 6 (December 1923): 699–700, which lists new regulations; and Notes from the Chief of Infantry, "Field Manuals," *Infantry Journal* 30, no. 4 (April 1930): 418–421, which discusses a new system of field manuals replacing some regulations.

47. Captain Harold D. Shannon, USMC, "Artillery in Landing Operations," *Field Artillery Journal* 24, no. 5 (November–December 1934): 515–537; First Lieutenant W. H. Kennett, Field Artillery, "Maintenance of the Truck-Drawn Battery," *Field Artillery Journal* 24, no. 4 (July–August 1934): 381–401; and Lieutenant Colonel William G. Livesay, Infantry, "Shuttling," *Infantry Journal* 47, no. 1 (January–February 1940): 31–33.

48. Lieutenant Colonel Spaulding led the call for new doctrine in his 1920 article in *Infantry Journal*. He did not specify a particular doctrine but that "we must get at our principles by a study of what actually happened." Spaulding, "Tactics of the War with Germany," *Infantry Journal* (September 1920): 228.

49. Two of these articles, from 1933 and 1934, discussed the challenge of the duality of fire and maneuver, and discussed them as incompatible: Colonel Albert S. Williams, Infantry, "Our Present Tactical Doctrine," *Infantry Journal* 40, no. 2 (March–April 1933): 97; and Lieutenant Colonel J. M. Scammel, National Guard, "The Infantry Division: A System for Determining Its Organization," *Infantry Journal* 41, no. 2 (March–April 1934): 111–116.

50. For example, a September–October 1932 article in *Cavalry Journal* asked for the human element to be added to the doctrinal discussion of estimates of the situation. Colonel Weston Jenkins, 390th Infantry, "The Imponderables in an estimate of the Situation: As Illustrated by Stonewall Jackson's Valley Campaign," *Cavalry Journal* 41, no. 173 (September–October 1932): 33–39.

51. "Field Service Regulations: Study of Combat Principles," *Infantry Journal* 17, no. 5 (November 1920): 480–482, discussed what new regulations should be written, how they should be taught, and the general role of the professional schools. Bernard Lentz, "A Decade of Army Schools," *Cavalry Journal* 41, no. 173 (September–October 1932): 46–48, used *Cavalry Journal* as a platform for his critique of both doctrine and officer education. Major John D. Townsend, "Practical Employment of Field Artillery," *Field Artillery Journal* 42, no. 5 (September–October 1935): 416–418, reads like a school problem from Sill or Leavenworth.

52. Colonel Ralph Talbot Jr., Field Artillery, "The Defensive-Offensive Maneuver," *Field Artillery Journal* 27, no. 2 (March–April 1937): 112–122.

53. "Tactical Employment of the Mechanized Division (Tentative)" (Command and General Staff School Press, 1937), CARL curriculum archives, 1937–1938 class.

54. *Manual for Commanders of Large Units* served as the guide for corps and army commanders and staff officers from 1930 through World War II. These manuals are examined below.

55. In the 1939 and 1941 editions, *"ultimate objective"* was italicized. U.S. War Department, *Field Service Regulations, United States Army, 1923* (Washington, DC: Government Printing Office, 1923), 77; U.S. War Department, *Tentative Field Service Regulations, Operations FM 100-5* (Washington, DC: Government Printing Office, 1939), 27; U.S. War Department, *Field Service Regulations, War Department, FM 100-5, May 22, 1941* (Washington, DC: Government Printing Office, 1923), 22; U.S. War Department, *War Department Field Manual FM 100-5, Field Service Regulations, Operations, 15 June 1944* (Washington, DC: Government Printing Office, 1944), 32. These manuals hereafter cited as 1923 *FSR*, 1939 *FSR*, 100-5 (1941) and 100-5 (1944).

56. 1923 *FSR*, iii. See very similar comments in the 1939 *FSR*, ii, an expanded version which retained the meaning in 100-5 (1941), ii, and a statement identical to the 41 statement in 100-5 (1944), ii.

57. The manuals from 1923 and 1939 used "principles"; those from 1941 and 1944 used "objectives."

58. Even Russell Weigley summarized this sentiment into a concise statement of the army's educational programs that the "emphasis always was on the intractability of modern strategic problems to any solution save that of overwhelming power." Russell F. Weigley, "The Interwar Army, 1919–1941," in Kenneth J. Hagan and William R. Roberts, eds., *Against All Enemies: Interpretations of American Military History from Colonial Times to the Present* (New York: Greenwood, 1986), 269. Quote in text from Weigley, "Interwar Army," 258.

59. 1923 *FSR*, 1939 *FSR*, and 100-5 (1941). For a discussion of the alterations in doctrine in the 1923 and 1939 versions, see Odom, *After the Trenches*.

60. To establish if the essence of army doctrine continued unchanged in major form from 1923 through 1944, the doctrine was compared across all four editions, using the discussions of types of organizations; command and control; the concept of combined arms; the functions of the infantry, artillery, and cavalry branches; the function of tanks and mechanized forces; the role of airpower; the principles of land combat; and the concepts of offensive operations.

61. 1923 *FSR*, iii.

62. The army, the next level, had both operational and administrative functions. The army group, consisting of two or more armies, was necessary only under conditions of extended frontages. The general headquarters exercised control over all subordinate formations, including the services of supply at the theater level. 1923 *FSR*, 1–2.

63. 1923 *FSR*, 4.

64. Ibid., 4–5.

65. Subordinate staff officers were referred to the *Staff Manual* for additional guidance. Ibid., 5.

66. Ibid., iii.

67. Ibid., 11–13.

68. Ibid., 13.

69. Ibid., 14–15.

70. Ibid., 17–19.

71. As examined below, the attack mission became gradually more and more marginal. Ibid., 17–24.

72. Ibid., 77.

73. Ibid., 77–78.

74. Ibid., 88–89.

75. Ibid., 96.

76. Ibid., 97.

77. For background, see Ferrell, *America's Deadliest Battle.*

78. 1923 *FSR,* 79.

79. The 1923 version used language familiar to the authors of "Tactical Note No. 7"—the "stabilized front" and "open warfare." These forms of combat exist in all four editions of the manual, with only minor alterations in execution. The penetration of the front, either in a stabilized environment or in a localized attack, was necessary to generate the war of movement or open warfare where initiative and rapid decision making would create the conditions for the destruction of the enemy force. See previous discussion of "Tactical Note No. 7." These phrases are in 1923 *FSR,* 90 and 96.

80. 1923 *FSR,* 79.

81. See Odom, *After the Trenches,* for a discussion of the different writing environments of the 1923 and 1939 FSRs. His conclusion, 241–242, that the 1939 edition was flawed due to a lack of a doctrine development system in the army is based on the assumption that the *FM 100-5* 1941 and 1944 editions were significantly different from the 1923 and 1939. As shown below, this assumption is not substantiated by a direct comparison of the doctrine or by a comparison of warfare itself in its 1918 and 1944 stabilized front forms. The purpose of land combat operations; the mandate for combined arms; almost all of the discussion of infantry, artillery, and cavalry; the differentiation of command from staff; the use of principles; and much of the discussion of the offensive remained nearly identical to the 1923 *FSR.* The purpose of land combat operations is found in 1939 *FSR* on 27; the mandate for combined arms on ii and 5; the discussion of infantry, artillery, and cavalry on 5–13. The differentiation of command from staff is in ch. 4, 33–37, and the use of principles on ii.

82. The section of combat in woods now contained a discussion of combat in urban areas. See 1939 *FSR,* Contents.

83. See 1939 *FSR,* 163–164 and 165–166.

84. Discussion of mechanized cavalry is in ibid., 9–10. Use of "stabilized front" is on 154, and "moving situations" is on 142.

85. Ibid., 14–148.

86. Ibid., 15–17.

87. The writing of the 1941 and 1944 versions of this critical manual has never been studied by any military historian. Christopher Gabel, in his preface to the reprint edition of *FM 100-5* (1941), called the manual a classic piece of doctrine-writing, remarkable for its clarity of concept and prose. He is correct, but how the manual was written, and under what bureaucratic environment, remains undiscovered country.

88. The description of infantry remained intact, but now the weapons of the infantry were explicitly the rifle, the bayonet, the automatic rifle, and the machine gun. However, it was thought sound to mention that the entrenching tool was also an "essential article of equipment." *100-5* (1941), ii, 2–3, 6, and 41.

89. Now divided into sixteen chapters, this version retained chapters on organization, arms and services, command, intelligence, and reconnaissance at the start of the manual. A new very short chapter, titled "Leadership," was added before the chapter on command. Particular forms of operations continued to be the next section, with security, halts, and troop movements chapters. Ibid., "Contents," iii–v.

90. The field artillery section was moved behind the discussion of cavalry. Ibid., 8–10.

91. One alteration to the 1923 and 1939 editions was the addition that cavalry could be assigned to work as part of an infantry division, or could be made an organic component, being named divisional cavalry. Ibid., 6–8.

92. Ibid., 22–23.

93. Ibid., 22–30. Parts of this chapter were adopted from portions of earlier chapters on combat orders, information (intelligence), and transmission of orders.

94. Much of the infantry division discussion, itself only two pages long, was a discussion of the differences between the square and triangular divisions. Ibid., 253–254. The cavalry division discussion included more detail on the execution of the cavalry missions contained in the 1923 and 1939 FSRs, with the addition of a new task—the delay. Ibid., 257–262.

95. The motorized division, destined never to be fielded in combat, was a discussion of a new form of division that had internal to assigned structure the motor transportation necessary to simultaneously move the entire division. Ibid., 255–257; see also Maurice Matloff, "The 90 Division Gamble," in Kent Roberts Greenfield, ed., *Command Decisions* (Washington, DC: Office of the Chief of Military History, 1959; reprint ed., 1977), 374.

96. *100-5* (1941), 263–277. The World War II experience did not match these expectations.

97. For example, in the *Truppenführung* appears: "In spite of technique, the worth of the man is the decisive factor." In *FM 100-5* this became "in spite of the advances in technology, the worth of the individual man is still decisive." Several sections of the *FM 100-5* chapter on leadership are not addressed in the German manual and appear to be wholly an invention of the authors of the American manual, including comments on reward: "The commander should promptly extend recognition for services well done, lend help where help is needed, and give encouragement in adversity." The German version stated, with no American counterpart: "In all situations every leader must exert, without evasion of responsibility, his whole personality. Willing and joyful acceptance of responsibility is the distinguishing characteristic of leadership." Direct, phrase-by-phrase comparison of *FM 100-5* (1941) and *Truppenführung*, 1933. See *100-5* (1941), 1–21, and Report no. 14,507, translation of *Truppenführung* published by staff and faculty of CGSS, in 1936 or 1937, 1–6. Document available in CARL, with signature of Lieutenant Colonel F. W. Milburn, an instructor at Leavenworth from 1934 to 1938.

98. *100-5* (1941), 12–14.

99. Ibid., 101–103.

100. Ibid.

101. Ibid., stabilized front section on 124, war of movement section at 112–116.

102. Michael D. Doubler, *Closing with the Enemy: How GIs Fought the War in Europe* (Lawrence: University Press of Kansas, 1994), 12.

103. The remainder was a discussion of the independent nature of the air forces and their need to gain air superiority. *100-5* (1944), 20–26. Additionally, the motorized division section was replaced by a light division section, antitank forces above the division were addressed in a new section, and the chapter on aerial movement of forces became "Airborne Troops."

104. *100-5* (1941), 18–21, and *100-5* (1944), 27–31.

105. There was no discussion of the interface between political aims and military actions. The only mention of what is today considered to be a significant portion of military competence is that the theater commander in chief "draws up and issues strategical plans in accordance with the general policies prescribed by the President." U.S. War Department, *Manual for Commanders of Large Units* (Washington, DC: Government Printing Office, 1930), 7.

106. See Odom, *After the Trenches*, 118–123, for a brief discussion of the origin and criticism of the *MCLU*. In a manner similar to his selection of the 1923 and 1939 *FSRs*, Odom did not research or analyze the 1942 version of the *MCLU*, FM 100-15, for *After the Trenches*.

107. Odom, *After the Trenches*, 120–121.

108. *MCLU*, analysis of army in the offensive, 21–22, revealed the prescription "continue to press the enemy" as the solution to the transition to exploitation. The corps in the offense, 31–35, and division in the offense, 41–51, offered very few practical techniques for success. This manual, only issued as provisional, had three minor alterations in 1936 and was entirely replaced with a June 29, 1942, edition, which bore little resemblance to the 1930 edition.

109. *FM 100-15* (1942), ii. Italics in original.

110. *100-15* (1942), breakthrough discussion on 33–37, larger armored units on 93–99.

111. Divisional numbers from Matloff, "90 Division Gamble," 374.

112. For the early works, see GSS, *Combat Orders* (GSSP, 1920); and GSS, *Command, Staff and Tactics* (GSSP, 1923).

113. GSS, *Field Service Staff Manual (Tentative)* (GSSP, 1925), instructions stated on introduction page.

114. These principles included discussions of purposes of staffs, staff authorities, staff coordination, responsibilities, control, functions and duties, and the role of the chief of staff. The remainder of this section discussed subordinate divisions of the staff and specific duties of staff divisions, personnel, intelligence, operations, and training and supply. *Field Service Staff Manual (Tentative)*, 1925, 1.

115. This manual actually only consisted of chapter 1, "Staff Principles and Functions." U.S. War Department, *Staff Officers' Field Manual* (Washington, DC: Government Printing Office, 1928).

116. *Staff Officers' Field Manual*, 1928, definition on 1, block quote on 4.

117. The introductory material, including staff functions and principles, now took some twenty-five pages. U.S. War Department, *Staff Officers' Field Manual* (Washington, DC: Government Printing Office, 1932), definition on 1, functions on 4.

118. "Staff Officers' Field Manual, Part One: The Staff and Combat Orders," Draft Prepared by CGSS, June 13, 1940. Copy located in CARL. U.S. War Department, *FM 101-5, Staff Officers' Field Manual: The Staff and Combat Orders* (Washington, DC: Government Printing Office, August 19, 1940), with changes 1–10. U.S. Department of the Army, *FM 101-5, Staff Officers' Field Manual: Staff Organization and Procedure* (Washington, DC: Government Printing Office, July 1950).

119. Change 1, March 24, 1942, added air forces to the discussion of command relationships and staff officer positions. Change 2, May 1, 1942, added functions to the staffs. Change 3, July 27, 1942, added a special service officer, responsible for morale and recreation. Change 4, July 30, 1942, changed "date and hour" to "time and date" and specified the use of Greenwich Mean Time for all orders where units were in different time zones. Change 5, September 8, 1942, added an automotive officer to the G4 staff. Change 6, January 25, 1943, rescinded change 5 and renumbered several paragraphs. Change 7, February 3, 1943, added two forms to the annexes, a form on intelligence instructions, and a form on reconnaissance instructions. Change 8, April 6, 1943, added a bomb disposal staff officer. Change 9, July 28, 1944, modified specific instructions for the engineer staff officer. Change 10, September 9, 1944, the last modification until the new version was published in 1950, modified the tasks of the bomb disposal and ordnance staff officers. All changes were issued by the War Department.

120. *FM 101-5, Staff Officers' Field Manual,* 1940, 3.

121. Major General Ernest Hinds, "Graduation Address to the Classes at the Field Artillery School, June 14, 1924," *Field Artillery Journal* 14, no. 5 (September–October 1924): 469–475.

122. Odom's dissertation used this title. William O. Odom, "The Rise and Fall of U.S. Army Doctrine, 1918 to 1939" (Ph.D. diss., Ohio State University, 1995). His later book was *After the Trenches: The Transformation of U.S. Army Doctrine.*

Chapter 3. The Leavenworth Mission: Knowledge, Problem Solving, and Confidence

1. Green diary for May 1918, Fay Brabson papers, MHI. Fiske was Harold B. Fiske, instructor at Leavenworth in the years before World War I; he led the training section of the AEF General Staff. Brabson's daily diary has not been used by historians, in part due to the nearly indecipherable handwriting. This is unfortunate, as he kept a nearly daily journal his entire life, including instructor duty at Langres and as a member of the 1919 faculty at Leavenworth.

2. Quoted in Ed Cray, *General of the Army: George C. Marshall, Soldier and Statesman* (New York: W. W. Norton, 1990), 37.

3. Charles Bundel, "Lecture to Course, School of the Line," "The Solution of Map Problems—The Estimate of the Situation," September 17, 1919, in Charles Bundel, "Graduation Address," Fort Leavenworth course, June 20, 1938, in *Selected Professional Papers of Chas. M. Bundel* (Fort Leavenworth: Command and General Staff School Press, 1939), 174.

4. Bundel, *Selected Papers,* 122.

5. Director, General Staff School, *Annual Report,* 1921–1922, 49–50.

6. See Shimon Naveh, *In Pursuit of Military Excellence: The Evolution of Operational Theory* (London: Cass, 1997), xviii and ch. 1; U.S. Department of Defense, Joint Staff, *Joint Publication 1-02, Department of Defense Dictionary of Military and Associated Terms* (Washington, DC: Joint Staff Electronic Library, JEL CD-ROM, February 2000, manual dated March 23, 1994), 327. For an exploration of the issue, see Michael R. Matheny, "Development of the Theory and Doctrine of Operational Art in the American Army, 1920–1940" (Master's thesis, School of Advanced Military Studies, U.S. Army Command and General Staff College, April 1988).

7. Colonel Wallace P. Franz, "The Art of War: Theory and Practice," *Art of War Quarterly* 2 (Carlisle Barracks, PA: U.S. Army War College, September 1983): 121–124. Operational excellence quote on 124, anticipation discussion on 121.

8. Major Stuart Heintzelman, "Notes of a Conference," MHI, AWCCA, Box Curriculum 1919–1920, Volume 6 (VI), Special Course, Volume 8 (VIII): Field Exercises, Course at the General Staff College, 1919–1920. VII War Game, 1–3, quote on 2.

9. See Donald A. Schön, *The Reflective Practitioner: How Professionals Think in Action* (New York: Basic Books, 1983), and *Educating the Reflective Practitioner: Toward a New Design for Teaching and Learning in the Professions* (San Francisco: Jossey-Bass, 1987).

10. Schön, *Reflective Practitioner,* xi, 8.

11. Ibid., 13. Schön's theory of educating practitioners is a descendant of the theories of John Dewey and Edward Lee Thorndike, educational theorists of the early twentieth century. Dewey, whom Schön frequently cited, believed in the value of learning through experience. For examples of Dewey's influence on Schön, see Schön, *Reflective Practitioner,* 16–17, 32–33,

312–313. Dewey's works included John Dewey, *Democracy and Education: An Introduction to the Philosophy of Education* (New York: Macmillan, 1916, reprint ed. Free Press, n.d.); *How We Think* (Boston: D.C. Heath, 1910, reprint ed. Mineola, NY: Dover, 1997); and especially *Experience and Education* (New York: Macmillan, 1944). For Dewey's role, see Harold W. Stubblefield, *Towards a History of Adult Education in America: The Search for a Unifying Principle* (New York: Croom Helm, 1988), 6–7; Joan S. Stark and Lisa R. Lattuca, *Shaping the College Curriculum: Academic Plans in Action* (Boston: Allyn and Bacon, 1997), 70. The Command and General Service Schools Library held copies of Dewey's most important works. Arguably more influential on the education at Leavenworth was the educational psychologist Edward Thorndike. Thorndike's analysis, couched in the scientific terminology of the Progressive Era, was based on an assessment that human skills are developed most profoundly in experiences. Like Dewey, he believed that simple passive learning could never be as effective as practical application of learned skills. See Edward Lee Thorndike, *Educational Psychology, Volume 2: The Psychology of Learning* (New York: Teachers College, Columbia University, 1926), ch. 6, "The Improvement of Mental Functions by Practice." The Command and General Service Schools Library held copies of several works by Thorndike. The 1936 Command and General Staff School text for faculty, *The Art of Instructing*, extensively cited Thorndike. Although citing educational theorists was not a common occurrence in the interwar professional journals, there were at least three citations, one of Thorndike, one of Flexner, and one of Harold Rugg of the University of Chicago. For Thorndike, see Captain Elbridge Colby, Infantry, "Duty with Troops," *Infantry Journal* 20, no. 2 (February 1922): 127–132. For Flexner, see Lieutenant Colonel Bernard Lentz, Infantry, "A Decade of Army Schools," *Infantry Journal* 39, no. 5 (September–October 1932): 355–357; Flexner is cited on 356. For Rugg, see Major Frederick L. Pond, 112th Infantry (Penn. National Guard), "The Supervision of Training," *Infantry Journal* 36, no. 1 (January 1930): 52–56; citation of Rugg on 54–55.

12. The Command and General Staff Course for regular army officers was not the only course at Leavenworth during the interwar period, although it was by far the most significant. A correspondence course existed to both prepare officers anticipating assignment as students and instruct those who were not selected. Initially called the Mailing List, this course by 1923 had become the "D" course, or the Correspondence Course, and educated some 5,000 students at a time. *Annual Report, 1923*, 6–7. See *Instruction Circular No. 1, The General Service Schools, Fort Leavenworth, Kansas, 1 July 1924* (Fort Leavenworth: General Service Schools Press, 1924), section III, for discussion of correspondence school. In the late 1920s, the course was renamed the Command and General Staff Extension Course and became a loosely enforced prerequisite for attendance at the Special Resident Course for National Guard officers. By 1930, this course graduated only slightly more than 100 officers each year. *Annual Report, 1929–1930*, 8. A special resident course for National Guard and other selected officers annually brought a small group of students to Leavenworth in the 1920s and 1930s. Usually of twelve weeks' duration, the course offered a condensed version of the regular army resident course and acquainted officers of the National Guard with mobilization duties as general staff officers. This course was usually attended by some three dozen National Guard and Organized Reserve officers. *Annual Report, 1929–1930*, 8. Also see *Instruction Circular No. 1, 1924*, Section IV, for discussion of special course.

13. Director, School of the Line, *Annual Report*, 1920, 20.

14. Director, GSS, *Annual Report*, 1920, 14–15.

15. Director, General Staff Course, *Annual Report*, August 20, 1920, 15.

16. Brigadier General Hanson E. Ely, "Address at Opening of the General Service Schools" (GSSP, 1922), 5.

17. Brigadier General Charles M. Bundel, "Remarks at Graduation, the Command and General Staff School," June 20, 1938, in *Selected Professional Papers*, 122.

18. *Schedule for 1919–1920*, General Staff School, Fort Leavenworth, Kansas, October 1, 1919, 2–8. AEF documents were used as student references in at least four of these lectures and conferences in just the first month of instruction.

19. Bundel had commanded an artillery brigade in combat but had no experience at echelons above brigade in the AEF.

20. The earlier development of the problem-solving pedagogy is discussed in Chapter 5.

21. *Annual Report*, 1921–1922, 2.

22. CGSS, "Bulletin No. 1, Subject: Textbooks," dated August 15, 1934 (CGSSP). Available in CARL Archives, CGSS curricular archives. For examples of school texts, see GSS, *Combat Orders* (GSSP, 1920); GSS, *Command, Staff, and Tactics* (GSSP, 1923); GSS, *Combat Orders* (GSSP, 1925); CGSS, *Command and Staff Principles (Tentative)* (CGSSP, 1937); and CGSS, *Combat Orders (Tentative)* (CGSSP, 1939).

23. For just one example, see "Old Grad," "Keeping Up," *Infantry Journal* 45, no. 4 (July–August 1938): 356.

24. CGSS, *Tactical Employment of the Mechanized Division (Tentative)* (CGSSP, 1937), Contents.

25. *Mechanized Division*, 13–18.

26. For example, the faculty added a course titled "Communist Warfare" in 1920, "touching upon problems and solutions arising out of internal strife and domestic disorders." Director, General Staff School, *Annual Report*, 1920, 16.

27. United States War Department, General Order No. 30, August 2, 1923. Also see *Annual Report*, GSS, 1923, 14–15. The school changed its name when the two-year course became a single one-year course. The School of the Line and the General Staff School combined became the Command and General Staff School effective with a War Department General Order of August 2, 1923. This name change lasted through World War II and into the early 1950s, after which the institution became the Command and General Staff College, responsible for teaching the Command and General Staff Officers Course.

28. United States War Department, *Field Service Regulations, United States Army, 1923* (Washington, DC: Government Printing Office, 1924), iii.

29. Charles M. Bundel, "The Solution of Map Problems," Lecture: The Estimate of the Situation, September 17, 1919, in *Selected Professional Papers*, 173. See biography of Brigadier General Charles Michael Bundel in *Field Artillery Journal* 24, no. 6 (November–December 1934): 582.

30. Charles M. Bundel, "Talk to Faculty, August 31, 1937," in Bundel, *Selected Professional Papers*, 89–90.

31. Brigadier General Hanson E. Ely, "Address at Opening of the General Service Schools" (GSSP, 1922), 13.

32. Brigadier General Charles M. Bundel, "Remarks at Graduation, the Command and General Staff School," June 20, 1938, in *Selected Professional Papers*, 122.

33. See Charles B. MacDonald, *The Siegfried Line Campaign: The United States Army in World War II, European Theater of Operations* (Washington, DC: Center of Military History, United States Army, 1984), 106–109; and Donald E. Houston, *Hell on Wheels: The 2d Armored Division* (Novato, CA: Presidio, 1977), 271–274.

34. Ernest N. Harmon, with Milton MacKaye and William Ross MacKaye, *Combat Commander: Autobiography of a Soldier* (Englewood Cliffs, NJ: Prentice Hall, 1970), 209–210.

35. CGSS, *Schedule for 1934–1935, First Year Course*, 7.

36. CGSS, *1934–1935, First Year Class: Command Course, G-2 Course, Text* (CGSSP, 1935), 1, and *Schedule for 1934–1935, First Year Course,* 7.

37. Although the course material for the first year focused on the division, by the mid-1930s a mechanized brigade was used for some problems as a substitute for the infantry division.

38. After being updated with a changed situation, which concluded by 8:30 A.M. on May 22, the students were then required to submit individual responses to the new situation. The solution provided by the school included the "actions taken and instructions given by the mechanized brigade S-2, S-4, motor officer, and S-3." They had until 11:00 A.M. that day to turn in their assignments for grading. *First Year Class: Command Course,* 265–266, 267–268.

39. CGSS, *1935–1936, Second Year Class: Command Course, G-2 Course, Text* (Fort Leavenworth, KS, 1936), 1–8, and *Schedule for 1935–1936, Second Year Course,* 7.

40. Graduation was scheduled for June 25, 1936, but two of the last weeks were dedicated to a command post exercise, and two other weeks to presentations by the students of their individual and group research projects, so the final map maneuver was scheduled for May 12, 14, and 15, 1937. *Schedule for 1935–1936, Second Year Course,* 18.

41. *1935–1936, Second Year Class: Command Course,* 437–449. That the faculty needed thirteen pages of closely typed text to describe the problem and requirements is an indicator of the increased complexity. The problem statement for two years before required merely one page.

42. *Annual Report,* 1921–1922, 16.

43. *Annual Report,* Assistant Commandant, 1921–1922, 23–24.

44. Director, General Staff School, *Annual Report,* 1921–1922, 49–50.

45. Charles M. Bundel, "Some Essentials of Leadership," Lecture to the Command and General Staff School, May 27, 1937, in Bundel, *Selected Professional Papers,* 70–71 and 74–75.

46. Letter, John McAuley Palmer to George A. Lynch, May 21, 1938, quoted in Larry I. Bland, ed., *The Papers of George Catlett Marshall, Volume 1: The Soldierly Spirit, December 1880–June 1939* (Baltimore: Johns Hopkins University Press, 1981), 599–600.

47. "Mercutio," "Canned Commanders," "Cerebrations," *Infantry Journal* 42, no. 3 (May–June 1935): 269.

48. "C.T.T.," "Banned Commanders," "Cerebrations," *Infantry Journal* 42, no. 4 (July–August 1935): 363.

49. "G.I.," "Non-Conformists Get a Break," "Cerebrations," *Infantry Journal* 42, no. 6 (November–December 1935): 566–567.

50. "Singlebars," "Canned Commanders—Continued," "Cerebrations," *Infantry Journal* 43, no. 1 (January–February 1936): 74–75.

51. Major R. M. Johnston, Historical Section, GHQ, AEF, "Staff and Command," *Infantry Journal* 16, no. 1 (July 1919): 88–92. Quote on 92.

52. "General Gripe," "Wishful Thinking," *Cavalry Journal* 49, no. 4 (July–August 1940): 349–359. Quote on 349.

53. CGSS, "Summary of Schedule (by Courses)" (CGSSP, n.d.), CARL, typescript located in files for CGSS, 1935–1936, "Schedules." Also see CGSS, *Index to School Problems, Series 1919–1920 to 1932–1933* (CGSSP, 1933), passim; *Course Schedules* for 1928–1929, 1929–1930, 1934–1935, and 1935–1936, located in CARL. The quantification done from this source is supported by Boyd L. Dastrup, who, although using a different categorization, states that in 1938–1939 "practical work accounted for 744 out of 1073 scheduled hours for the (single) year"; Dastrup, *The U.S. Army Command and General Staff College: A Centennial History* (Manhattan, KS: Sunflower University Press, n.d., c. 1982), 76.

54. Examples drawn from analysis of conferences ST 203, 205, 207, 211, 214, and 215 in CGSS, *1929–1930, Second Year Course Conferences: Command, Staff and Logistics; Strategy; Military History; Field Engineering; Military Intelligence; Methods of Training; Military Geography; Political Economy* (CGSSP, 1930), 196–234.

55. 1923 *FSR*, 4.

56. Ibid., 5.

57. GSS, *Command, Staff, and Tactics*, special ed. (GSSP, 1923), 22–24.

58. CGSS, *Command and Staff Principles (Tentative)* (CGSSP, 1937), 3, 14–15.

59. An issue of grave concern frequently at the Army War College. Of course, there the officer students received little formal education in the issues they were asked to resolve for the General Staff. Mobilization, manpower management, and training the mobilizing force were often discussed and analyzed at the War College but not formally educated as such.

60. CGSS, *Schedule for 1929–1930: Second Year Course* (CGSSP, 1929).

61. Harbord Board Report, *Memorandum*, dated July 21, 1921, MHI, AWCCA, 114 et seq., 2–3.

62. Marvin A. Kreidberg and Merton G. Henry, *History of Military Mobilization in the United States Army, 1775–1945*, Department of the Army Pamphlet no. 20-212 (Washington, DC: November 1955), 381–382.

63. Harbord Board, *Memorandum*, 2–3.

64. Paul A. C. Koistinen, *Planning War, Pursuing Peace: The Political Economy of American Warfare, 1920–1939* (Lawrence: University Press of Kansas, 1998), 42.

65. Ibid., 12.

66. The best secondary source on this issue is Harry Richard Yarger, "Army Officer Personnel Management: The Creation of the Modern System to 1939" (Ph.D. diss., Temple University, 1996).

67. Adjutant General, Letter to Commandant, General Service Schools, Fort Leavenworth, Kansas, "Consolidation of the General Service Schools, Fort Leavenworth," dated July 12, 1922. Located in NAII, RG 407, Office of the Adjutant General Central Files, Box 811, folder 352.01 (7-12-22) to (2-4-22). McGlachlin Report, found in NAII RG 407, Bulky Files, 352.01 (2-24-22) (1) "Report of Board of Officers re: Study of Army School System." See base report, "Report of Proceedings of a Board of Officers Appointed to Study the Army School System," February 4, 1922. Comments on length of course and mission on 6.

68. To accomplish this first change, during the 1922–1923 school year the old second-year course and the new single-year course were conducted simultaneously.

69. In his *Annual Report, 1922–1923*, 7, Major General Ely forecasted the resumption of the two-year program after "at least three or four years." In his *Annual Report, 1928–1929*, 8, Brigadier General Edward King recalled the reasoning behind the adoption of the one-year course and expressed optimism that the new two-year course would overcome the educational deficiencies of the one-year program.

70. G3 Division, War Department General Staff, Memorandum for the Chief of Staff, "Subject: Two-Year Course at the Command and General Staff School," dated December 10, 1927. Document in NAII, RG 407, Office of the Adjutant General Central Files 1926–1939, General Files, Box 2045, 352.01 (12-21-27) to 352.01 (8-13-26).

71. Proceedings of Conference of Corps Area and Division Commanders held at Washington, D.C., June 1927, located in NAII RG 407, Office of the Adjutant General, Central Decimal Correspondence File, Bulky Packages, Box 520, PI-17 Entry 37 352.01 6-2-27. See 107–110.

72. This board consisted of Major General Hanson E. Ely, former commandant of Leav-

enworth from 1921 to 1923; Major General Douglas MacArthur, then a corps area commander; Brigadier General Edward L. King, the current Leavenworth commandant; and Brigadier General Frank Parker from the War Department General Staff. Ely Board, NAII, RG 165, War Department General Staff, G1 (Personnel) Numerical File, 1921–1942, 12311–12675, Box 85, folder 12585–12600. Although this file is from 1932, it contains a copy of the results of the Ely board from 1927.

73. To make this possible, two courses would run simultaneously, the second-year course to graduate in 1929, with a student body of "about 80 students," and the first one-year course, with 120 students. G3 Division, War Department General Staff, Memorandum for the Chief of Staff, "Subject: Two-Year Course at the Command and General Staff School," dated December 10, 1927. Document in NAII, RG 407, Office of the Adjutant General Central Files 1926–1939, General Files, Box 2045, 352.01 (12-21-27) to 352.01 (8-13-26).

74. Omar Bradley referred to the War College as "like a graduate seminar or a contemporary think tank." See Omar N. Bradley and Clay Blair, *A General's Life: An Autobiography* (New York: Simon and Schuster, 1983), 74. Also see Edward S. Miller, *War Plan Orange: The U.S. Strategy to Defeat Japan, 1897–1945* (Annapolis: Naval Institute Press, 1991), chs. 1 and 2. The documents from these studies are located in MHI, AWCCA. The files for 1932–1933 are in folder 391-8, the 1933–1934 files are in 401-8, for 1934–1935 in 1-1935-8, and for 1935–1936 in 1-1936-8. Yarger, "Army Officer Personnel Management," drew my attention to these critical documents.

75. "G-1, Report of Committee No. 8, Subject: Promotion, Separation, and Assignment of Regular Army Officers in Time of Peace: Modifications to Develop an Efficient and Well Balanced Officer Personnel," Course at the Army War College, 1932–1933, folder 391-8, MHI.

76. "Report of Committee No. 8," 1932–1933, 11.

77. Ibid., 12–13.

78. Ibid., 13–15.

79. "G-1, Report of Committee No. 8, Subject: Promotion, Separation, and Assignment of Regular Army Officers in Time of Peace: Modifications to Develop an Efficient and Well Balanced Officer Personnel," Course at the Army War College, 1933–1934, folder 401-8, MHI, 9–12 and notes of discussion.

80. "G-1, Report of Committee No. 8, Subject: Promotion, Separation, and Assignment of Regular Army Officers in Time of Peace," Course at the Army War College, 1934–1935, folder 1-1935-8, MHI, passim.

81. "Report of Committee No. 8," 1934–1935, 40–43.

82. Major General Andrew Moses, War Department General Staff G-1, "Confidential Memorandum for the Chief of Staff, Subject: Length of course at the Command and General Staff School," dated April 22, 1932, located in NAII, RG 165, War Department General Staff, G-1 (Personnel) Numerical File, 1921–1942, 12311–12675, Box 85, folder 12585–12600. Numbers 3 and 4.

83. See the very extensive staff study documents in NAII, RG 165, War Department General Staff, G-1 (Personnel) Numerical File, 1921–1942, 12311–12675, Box 85, folder 12585–12600. Quote is from Major General Geo. Van Horn Moseley, Deputy Chief of Staff, "Memorandum from A.C. of S., G-1, Subject: Length of Course at the Command and General Staff School," dated June 1, 1932.

84. Note from Brigadier General Andrew Moses, War Department General Staff G1, October 31, 1932, filed in NAII, RG 165, War Department General Staff, G1 (Personnel) Numerical File, 1921–1942, 12311–12675, Box 85, folder 12585–12600.

85. Although a thorough review of all appropriate documents in RG 407 in the National Archives was conducted, no record of how this decision was staffed has yet emerged.

86. "G-1, Report of Committee No. 8, Subject: Promotion, Separation, and Assignment of Regular Army Officers," Course at the Army War College, 1935–1936, folder 1-1935-8, MHI, 7–9, 17–18.

87. Army War College, "Report of Committee No. 8, Promotion, Separation and Assignment of Regular Army Officers in Time of Peace" (Washington, DC: Army War College, November 3, 1934), 41–42.

88. Letter, Adjutant General's Office, dated January 2, 1935 (A.G. 325.01 [12-24-34]), referred to in *CSFG*, 6.

89. *Annual Report*, 1935–1936, 10.

90. For biography of Groves, see Vincent C. Jones, "Groves, Leslie Richard," in Roger J. Spiller and Joseph G. Dawson III, eds., *Dictionary of American Military Biography*, vol. 1 (Westport: Greenwood, 1984), 415–419. For Spaatz, see Roger Beaumont, "Spaatz, Carl Andrew," in ibid., vol. 3, 1030–1032.

91. *Annual Report*, 1935–1936, 10, 11, and 13.

92. See *Annual Reports*, 1936–1937 through 1938–1939.

93. *Annual Report*, 1924–1925, 10.

94. "Notes of Discussion following Conference of Committee No. 8, G-1, 10/26/32," in "Report of Committee No. 8, Promotion, Separation, and Assignment of Regular Army Officers in Time of Peace: Modifications to Develop an Efficient and Well Balanced Officer Personnel, Course at the Army War College, 1932–1933, G-1," 5, MHI, AWCCA.

95. See Director, GSS, *Annual Report*, 1922–1923, 34–35, for an impassioned plea to return to the two-year program.

96. Frank E. Emery Jr., "What Should Be the Plan of Education for Officers of the Army" (CARL: Student Research Paper, n.d. but c. 1928–1929), 5 and 10.

97. This discussion is assessed in Chapter 7. J. P. Cromwell, "Are the Methods of Instruction Used at This School Practical and Modern? If Not, What Changes Are Suggested?" (CARL: Student Research Papers, May 27, 1936), 16.

98. George Catlett Marshall, "Memorandum for the Deputy Chief of Staff, April 13, 1937," in Bland, *Papers, Volume 1*: 533.

99. Marshall also recommended McNair look into the training procedures at Maxwell Airfield for an update before assuming command at Leavenworth. George Catlett Marshall, "Letter to Brigadier General Lesley J. McNair, February 23, 1939," in Bland, *Papers, Volume 1*, 702–703. Timothy K. Nenninger criticizes Marshall's comment in "Creating Officers: The Leavenworth Experience, 1920–1940," *Military Review* 69, no. 11 (November 1989): 67–68.

100. George Catlett Marshall, "Letter to Brigadier General Lesley J. McNair, May 3, 1939," in Bland, *Papers, Volume 1*, 714.

101. George Catlett Marshall, "Letter to Brigadier General Lesley J. McNair, August 7, 1939," in Larry I. Bland, Sharon R. Ritenour, and Clarence E. Wunderlin Jr., eds., *The Papers of George Catlett Marshall, Volume 2: "We Cannot Delay," July 1, 1939–December 6, 1941* (Baltimore: Johns Hopkins University Press, 1986), 30–31.

102. George Catlett Marshall, "Letter to Brigadier General Lesley J. McNair, August 16, 1939," in Bland, *Papers, Volume 2*, 36–37.

103. George Catlett Marshall, "Letter to Brigadier General Lesley J. McNair, January 24, 1940," in Bland, *Papers, Volume 2*, 144–145.

104. *Annual Report*, 1938–1939, appendix 2.

105. Ibid., appendix 2, 13.

Chapter 4. The Leavenworth Staff and Faculty

1. Perhaps one of the finer efforts by historians to assess the influence of faculty on officer education is David C. Evans and Mark R. Peattie, *Kaigun: Strategy, Tactics, and Technology in the Imperial Japanese Navy, 1887–1941* (Annapolis: Naval Institute Press, 1997), 69–74 and passim. Epigraph from "A Young Graduate," "The Leavenworth Course," *Infantry Journal* 30, no. 6 (June 1927): 589–600, quote from 589. Attributed "almost certainly" to Eisenhower by Timothy K. Nenninger, "Creating Officers: The Leavenworth Experience, 1920–1940," *Military Review* (November 1989): 58–68, endnote 8, where he cites materials from the Eisenhower Library in Abilene, Kansas.

2. This view is contested by Brian McAllister Linn, "Transforming Defense in Peace: A Historical Perspective," paper delivered at the twelfth Annual Strategy Conference, "Transforming Defense in an Era of Peace and Prosperity," U.S. Army War College, April 17–20, 2001.

3. U.S. Army, Command and General Staff College, *A Military History of the U.S. Army Command and General Staff College, 1881–1963* (Fort Leavenworth, KS: U.S. Army Command and General Staff College, n.d.), 30–41. Also see the digest of Adjutant General Orders in *CSFG*, 9.

4. *Annual Reports*, 1919 through 1940.

5. The duties of the senior faculty were described in General Orders No. 5, September 14, 1920, of the GSS. Orders are reproduced in their entirety in appendix A, *Annual Report, 1920–1921*, 14.

6. Herbert Brees served as the assistant commandant from 1925 through 1929, then as commandant from 1935 through 1936; Charles Bundel was director of the General Staff School from 1923 to 1924, then commandant from 1936 through 1939; Joseph McAndrew returned as course director from 1933 through 1936, then assistant commandant until 1937; Troup Miller served as director of the second-year class in 1934 through 1936; and Lesley McNair returned as commandant in 1939. Data drawn from *Annual Reports*, 1919 through 1940.

7. Records of the 1924 Educational Advisory Board in NAII, RG 407, Office of the Adjutant General Central Files, Box 806, Folder 352 (11-3-24) to (10-30-24), Report of 1924 EAB.

8. See Elvid Hunt, *History of Fort Leavenworth, 1827–1937*, 2nd ed. brought up to date by Walter E. Laurence (CGSSP, 1937), charts between 158 and 159.

9. Mark M. Lowenthal, "Middleton, Troy M.," in Roger J. Spiller and Joseph G. Dawson, eds., *Dictionary of American Military Biography*, vol. 2 (Westport: Greenwood, 1984), 765–768. Also see Frank James Price, *Troy H. Middleton: A Biography* (Baton Rouge: Louisiana State University Press, 1974), 87–88.

10. Only the school adjutant, Major Thomas Lowe, had graduated only from the School of the Line. Of the remaining sixty-seven officers, two had graduated from Leavenworth before World War I: the commandant, Brigadier General Harry Smith, class of 1913, and Lieutenant Colonel Oliver Robinson, class of 1915, an instructor. Of the remaining faculty, three had graduated from the one-year General Staff Course in 1920. With the start of the normal two-year course, four were graduates of 1921, thirteen from 1922, and fifteen from the general staff class of 1923. After the transition to a single-year class, fifteen, including two instructors given credit for the course they taught, graduated in 1923, and the remaining fifteen were immediately assigned to instructor duty from the class of 1924. Price, *Middleton*, 90. *Annual Report*, 1924, 11. Calculations for the faculty for academic year 1924–1925 from the *Annual Reports* of 1920 through 1925 and from CSFG. The two instructors given diplomas for the

course they taught were Colonel Lytle Brown and Major Cassius Dowell. The practice of granting diplomas to instructors was a short-lived phenomenon, developed to overcome some of the turbulence of the immediate post–World War I years. It had ended by 1924.

11. Price, *Middleton*, 87–90.

12. The workload was the subject of official investigations and studies, including an inspector general investigation in May 1939. Having inspected the work being done, and scheduled for execution at Leavenworth, the inspector general reported to the adjutant general that the number of instructors at Leavenworth should not be reduced, despite the issues raised by protective mobilization. Among the tasks the inspector general listed were, in addition to the normal load of instruction, rewriting all extension courses, to be distributed over the next three years, a complete rewrite of the *Staff Officers' Field Manual*, a revision of the *FSR*, and, after the revision of the *FSR*, a "necessary rewrite of all school texts." Memorandum, Major General W. L. Reed, Inspector General, to Adjutant General, "Subject: Instructors," dated December 4, 1939, in NAII, RG 407, Office of the Adjutant General Central Files, Box 1920, folder 210.63 C&GS School (1-1026) Section 2 to 352.07 C&GS School (6-22-38) (3).

13. Director, School of the Line, *Annual Report*, 1920, 26.

14. Ibid., 19.

15. Captain Francis G. Bonham, Infantry, "The Military Instructor" [part one], *Infantry Journal* 29, no. 4 (October 1926): 355–365; Captain Francis G. Bonham, *Infantry*, "The Military Instructor" [part two], *Infantry Journal* 29, no. 5 (October 1926): 493–501; "The Instructor," *Cavalry Journal* 49, no. 1 (January–February 1940): 65–66.

16. I. B. Holley Jr., "Training and Educating Pre–World War I United States Army Officers," in Elliott V. Converse, ed., *Forging the Sword: Selecting, Educating, and Training Cadets and Junior Officers in the Modern World* (Chicago: Imprint, 1998).

17. This policy stayed in effect for the next two decades with only minor revisions. NAII, RG 165, Records of the War Department General and Special Staffs, War College Division and War Plans Division, General Records. General Correspondence, July 1919–October 1920, 8251–8400 Box 42, Entry 279, Letter from Director, War Plans Division, G.S. to Commandant, General Service Schools, Fort Leavenworth, Kansas, "Subject: Policy Regarding detail of instructors at the General Service Schools," dated December 10, 1920. [Box is incorrectly labeled; should read 8051–8400. Correction of mistyped label requested during March 2007 research visit to archives.]

18. Policy letter is reproduced verbatim in *Annual Report, 1920–1921*, 10.

19. See comment on his father's selection as an instructor at Leavenworth in 1910 from letter of Laurence Halstead Jr. to Richard Sommers, February 26, 1973, Halstead Family Papers, MHI.

20. Letter and "indorsements" from Commandant, Fort Leavenworth to Adjutant General, War Department GS, "Subject: Instructors for the General Service Schools," Fort Leavenworth, Kansas, dated February 29, 1924, located in NAII, RG 407, Office of the Adjutant General Central Files, Box 1108, folder C&GS School, 210.63 (8-13-24 to 12-27-23).

21. Letter and "indorsements" from Commandant Fort Leavenworth to Adjutant General, War Department, "Subject: Instructors for the Command and General Staff School," dated March 10, 1924, located in NAII, RG 407, Office of the Adjutant General Central Files, Box 1108, folder C&GS School, 210.63 (8-13-24 to 12-27-23).

22. Telegram from Adjutant General, War Department, to Commandant, Fort Leavenworth, reference Major George L. Wertenbaker, dated March 24, 1924, located in NAII, RG 407, Office of the Adjutant General Central Files, Box 1108, folder C&GS School, 210.63 (8-13-24 to 12-27-23).

23. See, for example, the records for the 1928 instructor detailing in NAII RG 407, Office of the Adjutant General Central Files, Box 1916, folder 210.63 C&GS School (12-8-27) to 210.63 C&GS School (10-20-27) (2); the 1932–1933 replacement cycle in NAII RG 407, Office of the Adjutant General Central Files, Box 1909, folder 210.63 C&GS School (1-25-32) (1) Section 2 to 210.63 C&GS School (10-27-31) (1); and the 1938–1939 selection process in NAII RG 407, Office of the Adjutant General Central Files, Box 1886, folder 210.63 C&GS School (11-4-37) (1) to 210.63 C&GS School (8–19–37) Section ___ [blank on folder in records].

24. Entire series of communications, some fifteen in number, on the Brees case in NAII, RG 407 Office of the Adjutant General Central Files, Box 1108, folder C7GS School 210.63 (8-13-24) to (12-27-23) part 3.

25. Another example is the case of an anticipated simultaneous three-senior-officer movement from Leavenworth: the commandant, the assistant to the commandant, and the director of the Command and General Staff School, all to be moved in 1929. Located in NAII, RG 407, Office of the Adjutant General, Central Files, Box 1915, folder 210.63 C&GS School (4-25-29) (1) Section 2 to 210.63 C&GS School (3-5-28).

26. Colonel Howell complained in his annual report for 1920–1921 that thirteen members of the faculty were ordered to depart Fort Leavenworth under instructions dated December 24, 1920. The departure in midyear of perhaps one-quarter of the faculty must have imposed a great strain on the instruction. To alleviate the strain, twenty-four selected students from the Staff School class assisted the instructors of the School of the Line that academic year. *Annual Report*, Director, General Staff School, 1920–1921, 18–19.

27. Ibid., 19.

28. *Annual Report*, 1922, 8.

29. Identification of honor and distinguished graduates began with the elimination of the initial two-year program. For the faculty of 1924–1925, recent graduates were selected from all three levels of course evaluation, honor graduates (the top 10 percent of the course), distinguished graduates (the next 15 percent of the class), and simple graduates (the other 75 percent). However, the selection of students from the class of 1924 was predominantly from the honor graduates (47 percent of the newly assigned instructors) and distinguished graduates (another 20 percent of the new teachers). Normal graduates were only one-third of those selected to be retained as instructors. Calculations from *Annual Reports*.

30. U.S. Army War College, "Report of Committee No. 8. Subject: Promotion, Separation and Assignment of Regular Army Officers in Time of Peace: Modifications to Develop an Efficient and Well Balanced Officer Personnel, October 26, 1932" (Washington, DC: U.S. Army War College, 1932–1933), 18. Document available in MHI, AWCCA, 391-8.

31. Fourteen officers, or 41.2 percent of all corps commanders. Six future corps commander instructors taught in one year, five taught in four years, four taught in three of the interwar years, two in five years, and in one year there was only one future corps commander on the staff. Robert H. Berlin, *U.S. Army World War II Corps Commanders: A Composite Biography* (Fort Leavenworth, KS: Combat Studies Institute, CGSC, 1989), data from table 2, 11.

32. CSFG; John S. D. Eisenhower, *Yanks: The Epic Story of the American Army in World War I* (New York: Free Press, 2001), 207–208; James G. Harbord, *The American Army in France, 1917–1919* (Boston: Little, Brown, 1936), 444, 448; James J. Cooke, *Pershing and His Generals: Command and Staff in the AEF* (Westport: Praeger, 1997), 149; CSFG, Spiller, *Dictionary*, vol. 1, 279–280; *Who Was Who in American History—The Military* (Chicago: Marquis Who's Who, 1975), 74, 156–157, 306–307, 536, 594; Arlington Cemetery website at

www.arlingtoncemetery.com/heintszelman.htm; *Dictionary of American Fighting Ships* website at www.hazegray.org/danfs/auxil/ap159.htm; Christopher Tunney, *A Biographical Dictionary of World War II* (New York: St. Martin's, 1972), 124; Chief Warrant Officer Ely J. Kahn Jr., *McNair: Educator of an Army* (Washington, DC: Infantry Journal, 1945). See biography of Brigadier General Charles Michael Bundel in *Field Artillery Journal* 24, no. 6 (November–December 1934): 582. For listings of most of these officers in their AEF positions, see Order of Battle of the United States Land Forces in the World War: American Expeditionary Forces: General Headquarters, Armies, Army Corps, Services of Supply, Separate Forces, vol 1, (Washington, DC: United States Army Center of Military History, 1937, facsimile reprint 1988), 81, 150, 268, and Order of Battle of the United States Land Forces in the World War: American Expeditionary Forces: Divisions, vol. 2 (Washington, DC: United States Army Center of Military History, 1937, facsimile reprint, 1988), 1, 21, 75, 140, 192, 338, 366, 418.

33. CSFG. In the immediate postwar period, a small number of officers received graduation credit form the course while serving as instructors. *Annual Report*, 1924, 11.

34. Lucian K. Truscott Jr., *The Twilight of the U.S. Cavalry: Life in the Old Army, 1917–1942*, ed. Lucian K. Truscott III (Lawrence: University Press of Kansas, 1989), 150.

35. See Charles M. Bundel, "Talk to Faculty, August 31, 1937," in Charles M. Bundel, *Selected Professional Papers of Chas. M. Bundel* (CGSSP, 1939), block quote on 91; TEAMWORK comment from Charles M. Bundel, "The Preparation of Problems, April 7, 1920," *Selected Papers*, 239–241, quote on 239. Bundel's views on the dominance of artillery can be clearly seen in Lieutenant Colonel Charles M. Bundel, "Some Important and Timely Problems for the Field Artilleryman," *Field Artillery Journal* 11, no. 6 (November–December 1921): 581–592, especially his discussion on 583–584, where the phrase "hammering attack" was used.

36. Data drawn from *Annual Reports*, 1919–1940.

37. *Annual Report*, 1919–1920.

38. Muir's command is identified in *United States Army in the World War, 1917–1919, General Orders, GHQ, AEF*, vol. 16 (Washington, DC: Center of Military History, United States Army, 1948, 1992). Also see U.S. Army War College, Historical Section, *Order of Battle of the United States Land Forces in the World War, Volume I: American Expeditionary Forces, Armies, Army Corps, Services of Supply*, and *Volume II: American Expeditionary Forces, Army Divisions* (Washington, DC: Center of Military History, facsimile rpt. ed. 1988, orig. printed 1937), for detailed listing of officer assignments. For Muir, see *Order of Battle*, vol. 1, 268.

39. For Drum, *Order of Battle*, vol. 1, 81, and Spiller, *Dictionary*, 695–699. For Naylor, *Order of Battle*, vol. 1, 341, and AEF GHQ 1918 General Order No. 219. For Eltinge, see *Order of Battle*, vol. 1, 1.

40. Spiller, *Dictionary*, 695–699, on Lesley J. McNair; and 1000–1003 on Walter C. Short.

41. *Order of Battle*, vol. 1, 81.

42. For Catron, *Order of Battle*, vol. 1, 337. For Beebe and Miller, *Order of Battle*, vol. 1, 193; *Annual Report*, 1919–1920; *Army Register*, 1930; and *Army Directory*, 1 July 1918 and 1 November 1918. For additional information see Hugh Aloysius Drum et al., *Operations of the First Army* (Bar-sur-Aube, France: First Army Headquarters, AEF, 1919), located in Special Collections, CARL, Fort Leavenworth, KS.

43. For Brabson, *Order of Battle*, vol. 2, 392; for Chaffee, vol. 1, 237 and 326, and Spiller, *Dictionary*, 164–167.

44. *United States Army in the World War, 1917–1919, General Orders, GHQ, AEF*, vol. 16 (Washington, DC: Center of Military History, United States Army, 1948, 1992), passim.

45. *Annual Report*, 1920, 5–6.

46. *Annual Report,* 1920–1921, 4–5.

47. *Annual Report,* Director, General Staff School, 1920–1921, 19–20.

48. *Annual Report,* 1923–1924, 6.

49. For example, see Charles Bundel, "Lecture on the Solution to Map Problems—The Commander—Decisions," September 17, 1919, in Bundel, *Selected Papers,* 211.

50. Ibid., 212.

51. The first several classes after Leavenworth reopened used roughly mimeographed texts hastily assembled by the faculty. Not until 1923 was the commandant able to report that the task of rewriting and publishing the required texts was completed and the faculty could again focus on instruction rather than attempting to both teach and write. *Annual Report,* 1923.

52. Army Service Schools, "Memorandum No. 185, Subject: Explanation of Course and Other Pertinent Comments, August 12, 1919," CARL, Curriculum Files, Hanging Files, 1919–1920, 1.

53. "Memorandum No. 185," 1.

54. Ibid., 4.

55. Timothy K. Nenninger, *The Leavenworth Schools and the Old Army: Education, Professionalism, and the Officer Corps of the United States Army, 1881–1918* (Westport, CT: Greenwood, 1978), 90–91, discusses the role of Arthur L. Wagner in the development of instruction at Leavenworth.

56. "Memorandum No. 185," 2.

57. For the academic year 1920–1921, 17 new instructors were assigned, 65 percent with AEF experience. The next year, 1921–1922, of 22 new instructors, 78 percent were AEF veterans. In 1922 to 1923, there were 21 new instructors; only 53 percent were from the AEF, but including the retained instructors, the instructors with AEF experience totaled 63 percent of the faculty. The proportion of AEF experienced faculty was still significantly higher than the average field-grade officer population of 37 percent AEF. Assessment from *Annual Reports,* 1919–1920 through 1923–1924.

58. Beginning in 1927, a small number of faculty were not veterans of any type with World War I experience, whether in France or in the United States or elsewhere. These officers, initially primarily medical and judge advocates general, joined the army after 1918. At the end of the interwar period, officers commissioned after 1918 had reached 21.5 percent of the faculty. Even given the presence on the faculty in 1939 of 21.5 percent who had joined the army since 1918, the veterans of the war were still 36.7 percent of the total faculty population. Remove these "new" officers and the veteran percentage increases to 46.8 percent of the faculty who had been in the Army in 1918. Assessment from *Annual Reports,* 1919–1920 through 1939–1940.

59. Of the field-grade officers actually remaining on active duty in the entire army in November 1939, what was the percentage with AEF experience? By sampling officers, this time randomly selected from pages of the October 1939 list, and examining the proportion of AEF experience, non-AEF active service in 1918 and those who were not yet in commissioned service, an accurate assessment is possible. In 1939, the Leavenworth faculty represented AEF experience at twice the rate of the overall officer population, with a shrinking of experience of only 3 percent since 1919. Numbers taken from assessment of randomly selected pages, *List,* September 1, 1929: 174, 199, 206, 207, 208, and 274; from the *List* of October 20, 1934: 180, 199, 236, 265, 285, and 292; the *List,* October 20, 1939: 197, 177, 228, 206, 350, and 259. For details on survey techniques, see Peter J. Schifferle, "Anticipating Armageddon: The Leavenworth Schools and U.S. Army Military Effectiveness, 1919 to 1945" (Ph.D. diss., University of Kansas, 2002), 121–127.

60. The faculty in 1939–1940 included 79 officers. Of these, 29 (37 percent) had served in the AEF; 33 (42 percent) field-grade officers had been on active service in 1918, but had served only in the United States or non-AEF overseas assignments. The remaining 17 (21 percent) field-grade officers had not yet been commissioned as army officers in November 1918. If only officers with active service during World War I are considered, the percentage of officers with AEF experience was 47 percent, still markedly higher than the population mean of 37 percent, based on the analysis of the November 1918 list. *List,* October 20, 1939.

Chapter 5. *The Applicatory Method*

1. As Captain Elbridge Colby explained in a 1922 *Infantry Journal* article, the Infantry School made extensive use of the applicatory method in both its basic and advanced officer courses. Captain Elbridge Colby, Infantry, "Teaching Methods at the Infantry School," *Infantry Journal* 20, no. 3 (March 1922): 284–289.

2. The educational theory of P. Jarvis is summarized in Sharan B. Merriam, Rosemary S. Caffarella, and Lisa M. Baumgartner, *Learning in Adulthood: A Comprehensive Guide* (San Francisco: Jossey-Bass, 2007), 100–103.

3. Extensive use of the applicatory method is a subject of some discussion among educational theorists. In the 1980s, education theorist Donald A. Schön described the challenge facing those who taught skills of practical application. Drawn from Donald A. Schön, *Educating the Reflexive Practitioner: Toward a New Design for Teaching and Learning in the Professions* (San Francisco: Jossey-Bass, 1987), 83–87.

4. GSS, *Instruction Circular No. 1,* Series 1924–1925 (GSSP, 1924), 14.

5. Timothy K. Nenninger, *The Leavenworth Schools and the Old Army: Education, Professionalism, and the Officer Corps of the United States Army, 1881–1918* (Westport, CT: Greenwood, 1978), 37–48. Nenninger gives significant credit to Swift. T. R. Brereton, *Educating the U.S. Army: Arthur L. Wagner and Reform, 1875–1905* (Lincoln: University of Nebraska Press, 2000), gives more credit to Wagner.

6. Brereton, *Educating,* 62–64.

7. Nenninger, *Leavenworth Schools,* 45–48.

8. Letter, George C. Marshall to Brigadier General John McAuley Palmer, May 27, 1938, in Bland, *Papers of George Catlett Marshall,* vol. 1, 599. For the controversy on map problems, see Brereton, *Educating,* 58–59.

9. Quoted in Brereton, *Educating,* 60–62.

10. Nenninger, *Leavenworth Schools,* 70–90. Bell quoted on 71.

11. Ibid., 74.

12. *Commandants, Staff, Faculty, and Graduates of The Command and General Staff School, Fort Leavenworth, Kansas, 1881–1939* (Fort Leavenworth, KS: Command and General Staff School Press, 1939), hereafter cited as CSFG.

13. Ed Cray, *General of the Army: George C. Marshall, Soldier and Statesmen* (New York: W. W. Norton, 1991), 36.

14. The assignment records are located in CARL in the CGSS files, organized by academic year. They are, unfortunately, incomplete.

15. Information from blueprint series titled "Plan of the Command and General Staff School Buildings, Fort Leavenworth, Kansas, March 1931." Blueprints located in CARL. For information on the postmobilization facilities, see *Information for Instructors, Instruction Cir-*

cular No. 2, June 1944 (CGSS, 1944), 12–13. Dates of construction from Elvid Hunt, *History of Fort Leavenworth, 1827–1937*, 2nd ed. brought up to date by Walter E. Laurence (CGSSP, 1937), 269.

16. Hunt, *History*, and Lucian K. Truscott Jr., *The Twilight of the U.S. Cavalry: Life in the Old Army, 1917–1942* (Lawrence: University Press of Kansas, 1989), ch. 6.

17. Numerous articles, frequently sponsored by the Leavenworth faculty, appeared in the interwar journals. Most explicit was an article penned by D. D. Eisenhower, under the pen name "A Young Graduate," "The Leavenworth Course," *Infantry Journal* 30, no. 6 (June 1927): 589–600, and two articles reprinted widely in other journals by Major Stuart C. Godfrey, C.E., "Command and General Staff School," *Field Artillery Journal* 16, no. 6 (November–December 1926): 619–627. Godfrey also wrote, under the pen name "A," "Command and General Staff School," *Field Artillery Journal* 16, no. 5 (September–October 1926): 515–523. The "A" articles were republished in *Cavalry Journal* 35, no. 144 (July 1926): 412–417, and originally in *The Military Engineer*. A review of these articles was published in *Infantry Journal* 28, no. 5 (May 1926): 562–563. The "A" articles were written in the form of four letters from "A," a student, to "B," a prospective student, about the Leavenworth schools. Similar articles were published in the Notes from the Chief of Cavalry column in *Cavalry Journal* and in editorials in *Field Artillery Journal* and *Infantry Journal*. For example, see Notes from the Chief of Cavalry, "Advice to students at the Command and General Staff School," *Cavalry Journal* 44, no. 191 (September–October 1935): 58–59. For the connection of one author with the faculty, see Carlo D'Este, *Eisenhower: A Soldier's Life* (New York: Henry Holt, 2002), 183.

18. "A Young Graduate," "Leavenworth Course," 589–600; Godfrey, "Command and General Staff School," *Field Artillery Journal* 16, no. 6 (November–December 1926): 619–627; and "A," "Command and General Staff School," *Field Artillery Journal* 16, no. 5 (September–October 1926): 515–523.

19. "A," "Command and General Staff School," *Cavalry Journal* 35, no. 144 (July 1926): 416. Italics in original.

20. See "Young Graduate," "Leavenworth Course," 591.

21. For a typical criticism, see Major L. D. Davis, Infantry, "A-B-C's of Leavenworth," *Infantry Journal* 23, no. 1 (July 1923): 21–26. Discussion of boring lectures on 25. For a brief analysis of instructor competency in a subject, see "A," "Command and General Staff School," *Cavalry Journal* 35, no. 144 (July 1926): 413.

22. "A," "Command and General Staff School," *Cavalry Journal* 35, no. 144 (July 1926): 412–413, and "A Young Graduate," "Leavenworth Course," 595–596. Also see "The Instructor," *Cavalry Journal* 49, no. 1 (January–February 1940): 65–66. The conference was a full audience participation event, not simply a lecture with questions and answers. On occasion, the questions provoked unexpected exchanges. "An engineer in our class was asked by an infantry instructor, 'How did the Engineers fight?' Answer: 'They fight like infantry, and they fight like h—!'" "A," "Command and General Staff School," *Cavalry Journal* 35, no. 144 (July 1926): 412.

23. "A," "Command and General Staff School," *Cavalry Journal* 35, no. 144 (July 1926): 413.

24. "A Young Graduate," "Leavenworth Course," 595–596.

25. Ibid., 594–595.

26. For the comment about all participants in a conference actually participating, see "The Instructor," *Cavalry Journal* 49, no. 1 (January–February 1940): 65–66. Also see Captain Francis G. Bonham, "The Military Instructor," *Infantry Journal* 29, no. 4 (October 1926):

355–365, and part two, "The Military Instructor," *Infantry Journal* 29, no. 5 (November 1026): 493–501. Bonham, a 1931 Leavenworth graduate, discussed in great detail the need to master the subject while providing interesting and stimulating instruction, including practical problem solving. Although his examples were from close-order drill and rifle marksmanship, his techniques appear to have been part of the instruction at Leavenworth.

27. "A," "Command and General Staff School," *Cavalry Journal* 35, no. 144 (July 1926): 417.

28. See CGSS, *Schedule(s) for 1928–1929, First Year Course; 1929–1930, Second Year Course; 1934–1935, First Year Course;* and *1935–1936, Second Year Course* (CGSSP, 1928, 1929, 1934, 1935). The differences among these educational environments were described for the students in *Instruction Circular No. 1,* issued to each student upon arrival. Exercises were "used to give students practice in the technique of certain subjects of instruction. They [were] used mainly in practicing the technique of combat orders" from *Instruction Circular No. 1, Series 1935–1936* (CGSSP, 1935), 17. Similar definitions are found in *Instruction Circular No. 1, Series 1926–1927,* 15.

29. "A Young Graduate," "Leavenworth Course," 594.

30. The evaluation's effect on the education is the subject of the next chapter. For a synopsis of the frequency of "pay problems," see Truscott, *Twilight,* 145–146.

31. *Instruction Circular No. 2, Series 1935–1936,* 20. For the blueprints of Building 52, see "Plans of the Command and General Staff School Building and Proposed Annex, March 1931," located in CARL blueprints archive.

32. For examples, see GSS, *Instruction Circular No. 1,* July 1, 1924, 16; *Instruction Circular No. 1,* July 1, 1926, 13, 15; CGSS, *Instruction Circular No. 1,* July 1, 1935, 17; and CGSS, *Instruction Circular No. 2,* July 1, 1935, 17.

33. Charles M. Bundel, "The Solution of Map Problems: The Estimate of the Situation," Lesson Sheet for Afternoon Conference, September 17, 1919, in *Selected Papers,* 192–195, is one example.

34. The eight types of solution from 1924 *Instruction Circular No. 1,* 48.

35. Examples from 1932–1933 CGSS Problems, from *The Command and General Staff School, Index to School Problems,* Series 1919–1920 to 1932–1933 (CGSSP, 1933), 66.

36. *Instruction Circular No. 2, Series 1935–1936,* 17–18, quote on 17. The challenge map maneuvers presented to keeping all students gainfully employed was discussed by Major W. G. Simmons in "The Relative Value of Lectures, Conferences, Map Problems, Map Exercises, and Map Maneuvers in a Course of Instruction within a Proposed Plan for Their Coordinated Use" (CARL: Student Research Papers, 1932), 25–26.

37. There is no evidence in the record that Leavenworth adapted the exercises to a true Red force in the interwar period. With mobilization, and especially after Pearl Harbor, specific instruction in the Axis military forces became a matter of course. Lieutenant Colonel Merrill E. Spalding, Infantry, "Down the Road," *Infantry Journal* 38, no. 5 (July–August 1931): 336–338.

38. The 1932 version was titled *Manual for Umpires of Field Maneuvers (Provisional).*

39. *Instruction Circular No. 2, Series 1935–1936,* 17–18, quote on 18.

40. See Cromwell, "Methods of Instruction," 18, for comments on the challenge of only knowing student requirements on the morning of the exercise.

41. *Instruction Circular No. 2, series 1935–1936,* 17–18.

42. Ibid., 19.

43. See *Instruction Circular No. 1,* 1924, 56, and *Instruction Circular No. 2, Series 1935–1936,* 17–20.

44. 1923 *FSR*, 28, 32, 41, 55, 72, and 77.

45. Ibid., 77.

46. Ibid.

47. Ibid., 84, 88, 93, 95, 96.

48. Army Service Schools, "The General Staff School Schedule for 1919–1920, dated October 1, 1919," Fort Leavenworth, Kansas, 1919, marked "issued to instructors only," 1, 2–23.

49. Students, U.S. Army Command and General Staff School, *The Horseshoe*, 1926 (Mimeograph, Fort Leavenworth, KS: 1926), cartoon on 15; overheard remarks on 49. Available in CARL, curricular files for 1926.

50. Director, GSS, *Annual Report*, 1920–1921, 24.

51. See, for example, *Instruction Circular No. 2*, 1935.

52. Director, School of the Line, *Annual Report*, 1921–1922, 57.

53. J. A. McAndrew, *The Art of Instructing: Prepared Especially for the Information of Instructors at the Command and General Staff School* (CGSSP, 1936), 16.

54. McAndrew, *The Art of Instructing*, 16–17.

55. Quoted in L. James Binder, *Lemnitzer: A Soldier for His Time* (Washington, DC: Brassey's, 1997), 60.

56. GSSP, *Instruction Circular No. 1* (GSSP, 1926–1927), 46–50.

57. CGSS, *Instruction Circular No. 2* (CGSSP, 1935), 25–28.

58. Ibid., 23–24.

59. *Annual Report*, 1928–1929, 9.

60. Henry Gerard Phillips, *The Making of a Professional: Manton S. Eddy, USA* (Westport, CT: Greenwood, 2000), 64.

61. Cited in Phillips, *Making of a Professional*, 63–64. For the original description by Collins, see J. Lawton Collins, *Lightning Joe: An Autobiography* (Baton Rouge: Louisiana State University Press, 1979), 56–57.

62. Ernest N. Harmon (other authors unknown), "Group Research Study: A Study of the Japanese Intelligence Service during the Russo-Japanese War," File No. 27, G 1932–33. Available at the Combined Arms Research Library website at http://comarms.ipac.dynixasp.com/ipac20/ipac.jsp?session=T228P85R37475.47382&profile=carlcgsc&source=~!comarms&view=subscriptionsummary&uri=full=3100001~!358307~!0&ri=1&aspect=subtab327&menu=search&ipp=20&spp=20&staffonly=&term=Study+of+the+Japanese+intelligence+service+during+the+Russo-Japanese+War&index=.GW&uindex=&aspect=subtab327&menu=search&ri=1#focus, accessed December 5, 2008; quote on 8.

63. Ernest N. Harmon, "Critical Analysis of the German Cavalry Operations in the Lodz Campaign to include the breakthrough at Brzeziny, with particular reference to the I Cavalry Corps," CGSS student research paper, May 12, 1933, available at the CARL website at http://comarms.ipac.dynixasp.com/ipac20/ipac.jsp?session=T228P85R37475.47382&profile=carlcgsc&source=~!comarms&view=subscriptionsummary&uri=full=3100001~!357991~!0&ri=4&aspect=subtab327&menu=search&ipp=20&spp=20&staffonly=&term=Harmon+German+Cavalry&index=.GW&uindex=&aspect=subtab327&menu=search&ri=4#focus, accessed December 5, 2008. Comments about weakness of cavalry on 23–24.

64. *Annual Report*, 1938–1939, Appendix 2.

65. Ibid.

66. Simmons, "Relative Value," 13, for survey numbers; quote from 32; "valuable time" from 24; 15 for instructor quality comment.

67. See Emery, "What Should Be the Plan," 5, and Cromwell, "Methods of Instruction," 12.

68. Analysis of charts in Hunt, *History*, 160–165. Some interpretation of these charts was

necessary, as the hours are reported in periods of two hours and half-days of four. Several individual classes and exercises also varied from the standard two- or four-hour schedule.

69. Orville Z. Tyler, Colonel of Infantry, U.S. Army, *The History of Fort Leavenworth, 1937–1951*, which brings up to date the *History of Fort Leavenworth 1827–1927* by Elvid Hunt, and 2nd ed. brought up to date 1827–1937 by Walter E. Lorence, Captain, Corps of Engineers, U.S. Army (CGSCP, 1951), 4.

70. "Mercutio," "Wanted — Ghosts," in "Cerebrations" column, *Infantry Journal* 43, no. 3 (May–June 1936): 265–266.

71. Major John H. Burns, Infantry, "Vitalize the Map Problem," *Infantry Journal* 44, no. 5 (September–October 1937): 412–414.

72. Lieutenant Colonel L. D. Davis, Infantry, "The Marking System at Leavenworth," *Infantry Journal* 42, no. 3 (March–April 1935): 117–118.

73. Lieutenant Colonel Bernard Lentz, Infantry, "A Decade of Army Schools," *Cavalry Journal* 41, no. 173 (September–October 1932): 46–48. Another critique of the applicatory method was that it was out of touch with the real life of an army officer in the 1930s. Perhaps not understanding the mission of the school, Major E. D. Cooke in 1935 accused the school of teaching about "corps artillery, tanks, chemicals and whatnots," when the reality for army officers was they lived and worked "in the bush leagues" where such things did not exist. Major E. D. Cooke, Infantry, "Curves and Fast Balls at Leavenworth," *Infantry Journal* 43, no. 5 (September–October 1936): 447–449. Quote from last paragraph on 449.

74. Memorandum, General George Catlett Marshall to Colonel Omar Bradley, March 30, 1940, in Larry I. Bland, Sharon R. Ritenour, and Clarence E. Wunderlin Jr., eds., *The Papers of George Catlett Marshall, Volume 2: "We Cannot Delay" July 1, 1939–December 6, 1941* (Baltimore: Johns Hopkins University Press, 1986), 182.

75. Extensive correspondence located in NAII, RG 407, Office of the Adjutant General, Central Files, 1926–1939, General Files, Box 2037, 352.01 (12-38-36) (1) Section 2 to 352.01 (11-7-35) (1) Section 1. Hereafter cited as RG 407, Box 2037.

76. Brigadier General Chas. M. Bundel, "1st Ind," date-stamped Jan 7 1937, RG 407, Box 2037.

77. Bundel, "1st Ind," RG 407, Box 2037, 3–4.

78. Bundel, "1st Ind," RG 407, Box 2037, 4–5.

79. Adjutant General, "2d Ind," not dated, RG 407, Box 2037. Underline of *"salient principles"* in original.

80. Major P. E. Peabody, Assistant Secretary, General Staff, Memorandum for the Adjutant General, "Subject: The Command and General Staff School," dated July 7, 1937, RG 407, Box 2037.

81. Colonel E. L. Gruber, Memorandum for the Deputy Chief of Staff, "Subject: Command and General Staff School," dated March 30, 1937, RG 407, Box 2037. Pencil notations are on 3.

82. For General Marshall's curtailed visit to Leavenworth, see Bland, vol. 2, 145, note 1.

83. A situation eloquently summarized by Brigadier General Bundel at the Command and General Staff School Opening Exercises on September 1, 1938, in Bundel, *Selected Professional Papers*, 10. The only exceptions to this rule were forces deployed on the border with Mexico and 15th Infantry in China.

84. Major H. H. Pfeil, A.G.D., "Why Leavenworth?" *Infantry Journal* 30, no. 1 (January 1927): 30–31.

85. McAndrew, *The Art of Instructing*, 1936, 18. Italics added.

Chapter 6. The Leavenworth Students

1. E. N. Harmon with Milton MacKaye and William Ross MacKaye, *Combat Commander: Autobiography of a Soldier* (Englewood Cliffs, NJ: Prentice-Hall, 1970), 14–56. Also see Omar N. Bradley and Clay Blair, *A General's Life* (New York: Simon and Schuster, 1983), chs. 6–9.

2. From 1935 through 1938, two Chinese Army officers attended the course in each year. The Philippine Army sent one officer in 1938 and two officers in 1939 and 1940. In addition to the officers of the new Philippine Army, Leavenworth had students from the Philippine Scouts, a formation of U.S. officers and Philippine soldiers. The Philippine Scouts sent two officers in 1928, one each in 1930, 1932, 1935, and 1938, and five in 1937. The Philippine Scout officers were frequently of Philippine ethnicity.

3. *Annual Report*, 1939–1940, 8; *Annual Report*, 1932–1933, Commandant, 6; and *CSFG*.

4. *Annual Report*, 1939–1940, 8, and *CSFG*.

5. Edward M. Coffman and Peter F. Herrly, "The American Regular Army Officer Corps between the World Wars," *Armed Forces and Society* 4, no. 1 (November 1977): 55–73.

6. From roster of graduates of 1925 from *Annual Report*, 1924–1925, 10–14, and Adjutant General's Office, U.S. Army, *The Army Register, 1923* (Washington, DC: Government Printing Office, 1923).

7. *Annual Report*, 1924–1925, 10–14.

8. Timothy K. Nenninger has researched the deaths of every officer at Fort Leavenworth in the period. Eight student officers died; two were suicides. Major Frank A. Turner died on June 15, 1924, and Lieutenant Colonel Emery T. Smith on December 3, 1924. Both officers were geographic bachelors, and both were suffering stress from their grades, according to the Line of Duty investigations. Turner's Line of Duty investigation is in NAII, RG 153, Judge Advocate General to the Adjutant General, July 23, 1924, 210.46. Smith's Line of Duty investigation is available in the same record group, January 9, 1925. Unpublished study provided to the author by Timothy K. Nenninger. Several students failed to complete the course each year. Some were identified as physically unable to complete the course, but the six deaths were identified as accidental deaths or deaths from illness. See *Annual Reports*, 1919 through 1928. Lucian K. Truscott Jr., *The Twilight of the U.S. Cavalry: Life in the Old Army, 1917–1942*, ed. Lucian K. Truscott III (Lawrence: University Press of Kansas, 1989), 140.

9. See, for example, Bradford Grethen Chynoweth, *Bellamy Park: Memoirs* (Hicksville, NY: Exposition, 1975), who called the course "the ordeal," 122–126; Frank James Price, *Troy H. Middleton: A Biography* (Baton Rouge: Louisiana State University Press, 1974), 89–96; Truscott, *Twilight*, 136–155; and many others.

10. Lois R. Dunn, "An Army Wife Goes to School," *Field Artillery Journal* 27, no. 4 (July–August 1937): 286–288.

11. Truscott, *Twilight*, 144.

12. Brigadier General Hanson E. Ely, Commandant, Fort Leavenworth, Kansas, "Address at the Opening of the General Service Schools" (GSSP), 1922), 8–19. Long quote on 19. Address is available in CARL.

13. Brigadier General H. A. Smith, Commandant, General Service Schools, "Address at Opening Exercises of the Command and General Staff School, Fort Leavenworth, Kansas, September 10, 1923" (GSSP, 1923), 8–12. Address is available in CARL.

14. Bundel, "Address to Opening Exercises," Command and General Staff School, in Charles M. Bundel, *Selected Professional Papers of Chas. M. Bundel* (CGSSP, 1939), 10–15.

15. Harry Richard Yarger, "Army Officer Personnel Management: The Creation of the Modern American System to 1939" (Ph.D. diss., Temple University, 1996), 188–189, n. 48.

16. NAII, RG 407, Office of the Adjutant General, Central Files, Box 1110, CGS School, Fort Leavenworth, Kansas 210.63 (11-21-23) to (10-25-23) folder 210.63 (11-13-23) Sections 1 and 2.

17. J. B. Crawford, as a staff study in support of a memorandum from the Chief of Coast Artillery to the War Department Adjutant General in December 1931. Available at NAII, RG 407, Office of the Adjutant General, Central Files, 1926–1939, 352.01 (7-18-33) (1) top 352.01 (2-1-32) Box 2041.

18. See NAII, RG 407, Office of the Adjutant General, Central Files, Box 1109, folder CGS School 210.63 Section 2, Memorandum dated December 22, 1924, from Adjutant General to Chiefs of all War Department Branches, "Subject: Apportionment of Student Officers, General Service Schools, 1925–1926 Course, and Policies Governing Their Selection."

19. Lieutenant Colonel F. A. Doniat, Field Artillery, "Recommendations for Leavenworth and the War College," *Field Artillery Journal* 27, no. 6 (November–December 1937): 455–456.

20. File for student selection process of 1922. NAII, RG 407, Office of the Adjutant General, Central Files, Box 1114, folder "General Staff College, Fort Leavenworth, Kansas."

21. NAII, RG 407, Office of the Adjutant General Central Files, 1926–1939, Box 1911, Extracts from the Efficiency Reports of . . . (1932–1934 C&GSS) file.

22. See topics of the Day, "Selection of Students for the Command and General Staff School," *Cavalry Journal* 37, no. 151 (April 1928): 275–276; Notes from the Chief of Cavalry, "Selection of Students for Command and General Staff School and the Army War College," *Cavalry Journal* 46, no. 5 (September–October 1937): 469–470; Varied Ground, "School Details," *Infantry Journal* 17, no. 3 (September 1920): 285–287; and Notes from the Chief of Infantry, "Policy on Command and General Staff School," *Infantry Journal* 30, no. 1 (January 1927): 63–64. Also "Field Artillery Graduates of General and Special Service Schools and Their New Assignments," *Field Artillery Journal* 27, no. 4 (July–August 1937): 300–301.

23. Dwight David Eisenhower, *At Ease: Stories I Tell My Friends* (Garden City, NY: Doubleday, 1967), 198–200, tells this story.

24. Kenneth S. Davis, *Soldier of Democracy: A Biography of Dwight Eisenhower* (Garden City, NY: Doubleday, Doran, 1945), 203, gives part of this story; Geoffrey Perret, *Eisenhower* (Holbrook, MA: Adams Media, 1999), 91–92, fills in more of the details.

25. See the spreadsheet NAII, RG 407, Office of the Adjutant General Central Files, Box 1109, folder CGS School 210.63 Section 2.

26. NAII RG 407, Office of the Adjutant General Central Files, Box 1894, 210.63 C&GS School (12-19-34) Section 1 "s"–"Z" to 210.63 C&GS School (12-19-34) Section 2.

27. Chynoweth, *Bellamy Park*, 101.

28. Ibid., 99.

29. William M. Hoge, oral history interview, conducted by Lieutenant Colonel George R. Robertson, 34. Located in William M. Hoge Papers, MHI.

30. Walter K. Wilson Jr., oral history interview, conducted by Dr. Paul Walker, January 1978, 43–44, 50. Interview located in Walter K. Wilson Jr. Papers, MHI.

31. Henry Gerard Phillips, *The Making of a Professional: Manton S. Eddy, USA* (Westport: Greenwood, 2000), 45. Also see Bradley, *General's Life*, 56, for a similar discussion.

32. Coffman and Herrly, "Regular Officer Corps," 56.

33. Harmon, *Combat Commander*, 50–56. Also Bradley, *General's Life*, 60–79.

34. Colonels were 191 of 201, lieutenant colonels 245 of 264. "Lists showing number of present Regular Army officers who are graduates and non-graduates of the various Army

schools," located in NAII, RG 407, The Office of the Adjutant General Central Files, Bulky Files, Box 1786, folder 352.07 (8-24-37). See chart on 5.

35. Ibid. See chart on 5.

36. Ibid.

37. Notes from the Chief of Infantry, "Field Officer Graduates of Fort Leavenworth," *Infantry Journal* 32, no. 2 (February 1928): 183–184.

38. "Invictus," "The Legion of the Lost," *Infantry Journal* 43, no. 6 (November–December 1936): 503–506. Quote on 503.

39. Colonel Rowan P. Lemly, Infantry, "Leavenworth or Bust," *Infantry Journal* 43, no. 1 (January–February 1936): 46–48.

40. "Competitor," "Leavenworth: At Home and Abroad," *Infantry Journal* 44, no. 5 (September–October 1937): 423–427.

41. "A Study of C&GSS Capacity to Educate All Army Officers," located in NAII, RG 407, Office of the Adjutant General Central Files, Box 1889, 210.63 C&GS School (1-2-37) Section 2 to 210.63 C&GS School (12-7-36).

42. Analysis from roster of graduates of 1938 from *Annual Report*, 1937–1938, 10–14, and Adjutant General's Office, U.S. Army, *The Army Register, 1935* (Washington, DC: Government Printing Office, 1935). Also Phillip S. Meilinger, *Hoyt S. Vandenberg: The Life of a General* (Bloomington: Indiana University Press, 1989), 18.

43. *Annual Report*, 1936–1937, 14.

44. *Annual Report*, 1937–1938, 9–10.

45. Major General W. L. Reed, Inspector General, Memorandum dated December 5, 1938, "Subject: Method of Selection of Students," NAII, RG 407, Office of the Adjutant General Central Files, Box 1883, 210.63 C&GS School (7-26-39) Section 3 to 210.63 C&GS School (11-7-38) Section 1.

Chapter 7. The Most Difficult Year of Their Careers

1. See discussion of suicides in Chapter 6. Epigraph from Ernest N. Harmon with Milton MacKaye and William Ross MacKaye, *Combat Commander: Autobiography of a Soldier* (Englewood Cliffs, NJ: Prentice-Hall, 1970), 50. Harmon may have believed there was a cut of 50 percent for the second year, but this was certainly no longer the case.

2. See, for example, Bradford Grethen Chynoweth, *Bellamy Park* (Hicksville, NY: Exposition, 1975), who called the course "the ordeal," 122–126; Frank James Price, *Troy H. Middleton: A Biography* (Baton Rouge: Louisiana State University Press, 1974), 89–96; Lucian K. Truscott Jr., *The Twilight of the U.S. Cavalry: Life in the Old Army, 1917–1942* (Lawrence: University Press of Kansas, 1989), 136–155; and many others.

3. Marshall, "Memorandum for the Deputy Chief of Staff, April 13, 1937," in Larry I. Bland and Sharon R. Ritenour, eds., *The Papers of George Catlett Marshall, Volume 1: The Soldierly Spirit, December 1880–June 1939* (Baltimore: Johns Hopkins University Press, 1981), 531–533. See Forrest C. Pogue, *George C. Marshall: Education of a General, 1880–1939* (New York: Viking, 1963), 314–315. Also see Maxwell Taylor, *Swords and Ploughshares* (New York: W. W. Norton, 1972), 30.

4. Timothy K. Nenninger, "Creating Officers: The Leavenworth Experience, 1920–1940." *Military Review* 69, no. 11 (November 1989): 61–62.

5. *Instruction Circular No. 1, The General Service Schools, Fort Leavenworth, Kansas, 1 July 1924* (Fort Leavenworth: General Service Schools Press, 1924), 6.

6. At least one student during the interwar period had a somewhat different perception of the GSEL and attendance at Leavenworth. In his memoir, Omar Bradley reminisced that he and his wife welcomed his *selection* to the Command and General Staff School because it would effectively guarantee his eventual promotion to colonel before mandatory retirement age and, therefore, a financially secure retirement. In actuality, as Bradley pointed out several pages later, selection to attend the school was only the first step toward entry into the senior ranks of the army. The student had to do well at Leavenworth to move forward. Omar N. Bradley and Clay Blair, *A General's Life: An Autobiography* (New York: Simon and Schuster, 1983), 60–61.

7. Memorandum dated November 1, 1932, "Subject: Recommendations to the Chief of Coast Artillery Relative to the General Service Schools," located in NAII, RG 407, Office of the Adjutant General Central Files, Box 2041, 1926–1939 General Files, 352.01 (7-18-33) (1) to 352.01 (2-1-32).

8. As reported to the army in War Department General Order No. 56, September 14, 1920, 1.

9. For the GSEL board process, see War Department General Order No. 16, December 3, 1928. For the procedures by 1935, see CGSS, *Instruction Circular No.1* (CGSCP), 1935), 9–10. Also see Policy Letter, War Department, Adjutant General's Office, January 5, 1922, reproduced in *Annual Report*, 1921–1922, 9–11, and comments by commandant on 14.

10. *Annual Report*, 1927–1928, lists 201 graduates, including two USMC officers, two Philippine Scouts, one officer who resigned since graduation, and one officer from Cuba. The selection of 407 officers for the 1928 GSEL is reported in War Department General Order No. 10, July 16, 1928.

11. Major General John W. Gulick, Chief, Coast Artillery, Memorandum dated December 20, 1931, "Subject: Operation of the Army Educational System with Special Reference to the Coast Artillery Corps," located in NAII, RG 407, Office of the Adjutant General Central Files, Box 2041, 1926–1939 General Files, 352.01 (7-18-33) (1) to 352.01 (2-1-32), quote on 2. Also see Major General Andrew Moses, Memorandum dated November 1, 1932, "Subject: Recommendations of the Chief of Coast Artillery Relative to the General Service Schools," in NAII, RG 407, Office of the Adjutant General Central Files, Box 2041, 1926–1939 General Files, 352.01 (7-18-33) (1) to 352.01 (2-1-32).

12. Colonel Thomas W. Hammond, "Why Not Keep the Door Open?" *Infantry Journal* 26, no. 3 (March 1925): 253–255.

13. Lieutenant Colonel Bernard Lentz, Infantry, "A Decade of Army Schools," *Infantry Journal* 39, no. 5 (September–October 1932): 355–357. This article was also published in *Cavalry Journal* 41, no. 173 (September–October 1932): 46–48.

14. Notes from the Chief of Infantry, "General Staff Eligible List," *Infantry Journal* 42, no. 4 (July–August 1935): 365.

15. Major General Johnson Hagood, "A Bas Eligibility," *Infantry Journal* 44, no. 1 (January–February 1937): 14–15.

16. "Zadig," "General Staff Eligible List," *Infantry Journal* 45, no. 1 (January–February 1938): 61.

17. Extensive file of memoranda, endorsements, and letters located in NAII, RG 407, Office of the Adjutant General Central Files, 1926–1939 General Files, Box 2037, 352.01 (12-38-36) (1) Section 2 to 352.01 (11-7-35) (1) Section 1.

18. Major General Malin Craig, "Report of the Chief of Staff of the Army," in *Report of Secretary of War, 1938* (Washington, DC: Government Printing Office, 1938), 35. Also see War Department "Bulletin 8, August 12, 1938."

19. Assistant Commandant, *Annual Report*, 1921–1922, 28.

20. This assessment is from initial work done on his dissertation through the University of Kansas by Michael Stewart.

21. Policy Letter, War Department, Adjutant General's Office, January 5, 1922, reproduced in *Annual Report*, 1921–1922, 9–11.

22. Practically, the Leavenworth faculty had resolved the issue. According to Brigadier General Bundel's 1936–1937 annual report, "With the exception of the distinctly less capable members of a class, all graduating are assumed to be academically fitted for higher education and are so recommended." *Annual Report*, 1936–1937, 15.

23. Assistant Commandant, *Annual Report*, 1920, 7–9.

24. Ibid. Eltinge's assignments to Leavenworth from *CSFG*.

25. Director, School of the Line, *Annual Report*, 1920–1921, 28. Brees, a three-time graduate of the school, in 1903, 1905, and one of the instructor-graduates in 1922, returned to Leavenworth in February 1935 as commandant. *CSFG*.

26. *Annual Report*, 1921–1922, 12–13.

27. The Lawrence Family Papers, MHI, contain Major Thompson Lawrence's final class standing memorandum. He stood ninth of 258 classmates in the class of 1924–1925, with a percentage of 89.96.

28. *Annual Report*, 1922–1923, 7–8.

29. Policy Letter, War Department, Adjutant General's Office, November 10, 1921, reproduced in *Annual Report*, 1921–1922, 8–9.

30. *Annual Report*, 1921–1922, 9.

31. See Harry P. Ball, *Of Responsible Command: A History of the U.S. Army War College* (Carlisle Barracks, PA: Alumni Association of the U.S. Army War College, 1983), 173, 191, 203, 235, 249, and 250, for graduating class sizes.

32. Robert H. Berlin, *U.S. Army World War II Corps Commanders: A Composite Biography* (Fort Leavenworth, KS: Combat Studies Institute Press, 1989), 11, and Harmon, *Combat Commander*, 50–57.

33. J. A. McAndrew (CGSS), *The Art of Instructing: Prepared Especially for the Information of Instructors at the Command and General Staff School* (CGSCP, 1936), 7.

34. Henry Gerard Phillips, *The Making of a Professional: Manton S. Eddy, USA* (Westport, CT: Greenwood, 2000), 45, 61–62.

35. McAndrew, *The Art of Instructing*, 18.

36. Letter, George S. Patton to Beatrice Patton, quoted in Martin Blumenson, *The Patton Papers, 1885–1940* (New York: Houghton Mifflin, 1972; reprint ed. Da Capo, 1998), 776. Patton was a geographic bachelor while attending CGSS.

37. Harmon, *Combat Commander*, 50, and many other memoirs compare the easy life at the War College with the arduous study needed at Leavenworth. Of course, although selection to the final General Staff Corps list was not made until one was a student at the War College, the most significant cut was in attaining the GSEL at Leavenworth, or at least that was the perception, if it was not actually true by the late 1920s.

38. Geoffrey Perret, *Eisenhower* (Holbrook, MA: Adams Media, 1999), 94–95. The quote is Perret's conclusion. His sources for Eisenhower's time at CGSS included two interviews from the Eisenhower Library and "The Leavenworth Course" by "A Young Graduate."

39. Perret, *Eisenhower*, 94–95.

40. See Chynoweth, *Bellamy Park*, 101.

41. For example, see General William M. Hoge, *Oral History Interview*, Senior Officers Debriefing Program, MHI, 45.

42. See Lieutenant General Walter K. Wilson, *Engineer Memoirs*, oral history, MHI, January 1978, 44; Hoge, *Oral History*, 45. CSFG, 56, lists Hoge's graduation year.

43. See *Instruction Circular No. 1*, 1924, 47–48.

44. *Annual Report*, 1921–1922, 12.

45. *Annual Report*, 1925–1926, 11.

46. Ibid., 12.

47. *Annual Report*, 1926–1927, 10. Also see NAII, RG 407, Office of the Adjutant General Central Files 1926–1939, Box 2048, 352.02 (1-17-28) to 352.31 (2-20-26) (1), file titled "Grading of Student Officers, School of the Line. Amendment of pars. 30, and 31, G.O. 128 WD. 1911."

48. *Annual Report*, 1927–1928, 10.

49. *Annual Report*, 1928–1929, 10.

50. Truscott, *Twilight*, 148.

51. *Annual Report*, 1938–1939, appendix 4.

52. *Annual Report*, 1939–1940, appendix 3, 3.

53. Assistant Commandant, *Annual Report*, 1920, 7.

54. Major Bernard Lentz, Infantry, "The Applicatory Method," *Infantry Journal* 20, no. 6 (June 1922): 604–609.

55. Major L. D. Davis, Infantry, "A-B-C's of Leavenworth," *Infantry Journal* 23, no. 1 (July 1923): 21–26.

56. Lieutenant Colonel L. D. Davis, "The Marking System at Leavenworth," *Infantry Journal* 42, no. 3 (March–April 1935): 117–118. Quote on 118.

57. "Mercutio," "A Gauge of Battle Leadership," in "Cerebrations," *Infantry Journal* 43, no. 5 (September–October 1936): 458.

58. "Anti-Gauge," "A Gage to the Gauge," in "Cerebrations," *Infantry Journal* 43, no. 6 (November–December 1936): 541.

59. See, for examples of student endorsement of the evaluation system, monographs of J. P. Cromwell (1936); Frank E. Emery Jr. (1929); and W. G. Simmons (1932).

60. Francis J. Heraty, "What Should Be the Plan of Education for Officers of the Army, Including a Discussion of Individual Study, the Special Service Schools, the Command and General Staff School, and the Army War College" (CARL: Student Research Papers, 1930), 3.

61. *Annual Report*, 1938–1939, Appendix 2.

62. Ibid.

63. Ibid.

Chapter 8. National Mobilization and the Leavenworth Schools

1. Christopher R. Gabel, *The U.S. Army GHQ Maneuvers of 1941* (Washington, DC: United States Army Center of Military History, 1992), 8–19.

2. CGSS, *Wartime History of the Command and General Staff School, 1939–1945* (CGSS, January 1945), 30 and chart 3. Also see David Eugene Johnson, "The United States Army Command and General Staff School during World War II: Transition to Necessity" (MMAS thesis, CGSC, 1985). The curricular files at CARL for this period are extensive, approximately 300 linear feet of documents.

3. Ernest N. Harmon with Milton MacKaye and William Ross MacKaye, *Combat Commander: Autobiography of a Soldier* (Englewood Cliffs, NJ: Prentice-Hall, 1970), 58.

4. Dates from Trevor N. Dupuy, Curt Jonson, and David L. Bongard, *The Harper Encyclopedia of Military Biography* (New York: HarperCollins, 1992), 316. For the role of the Armored Force, see Robert S. Cameron, *Mobility, Shock, and Firepower: The Emergence of the U.S. Army's Armor Branch, 1917–1945* (Washington, DC: U.S. Army Center of Military History, 2008), chs. 7–8.

5. Orville Z. Tyler Jr., *The History of Fort Leavenworth, 1937–1951* (Fort Leavenworth, KS: Command and General Staff College, 1951), 10–11.

6. See discussion of the number of graduates later in this chapter.

7. For this ANSCOL course, see CGSS, *Wartime History*, 25–27. This course educated officers for duties well above the division level.

8. The system of instruction used after mobilization began in 1940 had been anticipated in the 1920 commandant's report. Colonel LeRoy Eltinge, the deputy commandant, former deputy chief of staff of the AEF, complained that closure of the school for the war was "believed to be wrong." He commented that a wiser use of the resources at Leavenworth would be to maintain the courses but to redesign them as the "particular emergency would necessarily determine the character of the instruction." *Annual Report*, GSS, 1920, 9–10.

9. *Schedule, Special Class, 1940–1941*; and *Schedule, Ninth Special Course, July–September 1942*, CARL.

10. Tabulation from "Sixth Class Statistical Summary" and "Eleventh Class Statistical Summary," CARL.

11. CGSS, *Schedule: Eighth Special Course, May–July 1942* (CGSSP, 1942), 8–10.

12. See, for examples, *Schedule, Special Class, 1940–1941*; and *Schedule, Ninth Special Course, July–September 1942*, CARL.

13. Fifty-eight officers in the study-group divisions graduated from one of these first eleven courses, twenty-two (37.9 percent) serving in exactly the position for which they had been trained, evenly distributed among the four staff sections. Another four officers (7 percent) served in parallel positions, G2s as G3s or G1s as G4s, which Leavenworth grouped together for education, and another four (7 percent) served in nonparallel general staff positions. Nine officers (15.6 percent), educated to be specific staff officers, ended up as division chiefs of staff, and four (7 percent) served as general officers in the divisions. The second largest group, fourteen officers (24 percent), commanded regiments in combat.

14. Letter, George C. Marshall to Lesley J. McNair, April 9, 1940, in Larry I. Bland, Sharry R. Ritenour, and Clarence E. Wunderlin Jr., eds., *"We Cannot Delay," July 1, 1939–December 6, 1941*, vol. 2 of *The Papers of George Catlett Marshall* (Baltimore: Johns Hopkins University Press, 1986), 190–192.

15. Letter, George C. Marshall to General McNair, April 9, 1940, in Bland, *"We Cannot Delay,"* vol. 2, 192.

16. This included 73.1 percent, or 261 hours, in exercises of a total of 357 hours in the course. In Course Ten, the percentage was 77.3 percent. This analysis from "Program and Schedule" documents from General Staff Courses One through Twelve, located in CARL, Curriculum Files.

17. CGSS, *Program and Schedule, Eighteenth General Staff Course and Tenth Service Staff Course, Air Forces, Ground Forces, Service Forces, April–June 1944* (CGSSP, 1944).

18. All students, regardless of their specific staff section, participated in thirty-two of these events, although frequently role-playing specific staff officers. The other events, fifty-six, were unevenly divided among the G1, G2, G3, and G4 sections, with the G3 covering twenty-two subjects, the G2 seventeen. The G1 and G4 sections were combined for fifteen subjects, and the G1s received an additional seven subjects covering specific personnel issues. CGSS,

Comprehensive Survey of the Command and General Staff School, Wartime, 1940–1945
(CGSSP, October 1945), appendix E, Summary of Subjects, Applicatory Work, located in
CARL Archives.

19. See the "Statistical Summary of the 24th General Staff Class" in the Darrie Richards
Papers, MHI.

20. Although the exact ratio varied from class to class, the December 1942 class of 773
students contained 153 regular army, 151 National Guard, 386 Organized Reserves, and 71
Army of the United States officers, in addition to 12 other officers. "Statistical Summary of the
Eleventh General Staff Class, C.&G.S. School, December 17, 1942," document located in
11th GS Class files, CARL. By late 1944, the official statistical summaries of the General Staff
Course no longer even differentiated among RA, NG, ORC, or AUS officers. Statistics were
now maintained regarding branch affiliation, but distinctions between the components of the
officers were no longer recorded. See, for example, "Statistical Summary of the 20th General
Staff Class," *Twenty-First General Staff Program and Schedule, October 1944–January 1945*,
located in Philip F. Biehl Papers, MHI.

21. U.S. War Department, *Field Service Regulations, Operations, May 22, 1941* (Washington, DC: Government Printing Office, 1941); *Comprehensive Survey*, Appendix E, Summary
of Subjects, Applicatory Work, located in CARL. Also see the *Program and Schedules* for the
various General Staff Courses, CARL.

22. CGSS, "List of Graduates and Nongraduates of the Eighteenth General Staff Class, 6
June 1944" (CARL, Curricular Records, Eighteenth General Staff Class, 1944), 36. One of
the effects of shortening the course in 1941 was the abandonment of effective evaluation. Students continued to be evaluated, given grades for the course, and listed in an order of merit,
but this apparently had little to do with immediate assignments or future career patterns. The
grades continued to follow the same distribution described by the report of the commandant
at the end of the peacetime period, with the exception of the increase in the number of unsatisfactory or failing evaluations. See, for example, the statistical analysis in *Comprehensive Survey*, appendix C, Statistics, table 19.

23. *Wartime History*, 19–20.

24. *Comprehensive Survey*, appendix C, Statistics, table 11.

25. After the change to the courses in early 1942, the War Department required a report
from the commandant on each class, listing the graduates and nongraduates and giving reasons for each failure. These reasons, about twenty per course, are located in part 3 of the
"List(s) of Graduates and Non-graduates of the ## General Staff Class," Fort Leavenworth,
KS. Records include the Eighteenth, Nineteenth, Twentieth, and Twenty-Second Classes.
Material available in the Curricular Files, CARL. The failures were also tabulated by component, with less than 6 percent from the regular army, 15 percent from the National Guard, 58
percent from Organized Reserve officers, and 20.3 percent from Army of the United States officers. The Women's Army Corps officers accounted for slightly more than 1 percent of the total failures. *Comprehensive Survey*, appendix C, Statistics, table 12.

26. An army aviator, McNarney, a veteran of AEF general staff duty, an honor graduate of
the 1926 Leavenworth class, and a former instructor at the Air Corps School at Maxwell, had
taught at the Army War College from 1933 to 1935. Richard G. Stone Jr., "Joseph Taggart
McNarney," in Roger Spiller, Joseph G. Dawson III, and T. Harry Williams, eds., *Dictionary
of American Military Biography*, vol. 2 (Westport, CT: Greenwood, 1984), 702–705.

27. Tyler, *History*, 19.

28. Lieutenant General McNarney, Directive to Commandant, CGSS, January 6, 1943,
cited in ibid., 20 (footnote).

29. Ibid., 19–20.

30. An element of the changing instruction at Leavenworth was a name change from "Special Course" to "General Staff Course." Apparently made at the personal desire of Truesdell, this name change demonstrated an acceptance that the courses at Leavenworth would not return to the prewar normalcy at any time during the war. Until victory, the short course was the normal course and deserved an easily understood name. See *Schedule for the Ninth Special Course, July–September 1942*, CARL, which has Truesdell's handwriting scratching out the "Special" and replacing it with "General Staff." Starting with the next class, all documents referred to the course as the "General Staff Course."

31. Also different from the interwar courses was the missing word "Command" in the course title. For an example, see the Courses and Scope description in the *Program and Schedule, Twenty-First General Staff Class, October 1944–January 1945* (CGSSP), document located in the Philip F. Biehl Papers, MHI.

32. In the same conference, the G2 for the European theater command, Brigadier General E. L. Sibert, Leavenworth class of 1935, asked Major General Truesdell specifically for Leavenworth to matriculate Women's Army Corps officers as trained G2 staff officers, commenting that they were "less ambitious, more thorough, faster workers" than the male officers. Major General Karl Truesdell and Lieutenant Colonel G. W. R. Zethren, "Notes on Overseas Observation Trip—October–November 1943" (CARL Archives, Document No. N-5362, October–November 1943), 2.

33. Robert T. Finney, *History of the Air Corps Tactical School, 1920–1940* (Maxwell Air Force Base, AL: Research Studies Institute, USAF Historical Division, 1955; rpt. ed. 1992), 81–85, quote on 82.

34. See CGSS, *Instruction Circular No. 5*, February 6, 1943, "Organization of the Twelfth General Staff Course and the Fourth Services of Supply Course," located in CARL, Curricular Files, Twelfth General Staff Course, February to April 1943. See "Breakdown of Allotments to Commands, 18th GSC," no date, in CARL Archives, Curriculum Files, 18th General Staff Class, and "Sending Agencies and Number of Students, 19th GSC," no date, in CARL, Curriculum Files, 19th General Staff Class.

35. This logistics course, begun in July 1942, educated officers for logistical staff duty and is discussed in detail below.

36. By the Twenty-First General Staff Course, the antiaircraft students were instructed as a distinct group, with part of their classtime spent with the air forces officers, part with the Infantry Course students, and part on their own schedule. "Program and Schedule, Twenty-First General Staff Class: Air Forces Courses, Ground Forces Courses, Service Forces Courses, October 1944–January 1945," located in Philip F. Biehl Papers, MHI.

37. *Wartime History*, 55–56, lists the classes, students, and graduates through Class Twenty-Two. The graduates from Classes Twenty-Three through Twenty-Seven are available in documents labeled "List of Graduates and Nongraduates of the # General Staff Class." These documents are available in CARL, program of instruction hanging files for each class.

38. "Breakdown of Allotments to 'Commands,'" document located in 18th GS Class files, CARL.

39. *Wartime History*, 20–23.

40. John Sloan Brown, *Draftee Division: The 88th Infantry Division in World War II* (Lexington: University Press of Kentucky, 1986), 37–40, discusses divisional training programs.

41. In the eighteen months from January 1942 to June 1943, the Leavenworth faculty taught fifteen of the New Divisions classes. No division formed before January 1942 attended these courses; however, after that date, the majority of new divisions sent teams to the

Leavenworth classes. Thirty-six infantry, five armored, three airborne, and one cavalry division command and staff teams completed the course. *Wartime History*, 60.

42. Bell I. Wiley, "The Building and Training of Infantry Divisions," in Robert R. Palmer, Bell I. Wiley, and William R. Keast, *The Procurement and Training of Ground Combat Troops: The Army Ground Forces, United States Army in World War II* (Washington, DC: Office of the Chief of Military History, 1948), chart 1, between 434 and 435.

43. Application was 143 hours (81.7 percent) of the course time. CGSS, "Schedule, Fifth Course for Officers of New Divisions, June–July 1942" (CGSSP, 1942). Document located in New Division Courses, Curricular Files, CARL.

44. "Schedule, Fifth Course for Officers of New Divisions," 7.

45. CGSS, "Agenda for Discussion with CGs and CSs, 5th Group of New Divisions, June 7, 1942," document located in New Division Courses, Curricular Files, CARL.

46. Brigadier General Frank Camm attended the course as the executive officer of the division artillery but entered combat as commander of division artillery. Robert C. Wilson was the division G2 in combat but attended the New Divisions Course as General Parker's aide de camp. New Division Course records, CARL and the ETO Order of Battle documents.

47. The 65th Infantry Division had the same officers in the chief of staff, G1, G3, and G4 positions until after V-E Day. The 94th Infantry Division had the same division commander, chief of staff, G2, and G4. New Division Course records, CARL and the ETO Order of Battle documents. The 97th Infantry Division retained only the G4 from the course to combat. The 99th Infantry Division retained no officers in the same duty positions. Just as ineffective was the experience of 71st Infantry Division, which never attended a New Divisions Course, although it was formed in the same time period as these other divisions. New Division Course records, CARL and the ETO Order of Battle documents.

48. New Division Course records, CARL.

49. *Wartime History*, 56.

50. Quoted in ibid., 17.

51. Ibid., 14–19.

52. Two hundred and two officers graduated from nine ANSCOL classes in 1943 and 1944. Although army officers did not initially attend this course, in 1944 they began to attend as a refresher, as most of these relatively senior officers had graduated from a Leavenworth class before World War II. Eighty-six army officers, of whom twenty were "aviation pilots," graduated from these classes. Each class had one or two USMC officers, approximately ten navy officers, and, after February 1944, two or three Allied officers. *Wartime History*, 57. The purpose of these classes was to provide an orientation to selected civilian leaders on issues relevant to civilian support of the war effort. Although the second class was somewhat more successful, with eighty-eight graduates, this program was canceled in April 1943 after only four classes. Focused on material similar to the Service of Supply Course, the class consisted primarily of discussions with the Leavenworth instructors and had no practical application component. *Wartime History*, 61.

53. Ibid., 4–10.

54. Brigadier General Edmund L. Gruber came to Leavenworth when McNair became Chief of Staff of Army General Headquarters, Army Ground Forces, but died suddenly after only a few months at Leavenworth. He had been an instructor at the Field Artillery School, West Point, the Cavalry School, Leavenworth, and the Army War College and was a veteran of the AEF. Christopher Tunney, *A Biographical Dictionary of World War II* (New York: St. Martin's, 1972), 124. Also see Brooks E. Kleber, "Lesley James McNair," in Spiller, *Dictionary*, vol. 2, 695–699, and Ely J. Kahn Jr., *McNair: Educator of an Army* (Washington, DC: Infantry

Journal, 1945). Also see Edmund Louis Gruber hanging files, CARL. The next commandant was Brigadier General Horace H. Fuller, another AEF veteran, who had been an instructor from 1924 through 1927 and a military attaché to France until the collapse in June 1940. Tyler, *History*, 59; *CSFG*, 55, 30, 12. Also see R. Manning Ancell with Christine M. Miller, *The Biographical Dictionary of World War II Generals and Flag Officers: The U.S. Armed Forces* (Westport, CT: Greenwood, 1996), 109. The last wartime commandant was Major General Karl Truesdell, who assumed command of Fort Leavenworth in March 1942.

55. He retired from his position as commandant at Leavenworth shortly after V-J Day. Tyler, *History*, 66. Also see *Who Was Who in American History: The Military*, 594–595; *CSFG*, 14, 23, 28.

56. Senior officers who served as assistant commandants were Colonel Kinzie B. Edmunds, Cavalry (September 1938 to July 1941), Colonel Martin C. Shallenberger, Infantry (July 1941 to June 1944), and Brigadier General William A. Campbell, Field Artillery (August 1944 to September 1945). Edmunds was a 1922 School of the Line graduate and 1923 graduate of the General Staff Course. Shallenberger was a distinguished graduate of the 1927 one-year course, and Campbell graduated in 1934 from the two-year course. Edmunds was an instructor from 1923 through 1925. Shallenberger was first assigned as an instructor in 1939. Campbell was assigned as an instructor beginning in 1937. Tyler, *History of Fort Leavenworth, 1937–1951*, 66, and *CSFG*, 25, 29, 36, 42. The directors of the General Staff Course during World War II were Lieutenant Colonel Raymond E. McQuillan, Cavalry (August 1939 to June 1940), Colonel William Nalle, Cavalry (June 1942 to September 1943), and Colonel John H. Van Vliet, Infantry (August 1942 to January 1947). Colonel Van Vliet directed the General Staff Courses, the New Divisions Course, and then the Regular Course immediately after the war. All of these officers were graduates of Leavenworth: McQuillan was an honor graduate of the class of 1925, Nalle was a distinguished graduate of the class of 1924, and Van Vliet graduated in 1929. McQuillan was first assigned as an instructor in 1936 and Nalle had no prior instructor experience at Leavenworth, but Van Vliet had been an instructor from 1929 to 1933. With the exception of Nalle, seven of the eight senior officers involved in the formation, coordination, and execution of instruction at Leavenworth from 1940 through 1945 were graduates of the interwar course and had served as instructors before World War II. Of the eight, Nalle was assigned to a duty of responsibility for the shortest period—less than four months. Tyler, *History*, 67, *CSFG*, 11–14 and 31–39. The class of 1929 was the second class with no distinction for honor or distinguished graduates.

57. Analysis from CGSS, *Comprehensive Survey of the Command and General Staff School, Wartime, 1940–1945* (CGSS, October 1945), Appendix on Faculty Organization, compared to *CSFG* and *Annual Report, 1939–1940*, list of graduates.

58. Premobilization instructor strength from *Annual Report, 1939–1940*. *Wartime History* gives some data for instructors on 8–9.

59. Tyler, *History*, 69.

60. Discussion of problems of faculty management after mobilization from *Wartime History*, 8–9, cites eight letters from the commandant to the army adjutant general pleading for instructors in the year from August 1940 to October 1941.

61. These comments appear to have concerned both faculty and students, as the letters did not make any distinction. See Letter, George Catlett Marshall to Major General Harold R. Bull, September 8, 1942, and Memorandum for General McNair, December 7, 1942, in *"The Right Man for the Job," December 7, 1941–May 31, 1943*, vol. 3 of *The Papers of George Catlett Marshall*, Larry I. Bland and Sharon Ritenour Stevens, eds. (Baltimore: Johns Hopkins University Press, 1991), 349–350 and 478–479.

62. *Wartime History*, 35–36.

63. Ibid., 36–37.

64. Truesdell, "Notes on Overseas Observation Trip," 6, 3.

65. Major General Karl Truesdell and Lieutenant Colonel G. W. R. Zethren, "Notes on Overseas Observation Trip—October–November 1943" (CARL, Document No. N-5362, October–November 1943), 27.

66. *Wartime History* begins with a photograph ("The academic buildings of . . . Old Leavenworth") and then, on the next page, reproduces the photograph of the 1,000-seat lecture hall in Gruber Hall. Even the official history clearly demonstrates the grave difference between the small, collegial atmosphere of the 250 students in an annual class and the 1,000 students in a ten-week course. *Wartime History*, front-sheet photographs.

67. Maximum student population at Leavenworth from 1941 through 1945 was 1,015. This number was reached in the summer of 1944, when the General Staff Class, newly combined with the Service Staff Class, had 962 students, the ANSCOL had 30 students, and 23 students from Brazil and Peru attended a special Latin American pre–general staff course. See *Wartime History*, appendices B, C, and D.

Chapter 9. Few Leavenworth Graduates, a Global War's Needs

1. Headquarters, Services of Supply, European Theater of Operations, "Notes of Command and Staff Conference, 1 November 1943," 17–18. Document located in CARL, No. N 6542, 1 Nov 43.

2. Ibid., 18.

3. Marvin A. Kreidberg and Merton G. Henry, *History of the Military Mobilization in the United States Army, 1775–1945*, Department of the Army Pamphlet no. 20-212 (Washington, DC: Government Printing Office, 1955), and Kent Roberts Greenfield, Robert R. Palmer, and Bell I. Wiley, *United States Army in World War II: The Army Ground Forces, the Organization of Ground Combat Troops* (Washington, DC: Historical Division, United States Army, 1947). Also see Charles E. Kirkpatrick, *An Unknown Future and a Doubtful Present: Writing the Victory Plan of 1941* (Washington, DC: United States Army Center of Military History, 1990).

4. Kirkpatrick, *Victory Plan*, 8, Wedemeyer's early experience assessed on 7–10. A forthcoming book by Jim Lacey, *Keep from All Thoughtful Men*, from Naval Institute Press, scheduled for publication in the fall of 2010, properly criticizes Kirkpatrick's account and Wedemeyer's success. Jim Lacey provided the author with an advance copy of his manuscript in May 2009.

5. Kirkpatrick, *Victory Plan*, 11, 103.

6. The 215 division number is from ibid., 103.

7. Ibid., 104.

8. Ibid., 104–105.

9. Lacey also points out, accurately, that Wedemeyer's work had no influence on war production or industrial mobilization. It also had no effect on Leavenworth. Lacey, *Thoughtful Men*, ch. 2.

10. Total number of graduates given in CGSS, *Comprehensive Survey of the Command and General Staff School, Wartime, 1940–1945* (CGSS, October 1945), appendix C, table 22, located in CARL.

11. Although 599 Army Air Forces officers attended Leavenworth in Courses One through Eleven, they received little focused instruction on the application of airpower.

12. Total number of graduates given in *Comprehensive Survey*, appendix C, table 22, General Staff Class Matriculation Statistics, located in CARL. No other nation could match this educational output. One of Overy's main points was the U.S. commitment to airpower and the concomitant requirement, accepted by the United States, to devote training time and resources to the education of officers destined for staff jobs and not combat duty per se. See Richard Overy, *Why the Allies Won* (New York: W. W. Norton, 1995), 319.

13. Orville Z. Tyler Jr., *The History of Fort Leavenworth, 1937–1951*, which brings up to date *History of Fort Leavenworth, 1827–1927* by Elvid Hunt (CGSCP, 1951), gives a summary of this survey on 22–23. The August 1944 survey and a less comprehensive survey done two months earlier are no longer in existence at CARL.

14. This summary is based on comparison of the interwar program of instruction with the programs for the three-fold General Staff Course in the late World War II period.

15. Overy, *Why the Allies Won*, 225–227.

16. A copy of this roster, "Headquarters Twelfth Army Group, Subject: Order of Battle and Key Personnel Roster as of 15 December 1944," is on file at CARL.

17. Precise fills at the army level were adjutant general at 67 percent; artillery commanders at 67 percent; chief of staff and deputy chief of staff at 100 percent; G1, G2, G3, and G5 at 33 percent; and G4 at 67 percent.

18. Corps fills were G1 at 11 percent, G3 at 33 percent, and adjutant generals at 33 percent. G4 and G5 positions had no graduates of long courses.

19. Robert R. Palmer, "Reorganization of Ground Troops for Combat," in Greenfield, *Organization of Ground Combat Troops*, 364–382.

20. Hugh M. Cole, *The Lorraine Campaign: United States Army in World War II, European Theater of Operations* (Washington, DC: Historical Division, United States Army, 1950), 18.

21. See Palmer, "Reorganization," 364–382.

22. Cole, *Lorraine*, 373.

23. The number 1,575 is drawn from an analysis of the average age of graduating classes, the number of graduates, and the mandatory retirement age. It does not account for early retirements for health or for resignation. Therefore, 1,575 is an optimistic calculation—the reality was probably 100 or 200 lower. Analysis based on average age of each Leavenworth class from 1920 to 1940. The first three classes, 1920, 1921, and 1922, had all exceeded mandatory retirement age by 1944. The estimate was also based on the War College student committee assessment of a 3 percent per annum attrition of each graduating class, calculated with the actual total number of graduates of each class from 1920 through 1940 inclusive. See information on average age in CGSS, "Wartime History of the Command and General Staff School, 1939–1945" (CGSSP, January 1945), Average Age Chart. Calculations also based on CSFG, *Annual Report* of the Commandants, and a 1937 Staff Study in NAII, RG 407, Bulky Files, Box 17986, Folder 352.07 (8-24-37).

24. Linderman demonstrated that the soldiers and officers of the formations below division, the units that actually directly engaged the enemy ground forces, came from Main Street, USA, not from the professional army. Gerald F. Linderman, *Mirror of War* (Ann Arbor: University of Michigan Press, 1974). Also see his *The World Within War: America's Combat Experience in World War II* (Cambridge: Harvard University Press, 1999).

25. Raymond S. Beightler commanded 37th Infantry Division with distinction in the Pacific, and Raymond S. McLain eventually rose to command XIX Corps in the European theater. Edward M. Coffman, "The Duality of the American Military Tradition," *Journal of Military History* 64 (October 2000): 967–980. Information about Beightler and McCain is on 979.

26. Titles for general staff positions from abbreviations in Office of the Theater Historian, *Order of Battle of the United States Army, World War II: European Theater of Operations, Divisions* (Paris: December 1945), 585. Available at CARL, N-12472.1–3.

27. *FM 100-5* (1941), 23.

28. Ibid., 30.

29. Although all the collective biographies done to date focus on commanders, a full appraisal of divisional effectiveness, and therefore of a significant element of overall army effectiveness, must include the primary staff officers. Two examples of collective biographies are Robert H. Berlin, *U.S. Army World War II Corps Commanders: A Composite Biography* (Fort Leavenworth, KS: Combat Studies Institute, CGSCP, 1989), and Gary Wade, *World War II Division Commanders* (Fort Leavenworth, KS: Combat Studies Institute, CGSCP, 1983). Wade used a 25 percent sample of division commanders for his study. Berlin analyzed the career patterns of the thirty-four corps commanders. In current U.S. Army doctrine, control is the function of staffs; command is a function of the commander of each formation. "Control" is defined as supervision and observation to ensure adherence to instructions; "command" is more a function of leadership, will, and vision than routine observation and adjustment. See Headquarters, Department of the Army, *Operations, FM 3-0* (Washington, DC: Department of the Army, June 2001), 5–17 through 5–18.

30. See Palmer, "Reorganization," especially chapter 4 on the infantry division, chapter 5 on the armored division, and the last half of chapter 7 on the airborne division.

31. For the sampling technique, and for identification of the divisions, see Peter J. Schifferle, "Anticipating Armageddon: The Leavenworth Schools and U.S. Army Military Effectiveness, 1919 to 1945" (Ph.D. diss., University of Kansas, 2002), 40–51.

32. Assignment as of June 1945 of all the divisions graphically depicted in Headquarters, Army Ground Forces, *Report of Activities, Army Ground Forces: World War II* (Washington, DC: Office of the Commanding General, U.S. Army Ground Forces, January 1946), no page numbers, chart titled "Location of U.S. Divisions, June 1946."

33. The numerical analysis that follows included identification of the officers assigned to specific duties at the division and regimental levels. After identification, every roster of graduates of all the courses taught during the interwar period was compared with a list of the officers. Then the rosters of each mobilization course at Leavenworth were compared to the list. Additionally, officers' names were checked against the 1939 *Army Register* and 1939 *Army List* to determine if they were regular army, National Guard, or Organized Reserve officers. Several course rosters for the mobilization period also included biographical details, although none of this information was standardized in the period.

34. *Wartime History* lists all the graduation dates for courses One through Twenty-Two, 55–56.

35. Another division commander, Brigadier General James E. Wharton, CGSC class of 1933, assumed command of 28th Infantry Division in combat in France on August 13, 1944. While visiting the front lines later that day, a German sniper killed him. See 28th Infantry Division, *Historical and Pictorial Review of the 28th Infantry Division in World War II* (Camp Shelby, MI: 1946; reprint, Nashville, TN: Battery Press, 1980), no page numbers, photo and caption for Brigadier General Wharton approximately one-third from the front.

36. See ibid., photo and caption for Brigadier General Buchanan approximately one-third-from the front, discussion of his move to the 9th Infantry Division four pages before photo of General Wharton. Also see Omar N. Bradley and Clay Blair, *A General's Life: An Autobiography* (New York: Simon and Schuster, 1983), 109–110.

37. Marshall's comment to Patterson cited in Peter R. Mansoor, *The GI Offensive in Eu-*

rope: *The Triumph of American Infantry Divisions, 1941–1945* (Lawrence: University Press of Kansas, 1999), 58. Mansoor discusses the National Guard leadership situation on 57–59.

38. It is also possible that the perceived fascination with firepower resulted from having unusually well-educated officers in charge of divisional artillery during World War II. Another aspect of the firepower predominance question is the role of General McNair, an artilleryman, as the senior officer responsible for the training regimen of all army divisions.

39. William Westmoreland, the 1936 USMA graduate division chief of staff, related his career in *A Soldier Reports* (Garden City, NY: Doubleday, 1976), 12–26. Unfortunately, his early years in the memoir are nothing more than a listing of the great personalities he met in World War II. The source of commission of the remaining officer, the chief of staff of the 97th Infantry Division, is unknown, except that he was not a regular in 1939. Regular army status drawn from the 1939 *Army Register*. Duty as a division chief of staff from the U.S. Army Center for Military History, European Theater of Operations, Order of Battle website (see U.S. Army, Center for Military History, *Order of Battle of the United States Army, World War II: European Theater of Operations, Divisions*). Hereafter cited as USACMH ETO OOB; website available at www.army.mil/cmh–pg/documents/eto-ob/etoob_toc.htm. Accessed November 2, 2000, and April 20, 2001.

40. Of these five, two were veterans of the World War I era, one West Pointer, and one commissioned through the Organized Reserve system. One officer graduated from the Citadel in 1925, one from West Point in 1932, and the biographical data on the remaining officer are unknown.

41. Of the six without effective education for their duties, the two service professionals, West Point graduates of 1918 and 1923, perhaps had experienced enough staffs in their twenty-plus years of service to be effective chiefs of staff. The three very recent graduates of West Point, two from 1934 and one from the class of 1936, were undoubtedly more problematic as division chiefs of staff.

42. Lieutenant Colonel Fredie B. Butler Jr., CGSC class of 1940, was the G3 of 5th Armored Division from its commitment to the ETO in February 1944 through V-E Day.

43. Information from roster of graduates of General Staff Course Ten and the New Divisions Course Fifteen, both available at CARL, Curricula Files.

44. Information from New Division Course lists, General Staff Course rosters, and USACMH ETO OOB website.

45. Rosters of graduates from numerous postmobilization courses and the rosters from the ETO OOB of the USACMH website provided this assessment.

46. Information about RA commissions and West Point graduation from the 1939 *Army Register*. Identification of the staff officers from the USACMH ETO OOB website. Leavenworth attendance from the Leavenworth General Staff Course rosters.

47. Data drawn from USACMH ETO OOB website and a review of all rosters of Leavenworth courses for the period 1920–1945, as well as the 1939 *Army Register*.

48. Of the remaining eight nonregular regimental commanders, little is recorded.

49. The Army War College students in 1934 had also seen the need for educated, relatively senior regular army officers for postmobilization service as regimental commanders. "G-1, Report of Committee No. 8, Subject: Promotion, Separation, and Assignment of Regular Army Officers in Time of Peace," Course at the Army War College, 1934–1935, folder 1-1935-8, MHI 30–37.

50. Bradley, *General's Life*, 109.

51. This officer, Lieutenant Colonel Fredie Butler, served as the only G3 of 5th Armored Division, having graduated from the Leavenworth course in its very last peacetime course in

1940. He was the only staff officer below the rank of division chief of staff to attend Leavenworth before the war. Statistics on Leavenworth graduation drawn from several sources. For the peacetime years, 1920 through 1939, there exists a consolidated list of staff, faculty, and graduates. See *CSFG*. For the mobilization courses, there are partial lists, incomplete tabulations, and rosters from each of the twenty-seven graduating classes.

52. See the fascinating comparison offered by the student analysis in "G-1, Report of Committee No. 8, Subject: Promotion, Separation, and Assignment of Regular Army Officers in Time of Peace: Modifications to Develop an Efficient and Well Balanced Officer Personnel," Course at the Army War College, 1932–1933, folder 391-8, USAMHI, 18. According to this analysis, troop duty was the ninth-most desired of eleven possible assignments for high-quality regular army officers in 1932 and dead last in 1924.

53. Hugh M. Cole, *The Ardennes: Battle of the Bulge: United States Army in World War II, European Theater of Operations* (Washington, DC: Office of the Chief of Military History, United States Army, 1965), 434–435, and E. N. Harmon with Milton MacKaye and William Ross MacKaye, *Combat Commander: Autobiography of a Soldier* (Englewood Cliffs, NJ: Prentice-Hall, 1970), 229–232.

54. Collier listed as graduate of 1938 in *CSFG*, 52.

55. Cole, *Ardennes*, 440–441.

56. Ibid., 443.

57. This planning was on-again, off-again, as information and instructions form British and American higher headquarters changed late in the afternoon and early evening of December 24, 1944. See Cole, *Ardennes*, 565–566. A masterful depiction and analysis of the leadership of Collins in this case is in Harold R. Winton, *Corps Commanders of the Bulge: Six American Generals and Victory in the Ardennes* (Lawrence: University Press of Kansas, 2007), 270–277.

58. Cole, *Ardennes*, 567–570.

59. Ibid., 574.

60. Martin Blumenson, "Foreword" to Henry Gerard Phillips, *The Making of a Professional: Manton S. Eddy, USA* (Westport, CT: Greenwood, 2000), xi.

61. For more detail on this subject, an unpublished paper by Peter J. Schifferle, "World War I Practice on a World War II Battlefield," has been placed in CARL for reference. The author intends to pursue this issue in a later book-length study. The author delivered a paper that addressed this subject, in part, at the Society for Military History Conference in Ogden, Utah, in April 2008.

62. J. B. A. Bailey, *Field Artillery and Firepower* (Annapolis: Naval Institute Press, 2004), 320.

63. Captain Herbert W. Ehrgott, Corps of Engineers, "Power Plus Speed: The Essence of the Flanders Penetration," *Infantry Journal* 47, no. 4 (July–August 1940): 306–315; "The Battle of Picardy and the Double Penetration—Part I," *Infantry Journal* 43, no. 2 (March–April 1936): 113–123; and "The Battle of Picardy and the Double Penetration—Part II," *Infantry Journal* 43, no. 3 (May–June 1936): 227–232.

64. Ehrgott, "Power Plus Speed," 308–311, quote about maintaining superiority on 308, italics in original.

65. Shimon Naveh, *In Pursuit of Military Excellence: The Evolution of Operational Theory* (Portland, OR: Frank Cass, 1997, 2000), ch. 4; Karl-Heinz Frieser with John T. Greenwood, *The Blitzkrieg Legend: The 1940 Campaign in the West* (Annapolis: Naval Institute Press, 2005), 349–354; and Overy, *Why the Allies Won*, 63–100.

66. For the harnessing of American industrial capacity, see Paul A. C. Koistinen, *Planning War, Pursuing Peace: The Political Economy of American Warfare, 1920–1939* (Lawrence: University Press of Kansas, 1998), chs. 2 and 11; and Paul A. C. Koistinen, *Arsenal of World War*

II: *The Political Economy of American Warfare, 1940–1945* (Lawrence: University Press of Kansas, 2004), chs. 1, 4, 8, and 9. For some of the challenges faced by the German war production, see John Mosier, *The Blitzkrieg Myth: How Hitler and the Allies Misread the Strategic Realities of World War II* (New York: HarperCollins, 2003), 44–51.

67. Mansoor makes this point very effectively in *GI Offensive*.

68. A study done in 1973 by the Institute for Defense Analysis conducted a methodical study of the rates of advance of infantry divisions in World War II in both the Normandy and Siegfried Line campaigns. Institute for Defense Analysis, "Rates of Advance in Infantry Division Attacks in the Normandy–Northern France and Siegfried Line Campaigns" (Alexandria, VA: Institute for Defense Analysis, 1973), 11–14. These figures are not an average advance rate but rates for individual divisions actually conducting an attack.

69. John Mosier, *The Myth of the Great War: How the Germans Won the Battles and How the Americans Saved the Allies* (New York: HarperCollins, 2001), 279.

70. General George S. Patton Jr., "Conference on the Infantry Division, 20 November 1945, Opening Comments," USEFT Board no. 15, Organization, Equipment, and Tactical Employment of the Infantry Division, General Board, United States Forces, European Theater. Available from United States Army Center of Military History.

71. John Thomas Broom, "The Commander's Vision in Blue and Grey: The Roles of Adna R. Chaffee, James H. Wilson, and the American Civil War in the Development of American Armor Doctrine" (Ph.D. diss., Union Institute, 1993), 109, n. 29. For example, Major General J. Lawton Collins, commander of VII Corps, related a story of "probably the heaviest concentration on a single target during the war," when twenty battalions of artillery, more than 360 guns, fired on Hill 187 for three minutes during the Siegfried Line campaign near Aachen. General J. Lawton Collins, *Lightning Joe: An Autobiography* (Baton Rouge: Louisiana State University Press, 1979), 276. Also see Harmon, *Combat Commander*, 218–219, where Major General Ernie Harmon related a story of combined fighter-bomber and artillery support used in support of 2nd Armored Division in an attack in November 1944, support that allowed the division to make excellent initial progress. The attack bogged down on the second day due to German counterattacks and "repeated [German] artillery barrages."

72. Suisse Normande is the name applied to the high ground of southern Normandy, where the fighting around Mortain took place in August 1944.

73. Major Ralph A. Kerley, "Operations of the 2nd Battalion, 120th Infantry (30th Infantry Division) at Mortain, France, 6–12 August 1944 (Northern France Campaign) (Personal Experiences of a Company Commander): An Isolated Infantry Battalion Defending a Key Terrain Feature," Monograph Written for Advanced Infantry Officer's Class #1, 1949–1950, 16–17. Available at http://www.30thinfantry.org/Mortain-Operations.doc; accessed July 29, 2007.

74. Force array from Martin Blumenson, *Breakout and Pursuit: The United States Army in World War II, European Theater of Operations* (Washington, DC: Center of Military History, United States Army, 1961), map titled "Exploitation."

75. XIX Corps Demonstration, "2d Armored Division Tank-Infantry Assault of Tactical Locality and 30th Infantry Division, Infantry Assault of Fortified Village," December 10, 1944. Copy in CARL, File Number N-4770.

76. Stabilized-front operations were indeed much more costly than exploitation operations and can, by inference, be determined to actually be the more decisive of the two forms and also the more critical of the forms to eventual success. This is further demonstrated by the simple fact that, after the pursuit from the Normandy stabilized front, not only were the Germans able to reestablish another stabilized front; the Allies were themselves compelled to begin the costly and time-consuming reduction of this second stabilized front formed in less than a month.

77. For this part of U.S. effort in World War II, see Paul A. C. Koistinen, *The Military-Industrial Complex: A Historical Perspective* (New York: Praeger, 1980), and *Planning War, Pursuing Peace*.

78. This set of curricula is from Elliot W. Eisner, *The Educational Imagination: On the Design and Evaluation of School Programs*, 3rd ed. (Upper Saddle River, NJ: Prentice-Hall, 1994), ch. 4.

Conclusion

1. Robert R. Palmer and William R. Keast, "The Procurement of Officers," in Robert R. Palmer, Bell I. Wiley, and William R. Keast, *The Procurement and Training of Ground Combat Troops: The Army Ground Forces, United States Army in World War II* (Washington, DC: Office of the Chief of Military History, 1948), 91–92. Discussion of Protective Mobilization and September 8, 1939, declaration from Christopher R. Gabel, *The U.S. Army GHQ Maneuvers of 1941* (Washington, DC: Center of Military History, 1992), 9.

2. Frank James Price, *Troy H. Middleton: A Biography* (Baton Rouge: Louisiana State University Press, 1974), 90.

3. Hanson E. Ely, "Opening Address to Leavenworth Schools," September 1, 1923, in Hanson E. Ely, *A Series of Addresses and Lectures delivered by Major General Hanson E. Ely, United States Army* (GSSP, 1927), 11.

4. "Winston Churchill on Our Officer Corps," *Officer's Call* 1, no. 10 (1949 or 1950): 11–12, quote on 11. Thanks to Mike Stewart for this reference.

5. Major General Hanson E. Ely, "We Will Be Better Off Next Time," *Infantry Journal* 47, no. 6 (November–December 1940): 627.

6. Letter from Henry L. Stimson to Harry S. Truman, September 1, 1950, Huntington, Long Island, Truman Library, Truman Papers, President's Secretary's Files (PSF), Box 126, Folder: Military: Universal Training. I would like to thank Mike Stewart, currently researching the CGSS story in the post-1945 era, for this citation as well.

BIBLIOGRAPHY

Primary Sources

United States National Archives II, College Park, Maryland

Record Group 94, Adjutant General's Office, Central Decimal Files, Bulky Files, 1917–1925.
Record Group 120, Records of the American Expeditionary Forces (World War I).
Record Group 165, War Department General Staff, G1 Personnel, Numerical File, 1921–1942.
Record Group 407, Office of the Adjutant General Office, Central Files, 1917–1940.

*United States Army Military History Institute, Carlisle Barracks, PA, Army War
College Curricular Files, Individual Papers and/or Photograph Collections*

Biehl, Philip E.
Brabson, Fay W.
Chaffee, Adna R. Jr.
Conger, Arthur L. Jr.
Ely, Hanson E.
Daley, Arthur S.
Drum, Hugh A.
Fiske, Bernice
Halstead-Maus Family Papers
Hoge, William
King, Edward L.
Lawrence, Thompson, in the Lawrence Family Papers
Livesay, William G.
Nolan, Dennis E.
Rice, John Kirtland
Richards, Darrie
Short, Walter C.
Truesdell, Karl
Wallace, Fred C.
Waters, Jerome J.
Wilson, Walter K., Jr.

*U. S. Army, Command and General Staff College (CGSC) Records,
Combined Arms Research Library (CARL) Archives, Document Collection,
Fort Leavenworth, KS*

"Employment of the 2d Armored Division in Operation Cobra, 25 July–1 Aug. 44, a Research
Report." Lieutenant Colonel Glenn T. Pillsbury et al. Fort Knox, KY: Armored School,
May 1950.

"Fact Sheets on US Divs. AGF, 1945–1946." Washington, DC: Special Information Section, Office of Technical Information, Headquarters, Army Ground Forces, December 12, 1945. Document no. N-12472.3.

McLain, Raymond S. "XIX Corps Demonstration: 2d Armored Division Tank-Infantry Assault of Tactical Locality & 30th Infantry Division: Infantry Assault of Fortified Village." APC 270 (somewhere in France or Belgium): Headquarters, XIX Corps, December 10, 1944.

Report of the Department of the Army Board on Education System for Officers. June 15, 1949. "Eddy Board" report. Document no. R-13423.2–4.

Report of War Department Military Education Board on Educational System for Officers of the Army. February 1946. "Gerow Board" report. Document no. R-13423.1–3.

Translation of *Truppenführung*, published by Staff and Faculty of Command and General Staff School, Fort Leavenworth, 1936 or 1937. Report no. 14,507. Document available in CARL Library Collection. Catalog no. 355 T871.

U.S. Army Europe, Office of the Theater History. *Order of Battle of the United States Army, World War II: European Theater of Operations.* Paris: Office of the Theater Historian, 1945. Document no. N-12472.1–3.

United States Army, Headquarters, 1st Infantry Division. *Report of Breaching the Siegfried Line and the Capture of Aachen.* APO #1, U.S. Army, Headquarters, 1st Infantry Division, November 7, 1944.

Command and General Staff College (CGSC) Records, Combined Arms Research Library (CARL) Archives, 1917 through 1940, Fort Leavenworth, KS, Reports and Circulars

The Army Service Schools. *The General Staff School Schedule for 1919–1920, Dated October 1, 1919.* Fort Leavenworth, KS, 1919, marked "issued to instructors only." Curriculum Files, Hanging Files, 1919–1920.

U.S. Army Command and General Staff School. *Annual Report(s) of the Command and General Staff School, 1919–1920 through 1939–1940.* Fort Leavenworth, KS: Command and General Staff School Press, 1920–1940.

——. *1928–1929, First Year Course Conferences: Command, Staff and Logistics, Strategy, Military History, Field Engineering, Military Intelligence, Troop Leading, Methods of Training, Legal Principles.* Fort Leavenworth, KS: Command and General Staff School, 1928.

——. *1928–1929, First Year Course Conferences: Military Organization, Tactics and Techniques, Larger Units, Combat Orders.* Fort Leavenworth, KS: Command and General Staff School, 1928.

——. *1928–1929, First Year Course Conferences: Tactical Principles and Decisions, Discussion of Problems, Solution of Problems.* Fort Leavenworth, KS: Command and General Staff School, 1928.

——. *1929–1930, Second Year Course Conferences: Command, Staff and Logistics, Strategy, Military History, Field Engineering, Military Intelligence, Methods of Training, Military Geography, Political Economy.* Fort Leavenworth, KS: Command and General Staff School, 1930.

——. *1929–1930, Second Year Course Conferences: Military Organization, Tactics and Techniques, Larger Units, Tactical and Strategical Principles.* Fort Leavenworth, KS: Command and General Staff School, 1930.

——. *1934–1935, First Year Course: Problems*. Fort Leavenworth, KS: Command and General Staff School, 1935.

——. *1935–1936, Second Year Class: Command Course, G-2 Course, Text*. Fort Leavenworth, KS: Command and General Staff School, 1936.

——. *1935–1936, Second Year Class: G-3 Course, G-4 Course, Discussion of Problems, Text*. Fort Leavenworth, KS: Command and General Staff School, 1936.

——. *The Art of Instructing: Prepared Especially for the Information of Instructors at the Command and General Staff School*. Fort Leavenworth, KS: Command and General Staff School Press, 1936.

——. *Bulletin No. 1, Subject: Textbooks*. Fort Leavenworth, KS: Command and General Staff School, August 15, 1934.

——. *Class Schedules for 1916–1917 through 1939–1940*. Fort Leavenworth, KS: Command and General Staff School Press, 1917–1940.

——. *Commandants, Staff, Faculty, and Graduates of the Command and General Staff School, Fort Leavenworth, Kansas, 1881–1939*. Fort Leavenworth, KS: Command and General Staff School Press, 1939.

——. *Course Conferences. 1916–1917 through 1927–1928*. Fort Leavenworth, KS: Command and General Staff School, 1916–1928.

——. *Index to School Problems, Series 1916–1928*. Fort Leavenworth, KS: Command and General Staff School Press, 1917–1928.

——. *Index to School Problems, Series 1919–1920 to 1932–1933*. Fort Leavenworth, KS: Command and General Staff School Press, 1933.

——. *Instruction Circular No. 1, Series 1916 through Series 1928*. Fort Leavenworth, KS: Command and General Staff School Press, 1916–1928.

——. *Instruction Circular No. 1, Series 1926–1927, Series 1933–1934, Series 1935–1936*. Fort Leavenworth, KS: Command and General Staff School Press, 1926, 1933, 1935.

——. *Instruction Circular No. 2, Series 1916 through Series 1928*. Fort Leavenworth, KS: Command and General Staff School Press, 1916–1928.

——. *Instruction Circular No. 2, Series 1935–1936*. Fort Leavenworth, KS: Command and General Staff School Press, 1935.

——. *Study Course in Military Art: Questions Outlining the Direction Studies in Military Art Should Take*. Fort Leavenworth, KS: Command and General Staff School Press, 1935.

——. "Summary of Schedule (by Courses)" (Fort Leavenworth, KS: Command and General Staff School, n.d.), CARL Archives, typescript located in files for Command and General Staff School, 1935–1936, "Schedules."

Command and General Staff College (CGSC) Records, Combined Arms Research Library (CARL) Archives, 1941 through 1947

U.S. Army. Adjutant General's Office, Personnel Research and Procedures Branch, Personnel Research Section. *Survey of the Educational Program: The Command and General Staff College, Fort Leavenworth, Kansas*. Report and Recommendations on Program no. PR-4097. No place of publication. Date-stamped May 23, 1947.

——. Command and General Staff School. "Alphabetical List of the ## General Staff Class." Fort Leavenworth, KS: Command and General Staff School. These lists were published for the Thirteenth Class through the Twenty-Seventh Class in various forms.

——. "Comprehensive Survey of the Command and General Staff School: Wartime—

1940–1945, Volume 1 and Volume 2." Fort Leavenworth, KS: Command and General Staff School, October 1945.

———. "The Graduates of the General Staff and Services of Supply Staff Classes, 1941–1942–1943." Fort Leavenworth, KS: Command and General Staff School, February 15, 1943.

———. "Program and Schedule—Twelfth General Staff Course" through "Program and Schedule—Twenty-Seventh General Staff Course." Fort Leavenworth, KS: Command and General Staff School, various dates.

———. "Schedule First Course for Training Divisions, January–February 1942." Fort Leavenworth, KS: Command and General Staff School, n.d.

———. "Schedule: Second New Divisions Course, March–April 1942" through "Schedule: Fifteenth New Divisions Course, May–June 1943." Fort Leavenworth, KS: Command and General Staff School, various dates.

———. "Schedule Second Special Course" through "Schedule Eleventh Special Course." Fort Leavenworth, KS: Command and General Staff School, various dates.

———. "Schedule—Special Class, 1940–1941." Fort Leavenworth, KS: Command and General Staff School, n.d.

———. "Wartime History of the Command and General Staff School, 1939–1945." Fort Leavenworth, KS: Command and General Staff School, January 1945.

U.S. War Department. "Circular No. 188, The Command and General Staff School, Fort Leavenworth, Kansas, 12 May 1944." Washington, DC: Headquarters, War Department, May 12, 1944.

Command and General Staff College Records, Combined Arms Research Library (CARL) Archives, General Service Schools Lectures and Addresses, Fort Leavenworth, KS

Bundel, Charles M. *Selected Professional Papers of Chas. M. Bundel.* Fort Leavenworth, KS: Command and General Staff School Press, 1939.

Edmunds, Kinzie. "Lectures for Special Courses (CMTC), Business Men's Camp, July 1940." Bound typescript, CARL Archives, M308 E 73.

Ely, Hanson E. *A Series of Addresses and Lectures Delivered by Major General Hanson E. Ely, United States Army.* Fort Leavenworth, KS: General Service Schools Press, 1927.

King, Edward L. "Opening Address of the General Service School, 10 September 1928." Typescript, CARL Archives, King files.

Truesdell, Karl. "Graduation, Fort Leavenworth, September 12, 1942." Headquarters, Fort Leavenworth, September 4, 1942. Located in Ninth General Staff Course files, CARL Archives.

Command and General Staff College (CGSC) Records, Combined Arms Research Library (CARL) Archives, Fort Leavenworth, KS, School Texts

Brees, Herbert J. *Combat Orders.* Fort Leavenworth, KS: General Service Schools Press, 1920.

Bundel, Charles M. *The Solution of Map Problems.* Fort Leavenworth, KS: General Service Schools Press, 1921.

McNair, Leslie J., Maj. *Artillery Firing: Lectures to the Staff and Line Classes.* General Service Schools, Fort Leavenworth, October 1919. Fort Leavenworth, KS: Army Service Schools Press, 1919.

Price, X. H., CPT. *Text-book on Field Fortification: Course in Field Engineering.* Fort Leavenworth, KS: General Service Schools Press, 1920.

Smith, H. A., Col. *Military Government.* Fort Leavenworth, KS: General Service Schools Press, 1920.

U.S. Army, Command and General Staff School. *Checklist for Staff Officers: Field Manual.* Fort Leavenworth, KS: Command and General Staff School Press, 1935.

———. *Combat Orders (Tentative).* Fort Leavenworth, KS: Command and General Staff School Press, 1939.

———. *Command and Staff Principles (Tentative).* Fort Leavenworth, KS: Command and General Staff School Press, 1937.

———. *The Principles of Strategy for an Independent Corps or Army in a Theater of Operations.* Fort Leavenworth, KS: Command and General Staff School Press, 1936.

———. *Tactical Employment of the Mechanized Division (Tentative).* Fort Leavenworth, KS: Command and General Staff School Press, 1937.

U.S. Army, General Service School. *Combat Orders.* Fort Leavenworth, KS: General Service Schools Press, 1920.

———. *Combat Orders.* Fort Leavenworth, KS: General Service Schools Press, 1925.

———. *Command, Staff, and Tactics.* Fort Leavenworth, KS: General Service Schools Press, 1923.

———. *General Principles of Employment of Cavalry.* Fort Leavenworth, KS: General Service Schools Press, 1920.

U.S. Army, School of the Line. *General Tactical Functions of Large Units.* Fort Leavenworth, KS: General Service Schools Press, 1920.

Command and General Staff College (CGSC) Records, Combined Arms Research Library (CARL) Archives, Fort Leavenworth, KS, Student Papers

Cromwell, J. P. "Are the Methods of Instruction Used at This School Practical and Modern? If Not, What Changes Are Suggested?" May 27, 1936. Individual Research Papers Collection, 1936.

Emery, Frank E. Jr. "What Should Be the Plan of Education for Officers of the Army." n.d. Emery was a student from 1928 to 1930.

Harmon, Ernest N. "Critical Analysis of the German Cavalry Operations in the Lodz Campaign with Particular Reference to the I Cavalry Corps." May 12, 1933. Also available online in the CARL digital library.

———. "Study of the Japanese Intelligence Service during the Russo-Japanese War." 1933. Also available online in the CARL digital library.

Heraty, Francis J. "What Should Be the Plan of Education for Officers of the Army, Including a Discussion of Individual Study, the Special Service Schools, the Command and Staff School, and the Army War College." June 9, 1930. Individual Research Papers Collection, 1930.

Simmons, W. G. "The Relative Value of Lectures, Conferences, Map Problems, Map Exercises, and Map Maneuvers in a Course of Instruction with a Proposed Plan for Their Coordinated Use." 1932. Individual Research Papers Collection, 1932.

Command and General Staff College (CGSC) Records, Combined Arms Research Library (CARL) Archives, Fort Leavenworth, KS, Miscellaneous Material

Chandler, Rex. "Class of 1936–1937 C and GSS: A Series of Cartoons and Caricatures of the Headaches and Laughs of 1936–37." Undated mimeograph. CARL special collections, 355.0711 B433, 1937.

Colby, Elbridge. *Education and the Army*. Boston: Palmer, 1922.
"The Horseshoe, 1926." Yearbook compiled by General Eisenhower's class at the Command and General Staff School, 1925–1926. CARL special collection, M209 C.73 D4E 2F.
Military Service Publishing Company. *The Officers' Guide*. 4th ed. Harrisburg, PA: Military Service Publishing, 1941.
Siskind, R. K. *Analysis of Historical Barriers: The Siegfried Line*. Marina del Rey, CA: R & D Associates, February 1977.

U.S. Government Publications

Greenfield, Kent Roberts. *Army Ground Forces and the Air-Ground Battle Team Including Organic Light Aviation*. Study no. 35. U.S. Army, Army Ground Forces, Historical Division. Fort Monroe, VA: Office, Chief Army Field Forces, 1948.
Hunt, Elvid. *History of Fort Leavenworth, 1827–1937*. 2nd ed., brought up to date by Walter E. Lorence. Fort Leavenworth, KS: Command and General Staff School Press, 1937 [first edition c. 1926].
Ney, Virgil. *Evolution of the U.S. Army Division, 1939–1968*. Fort Belvoir, VA: United States Army Combat Developments Command, by Technical Operations, Combat Operations Research Group, January 1969.
Tyler, Orville Z. Jr. *The History of Fort Leavenworth, 1937–1951, Which Brings Up to Date History of Fort Leavenworth, 1827–1927, by Elvid Hunt*. Fort Leavenworth, KS: Command and General Staff College, 1951.
U.S. Army. Center of Military History. *Kasserine Pass Battles: Doctrines and Lessons Learned*. Vol. 2, pt. 3. n.d.
———. *Kasserine Pass Battles: Readings*, Vol. 1, pt. 1. n.d.
———. *Kasserine Pass Battles: Readings*, Vol. 1, pt. 2. n.d.
———. *Military Operations of the American Expeditionary Forces, Volume 9: United States Army in the World War, 1917–1919*. Washington, DC: Center of Military History, United States Army, 1948 [1990].
———. *Order of Battle of the United States Army, World War II: European Theater of Operations, Divisions*. Center for Military History. Available at www.army.mil/cmh-pg/documents/eto-ob/etoob_toc.htm. Accessed November 2, 2000, and April 20, 2001.
U.S. Army, Command and General Staff College. Website, available at www-cgsc.army.mil. Accessed April 9, 2001.
———. *A Military History of the U.S. Army Command and General Staff College, 1881–1963*. Fort Leavenworth, KS: U.S. Army Command and General Staff College, n.d.
U.S. Army, Command and General Staff School. *Truppenfuehrung*, Translation of German Troop Leading Manual, c. 1936.
U.S. Army, Headquarters, Army Ground Forces. *Report of Army Ground Forces Activities*. Washington, DC: Headquarters, Army Ground Forces, January 10, 1946.
U.S. Army War College. *Army Staff College Level Training Study, Final Report*. Carlisle Barracks, PA: U.S. Army War College, 5WPC768OE/Aug83, dated June 13, 1983.
U.S. Congress, House, Committee on Appropriations. *Reorganization of the Army: Hearings Before the Subcommittee of House Committee on Appropriations*. 66th Cong., 3rd sess. Washington, DC: Government Printing Office, 1921.
———. *Reorganization of the Army: Hearings Before the Subcommittee of House Committee on*

Appropriations, 67th Cong., 2nd sess. Washington, DC: Government Printing Office, 1922.

U.S. Congress, House, Committee on Military Affairs. *Report of the Secretary of War on Promotion and Retirement in Pursuance of the Provisions of Section 4 of the Act Approved July 2, 1926.* 69th Cong., 2nd sess. Washington, DC: Government Printing Office, 1926.

U.S. Congress, Senate. *The Army of the United States.* Presented by Mr. Sheppard. 76th Cong., 1st sess. Washington, DC: Government Printing Office, 1940.

U.S. Department of Defense, Joint Staff. Joint Electronic Library: JEL CD-Rom. Washington, DC: J-7 Joint Staff, February 2000.

United States Forces, European Theater. *Reports of the USFET General Boards.* Available at Center of Military History, Washington DC, 1945.

U.S. Naval War College. *Sound Military Decision.* Newport, RI: U.S. Naval War College, 1942.

United States, War Department. *Field Service Regulations, United States Army, 1923.* Washington, DC: Government Printing Office, 1923.

——. *Field Service Regulations, United States Army 1939 (Tentative).* Washington, DC: Government Printing Office, 1939.

——. *Field Service Regulations, Operations, FM 100-5, May 22, 1941.* Washington, DC: Government Printing Office, 1941. Reprint ed. Fort Leavenworth, KS: U.S. Army Command and General Staff College Press, 1992.

——. *Field Service Regulations, Operations, FM 100-5, 15 June 1944.* Washington, DC: Government Printing Office, 1944.

——. *A Manual for Commanders of Large Units (Provisional) with Changes, 1936.* Washington, DC: Government Printing Office, 1930 [1936].

——. *Report(s) of the Secretary of War to the President, 1917 through 1927.* Washington, DC: Government Printing Office, 1917–1927.

——. *Staff Officers' Field Manual Organization, Technical and Logistical Data, FM 101-10, 21 December 1944.* Washington, DC: Government Printing Office, 1944.

United States, War Department, Adjutant General's Office. *Official Army Directory, 1918 through 1940.* Washington, DC: Government Printing Office, 1918–1940.

——. *Official Army Register, 1917 through 1940.* Washington, DC: Government Printing Office, 1917–1940.

United States, War Department, Adjutant General's Office, Statistical and Accounting Branch. *Army Battle Casualties and Nonbattle Deaths in World War II: Final Report, 7 December 1941–31 December 1946.* Washington, DC: Office of the Adjutant General, n.d.

United States War Department, Historical Division. *Small Unit Actions.* Washington, DC: Historical Division, War Department, Facsimile reprint, Office of the Chief of Military History, 1982.

United States War Department, United States Army, American Expeditionary Force, First Army Headquarters. *Operations of the First Army.* Bar-sur-Aube, France: First Army Headquarters, AEF, 1919.

Wainstein, Leonard. *Rates of Advance in Infantry Division Attacks in the Normandy–Northern France and Siegfried Line Campaigns.* Paper no. P-990. Arlington, VA: Institute for Defense Analysis for Weapons Systems Evaluation Group, December 1973.

Wiley, Bell I. *Training in the Ground Army, 1942–1945.* Study no. 11. U.S. Army, Army Ground Forces, Historical Division. Fort Monroe, VA: Office, Chief Army Field Forces, 1948.

Autobiographies, Published Papers, and Memoirs

Ball, Edmund F. *Staff Officer with the Fifth Army: Sicily, Salerno, and Anzio.* New York: Exposition, 1958.

Bland, Larry I., and Sharon R. Ritenour, eds. *The Papers of George Catlett Marshall, Volume 1: The Soldierly Spirit, December 1880–June 1939.* Baltimore: Johns Hopkins University Press, 1981.

———. *The Papers of George Catlett Marshall, Volume 2: "We Cannot Delay," July 1, 1939–December 6, 1941.* Baltimore: Johns Hopkins University Press, 1986.

———. *The Papers of George Catlett Marshall, Volume 3: "The Right Man for the Job," December 7, 1941–May 31, 1943.* Baltimore: Johns Hopkins University Press, 1991.

———. *The Papers of George Catlett Marshall, Volume 4: "Aggressive and Determined Leadership," June 1, 1943–December 31, 1944.* Baltimore: Johns Hopkins University Press, 1996.

Bradley, Omar N., and Clay Blair. *A General's Life: An Autobiography.* New York: Simon and Schuster, 1983.

Brownlee, Romie L., and William J. Mullen. *Changing an Army: An Oral History of General William E. Depuy, USA Retired.* Carlisle Barracks, PA: United States Military History Institute, n.d. [1984?].

Bullard, Robert Lee. *Personalities and Reminiscences of the War.* New York: Doubleday, 1925.

Chynoweth, Bradford Grethen. *Bellamy Park.* Hicksville, NY: Exposition, 1975.

Collins, J. Lawton. *Lightning Joe: An Autobiography.* Baton Rouge: Louisiana State University Press, 1979.

Corlett, Charles L., Major General. *Cowboy Pete.* Ed. Wm. Farrington. Santa Fe, NM: Sleeping Fox, 1974.

Dean, William F., as told to William L. Worded. *General Dean's Story.* New York: Viking, 1954.

Eisenhower, Dwight D. *At Ease: Stories I Tell to Friends.* Garden City, NY: Doubleday, 1967.

Harbord, James G. *The American Army in France, 1917–1919.* Boston: Little, Brown, 1936.

———. *Leaves from a War Diary.* New York: Dodd, Mead, 1931.

Harmon, Ernest N., with Milton MacKaye and William Ross MacKaye. *Combat Commander: Autobiography of a Soldier.* Englewood Cliffs, NJ: Prentice-Hall, 1970.

Howze, Hamilton H. *A Cavalryman's Story: Memoirs of a Twentieth-Century General.* Washington, DC: Smithsonian Institution, 1996.

Kahn, Ely Jaques. *McNair, Educator of an Army.* Washington, DC: Infantry Journal, 1945.

March, Peyton C. *The Nation at War.* New York: Doubleday, Doran, 1932.

Marshall, George C. *Memoirs of My Services in the World War, 1917–1918.* Boston: Houghton Mifflin, 1976.

Masters, John. *The Road Past Mandalay.* New York: Bantam, 1961 [1979].

Palmer, John M. *America in Arms: The Experience of the United States with Military Organization.* New Haven: Yale University Press, 1941.

Pershing, John J. *My Experiences in the First World War.* Publ. c. 1931 as *My Experiences in the World War.* New York: Da Capo, 1995.

Stimson, Henry L., and McGeorge Bundy. *On Active Service in Peace and War.* New York: Harper and Brothers, 1947 and 1948.

Swain, Richard M. *Selected Papers of General William E. Depuy.* Fort Leavenworth, KS: Combat Studies Institute, U.S. Army Command and General Staff College, 1994.

Taylor, Maxwell. *Swords and Ploughshares.* New York: W. W. Norton, 1972.

Triplet, William S. *A Colonel in the Armored Divisions: A Memoir, 1941–1945.* Columbia: University of Missouri Press, 2001.

Truscott, Lucian K. Jr. *The Twilight of the U.S. Cavalry: Life in the Old Army, 1917–1942.* Edited by Colonel Lucian K. Truscott III. Lawrence: University Press of Kansas, 1989.

Vogel, Victor. *Soldiers of the Old Army.* College Station: Texas A&M University Press, 1990.

Wedemeyer, Albert C. *Wedemeyer Reports!* New York: Henry Holt, 1958.

Westmoreland, William C. *A Soldier Reports.* Garden City, NY: Doubleday, 1976.

Williams, Ben Ames, ed. *Amateurs at War: The American Soldier in Action.* Boston: Houghton Mifflin, 1943.

Wright, William M. *Meuse-Argonne Diary: A Division Commander in World War I.* Ed. Robert H. Ferrell. Columbia: University of Missouri Press, 2004.

Division Histories (World War I and World War II)

The 35th Infantry Division in World War II: 1941–1945. Atlanta: Albert Love Enterprises, rpt. ed., 2003 [orig. publ. c. 1946].

Battle Babies: The Story of the 99th Infantry Division in World War II. Nashville: Battery, 1985 [orig. publ. 1950].

Byrnes, Laurence G. *History of the 94th Infantry Division in World War II.* Nashville: Battery, 1982 [orig. publ. 1948].

Colby, John. *War from the Ground Up: The 90th Division in WWII.* Austin, TX: Nortex, 1991.

Fowle, Herb. *The Men of the Terrible Green Cross.* Hillsdale, MI: Herb Fowle, 1991.

Frankel, Nat, and Larry Smith. *Patton's Best: An Informal History of the 4th Armored Division.* New York: Hawthorn, 1978.

Historical and Pictorial Review of the 28th Infantry Division in World War II. Nashville: Battery, 1980 [orig. publ. 1946].

Hofman, George F. *The Super Sixth: History of the 6th Armored Division in World War II and Its Post-war Association.* Louisville, KY: Sixth Armored Division Association, 1975.

Houston, Donald E. *Hell on Wheels: The 2d Armored Division.* Novato, CA: Presidio, 1977.

Howe, George F. *The Battle History of the 1st Armored Division: "Old Ironsides."* Washington, DC: Combat Forces, 1954. Rpt. ed. Nashville: Battery, 1979.

Kahn, E. J. Jr., and Henry McLemore. *Fighting Divisions: Histories of Each U.S. Army Combat Division in World War II.* Washington, DC: Infantry Journal, 1946. Rpt. ed. Washington, DC: Zenger, 1979.

Kenamore, Clair. *From Vauquois Hill to Exermont: A History of the 35th Division of the United States Army.* St. Louis: Guard, 1919.

Koyen, Kenneth. *The Fourth Armored Division from the Beach to Bavaria: The Story of the Fourth Armored Division in Combat.* Nashville: Battery, 2000 [orig. publ. 1946].

The Legacy of the 4th Armored Division. Paducah, KY: Turner, 1990.

Le Tissier, Tony. *"Patton's Pawns": The 94th Infantry Division at the Siegfried Line.* Tuscaloosa: University of Alabama Press, 2007.

Paths of Armor: The Fifth Armored Division in World War II. Nashville: Battery, 1985 [orig. publ. 1950].

Rapport, Leonard, and Arthur Northwood Jr. *Rendezvous with Destiny: A History of the 101st Airborne Division.* Fort Campbell, KY: 101st Airborne Division Association, 1948 [enlarged ed. c. 1972].

Steward, Hal D. *Thunderbolt: The History of the 11th Armored Division.* Nashville: Battery, n.d. [1948].

Journal Articles

Complete serial run of *Cavalry Journal, Infantry Journal,* and *Field Artillery Journal,* from January 1919 through December 1940.

Hurley, Patrick J. "Remarks of Assistant Secretary of War at Graduation Exercises at Command and General Staff School." *Army and Navy Register* (June 29, 1929): 601.

Secondary Sources

Books

Abrahamson, James L. *America Arms for a New Century: The Making of a Great Military Power.* New York: Free Press, 1981.

Ambrose, Stephen E. *Eisenhower: Soldier, General of the Army, President-Elect, 1890–1952.* Vol. 1. New York: Simon and Schuster, 1983.

American Battle Monuments Commission. *American Armies and Battlefields in Europe: A History, Guide, and Reference Book.* Washington, DC: U.S. Government Printing Office, 1938.

Atkinson, James W. *The Soldier's Chronology.* New York: Garland, 1993.

Atkinson, Rick. *An Army at Dawn: The War in North Africa, 1942–1943.* New York: Henry Holt, 2002.

———. *Day of Battle: The War in Sicily and Italy, 1943–1944.* New York: Henry Holt, 2007.

Autry, Jerry. *General William C. Lee: Father of the American Airborne.* San Francisco: Airborne, 1995, 2005.

Badger, Anthony J. *The New Deal: The Depression Years, 1933–1940.* New York: Hill and Wang, 1989.

Bailey, J. B. A. *Field Artillery and Firepower.* Annapolis: Naval Institute Press, 2004.

Ball, Harry P. *Of Responsible Command: A History of the U.S. Army War College.* Carlisle Barracks, PA: Alumni Association of the United States Army War College, 1983.

Barr, Ronald J. *The Progressive Army: U.S. Army Command and Administration, 1870–1914.* New York: St. Martin's, 1998.

Bellafaire, Judith L., ed. *The U.S. Army and World War II: Selected Papers from the Army's Commemorative Conferences.* Washington, DC: Center of Military History, 1998.

Bender, Mark C. *Watershed at Leavenworth: Dwight D. Eisenhower and the Command and General Staff School.* Fort Leavenworth, KS: Command and General Staff College Press, 1990.

Berlin, Robert H. *U.S. Army World War II Corps Commanders: A Composite Biography.* Fort Leavenworth, KS: U.S. Army Command and General Staff College, Combat Studies Institute, 1989.

Binder, L. James. *Lemnitzer: A Soldier for His Time.* Washington, DC: Brassey's, 1997.

Bledstein, Burton J. *The Culture of Professionalism: The Middle Class and the Development of Higher Education in America.* New York: W. W. Norton, 1976.

Bloch, Marc. *Strange Defeat: A Statement of Evidence Written in 1940.* Trans. Gerard Hopkins. New York: Norton, 1968.

Blumenson, Martin. *Anzio: The Gamble That Failed.* Philadelphia: Lippincott, 1963.

———. *The Battle of the Generals: The Untold Story of the Falaise Pocket, the Campaign That Should Have Won World War II.* New York: Morrow, 1993.

———. *Bloody River: The Real Tragedy of the Rapido.* Boston: Houghton Mifflin, 1970.

———. *Breakout and Pursuit: United States Army in World War II, European Theater of Operations.* Washington, DC: Center of Military History, United States Army, 1961, 1993.

———. *Kasserine Pass.* New York: Berkeley, 1966, 1983, 2000.

———. *Sicily: Whose Victory?* New York: Ballantine, 1968, 1969.

Bonn, Keith E. *When the Odds Were Even: The Vosges Mountains Campaign, October 1944–January 1945.* Novato, CA: Presidio, 1994.

Braim, Paul F. *The Test of Battle: The American Expeditionary Forces in the Meuse-Argonne Campaign.* Newark: University of Delaware Press, 1987.

Brereton, T. R. *Educating the U.S. Army: Arthur L. Wagner and Reform, 1875–1905.* Lincoln: University of Nebraska Press, 2000.

Brogan, D. W. *The American Character.* New York: Alfred A. Knopf, 1944.

Brown, Anthony Cave. *Bodyguard of Lies: The Extraordinary Story Behind D-Day.* Guilford, CT: Lyons, 1975.

Brown, John Sloan. *Draftee Division: The 88th Infantry Division in World War II.* Lexington: University Press of Kentucky, 1986.

Brown, Richard C. *Social Attitudes of American Generals, 1898–1940.* New York: Arno, 1979.

Builder, Carl H. *The Icarus Syndrome: The Role of Air Power Theory in the Evolution and Fate of the U.S. Air Force.* New Brunswick, NJ: Transaction, 1996.

Bunting, Josiah. *The Lionheads.* New York: Popular Library, 1972.

Cameron, Craig M. *American Samurai: Myth, Imagination, and the Conduct of Battle in the First Marine Division, 1941–1951.* New York: Cambridge University Press, 1994.

Cameron, Robert S. *Mobility, Shock, and Firepower: The Emergence of the U.S. Army's Armor Branch, 1917–1945.* Washington, DC: Center of Military History, United States Army, 2008.

Carafano, James Jay. *GI Ingenuity: Improvisation, Technology, and Winning World War II.* Westport, CT: Praeger, 2006.

Chambers, John Whiteclay II. *To Raise an Army: The Draft Comes to Modern America.* New York: Free Press, 1987.

Chandler, Alfred. *The Visible Hand: The Managerial Revolution in American Business.* Cambridge: Belknap Press of Harvard University Press, 1977.

Citino, Robert M. *Armored Forces: History and Sourcebook.* Westport, CT: Greenwood, 1994.

———. *The Path to Blitzkrieg: Doctrine and Training in the German Army, 1920–1939.* Boulder: Lynne Rienner, 1999.

Clarke, Jeffrey J., and Robert Ross Smith. *Riviera to the Rhine: The United States Army in World War II, European Theater of Operations.* Washington, DC: Office of the Chief of Military History, United States Army, 1993.

Clifford, J. Garry, and Samuel R. Spencer Jr. *The First Peacetime Draft.* Lawrence: University Press of Kansas, 1986.

Coffman, Edward M. *The Hilt of the Sword: The Career of Peyton C. March.* Madison: University of Wisconsin Press, 1966.

———. *The Old Army: A Portrait of the American Army in Peacetime, 1784–1898.* New York: Oxford University Press, 1986.

———. *The Regulars: The American Army, 1898–1941.* Cambridge: Belknap Press of Harvard University Press, 2004.

———. *The War to End All Wars: The American Military Experience in World War I.* New York: Oxford University Press, 1968.

Cole, Hugh M. *The Ardennes: Battle of the Bulge: United States Army in World War II, European Theater of Operations.* Washington, DC: Center of Military History, United States Army, 1965, 1994.

Conrad, Clifton F., and Jennifer Grant Haworth, eds. *Revisioning Curriculum in Higher Education*. ASHE Reader Series. Needham Heights, MA: Simon and Schuster, 1995.

Converse, Elliott V., ed. *Forging the Sword: Selecting, Educating, and Training Cadets and Junior Officers in the Modern World*. Chicago: Imprint, 1998.

Cooke, James J. *Pershing and His Generals: Command and Staff in the AEF*. Westport, CT: Praeger, 1997.

Corum, James S. *The Luftwaffe: Creating the Operational Air War, 1918–1940*. Lawrence: University Press of Kansas, 1997.

———. *The Roots of Blitzkrieg: Hans von Seeckt and German Military Reform*. Lawrence: University Press of Kansas, 1992.

Cray, Ed. *General of the Army: George C. Marshall, Soldier and Statesman*. New York: W. W. Norton, 1991.

Crosswell, D. K. R. *The Chief of Staff: The Military Career of Walter Bedell Smith*. New York: Greenwood, 1991.

Cubic Applications. *Intermediate Level Education Needs Analysis*. Vol. 1. Report prepared in accordance with Federal Government Contract DABT65-98-D-0002. Leavenworth, KS: Cubic Applications, March 30, 2001.

Cuff, Robert D. *The War Industries Board: Business-Government Relations during World War I*. Baltimore: Johns Hopkins University Press, 1973.

Curry, Cecil B. *Follow Me and Die*. New York: Military Heritage, 1984.

Dastrup, Boyd L. *The U.S. Army Command and General Staff College: A Centennial History*. Manhattan, KS: Sunflower University Press, n.d., c. 1982.

Daugherty, Leo. *The Battle of the Hedgerows: Bradley's First Army in Normandy, June–July 1944*. Osceola, WI: Zenith, 2001.

Davis, Clark. *"Company Men": White-Collar Life and Corporate Culture in Los Angeles, 1892–1941*. Baltimore: Johns Hopkins University Press, 2000.

D'Este, Carlo. *Eisenhower: A Soldier's Life*. New York: Henry Holt, 2002.

———. *Patton: A Genius for War*. New York: HarperCollins, 1995.

Dewey, John. *Experience and Education*. New York: Macmillan, 1944.

Doubler, Michael D. *Busting the Bocage: American Combined Arms Operations in France, 6 June–31 July 1944*. Fort Leavenworth, KS: Combat Studies Institute, U.S. Army Command and General Staff College, 1988.

———. *Closing with the Enemy: How GIs Fought the War in Europe, 1944–1945*. Lawrence: University Press of Kansas, 1994.

Doughty, Robert A. *Breaking Point: Sedan and the Fall of France, 1940*. Hamden, CT: Archon, 1990.

———. *The Evolution of U.S. Army Tactical Doctrine, 1946–1976*. Combat Studies Institute, U.S. Army Command and General Staff College, 1979.

———. *The Seeds of Disaster: The Development of French Army Doctrine, 1919–1939*. Hamden, CT: Archon, 1985.

Dumenil, Lynn. *Modern Temper: American Culture and Society in the 1920s*. New York: Hill and Wang, 1995.

Dupuy, Trevor N. *A Genius for War: The German Army and General Staff, 1807–1945*. Fairfax, VA: Hero, 1984.

———. *Numbers, Prediction, and War: Using History to Evaluate Combat Factors and Predict the Outcome of Battles*. New York: Bobbs-Merrill, 1979.

Dupuy, Trevor N., Curt Johnson, and David L. Bongard. *The Harper Encyclopedia of Military Biography*. New York: HarperCollins, 1992.

Eiler, Keith E., ed. *Wedemeyer on War and Peace*. Stanford: Hoover Institution, 1987.

Eisenhower, John S. D. *Yanks: The Epic Story of the American Army in World War I*. New York: Free Press, 2001.

Eisner, Elliot W. *The Educational Imagination: On the Design and Evaluation of School Programs*. 3rd ed. Upper Saddle River, NJ: Prentice-Hall, 1994.

Eisner, Marc Allen. *From Warfare State to Welfare State: World War I, Compensatory State Building, and the Limits of Modern Order*. University Park: Pennsylvania State University Press, 2000.

Evans, David C., and Mark R. Peattie. *Kaigun: Strategy, Tactics, and Technology in the Imperial Japanese Navy, 1887–1941*. Annapolis: Naval Institute Press, 1997.

Farwell, Byron. *Over There: The United States in the Great War, 1917–1918*. New York: Norton, 1999.

Fass, Paula S. *The Damned and the Beautiful: American Youth in the 1920s*. New York: Oxford University Press, 1977.

Ferrell, Robert H. *America's Deadliest Battle: Meuse-Argonne, 1918*. Lawrence: University Press of Kansas, 2007.

———. *Collapse at Meuse-Argonne: The Failure of the Missouri-Kansas Division*. Columbia: University of Missouri Press, 2004.

Finlayson, Kenneth. *An Uncertain Trumpet: The Evolution of U.S. Army Infantry Doctrine, 1919–1941*. Westport, CT: Greenwood, 2001.

Finnegan, John Patrick. *Against the Specter of a Dragon: The Campaign for American Military Preparedness, 1914–1917*. Westport, CT: Greenwood, 1974.

Finney, Robert T. *History of the Air Corps Tactical School, 1920–1940*. Maxwell Air Force Base, AL: Air Force History and Museums Program, 1998.

Florence, Ronald. *The Perfect Machine: Building the Palomar Telescope*. New York: Harper-Perennial, 1995.

Frieser, Karl-Heinz. *The Blitzkrieg Legend: The 1940 Campaign in the West*. Annapolis: Naval Institute Press, 2005.

Fukuyama, Francis, and Abram N. Shulsky. *The "Virtual Corporation" and Army Organization*. Santa Monica, CA: RAND, 1997.

Gabel, Christopher R. "The Lorraine Campaign: An Overview." Fort Leavenworth, KS: Combat Studies Institute, 1985.

———. *Seek, Strike, and Destroy: U.S. Army Tank Destroyer Doctrine in World War II*. Fort Leavenworth, KS: Combat Studies Institute, U.S. Army Command and General Staff College, 1985.

———. *The U.S. Army GHQ Maneuvers of 1941*. Washington, DC: United States Army Center of Military History, 1992.

Gaff, Alan D. *Blood in the Argonne: The "Lost Battalion" of World War I*. Norman: University of Oklahoma Press, 2005.

Geffen, William, ed. *Command and Commanders in Modern Warfare: The Proceedings of the Second Military History Symposium, U.S. Air Force Academy, 2–3 May 1968*. Washington, DC: U.S. Air Force Academy, 1969.

Gilbert, Felix, and Stephen R. Graubard, eds. *Historical Studies Today*. New York: Norton, 1972.

Gillie, Mildred H. *Forging the Thunderbolt: A History of the Development of the Armored Force*. Harrisburg, PA: Military Service Publishing, 1947.

Gole, Henry G. *The Road to Rainbow: Army Planning for Global War, 1934–1940*. Annapolis: Naval Institute Press, 2003.

Gorman, Paul F. *The Secret of Future Victories.* Fort Leavenworth, KS: U.S. Army Command and General Staff College Press, 1994.

Gott, Kendall D. *Mobility, Vigilance, and Justice: The U.S. Army Constabulary in Germany, 1946–1953.* Fort Leavenworth, KS: Combat Studies Institute Press, 2005.

Gray, Colin S. *Strategy for Chaos: Revolutions in Military Affairs and the Evidence of History.* London: Frank Cass, 2002.

Greenfield, Kent Roberts, ed. *Command Decisions.* Washington, DC: Office of the Chief of Military History, United States Army, 1960.

Greenfield, Kent Roberts, Robert R. Palmer, and Bell I. Wiley. *The Organization of Ground Combat Troops: The Army Ground Forces, United States Army, in World War II.* Washington, DC: Historical Section, United States Army, 1947.

Griffith, Robert K. Jr. *Men Wanted for the U.S. Army: America's Experience with an All Volunteer Army between the World Wars.* Westport, CT: Greenwood, 1982.

Gropman, Alan, ed. *The Big "L": American Logistics in World War II.* Washington, DC: National Defense University Press, 1997.

Grotelueschen, Mark Ethan. *The AEF Way of War: The American Army and Combat in World War I.* New York: Cambridge University Press, 2007.

———. *Doctrine under Fire: American Artillery Employment in World War I.* Westport, CT: Greenwood, 2001.

Gruber, Carol S. *Mars and Minerva: World War I and the Uses of Higher Learning in America.* Baton Rouge: Louisiana State University Press, 1975.

Gudmundson, Bruce I. *On Armor.* Westport: Praeger, 2004.

Hagan, Kenneth J., and William R. Roberts, eds. *Against All Enemies: Interpretations of American Military History from Colonial Times to the Present.* New York: Greenwood, 1986.

Hallas, James H. *Squandered Victory: The American First Army at St. Mihiel.* Westport, CT: Praeger, 1995.

Harbord, James G. *America in the World War.* Boston: Houghton Mifflin, 1933.

Harrison, Gordon A. *Cross-Channel Attack: United States Army in World War II, European Theater of Operations.* Washington, DC: Center of Military History, United States Army, 1951.

Hart, Russell A. *Clash of Arms: How the Allies Won in Normandy.* Boulder: Lynne Rienner, 2001.

———. *Guderian: Panzer Pioneer or Myth Maker.* Washington, DC: Potomac, 2006.

Hart, Stephen Ashley. *Montgomery and "Colossal Cracks": The 21st Army Group in Northwest Europe, 1944–1945.* Westport, CT: Praeger, 2000.

Hawley, Ellis W. *The Great War and the Search for Modern Order: A History of the American People and Their Institutions, 1917–1933.* 2nd ed. Prospect Heights, IL: Waveland, 1992 [reissued 1997].

Heefner, Wilson A. *Twentieth Century Warrior: The Life and Service of Major General Edwin D. Patrick.* Shippensburg, PA: White Mane, 1995.

Heller, Charles E., and William A. Stofft. *America's First Battles, 1776–1965.* Lawrence: University Press of Kansas, 1986.

Herbert, Paul H. *Deciding What Has to Be Done: General William E. DePuy and the 1976 Edition of FM 100-5, Operations.* Fort Leavenworth, KS: Combat Studies Institute, U.S. Army Command and General Staff College, 1988.

Hittle, J. D. *The Military Staff: Its History and Development.* Harrisburg, PA: Military Service Publishing, 1949.

Hofmann, George F. *Cold War Casualty: The Court-Martial of Major General Robert W. Grow.* Kent, OH: Kent State University Press, 1993.

Hofmann, George F., and Donn A. Starry, eds. *Camp Colt to Desert Storm: The History of the U.S. Armored Forces.* Lexington: University Press of Kentucky, 1999.

Hogan, David W. Jr. *A Command Post at War: First Army Headquarters in Europe, 1943–1945.* Washington, DC: Center of Military History, United States Army, 2000.

Holland, Matthew F. *Eisenhower between the Wars: The Making of a General and a Statesman.* Westport, CT: Praeger, 2001.

Holley, I. B. Jr. *General John M. Palmer, Citizen Soldiers, and the Army of a Democracy.* Westport, CT: Greenwood, 1982.

———. *Ideas and Weapons.* New Haven: Yale University Press, 1953. Rpt. ed., Maxwell Air Force Base, AL: Air Force History and Museums Program, 1997.

Holzimmer, Kevin C. *General Walter Krueger: Unsung Hero of the Pacific War.* Lawrence: University Press of Kansas, 2007.

Horgan, Paul. *A Distant Trumpet.* New York: Farrar, Straus and Cudahy, 1951.

House, Jonathan M. *Combined Arms: Warfare in the Twentieth Century.* Lawrence: University Press of Kansas, 2001.

Howard, Michael, ed. *The Theory and Practice of War.* Bloomington: Indiana University Press, 1965.

Howe, George F. *Northwest Africa: Seizing the Initiative in the West: United States Army in World War II, Mediterranean Theater of Operations.* Washington, DC: Office of the Chief of Military History, United States Army, 1957.

Huelfer, Evan Andrew. *The "Casualty Issue" in American Military Practice: The Impact of World War I.* Westport, CT: Praeger, 2003.

Huntington, Samuel P. *Soldier and the State: The Theory and Politics of Civil-Military Relations.* Cambridge: Harvard University Press, 1957.

Hynes, Samuel, Anne Matthews, Nancy Caldwell Sorel, and Roger J. Spiller, advisory board. *Reporting World War II: American Journalism, 1938–1946.* New York: Literary Classics, 1995 [paperback ed. 2001].

Infantry Journal. *Infantry in Battle.* Washington, DC: Infantry Journal, 1939 [rpt. 1993].

Janowitz, Morris. *The Professional Soldier: A Social and Political Portrait.* New York: Free Press, 1971.

Johnson, David E. *Fast Tanks and Heavy Bombers: Innovation in the U.S. Army, 1917–1940.* Ithaca: Cornell University Press, 1998.

Johnson, Douglas V., II, and Rolfe L. Hillman. *Soissons 1918.* College Station: Texas A&M University Press, 1999.

Kanigel, Robert. *The One Best Way: Frederick Winslow Taylor and the Enigma of Efficiency.* New York: Penguin, 1997.

Kanter, Rosabeth Moss, Barry A. Stein, and Todd D. Jick. *The Challenge of Organizational Change: How Companies Experience It and Leaders Guide It.* New York: Free Press, 1992.

Kaufmann, J. E., and H. W. Kaufmann. *Fortress Third Reich: German Fortifications and Defensive Systems in World War II.* Cambridge, MA: Da Capo, 2003.

———. *The Sleeping Giant: American Armed Forces between the Wars.* Westport, CT: Praeger, 1996.

Keegan, John. *The First World War.* New York: Knopf, 1999.

Kennedy, David M. *Over Here: The First World War and American Society.* New York: Oxford University Press, 1980.

Kennedy, Robert M. *The German Campaign in Poland (1939).* Department of the Army. Pamphlet no. 20-255. Washington, DC: Government Printing Office, 1956.

Kier, Elizabeth. *Imagining War: French and British Military Doctrine between the Wars.* Princeton: Princeton University Press, 1997.

Killigrew, John W. *The Impact of the Great Depression on the Army.* New York: Garland, 1979.

Kington, Donald M. *Forgotten Summers: The Story of the Citizen's Military Training Camps, 1921–1940.* San Francisco: Two Decades, 1995.

Kirkpatrick, Charles E. *An Unknown Future and a Doubtful Present: Writing the Victory Plan of 1941.* Washington, DC: U.S. Army Center for Military History, 1990.

Knapp, George E. *Buffalo Soldiers at Fort Leavenworth in the 1930s and Early 1940s.* Fort Leavenworth, KS: Combat Studies Institute, U.S. Army Command and General Staff College, 1991.

Koistinen, Paul A. C. *Mobilizing for Modern War: The Political Economy of American Warfare, 1865–1919.* Lawrence: University Press of Kansas, 1997.

———. *Planning War, Pursuing Peace: The Political Economy of American Warfare, 1920–1939.* Lawrence: University Press of Kansas, 1996.

Kriedberg, Marvin A., and Merton G. Henry. *History of Military Mobilization in the United States Army, 1775–1945.* Washington, DC: Government Printing Office, 1955.

Kuhn, Thomas S. *The Structure of Scientific Revolutions.* 3rd ed. Chicago: University of Chicago, 1962 [1996].

Lacey, Jim. *Keep from All Thoughtful Men.* Annapolis: Naval Institute Press, forthcoming.

Lawren, William. *The General and the Bomb: A Biography of General Leslie R. Groves, Director of the Manhattan Project.* New York: Dodd, Mead, 1988.

Leach, William. *Land of Desire: Merchants, Power, and the Rise of a New American Culture.* New York: Vintage, 1993.

Lears, T. J. Jackson. *No Place of Grace: Antimodernism and the Transformation of American Culture, 1880–1920.* Chicago: University of Chicago Press, 1981.

Lengel, Edward G. *To Conquer Hell: The Meuse-Argonne, 1918.* New York: Henry Holt, 2008.

Leonard, Robert. *The Art of Maneuver: Maneuver-Warfare Theory and AirLand Battle.* Novato, CA: Presidio, 1991.

Liddell Hart, B. H. *The German General's Talk.* New York: Quill, 1979.

Linderman, Gerald F. *The Mirror of War: American Society and the Spanish-American War.* Ann Arbor: University of Michigan Press, 1974.

———. *The World Within War: America's Combat Experience in World War II.* Cambridge: Harvard University Press, 1997.

Linn, Brian McAllister. *The Echo of Battle: The Army's Way of War.* Cambridge: Harvard University Press, 2007.

———. *Guardians of Empire: The U.S. Army and the Pacific, 1902–1940.* Chapel Hill: University of North Carolina Press, 1997.

Lupfer, Timothy T. *The Dynamics of Doctrine: The Changes in German Tactical Doctrine during the First World War.* Leavenworth Papers no. 4. Fort Leavenworth, KS: Combat Studies Institute, U.S. Army Command and General Staff College, 1981.

Luvaas, Jay. *The Education of an Army.* Chicago: University of Chicago Press, 1964.

Lynn, John A. *Feeding Mars: Logistics in Western Warfare from the Middle Ages to the Present.* Boulder: Westview, 1993.

MacDonald, Charles B. *The Battle of the Huertgen Forest.* Philadelphia: University of Pennsylvania Press, 1963.

———. *The Last Offensive: United States Army in World War II, European Theater of Opera-*

tions. Washington, DC: Office of the Chief of Military History, United States Army, 1973, 1984.

———. *The Siegfried Line Campaign: United States Army in World War II, European Theater of Operations.* Washington, DC: Office of the Chief of Military History, United States Army, 1963, 1984.

———. *A Time for Trumpets: The Untold Story of the Battle of the Bulge.* New York: William Morrow, 1985.

Mansoor, Peter R. *The GI Offensive in Europe: The Triumph of American Infantry Divisions, 1941–1945.* Lawrence: University Press of Kansas, 1999.

Masland, John W., and Laurence I. Radway. *Soldiers and Scholars: Military Education and National Policy.* Princeton: Princeton University Press, 1957.

May, Ernest R. *Strange Victory: Hitler's Conquest of France.* New York: Hill and Wang, 2000.

McManus, John C. *The Deadly Brotherhood: The American Combat Soldier in World War II.* Novato, CA: Presidio, 1998, 2000.

McNally, Jeffrey A. *The Adult Development of Career Army Officers.* Westport: Praeger, 1991.

Mead, Gary. *The Doughboys: America and the First World War.* New York: Overlook, 2000.

Meilinger, Phillip S. *Hoyt S. Vandenberg: The Life of a General.* Bloomington: Indiana University Press, 1989.

Miller, Edward G. *A Dark and Bloody Ground: The Huertgen Forest and Roer River Dams, 1944–1945.* College Station: Texas A&M University Press, 1995.

———. *Nothing Less Than Full Victory: Americans at War in Europe, 1944–1945.* Annapolis: Naval Institute Press, 2007.

Miller, Robert A. *Division Commander: A Biography of Norman D. Cota.* Spartanburg, SC: Reprint Company Publishers, 1989.

Millett, Allan R. *The General: Robert L. Bullard and Officership in the United States Army, 1881–1925.* Westport, CT: Greenwood, 1975.

———. *Military Professionalism and Officership in America.* Columbus: Mershon Center of the Ohio State University, 1977.

Millett, Allan R., and Peter Maslowski. *For the Common Defense: A Military History of the United States of America.* New York: Free Press, 1984.

Millett, Allan R., and Williamson Murray, eds. *Military Effectiveness, Volume I: The First World War.* Boston: Allen and Unwin, 1988.

———. *Military Effectiveness, Volume II: The Interwar Period.* Boston: Allen and Unwin, 1988.

———. *Military Effectiveness, Volume III: The Second World War.* Boston: Allen and Unwin, 1988.

Millis, Walter, ed. *American Military Thought.* New York: Bobbs-Merrill, 1966.

———. *Arms and Men: A Study in American Military History.* New Brunswick, NJ: Rutgers University Press, 1956.

Mitchell, Vance O. *Air Force Officers: Personnel Policy Development, 1944–1974.* Washington, DC: Air Force History and Museums Program, United States Air Force, 1996.

Morelock, J. D. *Generals of the Ardennes: American Leadership in the Battle of the Bulge.* Washington, DC: National Defense University Press, 1993.

Mosier, John. *The Blitzkrieg Myth: How Hitler and the Allies Misread the Strategic Realities of World War II.* New York: HarperCollins, 2003.

———. *The Myth of the Great War: How the Germans Won the Battles and How the Americans Saved the Allies.* New York: HarperCollins, 2001.

Moskos, Charles C., John Allen Williams, and David R. Segal, eds. *The Postmodern Military: Armed Forces After the Cold War.* New York: Oxford University Press, 2000.

Mosley, Leonard. *Marshall: Hero for Our Times*. New York: Hearst, 1982.

Murray, Williamson, and Allan R. Millett, eds. *Calculations: Net Assessment and the Coming of World War II*. New York: Free Press, 1992.

———. *Military Innovation in the Interwar Period*. New York: Cambridge University Press, 1996.

Myer, Anton. *Once an Eagle*. Carlisle, PA: Army War College Foundation, 1968, 1997.

Naveh, Shimon. *In Pursuit of Military Excellence: The Evolution of Operational Theory*. Portland, OR: Frank Cass, 1997.

Nelson, John T. II. *General George C. Marshall: Strategic Leadership and the Challenges of Reconstituting the Army, 1939–1941*. Carlisle Barracks, PA: Strategic Studies Institute, U.S. Army War College, 1993.

Nenninger, Timothy K. *The Leavenworth Schools and the Old Army: Education, Professionalism, and the Officer Corps of the United States Army, 1881–1918*. Westport, CT: Greenwood, 1978.

Ney, Virgil. *Evolution of the U.S. Army Division, 1939–1968*. Fort Belvoir, VA: Headquarters, United States Army Combat Developments Command, January 1969.

Noble, Dennis L. *The Eagle and the Dragon: The United States Military in China, 1901–1937*. Westport, CT: Greenwood, 1990.

Odom, William O. *After the Trenches: The Transformation of U.S. Army Doctrine, 1918–1939*. College Station: Texas A&M University Press, 1999.

Ormrod, Jeanne Ellis. *Human Learning: Theories, Principles, and Educational Applications*. New York: Merrill, 1990.

Ossad, Steven L., and Don R. Marsh. *Major General Maurice Rose: World War II's Greatest Forgotten Commander*. New York: Taylor Trade, 2003.

Overy, Richard. *Why the Allies Won*. New York: W. W. Norton, 1995.

Palmer, Robert R., Bell I. Wiley, and William R. Keast. *The Procurement and Training of Ground Combat Troops: The Army Ground Forces, United States Army in World War II*. Washington, DC: Office of the Chief of Military History, 1948.

Pappas, George S. *Prudens Futuri: The U.S. Army War College, 1901–1967*. Carlisle Barracks, PA: Alumni Association of the U.S. War College, 1967.

Parker, Geoffrey. *The Military Revolution: Military Innovations and the Rise of the West, 1500–1800*. New York: Cambridge University Press, 1988, 1999.

Partin, John W., ed. *A Brief History of Fort Leavenworth, 1827–1983*. Fort Leavenworth: Combat Studies Institute, U.S. Army Command and General Staff College, 1983.

Pearlman, Michael D. *Warmaking and American Democracy: The Struggle over Military Strategy, 1700 to the Present*. Lawrence: University Press of Kansas, 1999.

Perret, Geoffrey. *Eisenhower*. Holbrook, MA: Adams Media, 1999.

———. *There's a War to Be Won: The United States Army in World War II*. New York: Random House, 1991.

Persons, Benjamin S. *Relieved of Command*. Manhattan, KS: Sunflower University Press, 1997.

Phillips, Henry Gerard. *The Making of a Professional: Manton S. Eddy, USA*. Westport, CT: Greenwood, 2000.

Pinar, William F., William M. Reynolds, Patrick Slattery, and Peter M. Taubman. *Understanding Curriculum: An Introduction to the Study of Historical and Contemporary Curriculum Discourses*. New York: Peter Lang, 1995.

Pogue, Forrest C. *George C. Marshall: Education of a General, 1880–1939*. New York: Viking, 1963.

————. *George C. Marshall: Ordeal and Hope.* New York: Viking, 1966.

Posen, Barry R. *The Sources of Military Doctrine: France, Britain, and Germany between the World Wars.* Ithaca: Cornell University Press, 1984.

Price, Frank James. *Troy H. Middleton: A Biography.* Baton Rouge: Louisiana State University Press, 1974.

Reardon, Carol. *Soldiers and Scholars: The U.S. Army and the Uses of Military History, 1865–1920.* Lawrence: University Press of Kansas, 1990.

Reardon, Mark J. *Victory at Mortain: Stopping Hitler's Panzer Counteroffensive.* Lawrence: University Press of Kansas, 2002.

Rogers, Clifford J., ed. *The Military Revolution Debate: Readings on the Transformation of Early Modern Europe.* Boulder: Westview, 1995.

Ropp, Theodore. *War in the Modern World.* Durham, NC: Duke University Press, 1959.

Rosen, Stephen Peter. *Winning the Next War: Innovation and the Modern Military.* Ithaca: Cornell University Press, 1991.

Rush, Robert Sterling. *Hell in Hürtgen Forest: The Ordeal and Triumph of an American Infantry Regiment.* Lawrence: University Press of Kansas, 2001.

Ryan, Garry D., and Timothy K. Nenninger. *Soldiers and Civilians: The U.S. Army and the American People.* Washington, DC: National Archives and Records Administration, 1987.

Schaffer, Ronald. *America in the Great War: The Rise of the War Welfare State.* New York: Oxford University Press, 1991.

Schön, Donald A. *Educating the Reflexive Practitioner: Toward a New Design for Teaching and Learning in the Professions.* San Francisco: Jossey-Bass, 1987.

————. *The Reflective Practitioner: How Professionals Think in Action.* New York: Basic, 1983.

Shaara, Jeff. *The Rising Tide: A Novel of World War II.* New York: Random House Ballantine, 2006.

Shafritz, Jay M., and Philip H. Whitbeck, eds. *Classics of Organization Theory.* Oak Park, IL: Moore, 1978.

Slotkin, Richard. *Lost Battalions: The Great War and the Crisis of American Nationality.* New York: Henry Holt, 2005.

Smith, Gene. *Until the Last Trumpet Sounds: The Life of General of the Armies John J. Pershing.* New York: John Wiley and Sons, 1998.

Smythe, Donald. *Pershing: General of the Armies.* Bloomington: Indiana University Press, 1986.

Spiller, Roger J., ed. *Dictionary of American Military Biography.* 3 vols. Westport, CT: Greenwood, 1984.

Stark, Joan S., and Lisa R. Lattuca. *Shaping the College Curriculum: Academic Plans in Action.* Boston: Allyn and Bacon, 1997.

Steele, Bret. *Military Reengineering between the World Wars.* Santa Monica: RAND, 2005.

Stelpflug, Peggy A., and Richard Hyatt. *Home of the Infantry: History of Fort Benning.* Macon, GA: Mercer University Press, 2007.

Stoler, Mark A. *George C. Marshall: Soldier-Statesman of the American Century.* New York: Twayne, 1989.

Stubblefield, Harold W. *Towards a History of Adult Education in America: The Search for a Unifying Principle.* New York: Croom Helm, 1988.

Sumida, Jon Tetsuro. *Inventing Grand Strategy and Teaching Command: The Classic Works of Alfred Thayer Mahan Reconsidered.* Baltimore: Johns Hopkins University Press, 1997.

Tate, James P. *The Army and Its Air Corps: Army Policy Toward Aviation, 1919–1941.* Maxwell Air Force Base, AL: Air University Press, 1998.

Thorndike, Edward L. *Educational Psychology, Volume 1: The Original Nature of Man*. New York: Teachers College, Columbia University, 1924 [orig. copyright 1913].

——. *Educational Psychology, Volume 2: The Psychology of Learning*. New York: Teachers College, Columbia University, 1925 [orig. copyright 1913].

——. *The Fundamentals of Learning*. New York: Teachers College, Columbia University, 1932.

Toner, James H. *Morals Under the Gun: The Cardinal Virtues, Military Ethics, and American Society*. Lexington: University Press of Kentucky, 2000.

Trask, David F. *The AEF and Coalition Warmaking, 1917–1918*. Lawrence: University Press of Kansas, 1993.

Traxel, David. *Crusader Nation: The United States in Peace and the Great War, 1898–1920*. New York: Vintage, 2006, 2007.

Tuchman, Barbara. *Stillwell and the American Experience in China*. New York: Macmillan, 1970.

van Creveld, Martin. *Fighting Power: German and U.S. Army Performance: 1939–1945*. Westport, CT: Greenwood, 1982.

——. *The Training of Officers: From Military Professionalism to Irrelevance*. New York: Free Press, 1990.

Waddell, Steve R. *United States Army Logistics: The Normandy Campaign, 1944*. Westport, CT: Greenwood, 1994.

Wade, Gary. *World War II Division Commanders*. Fort Leavenworth, KS: Combat Studies Institute, 1983.

Watson, Mark S. *Pre-War Plans and Preparations*. Washington, DC: Government Printing Office, 1950.

Weber, Max. *On Charisma and Institution Building: Selected Papers*. Ed. S. N. Eisenstadt. Chicago: University of Chicago Press, 1968.

——. *The Theory of Social and Economic Organization*. Translated by A. M. Henderson and Talcott Parsons. New York: Free Press, 1947 [1968 printing].

Weigley, Russell F. *The American Way of War: A History of United States Military Strategy and Policy*. Bloomington: Indiana University Press, 1973.

——. *Eisenhower's Lieutenants: The Campaign of France and Germany, 1944–1945*. Bloomington: Indiana University Press, 1981.

——. *History of the United States Army*. Enlarged ed. Bloomington: Indiana University Press, 1984.

Weinberg, Gerhard L. *A World at Arms: A Global History of World War II*. New York: Cambridge University Press, 1994.

Weingartner, Steven, ed. *Cantigny at Seventy-Five: A Professional Discussion: Proceedings of a Professional Discussion Held at the First Division Museum, Wheaton, Illinois, May 28–29, 1993*. Chicago: Robert M. McCormick Tribune Foundation, 1994.

White, Charles Edward. *The Enlightened Soldier: Scharnhorst and the* Militaerische Gesellschaft *in Berlin, 1801–1805*. Westport: Praeger, 1989.

Whitehorne, Joseph W. A. *The Inspectors General of the United States Army, 1903–1939*. Washington, DC: Office of the Inspector General and Center of Military History, United States Army, 1998.

Wiebe, Robert H. *Self Rule: A Cultural History of American Democracy*. Chicago: University of Chicago Press, 1995.

Wilson, John B. *Maneuver and Firepower: The Evolution of Divisions and Separate Brigades*. Washington, DC: United States Army Center of Military History, 1998.

Wilson, Theodore A., ed. *D-Day 1944*. Lawrence: University Press of Kansas, 1994.

Winterbotham, F. W. *The Ultra Secret.* New York: Dell, 1974.

Winton, Harold R. *Corps Commanders of the Bulge: Six American Generals and Victory in the Ardennes.* Lawrence: University Press of Kansas, 2007.

Winton, Harold R., and David R. Mets. *The Challenge of Change: Military Institutions and New Realities, 1918–1941.* Lincoln: University of Nebraska Press, 2000.

Yeide, Harry. *The Longest Battle: September 1944 to February 1945, from Aachen to the Roer and Across.* St. Paul, MN: Zenith, 2005.

Zieger, Robert H. *America's Great War: World War I and the American Experience.* New York: Rowman & Littlefield, 2000.

Zumbro, Derek S. *Battle for the Ruhr: The German Army's Final Defeat in the West.* Lawrence: University Press of Kansas, 2006.

Zunz, Olivier. *Making America Corporate, 1870–1920.* Chicago: University of Chicago Press, 1990.

Journal Articles

Barnett, Correlli. "The Education of Military Elites." *Journal of Contemporary History* 2, no. 3 (July 1967): 15–36.

Bielakowski, Alexander M. "General Hawkins's War: The Futures of the Horse in the U.S. Cavalry." *Journal of Military History* 71, no. 1 (January 2007): 127–138.

Coffman, Edward M. "The Long Shadow of *The Soldier and the State.*" *Journal of Military History* 55 (January 1991): 69–82.

Coffman, Edward M., and Peter F. Herrly. "The American Regular Army Officer Corps between the World Wars." *Armed Forces and Society* 4, no. 1 (November 1977): 55–73.

Dietrich, Steve E. "The Professional Reading of George S. Patton, Jr." *Journal of Military History* 53 (October 1989): 387–418.

Franz, Colonel Wallace P. "The Art of War: Theory and Practice." *Art of War Quarterly* 2 (September 1983): 113–126. Carlisle Barracks, PA: U.S. Army War College.

Gunsburg, Jeffrey A. "The Battle of Gembloux, 14–15 May 1940: The 'Blitzkrieg' Checked." *Journal of Military History* 64, no. 1 (January 2000): 97–140.

Holder, Leonard D., Lt. Gen. (ret.), and Williamson Murray. "Prospects for Military Education." *Joint Forces Quarterly*, no. 18 (Spring 1998): 81–90.

Hugh, Gil. "More than 'Officer U.'" *Soldiers: The Official U.S. Army Magazine* 54, no. 4 (April 1999): 32–35.

Irish, Kerry E. "Apt Pupil: Dwight Eisenhower and the 1930 Industrial Mobilization Plan." *Journal of Military History* 70, no. 1 (January 2006): 31–61.

Kirschner, Don S. "Publicity Properly Applied: The Selling of Expertise in America, 1900–1929." *American Studies* 29 (Spring 1978): 65–78.

Kohn, Richard H. "The Social History of the American Soldier: A Review and Prospectus for Research." *American Historical Review* 86, no. 3 (June 1981): 553–567.

Liaropoulos, Andrew N. "Revolutions in Warfare: Theoretical Paradigms and Historical Evidence—The Napoleonic and First World War Revolutions in Military Affairs." *Journal of Military History* 70 (April 2006): 363–384.

Linn, Brian M. "The American Way of War Revisited." With a response by Russell F. Weigley. *Journal of Military History* 66, no. 2 (April 2002): 501–533.

Mansoor, Peter R., and Kathy Cast Garth, eds. "*The Ten Lean Years* by Major General Robert W. Grow." *Armor Magazine* 96, no. 1 (January–February 1987): 22–30; no. 2 (March–April 1987): 25–33; no. 3 (May–June 1987): 21–28; and no. 4 (July–August 1987): 34–42.

Murray, Williamson. "Thinking about Innovation." *Naval War College Review* 54, no. 2 (Spring 2001): 119–129.

———. "Thinking about Revolutions in Military Affairs." *Joint Force Quarterly* (Summer 1997): 69–76.

Nenninger, Timothy K. "Creating Officers: The Leavenworth Experience, 1920–1940." *Military Review* 69, no. 11 (November 1989): 56–68.

———. "The Development of American Armor, 1917–1940: The World War I Experience." *Armor* 78, no. 1 (January–February 1969): 46–51.

———. "The Development of American Armor, 1917–1940: The Tank Corps Reorganized." *Armor* 78, no. 2 (March–April 1969): 34–38.

———. "The Development of American Armor, 1917–1940: The Experimental Mechanized Forces." *Armor* 78, no. 3 (May–June 1969): 33–39.

———. "The Development of American Armor, 1917–1940: A Revised Mechanization Policy." *Armor* 78, no. 5 (September–October 1969): 45–49.

———. "Leavenworth and Its Critics: The U.S. Army Command and General Staff School, 1920–1940." *Journal of Military History* 58 (April 1994): 199–231.

———. "'Unsystematic as a Mode of Command': Commanders and the Process of Command in the American Expeditionary Forces, 1917–1918." *Journal of Military History* 64, no. 3 (July 2000): 739–768.

Rainey, James W. "Ambivalent Warfare: The Tactical Doctrine of the AEF in World War I." *Parameters* 13, no. 3 (September 1983): 34–46.

———. "The Questionable Training of the AEF in World War I." *Parameters* 22, no. 4 (Winter 1992–1993): 89–103.

Richardson, William R. "Kermit Roosevelt Lecture: Officer Training and Education." *Military Review* 64 (October 1984): 22–34.

Shulimson, Jack. "Military Professionalism: The Case of the U.S. Marine Officer Corps, 1880–1898." *Journal of Military History* 60 (April 1996): 231–242.

Snider, Don M., and Gayle L. Watkins. "The Future of Army Professionalism: A Need for Renewal and Redefinition." *Parameters* 30, no. 3 (Autumn 2000): 5–20.

Weigley, Russell F. "Shaping the American Army of World War II: Mobility versus Firepower." *Parameters* 11, no. 3 (September 1981): 13–21.

Wilson, John B. "Mobility versus Firepower: The Post–World War I Infantry Division." *Parameters* 13, no. 3 (September 1983): 47–52.

Yingling, Paul. "A Failure in Generalship." *Armed Forces Journal* (May 2007). Available at www.armedforcesjournal.com/2007/05/2635198. Accessed July 1, 2007.

Unpublished Dissertations, Theses, and Monographs

Anderson, Philip. "Developing a Philosophy for Teaching at the Marine Corps University." Ph.D. diss., George Mason University, 1994.

Bielakowski, Alexander Magnus. "U.S. Army Cavalry Officers and the Issue of Mechanization, 1920 to 1942." Ph.D. diss., Kansas State University, 2002.

Broom, John Thomas. "The Commander's Vision in Blue and Grey: The Roles of Adna R. Chaffee Jr., James H. Wilson, and the American Civil War in the Development of American Armor Doctrine." Ph.D. diss., Union Institute, 1993.

Calhoun, Mark T. "Defeat at Kasserine: American Armor Doctrine, Training, and Battle Command in Northwest Africa, World War II." MMAS thesis, U.S. Army Command and General Staff College, Fort Leavenworth, Kansas, 2003.

Cockrell, Philip Carlton. "Brown Shoes and Mortar Boards: U.S. Army Officer Professional Education at the Command and General Staff School, Fort Leavenworth, Kansas, 1919–1940." Ph.D. diss., University of South Carolina, 1991.

Dale, Matthew B. "Professional Military Development of Major General Ernest R. Harmon." MMAS thesis, U.S. Army Command and General Staff College, Fort Leavenworth, Kansas, 2008.

Daley, John Leslie Sanderson. "From Theory to Practice: Tanks, Doctrine, and the U.S. Army, 1916–1940." Ph.D. diss., Kent State University, 1993.

Fullerton, Dan. "Bright Prospects, Bleak Realities: The U.S. Army's Interwar Modernization Program for the Coming of the Second World War." Ph.D. diss., University of Kansas, 2006.

Holzimmer, Kevin Conrad. "A Soldier's Soldier: A Military Biography of General Walter Krueger." Ph.D. diss., Temple University, 1999.

Jacobsmeyer, Paul J. "Intelligence in the American Expeditionary Force: The Experience of the Thirty-Second Division, September 1917–November 1918." MA thesis, University of Wisconsin, 1986.

Johnson, David E. "Fast Tanks and Heavy Bombers: The United States Army and the Development of Armor and Aviation Doctrine and Technologies, 1917 to 1945." Ph.D. diss., Duke University, 1990.

Johnson, David Eugene. "The United States Army Command and General Staff School during World War II: Transition to Necessity." MMAS thesis, U.S. Army Command and General Staff College, Fort Leavenworth, KS, 1985.

Macak, Richard J. Jr. "The United States Army's Second Year Courses: A Continuing Tradition in Educational Excellence." MA thesis, University of Kansas, 1988.

Matheny, Mike. "Development of the Theory and Doctrine of Operational Art in the U.S. Army, 1920–1940." MMAS thesis, School of Advanced Military Studies, U.S. Army Command and General Staff College, Fort Leavenworth, KS, 1988.

Miller, Robert Allan. "The United States Army during the 1930s." Ph.D. diss., Princeton University, 1973.

Morton, Matthew Darlington. "Men on 'Iron Ponies': The Death and Rebirth of Modern U.S. Cavalry." Ph.D. diss., Florida State University, 2004.

Nenninger, Timothy K. "The Development of American Armor, 1917–1940." MA thesis, University of Wisconsin, 1968.

———. "The Fort Leavenworth Schools: Postgraduate Military Education and Professionalization in the U.S. Army, 1880–1920." Ph.D. diss., University of Wisconsin, 1974.

O'Connell, Charles F. Jr. "The United States Army and the Origins of Modern Management, 1818–1860." Ph.D. diss., Ohio State University, 1982.

Odom, William O. "The Rise and Fall of U.S. Army Doctrine, 1918 to 1939." Ph.D. diss., Ohio State University, 1995.

Pohl, James William. "The General Staff and American Military Policy: The Formative Period, 1898–1917." Ph.D. diss., University of Texas, 1967.

Schifferle, Peter J. "Anticipating Armageddon: The Leavenworth Schools and U.S. Army Military Effectiveness, 1919–1945." Ph.D. diss., University of Kansas, 2002.

———. "The Prussian and American General Staffs: An Analysis of Cross-cultural Imitation, Innovation, and Adaptation." MA thesis, University of North Carolina, 1981.

Woodgerd, Michael. "'If You Don't Like This, You May Resign and Go Home': Commander's Considerations in Assaulting a Fortified Position." MSST thesis, Naval Postgraduate School, 1991.

Yarger, Harry Richard. "Army Officer Personnel Management: The Creation of the Modern American System to 1939." Ph.D. diss., Temple University, 1996.

Scholarly Papers

Jacobsmeyer, Paul J. "On the Edge of a Breakthrough: Semi-Open Warfare in the American Expeditionary Force — The Experience of the 32d Division (Michigan-Wisconsin National Guard)." Paper delivered at the annual meeting of the Society for Military History. Ogden, UT, April 2008. Copy in author's possession.
Kirkpatrick, Charles E. "Filling the Gaps: A Reevaluation of Officer Professional Education in the Inter-war Army, 1920–1940." Unpublished. Copy in author's possession.
Linn, Brian McAllister. "Transforming Defense in Peace: A Historical Perspective." Delivered at the twelfth Annual Strategy Conference of the U.S. Army War College ("Transforming Defense in an Era of Peace and Prosperity"). Carlisle Barracks, PA, April 17–20, 2001.

Internet Sources

"The 30th Infantry Division in World War II." Available at www.30thinfantry.org.
Combined Arms Research Library Website, Fort Leavenworth, KS. Available at www.cgsc. army.mil/carl.
Conetta, Carl. "We Can See Clearly Now: The Limits of Foresight in the Pre–World War II Revolution in Military Affairs (RMA)." Project on Defense Alternatives, March 2, 2006. Available at www.comw.org/pda/fulltext/0603rm12.pdf. Accessed July 1, 2007.
Lautenschlager, Karl. "The Tank as RMA: A Case Study in Real World Technical Revolution." Los Alamos National Laboratory. September 5, 2001. Available at http://web.mit. edu/SSP/seminars/wed_archives_01fall/lautenschlager.htm. Accessed July 1, 2007.
Military History Institute Website. Available at www.carlisle.army.mil/ahec/MHI.htm.
U.S. Army 2nd Armored "Hell on Wheels" Division Website. Available at www.2ndarmored hellonwheels.com.
U.S. Army Center of Military History Website. Available at www.history.army.mil.
Wilson, Peter A. "The Four RMAs (Ways of War) of the 20th Century: A Hegelian Cycle of Thesis and Antithesis?" PowerPoint briefing slides. Arroyo Center, CA: RAND, January 25, 2005. Available at www.tfpd.org/pdf/Wilson.MilTransPresentation.Apr2005.pdf. Accessed July 1, 2007.

INDEX

Adjutant General Corps, and Eisenhower, 129, 130

airpower, 28, 39, 48, 55; advocates of, 45, 93, 194; close air support, 51, 55, 180, 192, 194; combined arms, 7, 180, 182; curriculum, 169, 193, 194; doctrine, 53, 55, 56; failure of CGSS, 193–194; limited knowledge of, 168, 169, 187, 193; role in victory, 168–170, 187

Allen, Robert H., 91

American Expeditionary Force (AEF), 9–14, 15, 32, 36, 56, 65, 93, 119, 123, 161; basic operational concept functions in World War II, 183, 186; chiefs of staff in, 10; CGSS faculty, 88, 94, 193; command in, 10–13, 92; dominated by staff school graduates, 11 (*see also* Leavenworth clique); dual nature of warfare, 86, 98, 182, 183, 189, 190; 1st Army, 184; history of, 41, 66; incompetence of, 15, 98, 189, 190; instructors, 31, 94, 95, 98; Meuse-Argonne Campaign lessons, 13–16, 115–116, 180, 184–186, 188, 189; modern war, 8, 9, 41; operations of, 10–16, 61, 123, 186; origin of combined arms, 13, 36, 39, 47, 182; senior leaders in, 11; staff school at Langres, 11, 101; Tactical Note No. 7, 217n79; veterans of, 24, 87, 94, 97, 98, 186, 231n59

Anderson, Sir Kenneth A. N., 4

Anderson, Swede, 123

applicatory method, 62, 99, 121, 122, 148, 191; basis of CGSS mission, 65, 92–93; combat principles, 110–111; criticism of, 116–118, 119–121, 236n73; grading, 138, 143; journals, 20, 118, 146; official critiques, 119–121; practice of, 102–111, 121–122; problem solving, 107–116, 143; relative weight of curriculum, 223n53;

Schoen describes challenges of, 220n3; "school solution," 111–116; student confidence, 143, 191; student critiques, 116–118; tradition at Leavenworth, 101–102; value of, 121–122, 146; wartime courses, 152, 156

Armistice, 14, 39, 45, 94, 182, 184; AEF strength by, 24; Army commissioned strength by, 22, 135; Staff officer requirements by, 10

armored forces, 48, 55, 58, 60, 149. *See also* army units, U.S., armored divisions

Army, British, 5, 70; in World War I, 13; 6th Armored Division, 3, 4

Army, Chinese, officer students, 113, 237n2

Army, French, 27, 56; in World War I, 13

Army, German, 1, 4, 5, 8, 70, 71; *Afrika Korps*, 3; airpower, 182–183; cavalry, in World War I, 115; 1918 offensives of, 13; offensive operations in WWII, 60; reconnaissance battalion of 2d Panzer Division, 178–179; 2d Panzer Division, 178, 179. See also *blitzkrieg*

Army, Italian, 1, 5, 8

Army, Japanese, 1, 6, 8

Army, U.S., 9, 22, 135; Adjutant General, 81, 90, 91, 120, 128, 138, 140, 141; chief of staff of, 30, 50, 79, 81, 120, 129, 140; constabulary role of, 6, 9, 20, 46; general headquarters, functions in World War II, 216n62; Industrial College, 78, 159; lack of resources, 17–19, 25–26, 58, 61, 189, 192; motorized division, in World War II, 218n95; occupation in Germany, after World War I, 26, 88; Philippine Scouts, student officers, 237n2; reforms, 6, 10, 102

Army, U.S., airborne forces, 61, 151, 155, 172, 173, 192

and Harmon, 2, 241n37; and Howze, 3; length of CGSS, 79; mission of, 34; 1934 study of graduate utilization, 174; and Omar Bradley, 225n74; post-graduate assignments, 131, 132; pre-war planning, 167; selection process, 123–124, 126, 137, 140–141, 143, 146, 191; students and officer development system, 79, 88, 92, 96; studies by, 91; wartime courses, 159

Ward, Orlando, 3, 4, 12 (photo)

War Department, 12, 19, 22, 30, 59, 63, 67, 132, 133, 135, 138; and evaluation system, 143, 147; evaluation of grading, 119, 120, 142; experimentation, 29; faculty selection, 89–90; honor graduate system, 145–146; length of CGSS, 79; officer education, 33; policies on War College qualifications, 140; post-WWI education system, 33–34, 78; *Staff Officers Field Manual*, 58

War Department Adjutant General, and CGSS course length, 81

War Department G1, and CGSS course length, 81

War Department General Order No. 41, 78

War Department General Staff, 90, 110, 120, 128, 129, 162, 168; CGSS graduates, 131; doctrine, 46, 53; duties of, 32; *FSR* (1939), 53; Harmon on, 19; interwar policy, 21; manuals, 46; McGlachlin Board, 34; policy for officer education, 32, 80–81, 139–140; promotion, 124; reorganization of, 78; studies by, 79, 80–81; War College, 35

wargaming, 63, 66, 72, 98, 100. See also *kriegspiel*

War Plans Branch, 78. *See also* War Plans Division

War Plans Division, 2, 24, 168. *See also* War Plans Branch

Washington, George, 25

weapons: automatic, 50; howitzer, 41; M-1 Garand, 28; mortars, 38; rifle, 45

Wedemeyer, Albert C.: airpower, 168–169; critical appraisal, 248n4, 248n9

Weigley, Russell F., 216n58

Weinberg, Gerhard, 5

Wertenbaker, George L., 90

Westervelt Board, 213n19

West Point, 123, 130, 131, 175, 177; Class of 1915, 24; Harmon at, 1–2, 19; Howze at, 3; McNair at, 92; officer education system, 32, 34; proportions of officer assignments, 34, 125, 135, 176

Wilson, Walter K., 130–131

wives, of students, 125–126

Women's Army Corps, 245n32

Woolfley, Francis, 45

World War I, 6, 8, 14, 58, 124; casualties in, 15; experience is helpful in World War II, 5, 177, 180, 183, 184–186; Harmon in, 1–2; influence on education, 1, 6–7, 189; intensity of experience, 5, 9–17, 68; large formation combat similar to World War II, 180, 181 (photo), 184–187, 252n61; lessons of, 17, 188; planning in, 15; RMA, 7; special features of, 67; staff judgment, 7; staff work, 119; victory in World War II, 196

World War II, 5, 92, 149–166, 183, 185, 188; command and graduates, 170–174, 191, 192, 194; and large formation combat, 180, 181 (photo), 184–187, 252n61; lessons from World War I used in, 180, 184–186; reasons for U.S. victory, 196. *See also* Army and Navy Staff College Course; civilian course; faculty; mobilization; New Divisions Course; Service Staff Course; Special General Staff Course

CPSIA information can be obtained
at www.ICGtesting.com
Printed in the USA
BVOW10s1507301017
499010BV00009B/152/P